GENETICS
An Introduction for Dog Breeders

Jackie Isabell

Alpine
Blue Ribbon Books
Loveland, Colorado

Genetics: An Introduction for Dog Breeders
Copyright ©2002 Jackie Isabell

All rights reserved. No part of this book may be used or reproduced in any manner whatsoever, including electronic media, internet, or newsletters, without written permission from the publisher, except in the case of brief quotations embodied in critical reviews. For permission, write to Alpine Publications, Inc., P. O. Box 7027, Loveland, CO 80537.

Library of Congress Cataloging-in-Publication Data

Isabell, Jackie.
   Genetics : an introduction for dog breeders / Jackie Isabell.
     p. cm.
   Includes bibliographical references (p.).
   ISBN 1-57779-041-3
     1. Dogs--Genetics. 2. Dogs--Breeding. I. Title.

SF427.2 .I82 2002
636.7'0821--dc21   2002071721

This book is available at special quantity discounts for breeders and for club promotions, premiums, or educational use. Write for details.

The information contained in this book is complete and accurate to the best of our knowledge. All recommendations are made without guarantee on the part of the author or Alpine Publications, Inc. The author and publisher disclaim any liability with the use of this information.

Editing: Debbie Helmers
Design: Laura Claassen

First printing: 2002

1 2 3 4 5 6 7 8 9 0

Printed in the United States of America.

CONTENTS

Preface v

THE NATURE OF THE SPECIES

1. **Evolutionary Genetics** 1
   Origin of the *Canidae* • Genus *Canis* • The Domestic Dog—*Canis Familiaris*
   The Evolution of Breeds • DNA Discoveries • Domestication—Selective Evolution

2. **Behavioral Genetics** 19
   How Do Genes Affect Behavior? • The Environmental Impact
   Patterns of Behavior and Learning • Hereditary Canine Behavior

THE NATURE OF HEREDITY

3. **Cytogenetics** 37
   Cells • Those Paired Chromosomes • Cell Division • Chromosomal Variations

4. **Mendelian Genetics** 53
   Mendel and His Laws • Single-Gene Heredity • Types of Gene Action
   Alleles and Loci • Summary

5. **Molecular Genetics** 65
   DNA—What Is It? • Gene Expression • Copies and Miscopies • Genetic Engineering

6. **Quantitative Genetics** 81
   Continuous and Discontinuous Variance • Additive Gene Action
   Threshold Effects • Heritability • The Environment and Phenotype

7. **Population Genetics** 91
   Gene Frequency • Genetic Diversity

APPLICATIONS FOR BREEDERS

8. **Coat Colors and Markings** 103
   Color Alleles and Loci • Pigment • Loci with Two Alleles
   Loci with Multiple Alleles • Other Color Factors • Eye Color • Summary

9. **Coat Types and Qualities** 125
   Coat Types • Coat Qualities

10. **Structural Traits** 137
    The Head • The Body

11. Control of Genetic Disorders 147
Verifying a Genetic Basis • Incidence
Mode of Inheritance • Screening Methods

12. Congenital Disorders 157
Cleft Palate • Cryptorchidism • Swimmers' Syndrome • Hernias
Cardiac Abnormalities • Keep an Open Mind

13. Common Hereditary Problems 165
Bleeding Disorders • Epilepsy • Eye Disorders
Hypothyroidism • Skeletal Disorders

SELECTION

14. Selection—The Theories 191
Effects of Selection • Selection Procedures • Systems of Mating
Gathering Data • Choices

15. Selection—The Art 203
Why an Art? • Getting Acquainted with a Breed • A Firm Foundation
Charting a Course

16. Evaluation and Records 211
Puppies • Ongoing Evaluation • Some Final Thoughts

Appendix A. Breed Colors and Alleles 223

Appendix B. A Catalogue of Congenital and Hereditary Disorders (by Breed) 249

Notes 259

Bibliography 275

Glossary 285

Index 311

PREFACE

New discoveries in genetics have become commonplace in the news and popular magazines, including those publications devoted to dogs. At the 1995 American Kennel Club (AKC) delegates meeting, Dr. Robert J. Hritzo gave an update on the *canine genome project's* search for genetic *markers* and *anchor loci* to identify hereditary disorders in dogs; he also reported the identification of the gene that causes copper toxicosis in Bedlington Terriers.[1] Clearly, an understanding of this jargon and of the underlying concepts and principles is of growing importance to dog breeders. The breeder who understands genetics has a better chance of consistently producing sound, healthy puppies with desired breed temperament and aptitude and with fewer undesired genetic traits. Breed club members who understand genetics can initiate educational and control programs to improve the overall quality of their breed.

The objective of this book is to introduce breeders to basic genetic terms, principles, and concepts that will help them breed sounder, healthier dogs with better temperament and breed aptitude. The challenge in writing it was to share my own fascination with genetics and to weave its many different aspects into a simple, easy-to-understand primer that will help the breeder move on to more advanced material.

The chapters are arranged by four broad topics: The Nature of the Species; The Nature of Heredity; Applications for Breeders; and Selection.

In Part One, the nature of the genus *Canis* and the domestic dog (*Canis familiaris*) is explored through a look at evolutionary and behavioral genetics. They are more closely related than one would think because the process of domestication and selection for tameness appears to have surprisingly far-reaching effects upon anatomy and physiology. No other aspect of genetics is so sensitive to environmental effects as that involving behavior. Breeders can not only select for behavioral traits but also give nature a boost through modifying the environment.

Vocabulary is a key aspect of learning genetics, and the goal of Part Two, The Nature of Heredity, is to help breeders understand the basic terms and fundamental concepts of the science of heredity. These are described within the context of different areas of genetics—cytogenetics, Mendelian genetics, molecular genetics, and quantitative and population genetics. The discussion covers only those aspects that will help breeders understand these areas' interrelationships and possible roles in breeding.

Part Three, Applications for Breeders, gets down to the "nitty gritty" of applying the information in the preceding chapters to dogs. The inheritance of coat (color, markings, types, and qualities) and structural traits are discussed. The other three chapters focus on health-related aspects of heredity.

In Part Four, Selection, the three chapters examine the heart of dog breeding—the theories of selection, the art of selecting the individuals to be mated, and evaluating the results of breeding. In the final analysis of the results of a mating—that is, evaluating the litter—the breeder must consider many questions: What went right? What went wrong? What are the chances that these puppies are free of a genetic problem? Was that deformed puppy caused by a hereditary problem, or was it a chromosomal abnormality that is unlikely to occur again? Will these puppies be prepotent for strong toplines, or should this trait be reinforced? The answers to these questions help in planning the next generation. It is only through understanding what went right or wrong that the breeder can improve the odds of obtaining the desired traits more consistently. The answers are never simple, but the rewards of healthier dogs with desired breed structure and behavior are priceless.

A summary of breed colors and alleles can be found in Appendix A. Appendix B offers a list of congenital and hereditary disorders that have been identified in many breeds. Finally, an extensive glossary provides a quick reference for the reader.

It has been said of genetics that *anything that can go wrong will go wrong in someone*. An awareness of the intricate patterns of heredity is the only way to begin to realize why traits don't always fall into predictable dominant-recessive patterns. Understanding that there are varying degrees of dominance, polygenes, modifiers, and environmental effects enables breeders to select breeding-quality individuals and to plan matings that improve the chances of achieving their goals.

I would like to give special thanks to Portia Vance, a long-time friend and an experienced Airedale breeder, who played a special role in the development of this book. Portia believed that an understanding of genetics would help her as a breeder, but she found genetics both confusing and intimidating. As I tried to develop a book that breeders in her position could understand, Portia studied each chapter and provided feedback. She identified the places that needed clarification and illustration; she raised questions about aspects that I had not included, leading to the addition of some rather interesting material. In all, she gave exactly the kind of help needed to achieve this book's goal.

EVOLUTIONARY GENETICS

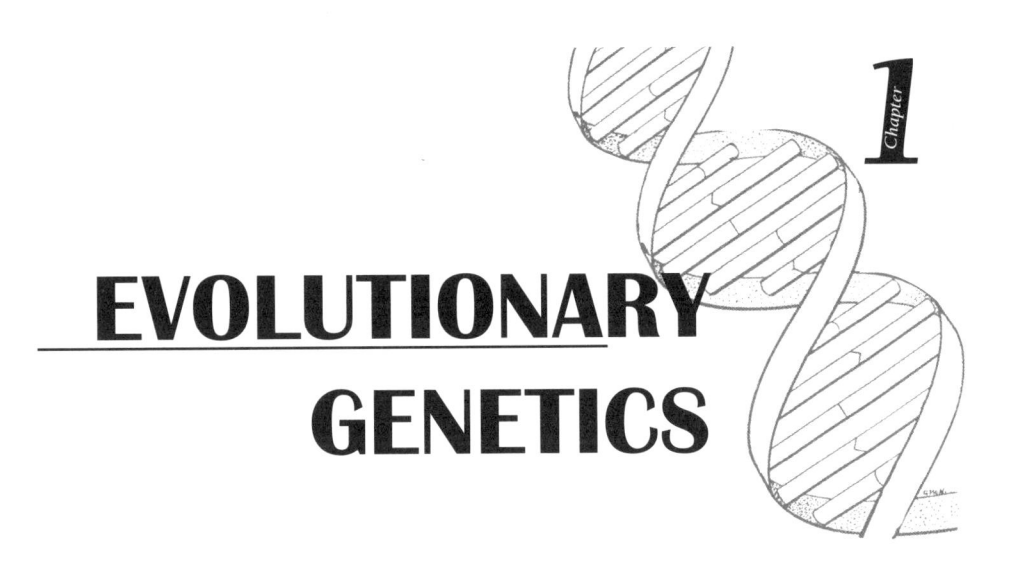

Chapter 1

When Charles Darwin's name is mentioned, the first word that comes to mind is *evolution*—the change in a population's genetic composition over time. The title of Darwin's great work published in 1859, *On the Origin of Species by Means of Natural Selection*, reflects his theory of *natural selection*—the natural process of differential survival and reproduction, also called *survival of the fittest*. Darwin pointed out that many are born, but only a fraction live to become parents. He concluded that many of those that lived long enough to reproduce had better survival traits, which they passed on to their offspring, and that these hereditary qualities eventually spread through the population. Any trait such as better immunity to disease, digestive efficiency, fertility, or parenting instincts improved not only the individual's chances of survival but also those of its progeny. Whenever individuals differ in one or more traits, natural selection merely reflects the value of such traits through their survival and reproduction.

Before the turn of the century, Gregor Mendel and others shed further light on the mysteries of heredity; these discoveries will be discussed later. In 1905, William Bateson, proposed that the new science should be known as *genetics* (from the Greek word *genesis*, meaning *origin*), a concept that grows ever more meaningful, for genetics is the root of all life sciences.

Genetics may be defined as the study of genes through their variation. As the understanding of heredity expanded, geneticists began to concentrate on different aspects. *Evolutionary genetics* focuses on the factors that alter a population's genetic composition over time. These factors—migration, mutation, natural selection, and random drift—are also important concepts of population genetics and are discussed in Chapter 7.

For many years, scientists believed that evolution was a very slow process, a gradual accumulation of the genetic differences that develop in reproductive isolation such as that observed by Darwin on the Galapagos Islands. It is now known that very minor mutations occur constantly, indicating that species are dynamic units, subject to constant change, and those mutations that improve the chances of survival and reproduction become spread through the population and contribute to evolutionary changes.

Evolution can occur with surprising swiftness when a species encounters something new and deadly in the environment. Mosquitos and other insects rapidly developed resistance to DDT because the few that survived became the only parents and passed on their resistance to their offspring.

Evolutionary changes can also occur instantly through chromosomal rearrangements. Mutations at the chromosomal level usually produce new species—if the individuals survive, of course.

Three patterns of evolution have been identified. (a) A single line may simply change over a period of time, maintaining genetic continuity throughout (*anagenesis*); this is caused by a combination of mutation, selection, and random drift. It may occur over centuries, as on the Galapagos Islands, or swiftly, as with DDT resistance. (b) Sometimes a single line gives rise to two or more contemporaneous species (*cladogenesis*); the cause is reproductive isolation plus mutation, selection, and random drift. (c) The third pattern (*reticulate evolution*) is produced by *species hybridization* (mating between two different species); this occurs in both plants and animals, especially in disturbed habitats. Many consider the red wolf an example of reticulate evolution, claiming it *originated* as a hybrid of the coyote and gray wolf.

Molecular genetics is revolutionizing our understanding of evolution. All organisms share certain features that suggest a single origin of life some 3 or 4 billion years ago, a stream of genetic continuity from the first replicating molecules of DNA. The best evidence of this is that many DNA sequences (genes) are shared by most living creatures. This "genetic conservation" often occurs with genes related to respiration and the metabolism of fats and carbohydrates. For example, there is a remarkable similarity of the DNA sequences that produce the enzyme enolase in life forms ranging from yeasts to mammals. The slight differences offer an interesting yardstick for comparing points of evolutionary divergence. The DNA sequence that produces enolase in humans is more like the sequence in monkeys and dogs than the sequence in chickens, yet all of these variant sequences produce the identical enzyme.[1]

ORIGIN OF THE *CANIDAE*

The earliest member of the *Canidae* (doglike species) family is *Hesperocyon gregarius*, known as the stem (ancestral) dog. It originated in the North American tropics about 67 million years ago. About 30 million years ago, the stem dog split into two branches. One branch, called the borophagines (*Borophagus*), consisted of mastiff-sized big-game hunters, that became extinct 2 1/2 million years ago when big game became scarce. The other branch, *Leptocyon*, were small-game hunters that could also metabolize vegetable matter—a clear survival advantage. This dietary flexibility enabled them to adapt to the changing environment and to diversified food sources. Over a few million years, the *Leptocyon* evolved into wolves, foxes, and other modern members of the family.[2]

The versatile doglike carnivores spread from the New World to the Old World during the ice ages, when the water levels of lakes and oceans fell as vast amounts of the earth's water froze into great sheets of ice. As the oceans retreated, dry land emerged between Asia and Alaska (the Bering Strait) and between New Guinea and Australia (the Torres Strait). Men and animals migrated across these land bridges, and the most adaptable became distributed worldwide. Many species—such as the horse, rhinoceros, and mammoth—that reached the American continents became extinct when the climate changed again.

The different species within the *Canidae* family have different numbers of chromosomes, ranging from 36 to 78.[3] For example:

- gray wolf *(Canis lupus)*   78
- maned wolf *(Chrysocyon brachyurus)*   76
- bush dog *(Speothos venaticus)*   74
- crab-eating fox *(Cerdocyon thous)*   74
- bat-eared fox *(Otocyon megalotis)*   72
- fennec fox *(Vulpes zerda)*   64
- arctic fox *(Alopex lagopus)*   50
- raccoon dog *(Nyctereutes procyonoides)*   42
- red fox *(Vulpes vulpes)*   36

Chromosomal analyses indicate that the *Canidae* evolved through a series of chromosomal aberrations—the splitting of one, loss of another, translocations, additions, and so forth. Tracing the changes, one by one, from ancestral species to modern has clarified the branches and ages of the family's evolutionary tree.[4]

GENUS *CANIS*

Taxonomy is the orderly classification of plants and animals according to their presumed natural relationships. The domestic dog's taxonomic name is *Canis familiaris*, meaning that it belongs to the order *Carnivora*, the family *Canidae* (doglike species), the genus *Canis*, and the species *familiaris*.

The problem with taxonomy is that phrase *presumed natural relationships*. As more is learned about these relationships, the classifications must be adjusted accordingly. Varying names may be the source of some confusion. For example, the gray wolf is normally identified as *Canis lupus*, and it is considered the stem (ancestral) form of the species. When discussing the gray wolf and its subspecies, the gray wolf may be identified as *Canis lupus lupus* to distinguish it from the subspecies such as *Canis lupus pallipes*, the Indian wolf. In fact, some writers now classify the domestic dog as *Canis lupus f. familiaris*. *Canis lupus* identifies the dog as a subspecies of the wolf, and the *f.* stands for *forma*, meaning *not a natural form*.[5]

Wayne divides the modern *Canidae* into sixteen *genera* (plural of *genus*) with thirty-six species.[6] The genus *Canis* consists of seven natural wild species and three domesticated species. The following are the wild species:

- side-striped jackal *(Canis adjustus)*
- golden jackal *(Canis aureus)*
- black-backed jackal *(Canis mesomelas)*
- Ethiopian wolf *(Canis simensis)*

- gray wolf *(Canis lupus)*
- red wolf *(Canis rufus)*
- coyote *(Canis latrans)*

The golden jackal inhabits a belt that stretches across northern Africa as well as northward to southeastern Europe and eastward to Central Asia and Thailand. The ranges of the golden and black-backed jackals overlap in East Africa. The black-backed and the side-striped jackals share the same general range to the south of the golden jackal's African range, though the first prefers open savannas, and the latter prefers the forests.

The Ethiopian wolf, a little-known endangered species, is also known as the Simian jackal or the Simian fox. However, it is more closely related to gray wolves and coyotes than to other African canids.[7]

The Old World and New World wolves are (or were) found throughout the northern hemisphere and are classified as a single species with many subspecies. The gray wolf exhibits so much physical variation that taxonomists cannot agree on the number of subspecies, and estimates range from twenty-four to thirty-six.[8]

In the New World, the relationship between the wolf and other wolflike species is uncertain. The fearsome dire wolf *(Canis dirus)* became extinct about 8,500 years ago when many of its big-game prey species died out. Although not much taller than the largest modern gray wolf, it weighed an estimated 20 percent more. The dire wolf is considered a branch of the early gray wolf rather than an ancestor.[9]

The coyote probably evolved from the wolf. This adaptable species has been extending its range and is now found as far south as Mexico City and as far north as Alaska as well as throughout most of the United States.

The endangered red wolf *(Canis rufus,* or *Canis niger* in earlier literature) is the subject of considerable controversy. According to Stains, zoologists cannot decide if it is a "proper species, subspecies of wolf, subspecies of coyote, coyote-dog cross, coyote-wolf cross, or even a dog-wolf cross." The red wolf's protected status and reintroduction to parts of its historical habitat is complicated by hybridization with coyotes. Exactly when the hybridization first happened poses an interesting question. Initially, it was believed that the hybridization was a very recent phenomenon brought about by diminishing habitat and increasing contact between the two species. However, analysis of the DNA from museum specimens of red wolves from about 1910 (before the hybridization was thought to be common) revealed that all were hybrids,

Figure 1–1. Gray wolf *(Canis lupus lupus)*. *Despite its name, the gray wolf's color ranges from solid black to solid white. Photo by Lisa Schnelzer.*

Figure 1–2. Coyote (*Canis latrans*). *Photo by J. R. Schnelzer.*

which some consider definitive evidence for the hybrid origin of the red wolf. Fossil records indicate that red wolves have inhabited the southeastern United States for about seven to eight thousand years. The size and dentition of some fossils are intermediate between the red wolf and the coyote, and Gipson suggests that there has been periodic interbreeding between the two species long before humans altered their habitat. In fact, it is believed that interbreeding occurred fairly often between all New World wolf species.[10]

The following species are classified as domesticated:
- domestic dog
- pariah dog
- dingo

What's this about other species of domestic dogs? The pariah dog (*Canis indicus*) is an ancient form of domestic dog that frequently reverts to a feral (wild) life. Although first identified as separate natural species, both the Australian dingo and the New Guinea dingo are now classified as feral domestic dogs with a common origin.[11]

Careful analysis of the ocean levels during the ice ages show that at no time was there a land bridge over which the dingo could have reached Australia. Humans reached Australia about 21,000 years ago, but the earliest confirmed dingo remains are about 3,000 years old. Thus, dingoes are believed to be the descendants of domesticated dogs brought to the isolated continent by humans. Later, they learned to live off the land as feral animals. The dingo's various taxonomic identifications include *Canis dingo*, *Canis familiaris dingo*, and *Canis lupus f. dingo*. Although red and black are the most common dingo colors, brown, yellow, cream, and white as well as dapples, brindle, and piebald are also mentioned. Oddly, all dingoes are black at birth, with a white tail tip, white feet, and sometimes a white patch on the nape of the neck.[12]

Already an endangered species at the time of its discovery in 1956, little is known of the New Guinea dingo, also known as the New Guinea Highland dog and the New Guinea singing dog. Its identifications include *Canis familiaris hallstromi* and *Canis lupus f. hallstromi*. It was soon discovered that this dog was a variety of the dingo that had adapted to the harsh mountain climate of New Guinea and had a greater affinity for humans than its Australian cousins. Furthermore, because of its size, conformation, and colors, it is considered a very close relative of the Shiba-Inu.[13]

Members of the genus *Canis* are characterized by similarity of structural and physiological *phenotype*—the observable and measurable expression of genetic traits.

Indeed, only the domestic dog exhibits major departures from the basic appearance. The physiological similarity is most obvious in reproduction. The copulatory tie has been observed in most members of the genus, and gestation in the bicornuate (horned) uterus lasts about sixty-three days. Sexual maturity occurs at about a year, though it may take up to three years in the larger species such as timber wolves. In general, canines produce one litter a year; the puppies' eyes open at about fourteen days, and they nurse for four to six weeks. Both parents share the task of raising the young. In the species that normally live in packs, the group also shares in the care of the young.[14]

A *hybrid* is the product of the mating of genetically differentiated forms, usually different species. A *species* is a group of individuals that share a common gene pool and are bound together by bonds of mating and heritage, and "among other things, the concept of species is based on the ability to produce fertile offspring when partners are freely chosen."[15]

This brings us to the crux of the problem with genus *Canis*. All members of the genus have 78 chromosomes, and moreover, the size and type of chromosomes as they appear on karyotypes (see Chapter 3) are also very similar. It is not too surprising that fertile hybrids are possible, but the fact that all members of the genus are completely interfertile makes them a zoological peculiarity.

Natural hybridization between species occurs in *hybrid zones,* which are regions where genetically distinct populations meet and produce progeny of mixed ancestry. The hybrids are typically less fit for survival and don't reproduce themselves. Occasionally, however, some find acceptance among one of the parental populations and produce offspring. In this way, the genes of the other species become dispersed among the adoptive population, a process called *introgression.*

Both planned and naturally occurring crosses between members of the genus *Canis* show complete interfertility. Jackals rarely cross species under natural conditions. In the Middle East, golden jackals and feral dogs share the same ecosystem but do not cross. Interbreeding between the side-striped jackal and the domestic dog has been reported. In a captive or a disturbed natural environment, however, species mating rituals are disrupted. In captivity, the New World coyote and the Old World golden jackal have been crossed and backcrossed to the parent species.[16]

The domestic dog is freely promiscuous. The deliberate crossbreeding of dogs with wolves is an ancient practice first recorded by Aristotle (385–322 B.C.). Later, Pliny (A.D. 23–79) wrote that the Gauls tied bitches in season to trees in the forest so they would be bred by wolves.[17] Eskimos and other northern people still do this occasionally.

Natural hybridization between dogs, wolves, and coyotes is well known in the United States and between dogs and dingoes in Australia. The coyote-dog hybrids are a special concern in the western United States because they are bolder and more aggressive toward livestock than the coyote.

The ranges of the New World wolf species (gray wolf and coyote) once covered most of North America, creating many hybrid zones. The fossil remains of many are intermediate between the species and are believed to indicate frequent hybridization.[18]

As DNA technology becomes more sophisticated, it is becoming possible to accurately identify hybridization and introgression. One DNA study of the Ethiopian wolf concluded that hybridization between female wolves and male domestic dogs had occurred in one population.[19]

Mitochondrial DNA (mtDNA), which is inherited solely through the mother, makes it possible to trace maternal descent. Recent studies of mtDNA have shown that gray wolves and coyotes along the U.S.-Canadian border have been enjoying illicit affairs. The frequency of coyote mtDNA among wolves ranges from 50 percent in Minnesota to 100 percent in Quebec. Because mtDNA is maternally transmitted, this means that hybrids are the offspring of coyote bitches and wolf males that have crossed back with the wolves. Most curiously, this seems to be a one-way affair because no wolf mtDNA has been identified in the coyote populations.[20]

THE DOMESTIC DOG—*CANIS FAMILIARIS*

The first question to be examined is what is the difference between domesticated, tamed, and feral? A *domesticated animal* belongs to a species that has been adapted to an intimate life in association with humans and often has been altered through human intervention. The dog is the most extreme example of the alteration of a domesticated species. A *tamed animal* is one in which the flight tendency has been eliminated and which has become emotionally stable and comfortable in the presence of humans; all of the *Canis* species are easily tamed when young. A *feral animal* belongs to a domesticated species that has reverted to the wild. The term applies to individual strays that have learned to survive through need as well as identifiable subspecies such as pariah dogs, Australian dingoes, and New Guinea dingoes.

Darwin speculated that the dog derived from wolves, jackals, or wild dogs, primarily because of the reports of species hybridization.[21] According to Chiarelli, it is possible "that different human populations domesticated different dog species, and then these different human populations came into contact with the different stocks of domesticated dogs that had been hybridized. This phenomenon of introgressive hybridization can explain the large variation existing among the actual living domestic dogs."[22]

Zeuner, an early authority on the history of domestication, believes that dogs were domesticated from a variety of wild canines, including the jackal.[23] Fox suggests another alternative:

> General (but unfounded) consensus holds that when it was first domesticated about 10,000 years ago, the dog was derived from a wolf, possibly the Asiatic wolf (*Canis lupus pallipes*). Archaeological records, however, show that a dingo-like canid was widespread throughout Europe in the Stone Age. It is my contention that the domestic dog was derived primarily from this prototype of *Canis familiaris*, and at different places and times this canid was crossbred with indigenous wolves to produce some of the more wolfish breeds, such as the malamute and the husky.[24]

The prehistoric dingo was smaller than the wolves but larger than the jackals. During the Mesolithic period, it inhabited northern Africa, Mesopotamia, and southern and western Asia.

Folklore and fiction abound with tales of the first tamed wolf and why it chose to associate with humans. However, dogs were probably domesticated many times and in many places during the prehistoric millennia. Fossil remains of humans with dogs or wolflike animals have been found on all continents, suggesting that the first bonds between human and wolf happened at more than one place and on more than one occasion. The range of phenotype among *Canis lupus* subspecies may have contributed to the earliest differences between strains of domestic dogs.

Domestication may have started with cooperative hunting, and this probably predates all other functions. Naaktgeboren reports a successful attempt to test this possibility by hunting with a tamed wolf.[25] From sporting dogs to tracking hounds, sight hounds, and terriers, hunting remains the dog's most universal function.

Zeuner suggests that scavenging behavior was also a factor—that is, a garbage clean-up crew has a definite utilitarian value.[26] All of the wild species feed on carrion and refuse, and so do dogs when given a chance, much to the dismay of their fastidious owners who toss the stinking carcass of a bird or rodent into the nearest dog-proof receptacle.

One other possibility must be mentioned. Macintosh described Gould's visit to a group of aborigines, few of whom had ever seen a white man, in the heart of the Gibson Desert in Western Australia. Gould counted nineteen dingoes in and around camp. The dingoes and aborigines slept huddled together for warmth. When Gould took a picture of this, the dingoes disappeared for several nights, and the aborigines spent cold nights until they returned.[27]

The role of the dingo in Australian aboriginal culture may be a valid window to the earliest bonds between humans and dogs. Fox summed it up when he wrote that dingoes tamed by Australian aborigines keep their camps clean of garbage, sleep next to humans, warn of intruders, and cooperate with hunting in a limited environment.[28]

Zeuner suggests that dogs were domesticated as early as 18,000 B.C. and that the first herding dogs were developed by 13,750 B.C. The main reason that it is so difficult to pinpoint where and when dogs first began their partnership with humans is because it is almost impossible to differentiate dogs from wolves in very early fossil remains. The only consistent difference between the skulls of dogs and wolves is the proportionally larger size of the wolf's teeth (except for the narrow-cheeked greyhound breeds and the brachycephalic breeds such as Bulldogs).[29]

The earliest evidence of *Canis familiaris* is a mandible found in Oberkassel, Germany, dated 14,000 B.C., a time near the end of the last Ice Age. A grave (12,000 B.C.) in Ein Mallaha, Israel, contains an elderly human, lying on his or her side, with a hand resting on a puppy's chest. The archaeological remains of dogs dating from 9000 to 7000 B.C. have been found in many parts of the world—from Europe and Asia to the southern tip of Chile.[30]

Among the most interesting of the prehistoric finds is the *tubary dog,* first identified in the remains of the Swiss lake dwellers. This tiny canine is considered the ancestor of the maltese-type toys and the small terriers. The dogs certainly could not have been used for hunting game animals, though they might have been useful for rodents. Perhaps they were also valued for companionship. The remains of two distinct types were identified in the Danish bog sites—8000–6000 B.C. The smaller is a tubary-type dog; the larger type is smaller than a wolf.[31]

By the time of the ancient Old World civilizations, dogs had evolved into several distinctive types. The earliest evidence of dogs in ancient Egypt is dated about 3500 B.C. At least three basic types—greyhounds, mastiffs, and sheepdogs—have been identified. The greyhound types portrayed in art exhibit considerable variety. Predynastic

Table 1–1. Prehistoric Dogs

Scientific Name	Description
Canis familiaris inostranzewi	Neolithic European breed Remains found in Denmark and Scotland Gray wolf plus some dingo or pariah dog cross Possible ancestor of Alsatian and northern sled-pulling breeds
Canis familiaris matris-optimae	Neolithic European breed Primitive sheepdog, probable ancestor of herding breeds
Canis familiaris intermedius	Neolithic European breed Remains found in Indus Valley, Austria, Switzerland Primitive hound, probable ancestor of hound breeds Strong resemblance to dingo and pariah dogs
Canis familiaris palustris	Neolithic European breed Remains found in Swiss lake dwellings, southern Britain, and others Known as tubary dogs Toy sized Probable ancestor of small terriers, maltese-type toys
Canis familiaris ladogensis	Toy-sized house dog
Canis familiaris spalleti	Remains found in Bosnia, Italy, Switzerland, Austria, and Germany Toy-sized house dog
Canis familiaris grajus	Neolithic greyhound type
Canis familiaris leineri	Neolithic greyhound x wolf type
Canis familiaris latifrons	Neolithic Algeria
Canis familiaris poutiatini	Senckenberg bog (9000 B.C.), Moscow area Possible ancestor of sheepdogs and hounds

art (4000–3000 B.C.) depicts dogs with both erect and lop ears. Later art depicts greyhound-type dogs with curled (spiral) tail and prick ears as well as some with pendulous tails and lop ears, similar to remains found in the Canary Islands. People of the Indus Valley civilization (about 3000 B.C.) had dogs of four distinct types—dingo, pariah, greyhound, and hound. Babylonian art (about 1950–1650 B.C.) depicts the immense mastiff-type dogs that they used for war.[32]

THE EVOLUTION OF BREEDS

OLD WORLD GROUPS

The evolution of breed phenotypes and their relationships has fascinated many, leading to theories of how they developed. Except for very distinctive types, opinion varies considerably, and what follows is simply an overview of the main points on which there seems to be general agreement. The first three groups (southern, northern, and mastiff) are very ancient types that share a common and relatively identifiable ancestral phenotype. Only one of the modern functional groups—sporting—is described in detail.

Southern Group

The southern group is believed to descend from one or both of the wolf subspecies that inhabit the warmer climates of the northern hemisphere. The historical range of the Indian wolf *(Canis lupus pallipes)* included India, Mesopotamia, and Arabia. Smaller than the gray wolf, it is the most doglike of the subspecies of wolves, and is easily tamed. It rarely howls but sometimes barks. The racy, lightly built Arabian wolf *(Canis lupus arabs)* inhabited the African deserts through Egypt and the Holy Land. From these stems, there are two primary branches: *(a)* the pariah or dingo types, and *(b)* the gazehounds.

Pariah or dingo group. Also called the primitive group, it is named for the pariah dog *(Canis indicus)* as well as for the dingoes it resembles. It bears a close resemblance to the Indian wolf *(Canis lupus pallipes)*. Because the ancient Egyptians used tamed jackals for hunting, the pariah group is the most likely to have hybridized with the tamed jackals during ancient times.

Pariah dogs were widespread in the ancient world—Mesopotamia, Egypt, Africa, and India. They were distinguished by a short curled tail and upright ears. Pariahs appear to have been highly regarded by Egyptians and are depicted in their art. The Bible, however, describes pariah dogs as urban scavengers, forming dangerous packs at times. Thus, some ancient pariahs developed domestic bonds with humans, but others survived in a semiferal state.

Information about modern pariah dogs is scanty, but Konrad Lorenz related some interesting information.

> Otto Koenig, who lately has studied Pariah dogs in Turkey . . . told me a very curious thing. The pariahs around Istanbul often live in close vicinity of domestic stock; chickens, goats, and sheep range free and unprotected, but they never touch them, even when very hungry. Even bitches with litters refrain from eating small chicks and newly born sheep. The survival value of this inhibition is obvious, as, in an area closely populated by humans and domestic animals, the dogs would soon be exterminated if they ever attacked livestock. The question, however, is how they learned not to do it. It is important to state in this connection, that unlike dingoes, Turkish pariah dogs prove to be completely amenable to a normally "civilized" house-dogs' education.[33]

The modern pariah dogs of India are urban scavengers. Their behavior varies considerably. Some are devoted pets that prefer to stay within a few hundred yards of home, others are home based but roam freely, and a third type are ownerless scavengers. The first two occasionally form temporary packs for hunting with owners. Structurally, the Indian pariah dogs exhibit a range of types: heavy extreme (sheep-guarding type); heavy medium (dingo type); light medium (collie type); light extreme medium (greyhound type); and small (toy type).

Pariah dogs are probably the most numerous canines in the world, but they are represented by the fewest recognized breeds. These include the Basenji, Pharaoh Hound, Ibizan Hound, and the Canaan Dog, which was developed from Israeli pariah dogs. The group also includes all hairless breeds. Among the toy breeds, the pariah group is represented by the diminutive Chihuahua.

Gazehounds. One of the earliest established types, the gazehound group includes all breeds that pursue game that is in sight. Some writers suggest that they stemmed from the lightly built desert wolf of Arabia (*Canis lupus arabs*), and others suggest either the pariah alone or in combination with the Arabian wolf.

Despite sizes that range from the Irish Wolfhound to the diminutive Italian Greyhound, all are characterized by their lean raciness and neatly folded rose ears. Other modern breeds include the Greyhound, Saluki, Afghan Hound, Scottish Deerhound, Borzoi, and Whippet.

Riddle traces the origin of the name *greyhound*, a breed that is rarely gray, to a decree of William the Conqueror after his conquest of England in 1066. William's law allowed gentlemen (landowners) to own bloodhounds (tracking hounds), but only men with *degrees*—the term for a title—could own the coursing breed, and they became known as *degreehounds*. This evolved into *greehound*, then greyhound.[34]

Northern Group

Nobody disputes that the gray wolf (*Canis lupus lupus*) is the origin of the northern group. The gray wolf—whose territory covers Asia, northern Europe, and North America—comes in black, white, and buff as well as gray. Height ranges from 26 to 38 inches and weight from 60 to 175 pounds.

Northern or spitz group. The spitz group is characterized by a curled tail and prick ears, and most have a thick, coarse, moderately longhaired coat. These sturdy dogs of medium size have been used for both hunting and draft since prehistoric times. The modern spitz breeds include the Alaskan Malamute, Siberian Husky, Samoyed, Russian Laika, Akita, Norwegian Elkhound, Finnish Spitz, Karelian Bear Dog, Chow Chow, Keeshond, and Shiba Inu.

The tubary dogs were an early branch of the northern group. They evolved into the spitz-type toys (Maltese, Pomeranian) and probably most terriers. The terriers lost the typical stop, but curled tails remain common.

Sheep-herding dogs. The herding sheepdogs have lost the distinctively curled tail and include the alsatian and collie types. The shaggy sheepdog breeds—Old English Sheepdog and Russian Ovtcharka—are also probable offshoots of the northern group.

Mastiff Group

The large, heavily built Tibetan wolf (*Canis lupus chanco*)—whose range includes Tibet, Persia, and northern India—is believed to be the ancestor of the Tibetan mastiff. This massive breed characterized by a blunt nose, drop ears, wooly coat, and loose skin is the prototype of all other mastiff-type breeds.

Mastiffs. The mastiff type was widespread and well-established in the ancient world, represented by the molossian of Greece and Rome and the hyrcanian of India. These were the great dogs of war that wore spiked collars when going into battle. They were also the guardians of home and livestock. The powerful medieval alaunt (ancestor of the Great Dane) helped bring down the dangerous bear and boar, and mastiffs were turned loose at night in the streets of Nantes to enforce the curfew.

The modern mastiff-type breeds include the Mastiff (obviously), Great Dane, Rottweiler, Saint Bernard, Newfoundland, and Bulldog. The toy forms include the Pekingese, Pug, and Boston Terrier.

Sheep-guarding dogs. The large breeds used to guard, rather than herd, sheep resemble mastiffs, though the smaller, racier breeds are believed to have either ancient crosses to the spitz and pariah types or more direct and recent crosses to the sheep-herding dogs.

Ancient shepherds apparently preferred white sheep-guarding dogs, probably so that they couldn't be mistaken for wolves. Several regions that developed the white sheep-guarding breeds also developed sheep-herding breeds of other colors. Thus, the Pyrenees produced the Great Pyrenees to guard and the Pyrenean Shepherd to herd, Italy the Maremma and Berganese Shepherd, and Poland the Chuvatch and Valee; Hungary produced the two white sheep-guarding breeds (Komondor and Kuvasz) and the sheep-herding Puli.

Scent hounds. The mastiff ancestry is evident in large, heavy, scent hounds such as the Bloodhound, with their massive wrinkled heads, jowls, and loose skin. These hounds are also characterized by pendulous ears. All European hound breeds are descended from the segusierhund, a collective name for the Gallic-Celtic running hounds. It is a long stretch from the Bloodhound to the Beagle, but all breeds in this group have pendulous ears. Other breeds include the Foxhound, Basset Hound, and so forth.

Sporting Group

The roots of the modern breeds known collectively as sporting dogs are among the most obscure, even though they are historically recent. After all, almost all dogs will hunt when given encouragement, and hunters didn't need a specialized gundog until after the invention of firearms. Most types can be traced to no farther back than the European Middle Ages. In addition, they evolved differently in Great Britain than they did on the European Continent.

Water dogs. The curly or corded coats of the water dogs suggest that they share an ancestry with the shaggy herding breeds. The oldest breeds are associated with fishing boats, where they retrieved articles lost overboard. This talent was later adapted to retrieving birds from water. The water dogs are represented by the Poodle, Irish Water Spaniel, American Water Spaniel, and Curly-Coated Retriever as well as the Portuguese Water Dog (shown in the working group). Toy forms include the toy Poodle and Bichon Frise.

Retrievers. The heavy bodies and wide heads with square muzzles of most water retrievers suggest mastiff ancestry, and this is known in the case of the Labrador Retriever, which was developed from the Newfoundland. Other breeds include the Golden Retriever and Chesapeake Bay Retriever.

Spaniels and setters. Medieval bird dogs indicated the presence of game by dropping to the ground (setting or couching). The birds could be flushed for falcons to capture, or the hunters could drop large nets over the birds and dog. Dogs that pointed game rather than dropping became entangled in the nets, and the trait was considered faulty until hunters began using firearms. The modern breeds, which are characterized by pendulous ears and silky coats, include all setters and most spaniels. Toy forms include the Cavalier King Charles Spaniel and Papillon, and many would include the American Cocker Spaniel.

Pointers. The Pointer is an English breed. The old hunting classics agree that the strength of the pointing trait came from the ancient Spanish Pointer, which was crossed with dogs that were used to locate and point hares for pursuit by greyhounds, and most references mention crosses to the foxhound for speed and range. Selective breeding developed an exclusive interest in game birds.

The Continental gundogs were developed as versatile hunters of both fur and feather that retrieve on land and in water as well as point. Most of the breeds were developed by crossing European scent hounds with pointers of English or Spanish origin. The Weimaraner's ancestry can be traced to a breed of deerhound brought from Egypt or Palestine by Louis IX; the Vizsla, also from western Asia and characterized by thin, pendulous ears, may share this deerhound ancestry.

Modern Show Groups

By now it should be obvious that the other modern show groups do not reflect ancestral families. The hound group includes representatives from the southern group (Greyhound, Saluki, Ibizan Hound), the northern group (Norwegian Elkhound), and the mastiff group (Bloodhound, Foxhounds). The toy group includes representatives from the southern group (Chihuahua, Chinese Crested, Italian Greyhound), the northern group (Maltese, Pomeranian), and the mastiff group (Pug). The working group includes representatives from the northern group (Akita, Alaskan Malamute, Samoyed) and the mastiff group (Great Dane, Great Pyrenees, Komondor, Newfoundland, Rottweiler). The terrier breeds include representatives from the northern group (most) and the mastiff group (Bull Terrier, Staffordshire Terrier). The non-sporting group includes representatives from the northern group (Keeshond, American Eskimo, Finnish Spitz, Tibetan Terrier) and the mastiff group (Boston Terrier, Bulldog). Only the herding group appears to share a common descent from the northern group. Finally, the sporting group appears to have no direct descent from any.

NEW WORLD DOGS

Very little is known about the pre-Colombian New World dogs except through the records of the early explorers, and those are not very helpful. Azua identified three breeds in pre-Colombian Mexico: (*a*) the hairless dog called the Xoloitzcuintli, (*b*) a dwarf dog called the Talchichi, and (*c*) a 15–18 inch (50–60 cm) dog known by various names.[35]

Although most native American cultures had several breeds—that is, locally distinct types—no serious systematic study of them was made until the early 20th century. Pferd identified seventeen breeds in fourteen different North and South American cultures. The breeds could be subdivided into three basic types:
- Large, wolflike, prick-eared, curled tail, northern (spitz) type; representatives include the Eskimo Dog and the Malamute
- Medium-sized, prick-eared, brush-tailed type that resembled the coyote
- Medium to small-sized terrier or toy type that showed considerable variation; modern representative is the Mexican Hairless [36]

On average, each cultural group was associated with three different breeds. Some breeds were found in up to six different groups, and others were found in only one.

The dogs filled a wide range of functions: hunting, draft (sled, travois), pack, guard, scavenger, wool producer, herding, and pet; at least four were kept for food.

DNA DISCOVERIES

With the development of DNA analysis, the experts were confident that it would be possible to confirm their theories of breed evolution and to clarify the relationships between dog breeds. The findings have been totally unexpected.

When Rodney Honeycutt compared the DNA of twenty-eight dog breeds, trying to establish the relationship between them, he discovered that the DNA of twenty-seven breeds couldn't be differentiated from that of a wolf. The DNA of the Italian Maremma (a sheep-guarding breed), however, was unique.[37]

Coppinger and Schneider summarized the findings of several unpublished papers, commenting that, of the eighteen breeds studied, there were greater mtDNA differences within single breeds than between the dogs and wolves. Furthermore, the wolflike husky breeds (Siberian, Eskimo, and Alaskan Malamute) were actually no more closely related to wolves than the Great Danes, Chihuahuas, Dachshunds, Bulldogs, and Poodles. They commented: "These data make wolves resemble another breed of dog." In fact, "there is less mtDNA difference between dogs, wolves and coyotes than there is between the various ethnic groups of human beings, which are recognized as belonging to a single species. The results are not surprising since, reproductively, wolves, coyotes, jackals and dogs are all interfertile, and cross-breeding still occurs in the wild between wolves, coyotes and dogs." Instead of shedding new light on the evolution of the domestic dog, it seems that the most modern genetic technology cannot conclusively identify the species from which they descended, though most authorities agree that dogs are descended from various subspecies of *Canis lupus*. However, as Coppinger and Schneider commented, "Until the matter is cleared up, we call the ancestor 'wolf' because it is the shortest word to type."[38]

DOMESTICATION—SELECTIVE EVOLUTION

The burning question of most dog fanciers is how did dogs evolve into such a varied species? The answer appears to lie in the process of domestication itself.

ENVIRONMENTAL EFFECTS

One of the most startling discoveries of modern zoo breeding programs is that identifiable, measurable differences between the zoo animals and their wild cousins develop within a few generations. It appears that removing any species from its natural environment leads to evolutionary changes in response to the altered environment.

Zoo foxes show striking structural changes after several generations of breeding in captivity: decreased brain weight, shortening of the facial skull, broadening of the skull base, and decreased muscular development. A similar decrease of brain size has been observed in experimental animals after a few generations in a captive environment.[39]

The most frequently observed physiologic changes in mammals are sexual precocity and disturbed heat cycles. For example, captive wild felines sometimes come into estrus more than once a year. A primary difference between dogs and their wild relatives is that the latter come into estrus only once a year.

Behavioral patterns are also disturbed. One of the most frequently observed alterations (and problems) in zoo animals is hypersexuality (excessive sexual interest or activity), which is common in zoo animals and which Hediger considers "one of the obvious phenomena of domestication." Mating ceremonials become simplified in captive animals. Interspecies matings are more common in captivity than in the wild, and interesting as they are, it must be remembered that these reflect sexually deviant behavior.[40]

BEHAVIORAL SELECTION

The genetic effect of active selection for tameness—that is, the domestication process—is even more dramatic than the passive effect of captivity alone. A modern attempt to domesticate a wild species of *Canidae* has opened a window on the evolutionary effects of domestication that may parallel those creating the domestic dog.

In 1958, Dmitry Belyaev, a Siberian geneticist, began selectively breeding silver foxes (a variant of the red fox that is black with silver-tipped guard hairs) for tameness to improve their manageability on commercial fur farms. The result of more than twenty generations has amazed everyone.

Behavior

The red fox *(Vulpes vulpes)* is an extremely nervous species. When first brought into captivity, the red fox displays a wide variety of psychotic symptoms: panic, aggressiveness, withdrawal, and other behavior indicating a very high level of fear. Generations of commercial breeding produced no significant changes of this inherent wild-type behavior. As with most behavioral traits, the foxes exhibited a range of defensive behavior, and some foxes were less fearful than others.[41]

The experimental population came from Siberian fur farm foxes, selecting six to eight-week-old cubs that showed no aggressive or fear response to humans. These were then graded on acceptance of food from hands, response to fondling and to call, and unrelated pairs with highest scores for domestic-type behavior were arranged.[42]

This could parallel the selective effect on wolves and other canines that survived by scavenging neolithic human communities—the less fearful ones would get more food and produce more offspring, which in turn would increase the survival value of tameness.

The behavior of the domesticated foxes is very similar to that of dogs and is becoming more so over succeeding generations. The foxes come when called and allow humans to pick them up for petting. Those with the highest domestication ratings even bark at the sight of humans and wag their tails in greeting.[43]

Nervous and Endocrine Systems

Genes produce proteins such as serotonin that interact with the nervous system to influence behavior. The tame foxes had higher serotonin levels in areas of the brain than the fur farm foxes, and the behavior may be related to the heredity of serotonin and similar substances that affect the nervous system.[44]

Selective breeding to reduce the fear response quickly affected the function of these endocrine glands and the total stress response of the foxes, and their stress-hormone levels became lower than those of the fur farm foxes. Stress, such as fear and pain, stimulates the production of the stress-response hormones (epinephrine, norepinephrine, and many others), which play a key role in genetic variance and evolution. Stress often eliminates the less fit; it also increases the frequency of chromosomal crossing over and the rate of mutations.[45]

Both serotonin and melanin (a pigment) are synthesized from the amino acid tryptophan. Thus, there is a link between the proteins that affect the nervous system and those that produce color. In a related study of commercial fur farm foxes of other color mutations, it was found that the size of the adrenal and pituitary glands in proportion to body weight appears to be reduced in the color mutations, with a corresponding reduction of activity and wildness. "When the genes of the black (nonagouti), blue, and chocolate [foxes] are combined in a single individual, their effects are somewhat additive, and the decrease in distance from the observer is roughly correlated with the ratio of adrenal weight to body weight."[46]

Reproductive Changes

Like their wild relatives, the fur farm vixens come into season from January to March and have shown no alteration of this pattern for about eighty years. Within this population, however, records showed that vixens that did not exhibit aggression and fear of human contact mated earlier during the breeding season and had larger litters. This suggested a modification of heredity that might be correlated with or characteristic of early stages of domestication.[47]

As with zoo animals, the foxes selected for tameness began to develop an altered reproductive cycle, coming into season twice a year. This was paralleled by decreased productive capacity; some did not mate, failed to conceive, had decreased lactation, or engaged in cannibalism. The selection for tameness had destabilized the foxes' reproductive cycle, and the changes had not yet stabilized into a new domesticated form.[48]

The selection for tameness also altered early embryonic development in the vixens: (*a*) passage of the ova through the oviducts and implantation of the embryos in the uterus was accelerated; and (*b*) the first cell divisions proceeded at a more rapid rate. It was suggested that more rapid implantation and embryonic development may be related to the higher rate of fertility in domesticated animals.[49]

Appearance

The most incredible results of selection for tameness are those that have altered the foxes' appearance. Structural changes include floppy ears, curled tails, short tails, protruding lower jaw, and shortened legs. Sometimes, the changes were not symmetrical; for example, one fox had three short legs and one of normal length.[50]

The following color mutations have appeared: singes, stars, white flanks, piebalds, brown mottling, blue tinge, and gray guard hairs. *Singes* are yellow spots near the eyes, behind the ear, on the flanks, and on the rump. The size of these spots varies, and the intensity ranges from almost colorless to yellow-brown. They "usually become well expressed by 2.5 months of age, when replacement of primary (juvenile) guard hairs with secondary (summer) [coat] concludes. With formation of the winter fur coat, 'singed' spots begin to disappear." The singes are a single-gene recessive. A single-gene mutation with incomplete dominance produces *stars* (white spots on the head) when heterozygous and white flanks when homozygous.[51]

The stars and singes appear to be repeated spontaneous mutations as only twelve of the eighty litters in which they appeared could be considered inbred; the other litters were very distantly related. There was a strong correlation between the mutations and the domesticity ratings.[52]

What Happened?

The selection for docile, tractable temperaments produced changes of reproductive cycles, stress response, behavior, and appearance. Think of it! In less than forty years of selection for tameness, Belyaev's foxes are well on the way to being a new domesticated canid species with a strong resemblance to dogs. Obviously, selection for tameness produces profound genetic changes. What is going on?

Commenting on the acceleration of implantation and embryonic development, Trut stated:

> This prompted the idea that genetic elements controlling the development and function of the neural system had, in all probability, evolved first as elements governing genetic activity and embryogenesis. The function of this control appears to be the most ancient and unique in the animal kingdom. Neural regulation of the whole organism is a later acquirement of the constellation of these elements.
>
> . . . The developmental systems are versatile: hormones and mediators carrying information from the neuroendocrine system are involved in gene activity regulation from the earliest embryogenesis. Here is a good case of the parsimony of Nature. While perfecting the regulation of genetic processes, evolution has also exploited them as integrative mechanisms of embryogenesis and behavior.[53]

A single alteration of the neuroendocrine system has a cascade effect that disturbs very ancient and fundamental genetic developmental systems. In other words, tinkering with the system produces a genetic earthquake.

The mechanisms are just beginning to be identified. A fox cub begins life as friendly and trusting as a puppy, soliciting attention and food from its mother. At the correct time, the genetic clock triggers the adult behavior, and the cub becomes a wary, solitary creature. In effect, Belyaev was selecting for foxes that had delayed behavioral maturation. Maturation, apparently, is linked with the production of dopamine, a neurohormone that is derived from dopa.[54] Dopa is also the precursor of the neurohormones epinephrine (adrenaline) and norepinephrine as well as the pigment melanin. Begin to see the cascade effect? Add to this the fact that the entire endocrine system is a delicately balanced mechanism that is characterized by feedback loops, and the destabilizing ripple effect begins to make sense.

REVIEW OF TERMS

The key to understanding genetics is learning the special terms. Once learned, you'll be able to read the material in popular literature and even some of the academic-type literature with comprehension. Before going on to the next chapters, be sure that you can understand the following terms:

>domesticated animal
>evolution
>feral animal
>genetics
>hybrid
>hybrid zone
>introgression
>natural selection
>phenotype
>species
>tamed animal

Chapter 2

BEHAVIORAL GENETICS

Nature or nurture—which determines behavior? The answer is neither one alone. No instinct is completely determined by heredity; no social, cultural, or learned behavior is purely environmental. Behavior always develops through the interaction of both hereditary and environmental factors.

Behavioral genetics is the study of organisms by means of both genetic and behavioral analysis; it is an interface between the two sciences. Like other hereditary traits, behavior is a phenotype that can be observed and measured. Unlike physical traits, behavioral phenotype influences the entire organism, making it the most dynamic of all hereditary traits as well as the most responsive to environmental changes.

HOW DO GENES AFFECT BEHAVIOR?

The precise way in which genes affect behavior is not yet clear, but knowledge is growing by leaps and bounds. What is known so far is tantalizing.

EFFECT ON STRUCTURAL TRAITS

The genes provide instructions for producing proteins, and some of those proteins play a role in behavior. Their first effect is to create the brain and nervous systems.

The structure of the brain and nervous system of a fruit fly is very different than that of a frog. The closer the relationship between animals, the fewer their structural differences. The brains and nervous systems of mammals such as dogs and wolves or humans and chimpanzees have many structural similarities.

The structural traits immediately set limits on the type of behavior that each creature can possibly achieve. The behavior of animals that are low on the evolutionary scale is almost completely *instinctive*—that is, programmed by the genes. Surprisingly, even fruit flies can learn to avoid shocks and to recognize different odors. This, too, is hereditary, and some strains learn more quickly and have better memories than others.[1] As the brain and nervous system become more sophisticated, behavioral patterns become more complex, and the potential for learned behavior increases.

THE GENETIC CALENDAR

Behavior is also attuned to a genetic time clock. Genes turn on the behavior appropriate for puberty, mating, and raising young. There are daily genes that influence the patterns of the feeding and the wake-sleep cycles. Annual cycles, such as mating and migration, respond to seasonal changes such as the length of daylight.

HORMONES AND BEHAVIOR

Genes produce many hormones that play important roles in behavior. Hormones are produced not only by the endocrine system but also by cells throughout the body. Although the endocrine system and the nervous system are anatomically distinct, the physiology of the systems are intricately interwoven. The nervous system is mediated by the endocrine system, and the endocrine system is controlled by the nervous system. The domesticated silver foxes described in Chapter 1 illustrate the complexity of these relationships.

Neurohormones—any biochemicals produced by or acting on nerve tissue—are produced in the brain as well as throughout the nervous system. They interact with *neurotransmitters*—substances that transmit nerve impulses across synapses—and influence behavior by initiating or modifying the transmission of nerve impulses. The neurotransmitters act in response to the environment. Fear, for example, floods the body with "fight-or-flight" neurohormones. Although the interplay of neurotransmitters is inherently an automatic, involuntary response, it can be modified in several ways. If an individual is repeatedly exposed to a frightening stimulus that never actually causes harm, the response becomes less intense or disappears. Humans can exert remarkable conscious control over their neurotransmitters through biofeedback techniques. Neurotransmitters are also modified by ingested substances. This can be beneficial in the case of mental disorders, and it can be harmful in the case of cocaine.

Arons studied the genetic variability of predatory behavior toward sheep in three breeds of dogs representing different functional types using neurochemical analysis. Siberian Huskies exhibit the complete predatory behavior pattern and are consistent killers of livestock. Border Collies represented the herding dogs that exhibit an inhibited predatory response. Shar Planinetz, developed to protect livestock, have low level of interest in sheep and exhibit little, if any, predatory behavior, and they had the lowest level of *catecholamines* (a group of biochemicals that function as neurohormones or neurotransmitters).[2]

Stress alters the levels of neurohormones such as norepinephrine, dopamine, and serotonin. An example of the heredity of stress-related neurohormone levels has been identified in a strain of genetically nervous Pointers. The dogs behave normally when not under stress, but freeze and exhibit other abnormal behavior in unfamiliar (stressful) situations. Comparative biochemical assays have found that these dogs have increased levels of norepinephrine and decreased serotonin and dopamine.[3]

Stress plays havoc with the endocrine system and even with the body's *homeostasis* (the ability to maintain physiological processes within normal limits despite varying external conditions). Furthermore, it sometimes impairs the immune system, leaving the individual vulnerable to infections that might have been easily overcome by normal body defenses. The incidence of cancer is higher during the five years following extreme stress, such as the loss of a loved one. The effect of long-term stress is less clear, but some permanent physiological damage is suspected. Many people who develop clinical depression under extreme stress must remain on antidepressants for years, sometimes for the rest of their lives. Symptoms of depression have been observed in chimpanzees, and the incidence appears to parallel that in humans, which is another indication of similar biochemistry.

Evidence that some mental disorders are related to disturbances of neurohormone levels is growing. Many drugs that are used to treat these disorders appear to act by restoring the normal balance of neurohormones. What is not clear is how much is genetically predetermined and how much is environmentally induced. Disorders such as schizophrenia and attention deficit disorder show such pronounced familial patterns that hereditary factors are suspected.

SOME HEREDITARY BEHAVIORAL DISORDERS

The specific mode of inheritance has been identified for only a few behavioral traits. In general, behavioral traits show the continuous variance typical of polygenic inheritance, and most single-gene traits that have been identified are related to neurological abnormalities or mental retardation.

Several single-gene neurological disorders have been identified in mice. The behavior of waltzer mice is characterized by head shaking, rapid circling, and irritability. A variant, Nijmegan waltzer mice, run in tight circles with both horizontal and vertical head shaking. Both are produced by single-gene recessives. Twirler mice, which circle and shake their heads in a horizontal plane, have a dominant gene that is lethal when homozygous.

In humans, a number of single-gene traits that produce mental retardation have been identified. Lesch-Nyhan syndrome is caused by a recessive gene on the X chromosome, and the gene interferes with normal purine metabolism. The victims are normal until their second year, when they begin to exhibit progressive motor defects and self-mutilation. Tay-Sachs disease is caused by an autosomal recessive gene that affects fat metabolism; children appear normal until about six months, when they develop progressive mental and physical

Figure 2–1. Smiling. *The aptitude for this charming trait is believed to be a simple hereditary dominant. Reprinted, by permission, from Virginia Alexander and Jackie Isabell,* Weimaraner Ways.

retardation followed by early death. Another single-gene recessive produces phenylketonuria (PKU), in which the inability to metabolize phenylalanine produces brain damage leading to severe mental retardation. This disorder demonstrates that there is some flexibility in genetically caused problems. If phenylalanine is eliminated from the diet during the developmental years, the child develops normally. The gene for Tourette's syndrome, another early onset disorder, is an autosomal dominant. The onset of Huntington's chorea, caused by a dominant gene with complete penetrance, usually occurs sometime during the victim's forties and fifties, with death following about fifteen years later.

THE ENVIRONMENTAL IMPACT

No other aspect of genetics is as sensitive to the environment as that of behavior. The intricate interplay between the environment and gene products begins before birth. Although environmental factors only occasionally alter the genes, they often modify the underlying genetic blueprint, and the phenotype does not necessarily reflect the genotype (genetic constitution). For example, a dog that has the genes for tight, well-arched feet may develop splayed feet through neglected nail trimming and living in a concrete-floored run, but the fault would not be passed on to the puppies.

ON STRUCTURAL TRAITS

The prenatal environment has a profound effect on embryonic development, including that of the nervous system and behavior. For example, alcohol abuse during pregnancy may produce infants with fetal alcohol syndrome, with abnormalities of anatomy and physiology as well as behavior. The same is true of many other substances. What is more surprising is that things such as dehydration, fever, insufficient oxygen, and viruses (such as parvovirus and German measles) as well as too much or too little of some vitamins can interfere with normal prenatal development (see Table 11–1).

The postnatal environment stimulates the release of biochemicals that, in turn, can modify phenotype. It has been shown that the phenotype of the brain can be altered by environmental factors. Rats, for example, developed significantly larger brains when raised in a stimulating environment *with* companions; neither the stimulating environment nor companions alone produced this effect. Decreased brain weight has been observed in animals such as foxes after several generations of breeding in captivity.[4]

An environmentally induced modification of the brain's phenotype that has been identified in humans is related to music. The cerebral (thinking) part of the brain is divided by a long fissure into right and left lobes (called hemispheres). It has long been recognized that specific types of memory and aptitude develop in specific lobes, though the functions are usually reversed in left-handed people. Recent studies have shown that in most people music perception is divided: The right lobe identifies musical intonation and melody, and the left lobe identifies rhythm. The situation is quite different in classically trained musicians. When playing or listening to the music, the brain-wave activity of musicians occurs almost exclusively in left hemisphere. In musicians, the portion of the bridge between hemispheres (the corpus callosum) that is associated with auditory processing was larger in the left hemisphere and smaller in the right than in nonmusicians. In addition, the structure had thicker nerve fiber between hemispheres. "The differences were especially striking among musicians who had started training before the age of seven."[5] Although musical aptitude is considered a hereditary trait, the age-related differences indicate that environmental influences (musical training) play a role in the brain's physical structure.

ON BEHAVIORAL TRAITS

Environmentally caused alterations of behavioral phenotype are more difficult to identify and to measure, but several studies indicate that this does occur.

Clarke and Schneider studied the effects of prenatal stress on the behavior of rhesus monkeys. They found that the eighteen-month-old offspring showed an increase of abnormal social behavior (mutual clinging) and a decrease of normal social behavior than the controls. The behavior suggests that the offspring of mothers stressed during pregnancy may show increased long-term sensitivity to stress.[6]

Petting and handling (gentling) of pregnant rats appear to stimulate their nervous systems to produce neurohormones that affect the developing embryos in a way that makes the offspring measurably more docile. Fox suggests that this handling may be a significant factor in the domestication process. Prenatal stress, on the other hand, consistently produced progeny that exhibited higher emotionality; similar effects were obtained by injecting the mother with adrenaline and ACTH. Several factors appeared to influence the susceptibility of the progeny to stress: (a) gender of offspring; (b) stage of pregnancy; and (c) strain (genetic difference). Even *premating* stress appeared to affect the behavioral phenotype of some.[7] All of this raises a question of the long-term consequences of shipping bitches for breeding.

In newborns, exposure to stress affects the subsequent response to psychological and physical stresses. One study suggests that there is a "hormonostat" that reacts to adrenal hormones during a specific developmental time period and that once set by a sudden elevation of hormones during this period the hormonostat will react differently in later life. Early handling stress appears to affect the autonomic nervous system; "the research evidence suggests that early handling not only resets the pituitary-adrenal axis but in some way influences autonomic tuning and temperament or emotionality."[8]

Fox described one study of this phenomenon:

> Pups were subjected to varied stimulation—exposure to cold, vestibular [balance] stimulation on a tilting board, exposure to flashing lights, and auditory stimulation—from birth until 5 weeks of age. The pups in the study differed from the controls in a number of ways including earlier maturation of EEG, lowered emotionality which enhanced problem-solving ability in novel situations, and dominance over controls in competitive situations. Analysis of their adrenal glands indicated a fivefold increase in norepinephrine, and studies of their heart rates indicated that a greater sympathetic tone was developed as a consequence of the early handling stress.[9]

A similar study with Siamese kittens produced similar results. Fox concludes that "early handling stress (or prenatal gentling), imprinting and socialization, and environmental enrichment (or deprivation) during sensitive and critical periods in early life represent the developmentally timed stages when appropriate input may dramatically influence development and later behavior."[10]

PATTERNS OF BEHAVIOR AND LEARNING

Behavior is characterized by a continuum that varies in degrees of flexibility. It ranges from completely programmed behavior to conscious learning. The types of behavior described here by no means cover the entire range of possible types that have been identified.

INSTINCTS

Instincts—also called *closed behavioral programs*—are natural patterns that are complete and functional the first time they are invoked. An egg-rolling instinct becomes active in the greylag goose from about a week before incubating her eggs to a week after hatching. She turns her eggs several times a day. If one rolls out of the nest, she reaches out, places her bill on the far side of the egg, and gently rolls it back. Any object that roughly approximates the size or shape of an egg (including beer bottles, light bulbs, and grapefruits) stimulates the programmed response. Once invoked, the entire egg-rolling pattern must be completed. If the egg is removed after she reaches for it (initiating the instinctive behavior), the goose still completes the pattern of retrieving an egg to her nest.

Although instincts are resistant to change, they may become modified over time. Herring gull chicks peck vigorously at the red spot on the parent's bill to stimulate the feeding response. When newly hatched, the chicks peck even more vigorously at a vertical, moving dowel with several red stripes. After several days, however, they become more discriminating and react only to the parent's red spot.

IMPRINTING

Imprinting is a rapid learning process that takes place early in the life of a social animal and activates a hereditary behavioral pattern. It is similar to instinct in that the behavior is innate, but unless activated within a limited period of time, the behavioral potential is lost. In many birds, for example, young males must be exposed to their species song before a certain age, or they lose the ability to learn it.

The most common type of imprinting is species identification. In *precocial species* (having a high degree of independence at birth) such as geese and deer, species imprinting occurs almost immediately. In *altricial species* (helpless at birth and requiring considerable parental care), imprinting occurs later.

Birds and animals raised by humans may not learn correct species identification. The classic example of imprinting was observed in geese, when newly hatched goslings immediately identified Konrad Lorenz as their parent and humans as their species. Species imprinting also occurs in mammals, sometimes very large ones. Hedinger commented that "if, as was once observed, it happens with a moose, the man concerned is in some danger."[11]

Species imprinting occasionally occurs between different animal species. Experiments with chickens, monkeys, and dogs indicate that they all show clear preference for creatures resembling those they are raised with. Chihuahuas raised with cats lacked species identification; when confronted with their own image in the mirror, they made no appropriate response.[12]

The breed preferences sometimes observed in domestic dogs may be a variant of species imprinting. At kindergarten training classes, one Weimaraner puppy refused to even look at the other puppies in her class, but when meeting other Weimaraners, she enthusiastically initiated social interactions.

Species identification plays an important role in mating. Bitches sometimes have a definite breed preference in mating, and among their own breed, may have a special liking for kennelmates. A particular fondness for a kennelmate of another breed may also influence mate preference. One Weimaraner bitch was aggressive toward all males except those that resembled her Kuvasz kennelmate. There is a range of individual promiscuity, of course, and some bitches will run off with any male. Mate preference is also linked with fertility. Bitches that have repeatedly failed to conceive with outside males often become pregnant when finally allowed to breed with kennelmates.

Imprinting occurs with other behavioral patterns. Cocker Spaniels at the Jackson Laboratory showed the expected talent for retrieving when tested between eight and ten weeks and then retested at thirty-two weeks. When not tested between eight and ten weeks, however, their retrieving performance was no better than that of other breeds, indicating that a critical period for imprinting the hereditary aptitude had passed.[13] Weimaraner breeders have observed that the genetic aptitude for swimming must be activated by about twelve weeks. After that time, the innate aptitude fades rapidly, and swimming becomes a learned behavior. Similarly, holding a live or freshly killed bird in the mouth at about seven weeks appears to elicit a strong lifelong interest in feathered game. The window for imprinting lasts for several months, but if neglected for too long, the desire to hunt feathered game must be induced by observing the excited behavior of other dogs.

CONDITIONING

Conditioning—also called *associative learning*—is the modification of behavior so that an act or response previously associated with one stimulus becomes associated with another.

Classical conditioning is a learned response to stimulus recognition. The behavior was first described by Ivan Pavlov. The sight or scent of food stimulates the reflexive flow of saliva. Pavlov rang a bell before feeding the dogs in his study. The dogs began to salivate at the sound of the bell, associating its ringing with food. A more natural example of classical conditioning is the avoidance of specific foods. Robins instinctively identify insects as appropriate food, but they learn that monarch butterflies have a terrible taste. They then avoid not only monarch butterflies but also other species that resemble monarchs.

Operant conditioning is a behavior learned through trial and error. If a certain behavior is rewarded repeatedly, the animal learns to perform the behavior for the reward. Rats and many other animals can learn to press a bar that releases a pellet of food. Some wild chimpanzees have learned to use twigs to catch termites and stones to crack hard-shelled nuts.

COMPLEX LEARNING

Many types of complex learning have been identified and studied. Most are related to intelligence, which is, again, a combination of genetic aptitude and environmental development.

Insight learning is also known as problem solving. One study of the problem-solving aptitude of laboratory rats and mice, wild brown rats, and wild and domesticated foxes (including different fur-color mutants) found some interesting differences. In all cases, the wild animals (which had been raised in captivity) showed greater aptitude than their domesticated counterparts, demonstrating the complex genetic component underlying problem-solving behavior.[14]

Many dog owners have observed differences in problem-solving aptitude. Some dogs are more talented (or more motivated) at opening gates than others. Hunting provides a wealth of opportunities to observe the ways dogs achieve their objectives. The most unorthodox solution I've ever observed took place at our club's informal training clinic. The owners of Brad, a retired 8-year-old show dog that had never done any hunting, finally gave him a chance to hunt birds. Brad found a pigeon almost immediately and went on a classic point. Suddenly, his eyes rolled to the left. He had scented another pigeon only a few feet away. Brad's dilemma was obvious. Instinct told him that the bird would not move while he maintained eye contact, and common sense told him that the second bird would probably fly away in a minute. He wanted *both* birds! Suddenly, he leaped to the second bird, killed it with a quick crunch, laid it down, leaped back before the first bird could fly away, and continued to point with every muscle quivering. Brad's solution would disqualify him in a field trial; in a real hunting situation, however, many hunters would applaud his ingenuity and appreciate the extra bird.

Behaviorists have observed that repeated experience with problem solving improves the speed of solving similar problems (called learning sets). In other words, a dog that has discovered how to open one type of gate is more apt to discover how to open another.

Highest on the evolutionary scale of learning is that of *observational learning*—the ability to learn by observing the behavior of another—which has a clear survival advantage. Prey species learn to run at alarm calls, and predator species learn how to hunt by observing the behavior of others, not necessarily of the same species. The aptitude for observational learning is well established in dogs, for both desired and undesired behavior. Field trainers know that puppies learn to hunt best when worked with an experienced dog. On the down side is that undesired behavior can also be learned; one stool-eating dog can spread the vice through a kennel like wildfire.

HEREDITARY CANINE BEHAVIOR

The canine species share many similar, genetically determined behavioral phenotypes such as use of the nose to locate prey, marking territorial boundaries, sleeping together, vomiting food to feed young, and tail wagging. All prefer a den for sleeping and for raising their young.

All of the species are easily *tamed*, though only the dog is easily *trained*. Stories of tamed wolves, coyotes, and dingoes are widespread. It was interesting to find an author, Cornelis Naaktgeboren, who described golden jackals as easy to tame if hand raised. He found their behavior similar to his dogs, except for a marked shyness toward strangers and social howling.[15]

SOCIAL RELATIONSHIPS

Social Organization

The greatest behavioral differences between the canine species are related to their social organization, and even those differences are not rigid. Although all join in packs at times, the circumstances under which they do so, the strength of the pack bonds, and the duration of the pack association varies. Three types of canine social organization have been identified:

- *Type I*. Solitary except for breeding and raising young (foxes)
- *Type II*. Permanent pair bonds with occasional pack bonds (coyote, jackal, dingo)
- *Type III*. Permanent pair and pack bonds (wolf)

Foxes, which belong to a different genus, are hunters of small game. Solitary animals usually fare better when food is scarce, and they need each other only for reproduction. This pattern has enabled foxes to survive, even to thrive, in close contact with humans in farming and suburban areas.

Wolves, with the most highly evolved social structure, have been the least able to adapt to human intrusion and environmental changes. Although they can survive on mice and occasional vegetable foods, their natural prey is large game, which requires cooperative hunting in packs.

Coyotes are unique among predator species in that they have actually expanded their range in this century. Like foxes, their normal prey is small animals. Unlike foxes, they form packs and hunt cooperatively when food is scarce, and they bring down large game.

Social Bonds

Canines form two types of social bonds. *Primary socialization* refers to social bonds that are established early in life. *Secondary socialization* refers to social bonds and relationships that are formed later. The ability to form and maintain primary and secondary social bonds is determined by heredity. In domestic dogs, the ability to form secondary social bonds has been greatly enhanced through selection.

The nature and permanence of social bonds are related to the type of heredity social organization. One study explored the primary and secondary social bonds using species representing the three types of social organization: type I, foxes; type II, jackals and coyotes; and type III, wolves. The young of all four species were hand-raised by humans. All developed primary social bonds with the person who raised them, which was indicated by active submissive greeting and passive submission to physical contact. The foxes had a low tolerance for physical contact, evading contact when possible and biting occasionally. After two years of age, some jackals and coyotes began to withdraw after a brief greeting, but the wolves continued to demonstrate clear enjoyment of close contact. Neither the jackals, the coyotes, nor the wolves ever displayed defensive or offensive aggression, whereas the foxes did so frequently.[16]

The capacity for secondary social relationships revealed even greater species differences. The foxes became consistently wary of strangers by four months. The jackals began to show fear of strangers between the ages of ten and twelve months. They became consistently aggressive toward men but only occasionally aggressive toward women. The coyotes remained friendly toward strangers, regardless of gender through their first year, then became increasingly hesitant.[17]

The wolves began to be wary of strangers between the ages of twelve and eighteen months. This wariness increased with age and was more pronounced in the males. If the person who raised the wolves introduced a stranger and the stranger remained in a passive squatting posture, the wolves gradually initiated a social approach. Interestingly, both sexes showed fear of and aggression toward adult male humans, never toward women or preadolescent males.[18]

BODY LANGUAGE

All canine species facilitate communication among themselves through *body language*—the position of the head, ears, and tail as well as general stance. Most studies of canine body language focus on the behavioral similarities such as the submissive, juvenile posture. However, Naaktgeboren points out that the behavioral inventory of "each species has its own peculiarities." If individuals of different species are confined together, they cannot understand each other's body language, and misunderstood cues often leads to physical fighting. He has observed that they "are capable of learning the language of other species, so that quarrels become less frequent." Different aspects of the body language appear to be inherited independently. Because of this, species hybrids acquire only parts of the language of each parent species, even littermates may not be able to communicate effectively.[19]

The mosaic inheritance of body language reveals an interesting aspect of species hybridization. Although there is no physiological barrier to mating between the canine species, the communication barrier sheds light on the preference for a mate of the same species—one who speaks the same language. It also explains the unique handicap of the hybrid offspring, who cannot communicate effectively with either parental species unless capable of *learning* the appropriate body language. This suggests that the coyote-wolf hybrids who successfully mated back with wolves must have been unusually clever individuals.

STAGES OF DEVELOPMENT

Critical periods are genetically set, age-related stages in which specific tasks must be accomplished. Specific events must occur during a narrow time window for an animal's hereditary behavioral development to progress normally. The onset and duration of these critical periods is a species characteristic that is genetically programmed. Failure to activate such genetically programmed behavior at one critical period may interrupt the entire sequence of development of later behavior, such as the song development of some birds.

Sensitive periods are the times of special vulnerability during which long-lasting behavioral effects can be caused by environmental factors such as maternal deprivation. The developmental time boundaries are less rigid than critical periods, and behavioral responses acquired during this period can be modified or even reversed, though never without some difficulty.

In 1946, the Jackson Laboratory (also called the Behavior Laboratory) at Bar Harbor, Maine, began a long-term study of dog behavior. One of the most important outcomes of the research was the identification of the critical stages (that is, periods) of

Figure 2–2. Neonatal Period. *Blind and deaf, the newborn puppy's basic task is survival.*

development. These stages, introduced to dog fanciers in Clarence Pfaffenberger's *The New Knowledge of Dog Behavior* in 1963, are well known throughout the English-speaking world of dog fanciers. The later modifications of these stages are less widely known. They are much more flexible than initially believed and are, therefore, now classified as sensitive periods.

Neonatal Period

During the neonatal period (the first fourteen days), the puppy functions entirely on reflexes. The brain is very immature, and only minimal neurological pathways exist. Development of neural pathways proceeds at a rapid pace.

Although the initial studies at Jackson Laboratory concluded that no learning takes place during the first twenty-one days, later studies confirmed (what many breeders had observed) that some type of learning does indeed occur. I have always handled my puppies a lot—they're so irresistible as they nuzzle and sniff—and it's so easy to cuddle one at a time while watching TV and switching with each commercial. The rare litters that I was too busy to do this with never seemed quite as outgoing and confident, and I've talked with many breeders who have had similar experiences. This is why I found the comments of Serpell and Jagoe particularly interesting:

> Nevertheless, it is well established that short periods of daily handling, as well as a variety of other strong or noxious physical stimuli, can have marked, long-term effects on the behavioural and physical development of some mammalian neonates, including puppies. These effects include accelerated maturation of the nervous system, more rapid hair growth and weight gain, enhanced development of motor and problem solving skills, and earlier opening of the eyes. In behavioural terms, canine neonates exposed to varied stimulation

Table 2-1. Sensitive Periods of Development

Period	Ends at Age—	Learning Task
Neonatal	14 days (plus-or-minus 3 days)	survival
Transitional	18 to 20 days	survival
Socialization	not distinct; often 6–8 weeks but sometimes up to 12 weeks	species identification, human bonding, learning
Juvenile	puberty or end of first year	secondary social bonds, place in pack, loyalty

from birth to five weeks of age were found to be more confident, exploratory and socially dominant when tested later in strange situations than unstimulated controls.[20]

Transitional Period

With the opening of their eyes at fourteen days (plus or minus three days), the puppies' world expands. They begin to respond to each other and to lift their bodies from the floor to take a wobbly step or two. Their tongues, curled to assist nursing, gradually flatten, and the puppies can begin to eat semisolid foods, which is especially helpful with hand-raised litters. The mother no longer needs to stimulate elimination.

Socialization Period

The onset of the socialization period is heralded by the connection of the auditory nerve pathways at about eighteen to twenty days. The boundary between the socialization and juvenile periods is not clear cut, but the upper limit for primary socialization occurs at about twelve weeks, with rather broad individual and breed variation.

Species identification. Two of the most important developmental learning tasks before the puppy are species identification and canine social behavior. The dam provides love, entertainment, nourishment, and discipline, and littermates provide exercise and companionship. During this period, the temperament of the dam influences the temperaments of the puppies as they begin to copy her attitude toward humans. Solitary puppies that have no contact with other dogs between three and seven weeks typically have poor social relationships. Although species identification is usually achieved by seven weeks, social contact with other dogs should be ongoing for the puppy to develop and master correct canine etiquette.

In general, dominance relationships between littermates develops after seven weeks and is not regarded as a problem. In some breeds (such as terriers), however, dominance conflicts may arise, and the breeder should be alert for developing problems. Any puppy that seems too submissive to another one should be removed from the litter several times a day, played with separately, and made to feel very special. Taking this time and effort with a puppy saves months of later work on socialization and development of self-confidence.

Human bonding. Socialization with humans is of critical importance during this period. Puppies that do not bond with humans have not had effective early socialization, and those that reach the age of ten weeks without sufficient human contact

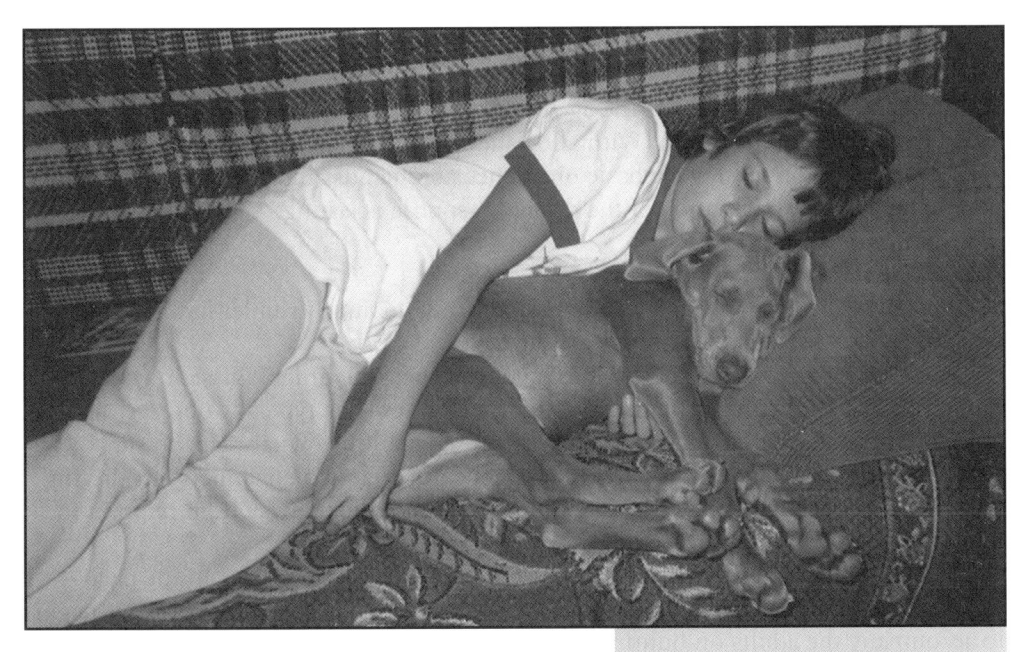

Figure 2–3. Human Bonding. *Canine-human bonding is a pleasurable developmental task. Reprinted, by permission, from Virginia Alexander and Jackie Isabell,* Weimaraner Ways.

begin to lose the potential to respond. Picking them up to move, worm, crate, or give a shot is not enough. If isolated from human contact, puppies become dog-oriented—the so-called kennel syndrome. Contact with and handling by both men and women is important. Puppies that have received socialization exclusively by humans of one gender often show a marked preference for that gender throughout their lives.

Based on the studies of Scott and Fuller, most breeders release their puppies to new owners at the age of six to eight weeks, and until recently, this has not been questioned. In one study of German Shepherds, puppies "separated from their mothers and nest sites (but not their littermates) at six weeks exhibited loss of appetite and weight, and increased distress, mortality and susceptibility to disease compared with pups that remained at home with their mothers until 12 weeks of age. Both groups, however, showed the same degree of socialization towards their human handlers."[21] This may not be true of all breeds and certainly does not occur with Weimaraners. Some breeders foster out the puppies they plan to keep from the age of seven to nine weeks because it seems to enhance the puppies' human bonding and trainability. Even a weekend away seems to make a difference.

Learning. Once the puppy can hear, learning proceeds at a very rapid rate. Positive and negative experiences during this period have lifelong consequences. Young wolves, coyotes, and dingoes venture from the den for the first time at twenty-one days. Trumler strongly urges breeders to be guided by natural canine developmental behavior by creating opportunities for the puppies to begin exploring their environment. Wire exercise pens are ideal for controlling the puppies and ensuring their safety. As he points out, this is the real difference between puppies raised within a home by devoted breeders and those produced by puppy mills; the home-raised puppies have a head start on winning friends, influencing humans, and making a mark in dogdom.[22]

The learning potential from the age of about seven to twelve weeks is phenomenal and rarely utilized to its fullest. With allowances for the short, immature attention span, the puppy can master the basic obedience commands, and once "imprinted" on the neural pathways, retention of the desired response is lasting.

Juvenile Period

Although the onset of the juvenile period is not distinct, Trumler has identified a sequence of age-related behavioral learning tasks.

At about four months, wild canines enter the "pecking order" phase in which the puppies establish their place within the litter. Puppy owners typically observe the onset of aggressive behavior, which must be repressed if the owner plans to stay in charge. During this phase, wild bitches teach the puppies "table manners" by driving them away from food. This is the time to practice taking food away from puppies to ensure that they do not become possessive.[23]

During the fifth and sixth months, puppies must learn their place in the pack—the "pack order phase." Pack bonds and loyalty are strengthened as the puppies begin to accompany the adults on hunting expeditions.[24]

For years, Weimaraner fanciers have puzzled over behavior that was not mentioned anywhere in the literature. The onset coincides with the loss of baby teeth at about four months and lasts for three or four months, and it is characterized by marked behavioral changes. The puppy that thought the world was wonderful and life was great suddenly becomes fretful and cranky. The bold self-confidence is suddenly gone. It is as if the puppy sees the world for the first time. The young Weimaraner examines a familiar room or a piece of furniture with apprehension. Could this be harmful? What can I do if it is? Familiar noises may suddenly become threatening. The puppy may be boisterous and rowdy at home but becomes docile and shy with strange people and situations. It is almost necessary to begin socialization all over again. Each situation and experience that the

Figure 2-4. Environmental Learning. *Puppies thrive in an enriched environment. This exercise pen contains a variety of toys and other articles to stimulate learning.*
Reprinted, by permission, from Virginia Alexander and Jackie Isabell, Weimaraner Ways.

Figure 2–5. Imprinting. *The experience of carrying a live or freshly killed bird stimulates the puppy's genetic bird-hunting behavior patterns—like observing a light turning on in the puppy's mind. If not imprinted at an early age, later contact rarely rouses such an immediate response.*
Reprinted, by permission, from Virginia Alexander and Jackie Isabell, Weimaraner Ways.

puppy finds overwhelming should be handled with supportive encouragement, minimizing all demands. The puppies are not as flexible or responsive to remedial socialization or environmental experience as they were earlier, and some puppies never recover their earlier stability.

Because of this it was particularly interesting to discover that similar behavior has been reported in young wolves as well as other dogs. It is described as "a second, sudden-onset phase of heightened sensitivity to fear-arousing stimuli at around 4–6 months of age."[25]

Behavior can be modified at all stages of development by changing the environmental factors. The optimal period for socialization and human bonding is from six to eight weeks, but these bonds must be reinforced. If well-socialized puppies are placed in a kennel at three to four months, they become shy of strangers—even their handlers—by six to eight months. Bonding contact must be maintained *at least* through the first year.[26]

Breeds that are naturally aggressive are less damaged by being raised in isolation than those that are naturally timid. Willis commented that the different breed responses to isolation indicate a genetic basis with an interaction between the genotype and the environment, "but we do not know if, within a breed, we can easily select for timidity or aggression."[27]

SOME BEHAVIORAL TRAITS

Trainability and Problem Solving

A key difference between a tame canine and a domesticated one is trainability. Dingoes can be tamed but not easily trained. Wolves are also easily tamed, even forming social bonds with humans as adults, but they cannot be readily trained.

Scott and Fuller reported that the ability to respond positively to training is highly individual and dependent on the training techniques used. The dog's emotional reaction proved important in training, either helping or inhibiting learning in all situations.[28]

A general principle of psychology is that reward (or punishment) increases motivation. At the Jackson Laboratory, the most effective motivational factor varied with different breeds. With Beagles, the best motivation was the inducement of food rewards and opportunities to explore. Basenjis were most motivated by the threat of restraint. Shelties responded best to the threat of punishment.[29]

The breeds studied by Scott and Fuller showed similar problem-solving ability *provided* that they were well motivated and fear was eliminated. However, once any dog learned to fail in problem-solving situations, it was difficult to stimulate enough motivation to solve even simple problems.[30]

Timidity and Anxiety

Some type of timidity occurs in every breed, suggesting that absolute fearlessness is not a survival trait. Excessive shyness with fear biting occurs in all breeds, but one study identified a pattern of simple dominant inheritance. In crosses of coyotes and Beagles, both the first and second generation offspring exhibited the coyote's typical timidity and shyness of strangers.[31]

Different types of fearfulness—that is, fear of strange objects, fear of strange dogs—appear to be inherited independently. Selection for confidence, therefore, must be done for each specific fear.

Hunting Traits

The hunting behavior of bird dogs involves multiple behavioral traits such as bird finding, eagerness, cooperation, speed, and style. Although hunting ability is definitely hereditary, identifying and measuring the genetic components in order to develop reliable selection criteria has presented problems.

Whitney experimented with many crosses between sporting and hound breeds (primarily Pointer and Bloodhound) to study the heredity of various aspects of hunting behavior. He found that crossbreds appeared to have as much bird interest as the bird-hunting parent but fell short in aptitude and style. He noted that the "quartering" hunting pattern of the bird dog was consistently lost in crossbreds.[32]

Marchlewski focused on the pointing trait in his analysis of crosses between English and German pointers—not quite the same thing as bird interest. He found that the crossbreds had greater pointing style than the German parent but never as much as the English parent and considered the pointing trait incompletely dominant.[33]

Whitney found that his crossbreds typically hunted with a high head, air scenting like a bird dog. Though they occasionally dropped their heads like the ground-scenting hound parent, none ever developed into a good ground trailer. Marchlewski also observed that his crossbreds had the high head carriage of the English Pointer rather than the ground-tracking tendency of the German dogs, which have tracking hounds in their heritage.[34]

In a wide variety of crosses between different breeds, Whitney found that the trait for giving voice on the trail was consistently dominant over mute tracking. In contrast, Marchlewski observed that the vocal hunting typical of the German gundogs "seems to be a recessive feature in relation to the silent manner of hunting typical to high class Pointers."[35]

A final consideration in the inheritance of hunting behavior is the role of the environment, in this case the interaction between dog and trainer. A skilled trainer can develop a moderately talented dog into a top performer, and training errors can ruin the most talented of dogs.

Breed-Specific Traits

There are few behavioral traits for which any breed is homozygous. Scott and Fuller observed breed-typical behavioral differences from birth through the first year. Puppies raised by mothers of different breeds generally exhibited their own breed-specific traits. Between-breed behavioral variance of behavior reflects genetic differences, provided the environmental components are similar.[36]

Despite breed-specific differences and aptitudes, all breeds retain broad general capacities for learning behavior that are not associated with the breed. For example, Weimaraners can learn to herd sheep, and Collies can learn to hunt deer.

Buchenauer reported that behavioral patterns such as temperament, nervousness, and aggressiveness showed relatively high heritability values; trainability and emotionality showed relatively low values. Selection experiments showed that remarkable changes in behavioral patterns could be achieved in a few generations. Selection for specific types of behavior can significantly modify a breed within a few generations.[37]

Genetic aptitude for specific tasks or breed functions is inherited independently, and no correlation between physical phenotype and behavioral phenotype has been identified. Although many breeds surpass wolves in specific behavioral traits for which the breed was developed, this has been accomplished at the expense of other traits, namely those related to independent survival.

REVIEW OF TERMS

behavioral genetics
conditioning
critical period
imprinting
instinct
neurohormones
neurotransmitters
observational learning
sensitive period

CYTOGENETICS

Cytogenetics is the study of genetics by visual analysis of chromosomes and chromosomal aberrations and of other cellular structures that are related to heredity. It combines the sciences of *cytology*—the study of the structure, function, development, and reproduction of cells—and genetics. The study of cells and the discovery that cellular structures contained the elements of heredity launched the science of cytogenetics in the early 20th century, and behavioral genetics soon followed. Today, it is the cytogeneticists who are developing cytogenetic maps—that is, identifying the locations of specific genes on the chromosome itself.

CELLS

Why start with cytogenetics? To begin with, as E. B. Wilson pointed out in 1925, "the key to every biological problem must finally be sought in the cell, for every living organism is, or at some time has been, a cell." Drlica adds: "The basic unit of life is the cell, an organized set of chemical reactions bounded by a membrane and capable of self-perpetuation. . . . With few exceptions, every cell contains all the information required for an independent existence; indeed, under the right conditions human cells can be removed from the body and grown in laboratory dishes."[1] Therefore, a good place to begin is with a look at cells, chromosomes, and cell division, as well as at some of the events that can alter the genetic information within the cell.

All in all, a *cell* (the smallest unit of living matter capable of self-perpetuation) is incredibly complex. Between periods of cell division, the genetic material is located within the cell nucleus, which is surrounded by the *cytoplasm*—everything enclosed by the cell membrane except the nucleus. (See Figure 3–2a on page 42.) The cytoplasm is virtually an industrial complex containing structures such as centrosomes, Golgi bodies, lysosomes, peroxisomes, mitochondria, and ribosomes. The ribosomes assemble enzymes and other protein molecules, many of which are stockpiled until needed. Other structures are responsible for assembling lipid (fat) molecules. Mitochondria not only play a role in the cell's energy cycle but also contain their own DNA. Raw material enters through the cell membrane; cell products and wastes exit in the same way.

Which came first, the gene or the cell membrane? To geneticists, this is not a frivolous question but one that some are seriously trying to answer. The issue is this: Cell membranes have pores that allow only atoms and relatively simple organic molecules to pass in or out, but genes are very large, complex molecules. So how did the genes get inside in the first place?

David Dreamer has come up with some promising leads while studying organic carbon molecules from an Australian meteorite. (Really! Life on Earth may have originated from an extraterrestrial source!) Grinding up the tarry substance, Dreamer examined it under a microscope: "It was a wonderful surprise—the whole slide began to fill with these beautiful little vesicles." The cell wall is made of fatty-type molecules called liposomes, which have an odd characteristic—groups of the molecules naturally arrange themselves into bubbles, and Dreamer's vesicles turned out to be liposomes. He believes that the first cells may have occurred in tide pools, where the wave action or the wet and dry tidal cycles could have weakened the bonding of naturally occurring liposomes enough for them to enclose large organic molecules. So far, Dreamer has developed a technique through which genetic material forms inside the bubbles; through another technique, he has developed genetic material that reproduces and evolves.[2]

THOSE PAIRED CHROMOSOMES

BACKGROUND

Genes, the basic units of heredity, come in packages called chromosomes, on which the genes are arranged in linear sequence like beads on a string. The most simple definition of a *chromosome* is that it is a linear sequence of genes. It is now known that each chromosome is actually one giant DNA molecule, consisting of hundreds to millions of genes. The arrangement or sequence of the genes on the chromosome is often critical, and alterations of that lineup can produce wholesale genetic changes.

By the end of the 19th century, scientists had observed stubby rods within stained cells, which they called *chromosomes* (using the Greek roots meaning colored bodies) and had described their behavior during cell division. Under an ordinary light microscope, the chromosomes become visible just before the cell divides, when the membrane containing the cell's nucleus disappears. After the cell completes division, the nuclear membrane reforms, and within the nucleus the chromosomes become indistinct. The development of electron microscopes revealed that chromosomes appear rodlike only during cell division; after cell division, the chromosomes uncoil into a mass of threadlike structures within the cell's nucleus.

In 1902, the study of heredity took a giant leap forward when Walter S. Sutton noticed that the behavior of chromosomes during reproductive cell division (meiosis) paralleled the behavior of Mendel's hypothetical units of heredity, and he suggested that these units were located on the chromosomes. Soon afterward, Thomas Hunt

Morgan experimented with the fruit fly *Drosophila melanogaster* (a species with only four chromosomes). He discovered linkage and the linear order of genes on the chromosomes. Chromosomal inheritance proved to be universal in life forms.

CHROMOSOME NUMBERS

The most primitive life forms—bacteria and blue-green algae—have only one chromosome. Cells with paired chromosomes represent a considerable jump on the evolutionary scale. Paired chromosomes, after all, are a prerequisite for sexual reproduction. The chromosomes in each pair usually have the same shape and length, and the genes on each are arranged in the same sequence and carry instructions for the same traits.

The number of chromosome pairs varies in different species, ranging from 2 to 220 pairs.[3] Interestingly, the number of chromosomes is quite unrelated to the organism's level on the evolutionary scale. The actual number of pairs seems to be less important than the size, shape, and number of genes on the chromosomes. Humans, for example, have 46 chromosomes (23 pairs), cats have 38 (19 pairs), and dogs have 78 (39 pairs).

HYBRIDS

Domestic dogs belong to the genus *Canis*, and other members of the genus also have 78 chromosomes: the golden jackal, coyote, gray wolf, red wolf. These species are so genetically similar that fertile male and female *hybrids*—the offspring of different species—are common.

Most matings between different species, however, are not capable of life. Not only must the chromosomes be similar in size, shape, and number but also must include enough similar genetic material to sustain life. Even then, interspecies hybrids are rarely fertile, though there are some notable exceptions. Both domestic cattle and American bison have 30 chromosome pairs, and the crosses (beefalo) occasionally produce fertile female hybrids. The chromosomes of domestic goats (30 pairs) and Barbary sheep (29 pairs) are enough alike to occasionally produce fertile males.[4]

The best-known hybrid, of course, is the mule—the offspring of a horse (32 pairs) and the donkey (31 pairs). Although occasional fertile females have been reported, Nicholas warns that the offspring should be tested genetically, because the one case he attempted to document proved very strange indeed. The mule was pastured with a Shetland mare. Three weeks after the mare gave birth, the mule appeared with a foal. Genetic analysis, however, established that her foal was the genetic twin of the Shetland mare's foal, meaning, of course, that this was another, albeit late, foal from the Shetland. The proximity of the Shetland mare had stimulated lactation in the mule (a phenomenon fairly common in mammals), and she readily adopted the latecomer.[5]

The reason that so few interspecies hybrids can occur is because of the different sizes and shapes of the chromosomes. It is vital that most of the genes on each paired chromosome match up with others that perform the same function. For example, if the first gene on a chromosome is responsible for producing a digestive enzyme, the first gene on the other chromosome must also be related to the same function. There is some flexibility, and if a gene product is not absolutely necessary for life, the offspring may mature to birth and might even enjoy normal health. If there are enough mismatches, however, the fertilized egg is doomed.

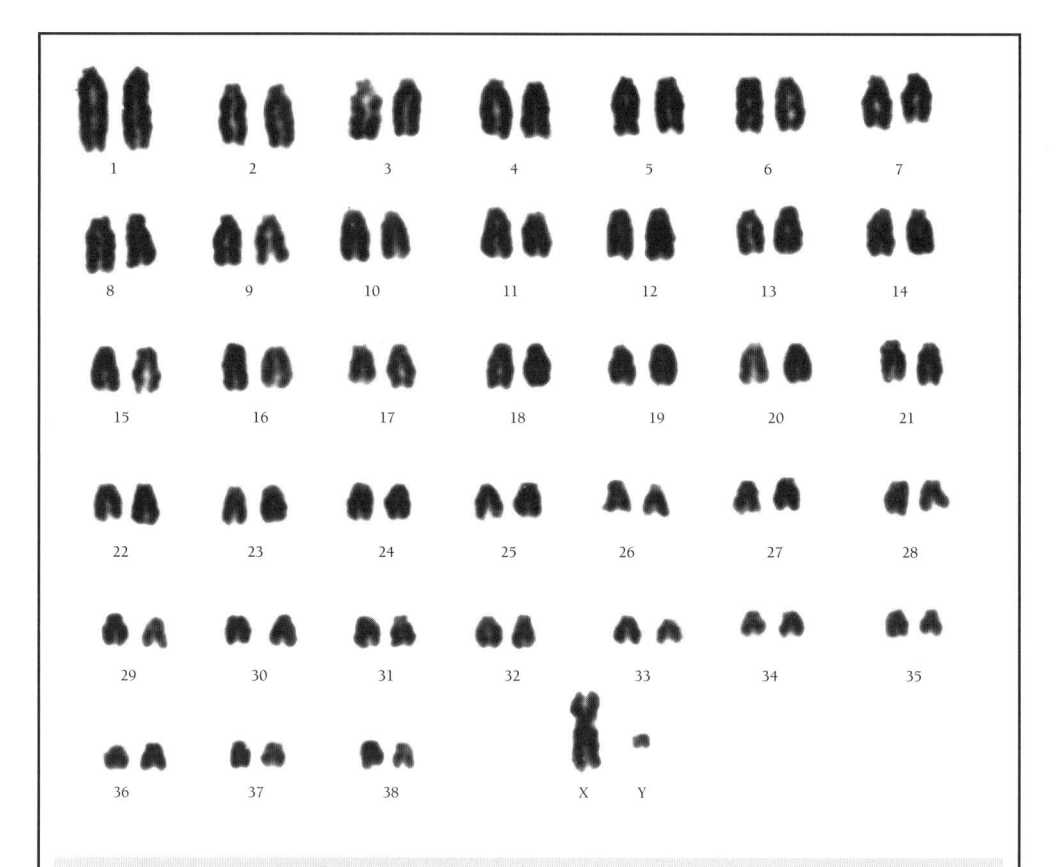

Figure 3-1. Canine karyotype. *The chromosomes coil and fold into distinctive shapes during cell division. The 76 autosomes are paired (38) in descending sequence of size. The 39th pair—the large X-shaped chromosome and its tiny companion on the bottom right—are the sex chromosomes, the difference indicating the cell was taken from a male (XY). Courtesy of Dr. Shirley Johnston.*

KARYOTYPES

One of the best techniques of viewing chromosomes is through a *karyotype diagram*, a special photograph showing the chromosomes of an individual or species. To prepare a karyotype, a photograph is taken of a cell (usually a cell arrested in metaphase of mitosis, after the chromosomes have doubled but are still joined). The cell is first treated with a stain, which bonds with certain proteins and produces patterns of light and dark bands indicating variations in protein (gene) sequences. The picture is then cut into pieces so that the chromosomes can be arranged by their relative length and the position of the centromere, which joins them. The centromere's position on the chromosome is an aid to identification of different species.

The chromosomes of each species have distinctive differences of shape and pattern. The bar patterns from the stain are also distinctive within each species and each individual, and this is the basis of "genetic fingerprinting."

THE GENOME

The *genome* is the complete *set* of chromosomes (DNA molecules) that specify the inherited characteristics of a species. In general, the set consists of one chromosome of each pair—that is, the set of chromosomes in a sperm or ova—which is known as the *haploid* set of chromosomes, whereas a cell with paired chromosomes is known as the *diploid* number. If the human genome were printed on standard typing paper in letters of average size, it would fill about two million pages and take about 415 feet of filing drawers.[6] Wow! And that's only one-half of the information in each diploid cell!

Progress in mapping the human genome makes the news quite often. The goal of the Human Genome Project is to determine the exact location of all genes plus their regulatory elements on their respective chromosomes. This worldwide project is expected to be completed in 2005.

Less well known is the canine genome project—the official name is the Canine Molecular Genetics Project (CMGP). The American Kennel Club, the Morris Animal Foundation, and the Orthopedic Foundation for Animals contributed funds to support the five-year project through March 1, 1995. The goal was to locate 400 DNA landmarks (markers) on the chromosomes and to use the linked markers to predict the inheritance of genetic disorders. The project not only surpassed expectations with the identification of 600 markers but also located the marker linked with copper toxicosis in Bedlington Terriers. Needless to say, the project's funding was renewed with the expectation of many more breakthroughs.[7]

CELL DIVISION

The most important concept related to cell division is that there are two types—mitosis and meiosis—and that each serves a different purpose. Cell division is an awesomely intricate process, and errors in the transfer of genetic information can occur at any stage.

MITOSIS—GROW AND MAINTAIN

Mitosis is the process of cell division that duplicates the chromosome pairs and apportions a set of each pair to the two daughter cells. This type of division creates new cells for growth, healing, and replacement of old cells. *Every* cell contains a complete set of chromosomes, and the chromosome numbers remain constant from one cell division to the next. Each time a cell divides, it must make an exact copy of itself. Even small errors in copying can have large consequences. The real wonder is the number of times cells divide without any mistakes. Errors of mitosis are not hereditary, though they may have serious consequences for the individual. Many types of cancer, for example, are characterized by uncontrolled cell division, because the genes regulating mitosis in canceous cells contain errors.

During *interphase* (the period after the cell was created through the beginning of the next cell division), the chromosomes within the nucleus are uncoiled and look like a mass of tangled threads. Near the end of this phase, the chromosomes are duplicated but remain joined at the *centromere*—the constricted region on the chromosome. While still joined, each chromosome strand is known as a *chromatid*, and the pair are *sister chromatids*.

Mitosis proceeds through the series of orderly stages shown in Figure 3–2.

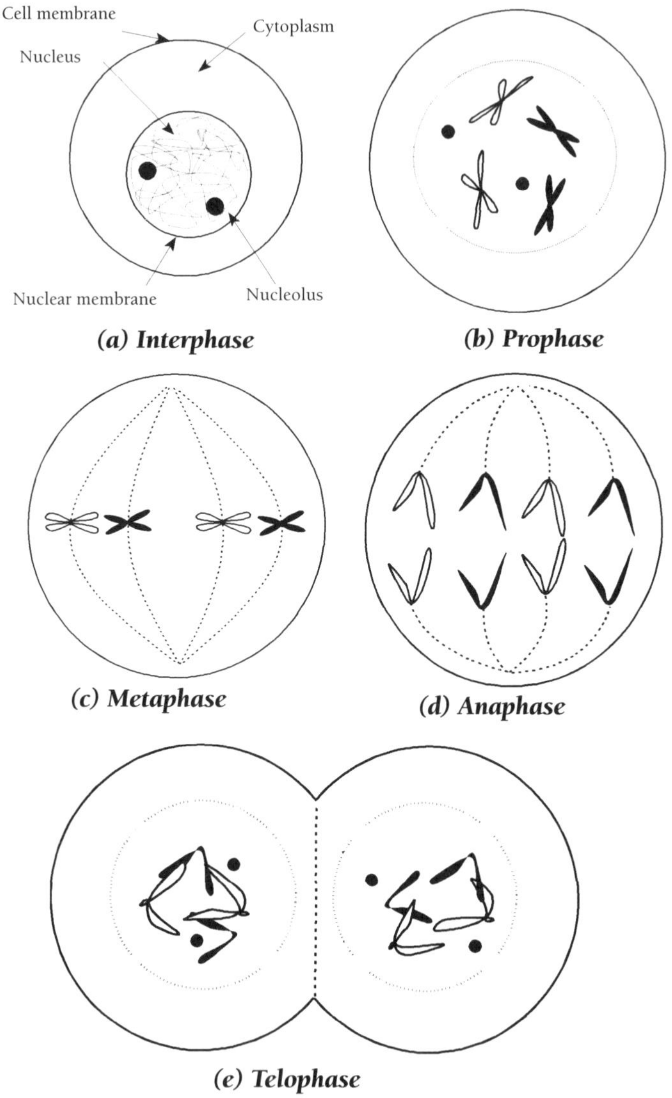

Figure 3–2. Mitosis.

(a) Interphase. The cell nucleus, enclosed in the nuclear membrane, is located at the cell's center and is surrounded by the cytoplasm. Just before cell division, within the nucleus, the chromosomes become visible as long, thin threads. The chromosomes have already divided into sister chromatids.

(b) Prophase. The chromosomes begin to shorten and thicken, becoming distinctly visible. The nuclear membrane breaks down, and the nucleoli disappear.

(c) Metaphase. The spindle structures become prominent, and the spindle fibers radiating from the poles become attached to the centromeres of each chromatid. The chromatids migrate and align on the center plane.

(d) Anaphase. The chromatids separate, and the spindle fibers draw each chromosome to opposite poles. The cell begins to constrict in the center.

(e) Telophase. When the chromosomes have drawn into separate clusters, the nuclear membranes form around each chromosome cluster. The cell membrane completes the division, and the daughter cells gradually separate.

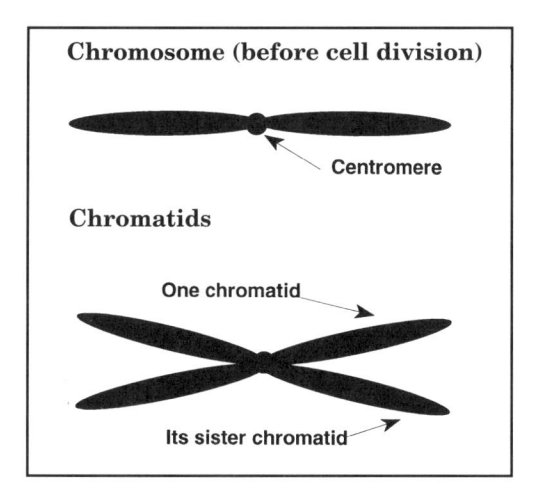

Figure 3–3. Chromatids.
After duplication but before separation, the new chromosomes remain joined at the centromere. While still joined, each chromosome strand is known as a chromatid, *and the pair are* sister chromatids.

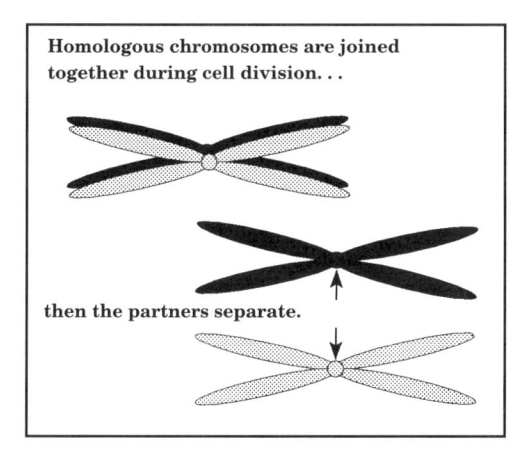

Figure 3–4. Homologous chromosomes.

MEIOSIS—PREPARE TO REPRODUCE

Meiosis is the process of cell division by which cells prepare for sexual reproduction by reducing the parental chromosome number by half—that is, from the diploid (paired) number to the haploid (unpaired) number. Meiosis occurs only in the *germ cells,* which are the cells that are related to sexual reproduction, found in the testes and ovaries of animals and in the anthers and ovaries of plants. The two-step division process produces *gametes,* which are mature germ cells. Gametes contain one unpaired (haploid) set of chromosomes and are capable of initiating the formation of a new individual by joining with another gamete to restore the diploid number of chromosomes.

The survival advantage of sexual reproduction is that it produces genetic diversity through new combinations that lead to variation of physical and behavioral traits. With asexual reproduction, such as that of an amoeba or a plant cutting, each generation is a genetically identical clone, and genetic changes can occur only through mutations.

Meiosis I (the first maturation division or reduction division) separates the *homologous chromosomes* (homo- means alike), those that form the diploid pairs. Unlike

Figure 3–5. Meiosis I.
The first maturation division or reduction division separates the homologous chromosomes (homo- means alike), those that form the diploid pairs.

(a) **Interphase.** *As with mitosis, the chromosomes within the nucleus become visible as long, thin threads. The chromosomes have already divided into sister chromatids.*

(b) **Prophase.** *The chromosomes begin to shorten and thicken, becoming distinctly visible. The nuclear membrane breaks down, and the nucleoli disappear. The homologous chromatids become closely aligned (synapsed in a zipper like fashion), producing a bundle of four homologous chromatids (called a tetrad).*

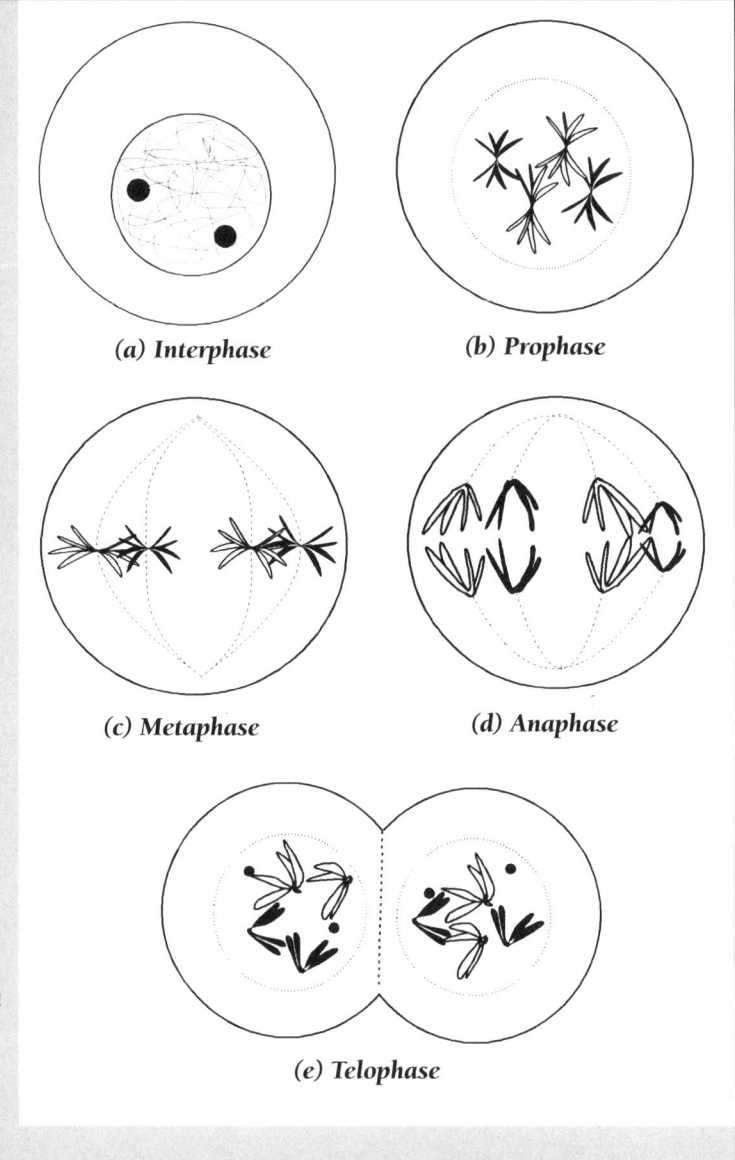

(a) Interphase

(b) Prophase

(c) Metaphase

(d) Anaphase

(e) Telophase

(c) **Metaphase.** *The tetrads, still joined, migrate and align on the center plane as the nuclear membrane disappears. Spindle fibers radiating from the poles become attached to the centromeres of each tetrad.*

(d) **Anaphase.** *The tetrads separate, but the chromatids remain joined at the centromere. The sister chromatids from each homologous pair are drawn to opposite poles.*

(e) **Telophase.** *When the sister chromatids have drawn into separate clusters, the nuclear membranes form around each cluster. The cell membrane completes the division, and the daughter cells gradually separate.*

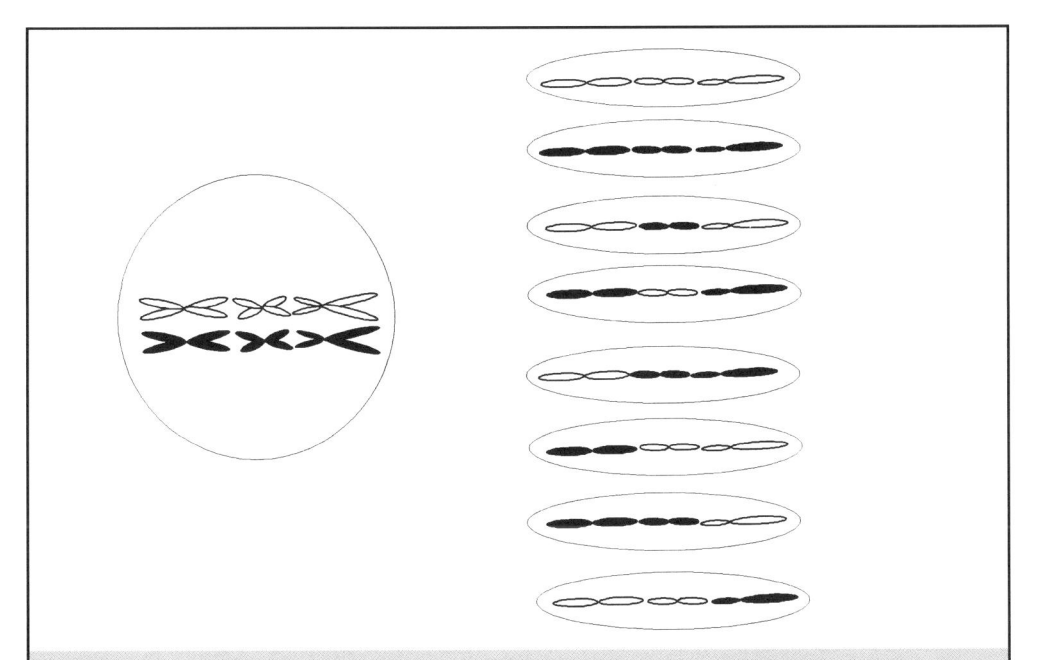

Figure 3–6. Random assortment. *Each germ cell begins with a diploid set of chromosomes, one of each set coming from each parent. Meiosis separates the parental pairs randomly. A germ cell with only three pairs of chromosomes could produce gametes with eight different chromosome combinations. Fertilization restores the chromosome pairs that have been separated by meiosis, and the above gametes could produce many different chromosome combinations.*

mitosis, the chromatids *remain joined at the centromere,* and each of the two new daughter cells receives only one chromosome of each pair.

Meiosis II (the second maturation division) is also known as *gametogenesis*—the creation of gametes. The chromatids separate at the centromeres, with one chromatid going to each daughter cell. The process differs slightly in males and females. In males, the process is known as *spermatogenesis*. Each division is equal, and the result is four viable sperm. In females, the process, known as *oogenesis,* produces three polar bodies and only one viable ovum or egg. The polar bodies have little or no cytoplasm and soon disintegrate, whereas the ovum has almost all of the cytoplasm, *which also contains some genetic material in the mitochondria.*

One of the most important features of meiosis is the random assortment of the chromosomes during metaphase. Each germ cell begins with a diploid set of chromosomes, one of each set coming from each parent. Meiosis separates the parental pairs randomly. When the chromosomes are drawn to different poles during metaphase, the only priority is that each set has a full complement of chromosomes. In this way, the parental chomosomes are randomly mixed. Chromosome 1 and chromosome 2 may have come from the paternal line, or chromosome 1 may be from the paternal line and 2 from the maternal line. The greater the number of chromosomes, the greater the number of possible combinations. The mathematical formula here is 2^n, with *n* representing the number of chromosome pairs. An organism with just three chromosomes,

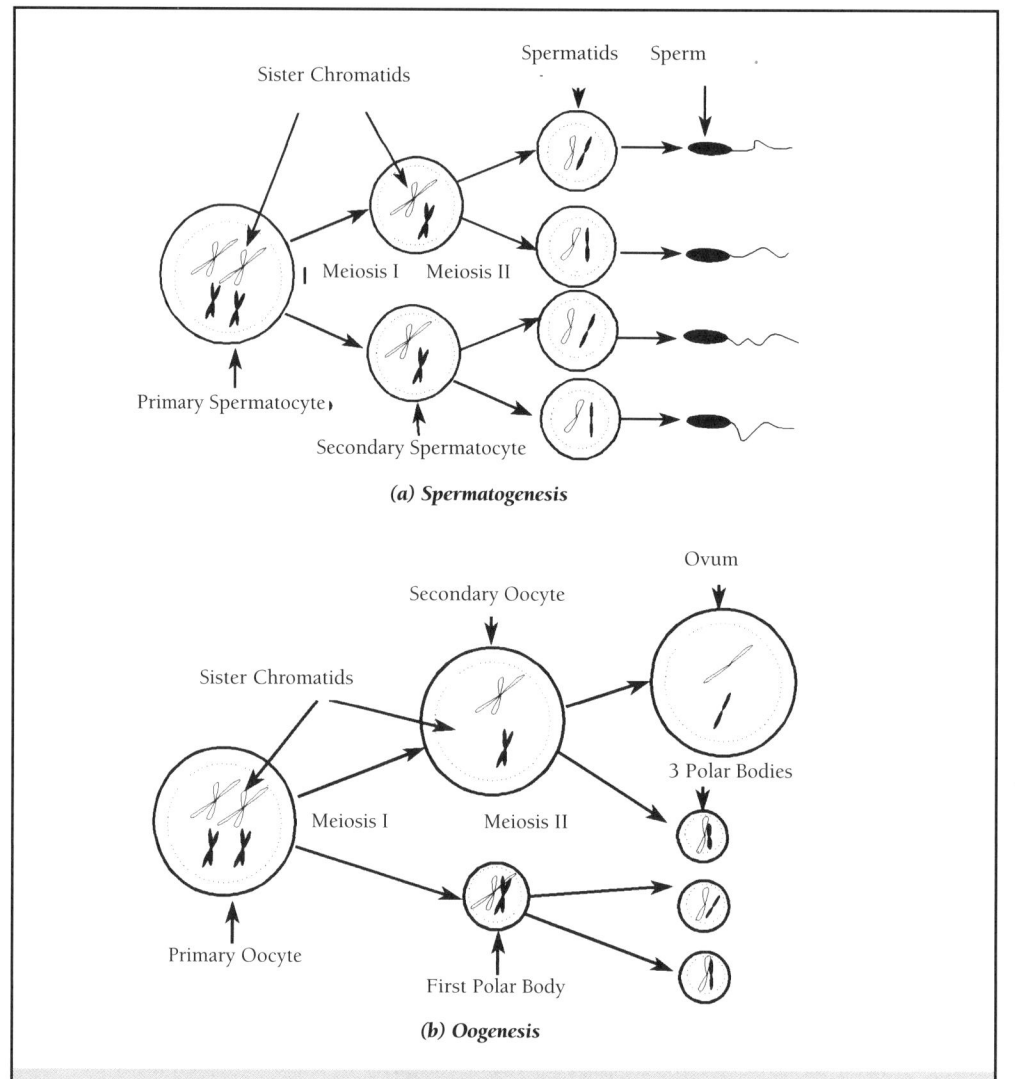

Figure 3–7. Meiosis II. Second reduction division or gametogenesis.

(a) Spermatogenesis. In males, the process is known as spermatogenesis. At the end of meiosis I, each cell is equal in size. In meiosis II, each of the cells again divides equally, producing a total of four cells called spermatids, which develop tails (flagella) and become active sperm.

(b) Oogenesis. In females, the process, known as oogenesis, proceeds somewhat differently. Instead of forming two identical cells during meiosis I, one cell—the secondary oocyte—receives most of the cytoplasm, and the other, known as a polar body, receives little. In meiosis II, the secondary oocyte divides unequally, producing the ovum and another polar body, and the first polar body divides into two, making a total of three. Only the ovum, containing almost all of the cytoplasm and the mitochondrial genetic material, is a functional gamete.

Cytogenetics   47

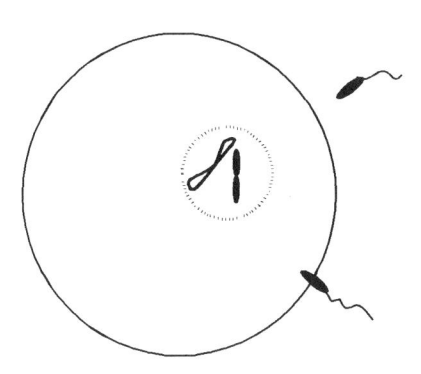

(a) The sperm penetrates the cell wall.

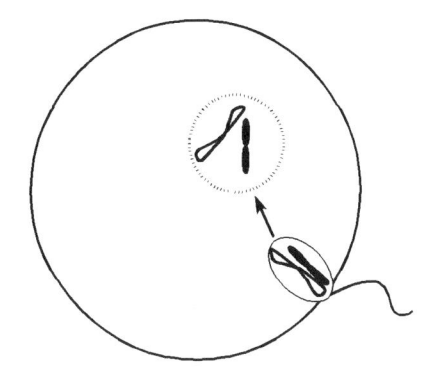

(b) The sperm nucleus (enlarged) approaches the ovum's nucleus.

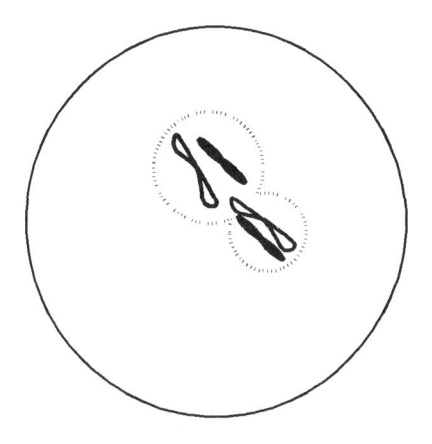

(c) The nuclei make contact.

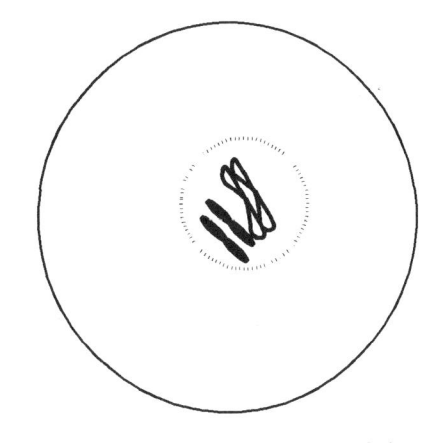

(d) The nuclear walls part, and the nuclei unite.

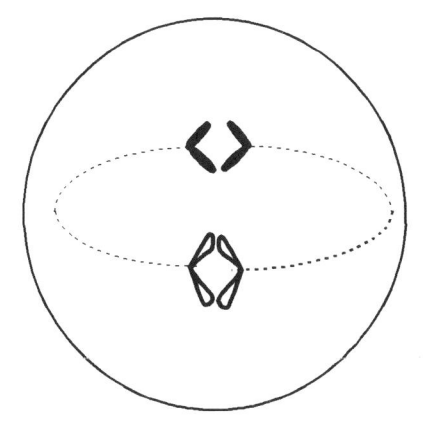

(e) The chromosomes align for the first mitotic cell division.

Figure 3–8. Fertilization.

2^3, could have eight possible chromosome combinations. Humans, with 23 chromosome pairs (2^{23}), have 8,388,608 different possible chromosome combinations. Dogs, with 39 chromosome pairs (2^{39}) have 549,755,813,888 possible chromosome combinations. (No wonder puppies often fail to look like either parent.)

TOGETHER AGAIN—FERTILIZATION

With the act of fertilization, the sperm penetrates the cell wall of the ovum, the two cell nuclei join, and the *zygote* (fertilized egg) has the full complement of paired chromosomes and genetic material. The zygote immediately forms a fertilization membrane that prevents the entrance of another sperm.

After fertilization, the cell begins to multiply by mitosis. The first few cells (stem cells) retain the same genetic potential as the fertilized egg—that is, each cell is capable of growing into a complete organism. In fact, if these early cells separate, the result is identical (monozygotic) twins.

The embryo continues to grow, and the early stages of development are characterized by the development (differentiation) of the organ systems and the main external features. At this stage, the embryo is very sensitive to injuries, which may alter its development and produce congenital defects; the type of deformity depends on type of cells injured and the stage of development. Unless the damage affects the reproductive cells, however, *the defect is not hereditary!*

During the later stages of development, the organism is known as a fetus, though there is no specific point at which the term first applies. The fetus continues to grow until ready to enter the world.

CHROMOSOMAL VARIATIONS

MIX AND MATCH

Crossing-Over

Crossing-over is the reciprocal exchange of segments of genetic material between homologous chromosomes during the prophase of cell division. The genes are still in the same sequence and location on the chromosome, but they are in new combinations.

With sexual reproduction, each parent contributes one chromosome of every pair to the progeny. Because they too received one chromosome from their parents, it is logical to

Figure 3–9. Crossing over. *Crossovers are a precise exchange of genetic material between chromatids.*

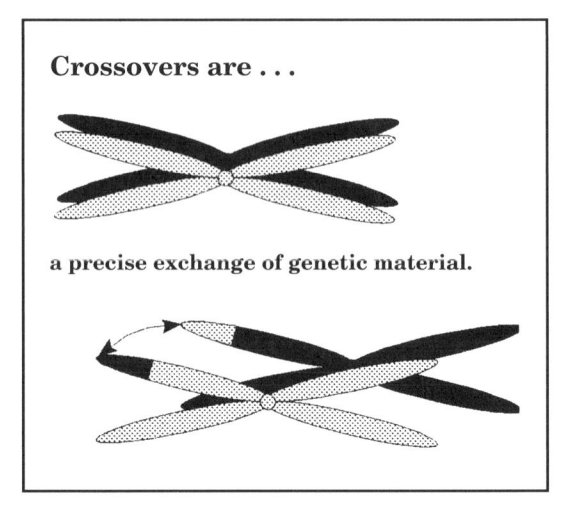

Crossovers are . . .

a precise exchange of genetic material.

picture a straight-line descent of chromosomes that are identical to those of one or another ancestor. This is possible but not likely because of crossing-over, and it becomes increasingly unlikely with each successive generation.

When first observed, geneticists believed that crossovers were very rare, as they are in mitosis. In meiosis, however, it is now known that crossovers occur quite often. Environmental factors (such as increased temperature and some drugs) are known to increase the frequency of crossing over. It has also been found that the frequency is significantly increased by maternal stress.[8]

Linkage

Linkage is the relationship between genes on the same chromosome that causes them to be inherited as a unit. Although crossing-over exchanges gene segments from one chromosome to another, the sequence of the genes along the chromosome's length remains the same. The strength of the linkage depends on the distance between the genes. The greater the distance between genes on the same chromosome, the greater the chances of separation during a crossover. If the genes are right next to each other, the chances of them being separated during a crossover are extremely low.

Linkage can lead to the increase of an undesirable trait in a breed of animals in which the selection for certain desirable traits is intense. Evidence has been presented in support of the hypothesis that the gene responsible for sharply defined spots in the Dalmatian is closely linked to the gene responsible for abnormally high levels of uric acid in the blood.

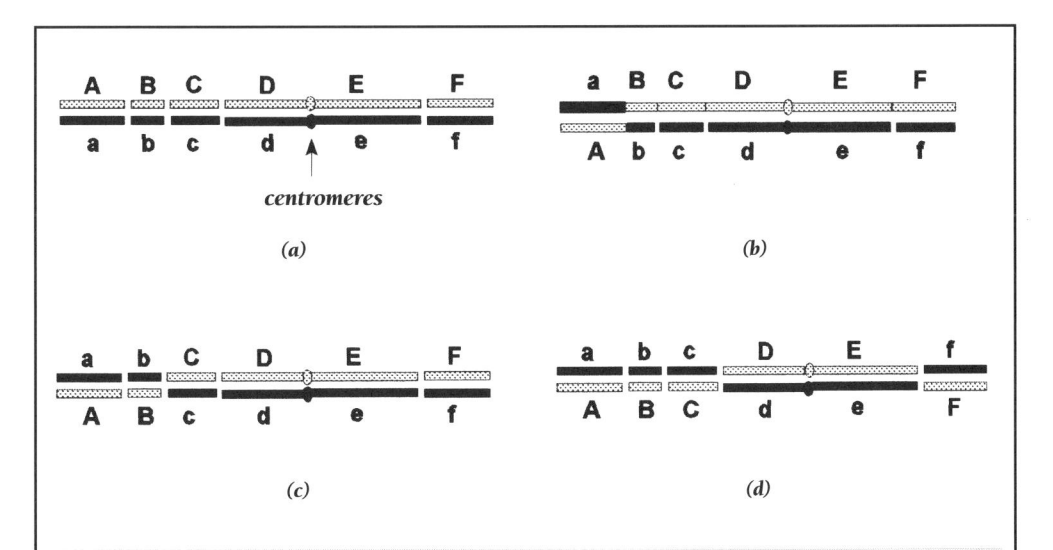

Figure 3–10. Linkage. *Although crossing over exchanges gene segments from one chromosome to another, the sequence of the genes along the chromosome's length remains the same. Almost any exchange will separate A and F; only one of these possible groups of crossovers will separate C and F. The closer the genes are located to each other, the smaller the chances of their being separated by a crossover. (a) The sequence of genes in a pair of chromosomes before crossing-over. (b) A reciprocal exchange of A and a. (c) A reciprocal exchange of AB and ab. (d) A reciprocal exchange of ABC and abc.*

Sometime in the breed's history, when selecting for the spotting pattern, breeders also unknowingly selected for the linked abnormal gene that was responsible for the uric acid defect. By the time the problem was identified, the breed was homozygous for the abnormal uric acid gene as well as the spotting gene. It was necessary to cross with another breed (Pointers were used) to obtain dogs that had the desired spotting gene and normal uric acid metabolism.[9]

MIX AND MISMATCH—ANOMALIES

Any irregularity in the structure of a chromosome or in the number of chromosomes that may alter embryonic development is known as a *chromosomal anomaly*, a *chromosomal aberration*, or a *chromosomal mutation*. An anomaly is not hereditary unless the germ cells that produce sperm and ova are affected.

Chromosomal abnormalities are surprisingly common. In humans, it has been estimated that as many as half of fertilizations involve chromosomal abnormalities. Most anomalies lead to early abortion of the embryo, and anomalies have been identified in 15 percent of spontaneous human abortions. One study of reproduction-related abnormalities in domestic animals identified them in all species studied; of the 264 dogs examined, abnormalities were detected in 17 (6.4 percent).[10] The death of an embryo or fetus does not always lead to an immediate, spontaneous abortion. A dead embryo is often reabsorbed; a dead fetus may be retained and become "mummified," and aborted later. One difficulty in identifying chromosomal aberrations in species that have multiple births (such as dogs) is that abnormal individuals are rarely aborted. When a mummified puppy appears at whelping, breeders rarely bother to have it examined for chromosomal anomalies.

Changes of Structure

Segments of a chromosome may be duplicated, deleted, inverted, or translocated, all of which alter the sequence of genes along the chromosome's length. (A *translocation* is the insertion of a segment into another part of the same chromosome or into a different chromosome.) Whether or not the rearrangement of genetic material is compatible with life depends on many factors, such as the function of the altered segment. Even if compatible with life, the change may not be compatible with reproduction. Nevertheless, such large-scale alterations have played an important role in evolution. The evolution of the family of *Canidae*, for example, has been traced by identifying the sequential changes in chromosomal structure over millions of years.

Variations of Number

Sometimes chromosomal aberrations involve complete sets of chromosomes. In general, the loss of chromosomes is incompatible with life, but additions are not always lethal.

As mentioned earlier, *diploid* means a set of paired chromosomes, and *haploid* means one-half of a diploid set of chromosomes. *Triploid (triploidy)* means three complete sets of chromosomes; *tetraploid (tetraploidy)* means four sets of chromosomes. Interestingly, tetraploidy tends to be both stable and fertile. In the plant kingdom, tetraploidy occurs fairly frequently, both naturally and artificially induced. Because they tend to be larger than their diploid cousins, many commercially important crop species are tetraploid. Although less common, tetraploidy also occurs in the animal kingdom.

Trisomy refers to the addition of an extra chromosome to one of the homologous pairs. One of the best-known examples in humans is trisomy 21 (referring to chromosome number 21), better known as Down's syndrome. Other examples in humans are trisomy 8, trisomy 13 (Patou's syndrome), trisomy 18 (Edward's syndrome), and trisomy 22 as well as trisomy of the sex chromosomes. Very few trisomic mammals are fertile, though women with Down's syndrome have produced children, and in 1986, a trisomic Simmental cow with a normal calf was reported.[11]

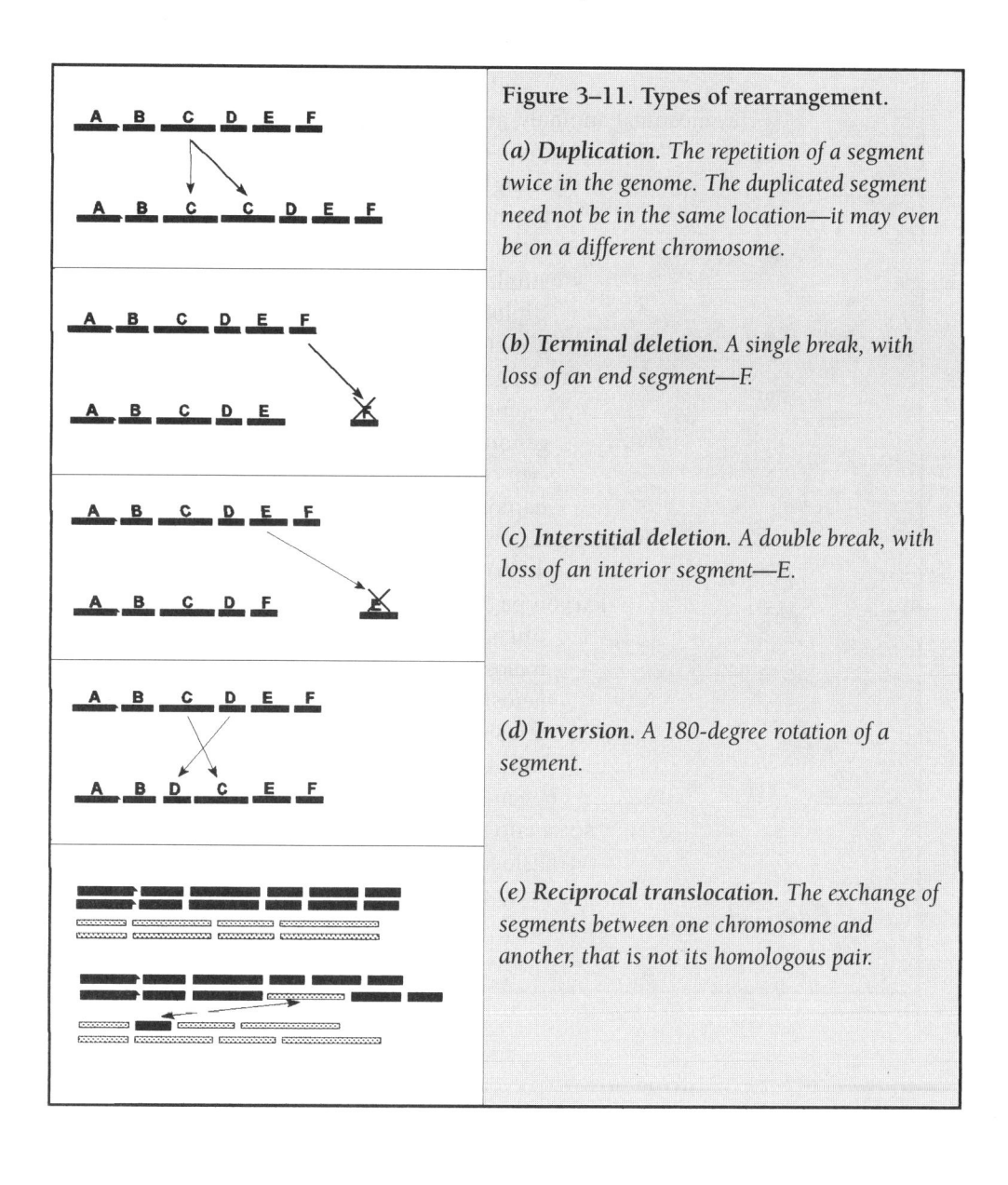

Figure 3–11. Types of rearrangement.

(a) *Duplication.* The repetition of a segment twice in the genome. The duplicated segment need not be in the same location—it may even be on a different chromosome.

(b) *Terminal deletion.* A single break, with loss of an end segment—F.

(c) *Interstitial deletion.* A double break, with loss of an interior segment—E.

(d) *Inversion.* A 180-degree rotation of a segment.

(e) *Reciprocal translocation.* The exchange of segments between one chromosome and another, that is not its homologous pair.

REVIEW OF TERMS

cell
chromosomal anomaly, aberration, or mutation
chromosome
crossing-over
cytogenetics
cytology
cytoplasm
diploid
gametes
gametogenesis
gene
genome
germ cells
haploid
homologous chromosomes
hybrid
karyotype diagram
linkage
meiosis
meiosis I
meiosis II
mitosis
oogenesis
spermatogenesis
translocation
zygote

Chapter 4

MENDELIAN GENETICS

MENDEL AND HIS LAWS

Gregor Johann Mendel (1822–1884), an Augustinian monk, is well known as the father of genetics. Often, the image arises of a humble monastic gardener, sowing his peas and making inspired observations. Mendel was, in fact, a highly educated teacher. He attended the University of Vienna where he studied mathematics and natural science from 1851 to 1854. Mendel returned to his home monastery at Brunn, where he taught these subjects and experimented with peas. Both teaching and research had to be put aside when Mendel became abbot of the monastery in 1868.

Mendel began his experiments with peas in 1856. He studied traits such as height, seed color, seed shape, and pod shape. Keeping careful records of his experiments, Mendel formulated the fundamental laws of heredity.

In 1865, Mendel reported his findings at a meeting of the Brunn Natural History Society. The following year, Mendel's paper, "Experiments with Plant Hybrids," was published in the society's proceedings. Mendel's work was never "lost" in the sense implied when its later "rediscovery" is mentioned. The society's proceedings were widely circulated (at least fifty-five European libraries and scientific societies received copies), and Mendel sent reprints to many leading botanists. Mendel or his work was mentioned in sixteen late nineteenth-century publications, including the *Encyclopedia Britannica*. Nevertheless, the world-shaking implications of his discoveries were not recognized immediately.

In 1900, sixteen years after Mendel's death, three scientists independently and almost simultaneously ran across his paper and repeated his experiments—Hugo de Vries (Netherlands), Carl Correns (Germany), and Erich von Ischermak-Seysenegg (Austria). They reached the same conclusions as Mendel, and the new science was off and running.

Mendel's most enduring contributions to the science of genetics are the laws of segregation and independent assortment. Although he formulated other laws, it is the first two that proved to be keystones of the new science.

The *law of segregation* states that the units of heredity exist in pairs, the pairs separate for reproduction, and each parent contributes one unit to the next generation. Mendel began with pure lines of peas that bred true for specific traits from one generation to the next, crossed the different strains, and observed the results. In genetic jargon, the *parental generation* is identified as *P*; the term for their offspring is *filial*. The first generation of descendants is called the *first filial* or F_1 *generation*, and the second generation is known as the *second filial* or F_2 *generation*. Mendel observed that, when crossing the purebred strains, some traits in the first generation (F_1) always resembled only one parent. When he crossed peas with white flowers with those with purple flowers, for example, all of the progeny produced purple flowers. In the second generation (F_2), though, the white color reappeared in about one-fourth of the flowers. The hereditary unit for white flowers had merely been masked by the purple, not destroyed. Knowing nothing about meiosis or genes, Mendel nevertheless deduced the separation of paired units of heredity and their reunion in the next generation. The segregation that Mendel obeserved occurs during meiosis, when the two genes of each pair end up on different gametes.

The *law of independent assortment* states that the inheritance of each paired unit is independent of the others. Mendel studied the inheritance of several traits and discovered that the inheritance of each trait was independent of others. The inheritance of seed color, for example, was unrelated to that of flower color. This also occurs during meiosis, as illustrated in Figure 3–6.

SINGLE-GENE HEREDITY

Mendelian genetics is sometimes defined as the study of *particulate* (that is, minute and separate particles) *heredity*, because it is characterized by easily classified units of heredity. It is also known as *single-gene heredity*, because each gene is inherited as a distinct unit and produces an identifiable effect. Two pairs of terms are fundamental to all descriptions and discussions of these units: homozygous and heterozygous; phenotype and genotype.

HOMOZYGOUS AND HETEROZYGOUS

This pair of terms simply describe whether the genes are *alike* (homo) or *unlike* (hetero). When the paired genes are identical, the genes are described as *homozygous*, and the individual is a *homozygote*. This identical pair means that all offspring will receive an identical gene for the trait. Therefore, in terms of genetic predictability, homozygosity insures that all progeny will carry one of those genes. Breeds that are characterized by a single color are homozygous for the color genes; Black and Tan Coonhounds are always black and tan, and Sussex Spaniels are always liver. If the genes are beneficial, homozygous pairs are highly desirable. Some genes produce undesirable traits, however, in which case homozygosity is a disadvantage.

Paired genes that are not identical are described as *heterozygous,* and the individual is a *heterozygote.* When the genetic material divides, the probability of a particular gene being passed to offspring is also divided in half.

PHENOTYPE AND GENOTYPE

This pair of terms differentiates between the genes that are expressed in the individual and the genes that may be transmitted to the next generation. *Phenotype* is often defined as the observable and measurable traits, and dog breeders tend to relate phenotype to traits judged in the show ring—that is, breed type, coat quality and color, and so forth. Geneticists, however, perceive phenotype as the *total* of all traits; this includes the molecular, cellular, anatomical, physiological, and behavioral traits that are expressed from conception to reproduction and death. The expression of phenotype is determined by a combination of genetic and environmental factors; for example, the genetic potential for height may not be expressed because of illness or malnutrition, or a genetically stable temperament my be damaged by isolation or abuse.

Genotype relates to the genetic constitution of an individual or group. When the genes of a pair are heterozygous (unlike), often the effect of only one of them can be identified in the phenotype, and the presence of the other gene is hidden. The genes that are not expressed in the phenotype are, nevertheless, passed on to the next generation. A growing number of the hidden genes that produce serious disorders can be identified by DNA analysis—someday it may be possible to analyze the entire genome.

Dog breeders' plans for matings are often based on traits that can be observed and measured—that is, the phenotype. The traits that the parents transmit to their puppies are determined by the genotype, however. The hidden traits are discovered only when they appear in the puppies, and therein lies the challenge of dog breeding.

PENETRANCE AND EXPRESSIVITY

Two important terms—penetrance and expressivity—describe variations of phenotypic expression.

The percentage (or proportion) of individuals with a given genotype that exhibit the associated phenotype is known as *penetrance*. For example, if 100 percent show the expected phenotype, the gene has 100 percent penetrance. If less than 100 percent show the phenotype, the genotype has *incomplete penetrance*. A good example of complete penetrance is the gene pair in dogs that produces either black pigment or brown.

Expressivity is the degree to which the genotype is expressed in the phenotype. An interesting example of the *variable expressivity* of a homozygous trait can be observed in dogs with the black-and-tan pattern. Within the same breed, variations of the size of the tan markings and the clarity of the facial points are common. Variations are even more pronounced when comparing different breeds such as the Cocker Spaniel and the Gordon Setter. Remember, they all have identical genes for the pattern, but the expressivity varies. Similarly, all Brittanies are piebald, but no two have identical markings.

TYPES OF GENE ACTION

The familiar dominant-recessive pattern of inheritance falls under Mendelian genetics. Complete dominance and recessiveness, however, does not always occur, even with single-gene heredity. Some genes are incompletely dominant. Others alter the typical patterns of heredity when they occur on the sex chromosomes or are lethal to the embryo when paired.

COMPLETE DOMINANCE

Mendel's law of dominance states that each trait is determined by two hereditary factors and that one always predominates. The latter is known as a *dominant* gene because, when heterozygous, it masks the presence of the unlike gene. The phenotypic effect is the same in both the homozygote and the heterozygote. A *recessive* gene, on the other hand, affects the phenotype only when it is paired with a matching (homozygous) recessive gene, and it is totally masked if paired with a dominant gene. Again, the gene pair that produced black and brown coat colors are a good example: A brown coat confirms that the dog is homozygous for the recessive brown gene, whereas a black coat indicates that the dog has at least one dominant black gene but could also carry a recessive brown gene.

Genetic checkerboards (Punnett squares) are a wonderful way to illustrate the inheritance of single genes. Remember, after meiosis, each gamete has only one chromosome from each pair. Each of those chromosomes will join with one from the other parent to form a new combination, and the checkerboards illustrate the different combinations that can occur. The letters above the square symbolize the gametes from one parent, and the letters on the left represent those from the other parent. Traditionally, the genes for a particular trait are designated by italicized letters, using a capital for the dominant gene and a lowercase letter for the recessive gene. In Figure 4–1, one parent contributes the genes *AA*, and the other contributes *aa*.

Figure 4–1. Genetic checkerboards (Punnett squares). *The letters above the square (AA) symbolize the gametes from one parent, and the letters on the left (aa) represent those from the other parent. Capital letters indicate dominant genes and lowercase letters indicate recessive genes.*

Dominant (AA) x Recessive (aa)

	A	A
a	Aa	Aa
a	Aa	Aa

Table 4–1.
Ratios of Dominant-Recessive Traits

Parents' Genotype	Offspring's Genotype Ratio			Offspring's Phenotype Ratio	
	BB	Bb	bb	Black	Brown
BB x BB	1	0	0	1	0
BB x Bb	1	1	0	1	0
BB x bb	0	1	0	1	0
Bb x Bb	1	2	1	3	1
Bb x bb	0	1	1	1	1
bb x bb	0	0	1	0	1

A good example of a simple dominant-recessive pair in dogs is the pair that determines black or brown coat color. The gene for black is dominant and is symbolized by B; the gene for brown is recessive and is symbolized by b. There are only three possible ways for the two genes to pair up—that is, only three possible genotypes:
- If the genotype is BB, the dog will be homozygous for the dominant trait, and the phenotype will be a black coat
- If the genotype is bb, the dog will be homozygous for the recessive trait, and the phenotype will be a brown coat
- If the genotype is Bb, the dog will be heterozygous, and the phenotype will be a black coat

The squares also illustrate the varying probabilities with different dominant-recessive combinations, which are called *Mendelian ratios*. The potential genotype and phenotype ratios produced by particular dominant-recessive combinations can be predicted, and the ratio of the offsprings' phenotype is also a clue to whether a particular trait is dominant or recessive. It is important to remember that these ratios are significant only in very large numbers. (Just think of how infrequently a litter has an equal number of males and females.)

Genotype of Parents — **Phenotype (Genotype) of Progeny**

B = dominant gene for black pigment
b = recessive gene for brown pigment

1. BB x bb

	B	B
b	Bb	Bb
b	Bb	Bb

100% black (Bb)

2. Bb x bb

	B	b
b	Bb	bb
b	Bb	bb

50% black (Bb)
50% brown (bb)

3. Bb x Bb

	B	b
B	BB	Bb
b	Bb	bb

50% black (Bb)
25% black (BB)
25% brown (bb)

4. BB x Bb

	B	B
B	BB	BB
b	Bb	Bb

50% black (BB)
50% black (Bb)

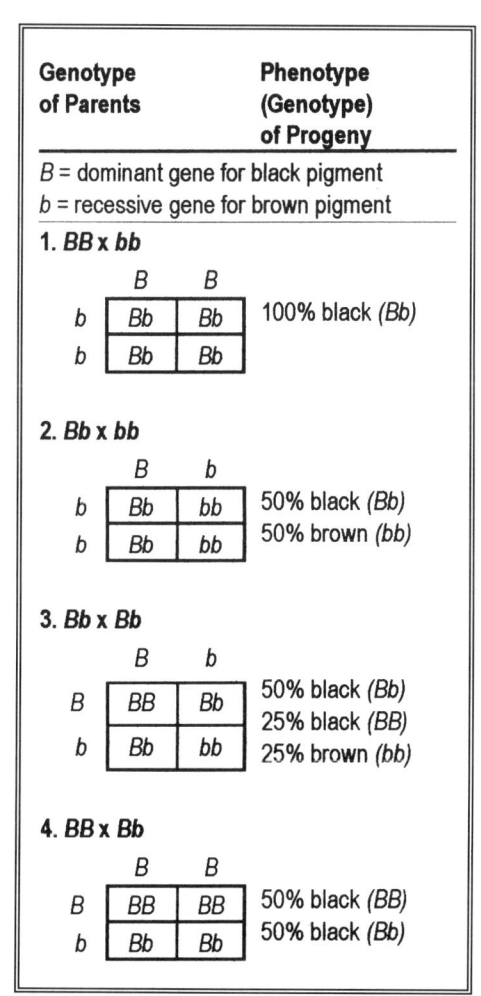

VARIATIONS OF DOMINANCE

Mendel's law of dominance did not prove to be absolute, for geneticists soon observed that many single-gene traits do not exhibit complete dominance. There are, in fact, varying degrees of dominance in which the expression of the recessive gene is not completely suppressed.

With *incomplete dominance*, the expression of a heterozygous pair produces an intermediate phenotype. In carnations, for example, the R gene produces red pigment, whereas the r gene produces no pigment. When homozygous RR, the flower is red; when homozygous rr, the flower is white. However, when the carnation is heterozygous Rr, the flower is pink.[1]

Figure 4–2. **Dominant-recessive genetic combinations.** *Different dominant-recessive genotype combinations of the parents produce different percentages of the phenotype and genotype of the progeny. In dogs, a good example is the gene pair that determines black or brown coat color.*

Figure 4–3. Incomplete dominance. *The inheritance of color in red (RR) and white (rr) carnations is an example of incomplete dominance.*

Red (RR) x White (rr)

	R	r
R	RR red	Rr pink
r	Rr pink	rr white

With *codominance,* the expression of a heterozygous pair produces a phenotype in which the activity of both genes can be identified in the phenotype by the presence of two *different* gene products. In sickle cell anemia, for example, the disease is caused by a variant type of hemoglobin in red blood cells: Hb^A produces normal hemoglobin, and Hb^S produces abnormal hemoglobin. Red blood cells with $Hb^A Hb^A$ never become sickle shaped; cells with $Hb^S Hb^S$ become sickled when the oxygen level decreases; and cells with $Hb^A Hb^S$ have both types of hemoglobin and become sickle shaped only under extremely low oxygen pressure.[2]

Suzuki and his coauthors point out that the nature of the two terms—incomplete dominance and codominance—is "somewhat arbitrary. The type of dominance depends on the phenotypic level at which the observations are being made." In other words, dominance relationships must be regarded as a spectrum of phenotypic expression rather than an either-or situation. The authors also point out that "complete

Figure 4–4. Codominance. *The inheritance of normal ($Hb^A Hb^A$) and abnormal ($Hb^S Hb^S$) hemoglobin with sickle-cell anemia is an example of codominance.*

Heterozygotes ($Hb^A Hb^S$)

	Hb^A	Hb^S
Hb^A	$Hb^A Hb^A$ never sickle	$Hb^A Hb^S$ rarely sickle
Hb^S	$Hb^A Hb^S$ rarely sickle	$Hb^S Hb^S$ frequently sickle

dominance and recessiveness are not essential aspects of Mendel's laws; those laws deal more with the inheritance patterns and genes than with their nature or function."[3]

Just think! If Mendel's peas had demonstrated such confusing qualities, the science of genetics may not have taken off for many years. In fact, the real miracle of Mendel's work is that he just happened to study seven traits that just happened to be dominant-recessive pairs on the seven different chromosomes of the garden pea (*Pisum sativum*). Suzuki and Griffiths compared his experiments with attempting to randomly push seven buttons in the dark and hitting a different one with each try; the probability of pushing a different one in each of seven tries is 0.61 percent.[4]

SEX LINKAGE

The pair of chromosomes that determines gender is unique. The chromosomes are so different that sex can be identified in karyotypes, where they are always placed as the last pair. In mammalian females, the largest paired chromosomes appear

	Female (XX) x Male (XY)	
	X	X
X	XX female	XX female
Y	XY male	XY male

Figure 4–5. Gender inheritance. *In mammals, the females have an XX chromosome pair, and the males have an XY pair.*

X-shaped and are, logically, called X chromosomes; thus, females have an XX chromosome pair. In males, one of the paired chromosomes is always smaller, containing fewer genes, and it is called the Y chromosome; males, therefore, have an XY pair. (Other patterns of gender inheritance, by the way, occur in the animal kingdom. In birds, for example, the females are XY, and the males are XX).

The X and Y chromosomes are known as the *sex chromosomes*, and a *sex-linked trait* is one that is produced by the genes on the X or Y chromosome. The more recent, and more precise, terms are *X-linked* and *Y-linked* traits. Curiously, *not one* of the sources in the lengthy bibliography at the end of this book gives an example of a Y-linked trait.

All other chromosomes are called *autosomes*, and an *autosomal trait* is one that is determined by a gene located on any chromosome other than the sex chromosomes. It is important to remember that some genes on autosomes are related to gender and that some of the genes on the sex chromosomes are related to other functions.

AUTOSOMAL DOMINANTS
- At least one parent in every generation has the disorder
- Affected parents may produce normal offspring
- Normal offspring from affected parents produce only normal offspring when mated to normals
- The incidence is about equal in males and females

AUTOSOMAL RECESSIVES
- The disorder skips generations
- Most affected individuals have normal parents
- All offspring of two affected parents have the disorder
- The incidence is about equal in males and females

SEX-LINKED RECESSIVES (X CHROMOSOME)
- The disorder skips generations
- Occurs only in males (50%) when both parents appear normal
- All offspring of two affected parents have the disorder
- Offspring of affected males and normal (unrelated) females are normal—all daughters are carriers
- Male offspring of affected females and normal males are affected but females are not—all daughters are carriers

---

Figure 4–6. Patterns of single-gene inheritance. *With hereditary disorders, patterns may help to identify the mode of inheritance.*

A sex-linked trait should not be confused with a *sex-limited trait,* which is one in which the visible expression is limited to one gender even though the genes may be carried by both parents. For example, the genetic expression of milk production is limited to females, and the number of descended testicles is limited to males.

The *XY* pair in the lower right corner of the karyotype in Figure 3–1 on page 40 clearly shows that the larger *X* chromosome has more genes than the *Y.* This means that the *X* chromosome has an additional segment of genetic material that has no corresponding segment on the *Y* chromosome. In females, the *XX* chromosomes are paired. In males, however, it is impossible for the genes on this segment of the *X* chromosome to have a corresponding gene on the *Y* chromosome, and traits located on this segment exhibit a different pattern of inheritance.

A heterozygous recessive gene that is located on the *X* chromosome is masked in all females because of the dominant gene on the other *X* chromosome. Males, however, have only one *X* chromosome, and they have no paired dominant to mask a recessive trait.

The best-known example of a recessive sex-linked trait is hemophilia, and interestingly, the heredity is the same in all species in which hemophilia has been identified. The gene carrying hemophilia is identified as X^h. There are five possible genotypes:
- *XX*—normal female
- *XX^h*—heterozygous female (carrier)
- *X^{h}X^h*—affected female with hemophilia
- *XY*—normal male
- *X^{h}Y*—affected male with hemophilia

LETHAL GENES

In general, a *lethal gene* is one that causes the death of the embryo or fetus when homozygous, though the term is sometimes applied to genes that are fatal during later life. Examples of lethal genes are the harlequin trait in the Great Dane and hairlessness in the Chinese Crested. When paired, these genes are simply incompatible with life.

ALLELES AND LOCI

Mendel's tidy system of paired dominant and recessive genes never allowed for the possibility that more than two genes could team up to form a pair. When geneticists discovered that more than two different genes could form pairs, it became necessary to add new terms to the language of genetics.

An *allele* (meaning "another form of") is any one of two-or-more alternative forms of a gene occupying the same position on a particular chromosome. "Depending on its structure, one gene of a pair may 'say' slightly different things about a trait. Each different molecular form of the same gene is called an allele."[5]

Locus (plural, *loci*) refers to the site or location the allele occupies on a chromosome. Many loci were given arbitrary identifications, such as Locus *A* and Locus *B*, long before genetic mapping became a possibility, and they designate a type of gene expression rather than the physical position on a chromosome. For example, most mammals have a pair of alleles for either black or brown pigment, and by custom,

Parents		Progeny Phenotype (Genotype)
	X	X^h
X	XX normal female	XX^h carrier female	25% normal males (XY) 25% affected males (X^hY) 25% normal females (XX) 25% carrier females (XX^h)
Y	XY normal male	X^hY affected male	

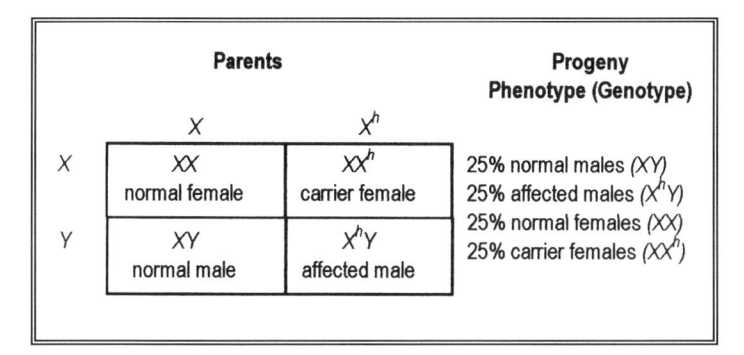

Figure 4–7. X-Linked Recessive Inheritance. *The gene that produces hemophilia is located on the X chromosome and is identified as X^h. The offspring of a normal male (XY) and carrier female (X^{xh}) could have four different genotypes.*

Locus B refers to their expression in all species. Obviously, the exact physical location of the pair could be on any chromosome and in any position. Alleles and loci are discussed in greater detail in Chapter 8.

The genes that determine many other expressions of color also have striking similarity in many mammals; dogs, cats, horses, rabbits, and mice, for example, have a Locus D, with alleles for dilution and nondilution of pigment, but some species have more than two alleles that can occupy that locus.

Mendel did not present the possibility of interactions between genes at different loci, which adds a whole new range of interesting possibilities.

A good example of interaction between different loci is demonstrated by the two that determine the basic colors and the shades of parakeets. The first locus determines whether the base color is green (G), which is dominant, or blue (g). The alleles at a second locus are known as the dark factors (the dominant D and recessive d). The alleles exhibit incomplete dominance and determine the shade of the basic green or blue colors. The two loci interact to produce the following colors:
- G–DD—olive green
- G–Dd—emerald green
- G–dd—light green
- ggDD—mauve (a dirty, pinkish gray)
- ggDd—cobalt blue
- ggdd—turquoise blue

(The dash after the G merely indicates that the second allele is unknown or uncertain—it has no effect on the phenotype.) The next time you look at a flock of parakeets, you should find it easy to identify the genotype of those that exhibit these basic colors.

Occasionally, alleles at a third locus influence the expression of a trait, and the beautiful violet color (V) in parakeets offers the clearest example of an interaction between three loci. Violet is masked by all of the above genotypes *except* the one that produces cobalt blue (ggDd), and the shade of violet is slightly more brilliant with the presence of two violet factors.

Violet is a popular color with parakeet hobbyists, and imagine that a breeder would like to selectively breed for the color. A pure strain, of course, is impossible, because the combination that produces cobalt blue is produced by heterozygous dark factors. The only combination that will consistently produce cobalt blue, therefore, is breeding a mauve parakeet (ggDD) to a turquoise parakeet (ggdd). To produce violets,

Figure 4–8. Blue color in parakeets. *In parakeets, the green color is produced by the dominant G allele, and all blues are homozygous for the recessive g allele. The different shades of blue color (mauve, turquoise, and cobalt) are produced different combinations of the dark-factor alleles (D and d), which are an example of incomplete dominance. Because cobalt blue (ggDd) is produced heterozygous dark factors, it is impossible to develop a strain that breeds true for that shade.*

Cobalt Heterozygotes (bbDd)

	bD	bd
bD	bbDD mauve	bbDd cobalt
bd	bbDd cobalt	bbdd turquoise

at least one of the parents would also have to carry the violet factor. Fortunately, mauve and turquoise birds that carry violet factors have a peculiar shimmering iridescence that a discerning eye can identify.

Similar three-allele combinations produce the spots in Dalmations and harlequins in Great Danes.

Further complicating the identification of hereditary patterns are *mimic effects,* in which two or more independently inherited alleles produce similar or identical phenotypes. Examples of mimic effects are abundant.

- In rabbits, two breeds are characterized by the rex coat (dense velvety fur) that is recessive to the normal coat in both breeds. However, when the two breeds are crossed, all of the progeny have normal fur, indicating that the rex alleles are not identical.
- Although most black German Shepherd Dogs are produced by a dominant allele, a recessive black allele has been identified at the same locus.
- In dogs, two different genotypes produce a yellow or a red coat—A^yA^yEE and A^sA^see; there is no way to identify the underlying genotype, but if the two are crossed, the puppies are black, with the genotype A^sA^yEe.

It is not unusual to read of conflicting evidence about the mode of heredity of some traits, particularly hereditary disorders; that is, it appears to be a dominant in one breed but recessive in another. Chances are that mutations in each breed

Figure 4–9. Violet color in parakeets. *The beautiful violet color in parakeets is produced by the dominant V allele, but the allele is masked by all combinations except the one for cobalt blue. It is possible, however, to improve the number of violet progeny by mating mauve and turquoise birds that carry the violet allele—DDVV and ddVV.*

Mauve (bbDDVV) and Turquoise (bbddVV)

	bDV	bDV
bdV	bbDdVV violet	bbDdVV violet
bdV	bbDdVV violet	bbDdVV violet

produced the same disorder, but the mutations did not occur at the same genetic locus.

SUMMARY

Mendel's first two laws—segregation and independent assortment—are the foundation of all of the genetic interactions described in this chapter, which are essentially the patterns of inheritance and expression of paired genes. The relationships are incredibly complex, but at the same time there is a wonderful underlying order that is consistent when the patterns are sorted out and identified.

Clearly, the expression of dominant-recessive pairs does not necessarily exhibit the either-or pattern identified by Mendel. When trying to identify the hereditary pattern of a trait, breeders must be aware of and consider many potential gene actions that may be responsible for the observed trait.

REVIEW OF TERMS

allele
autosome
dominant
expressivity
first filial generation (F_1)
genotype
heterozygous
homozygous
incomplete dominance
lethal gene

locus (loci)
mimic effect
parental generation (P)
penetrance
phenotype
recessive
second filial generation (F_2)
sex chromosomes
sex-limited trait
sex-linked trait

MOLECULAR GENETICS

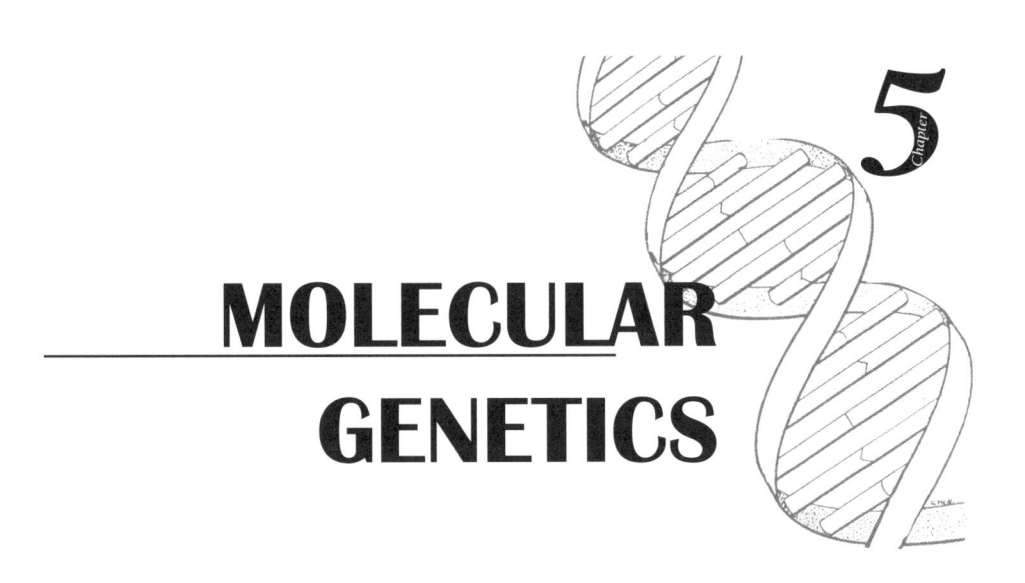

Chapter 5

Molecular genetics is the study of the structure and function of genes at the molecular level. The exciting discoveries in molecular genetics have become an integral part of most other biological disciplines and are revealing the secrets of life. This chapter is a *very simple* overview of molecular genetics, and the objective is to introduce terms and concepts that may be mentioned in the news and in popular literature.

The foundation of molecular genetics is the (relatively) simple molecule of *deoxyribonucleic acid*, better known as DNA. The presence of DNA in chromosomes was discovered early in the century, and in 1944, Oswald T. Avery, Colin M. McLeod, and Maclyn McCarty demonstrated that DNA is the basic genetic component of chromosomes. Even then, scientists failed to recognize its importance, considering DNA too simple and repetitive to control something as complex as heredity. It wasn't until 1953 that James Watson and Francis Crick identified the double-helix (double-spiral) structure of DNA, which earned them a Nobel Prize in 1962. "The breathtaking simplicity of the structure also enabled them to solve a long-standing riddle—how life can show unity at the molecular level and yet give rise to so much diversity at the level of whole organisms."[1] DNA occurs in all living organisms, except for a few viruses. Each DNA molecule carries the organism's genetic information and is capable of self-replication. Since the discovery that DNA holds the key to heredity, the understanding of genetics has virtually exploded.

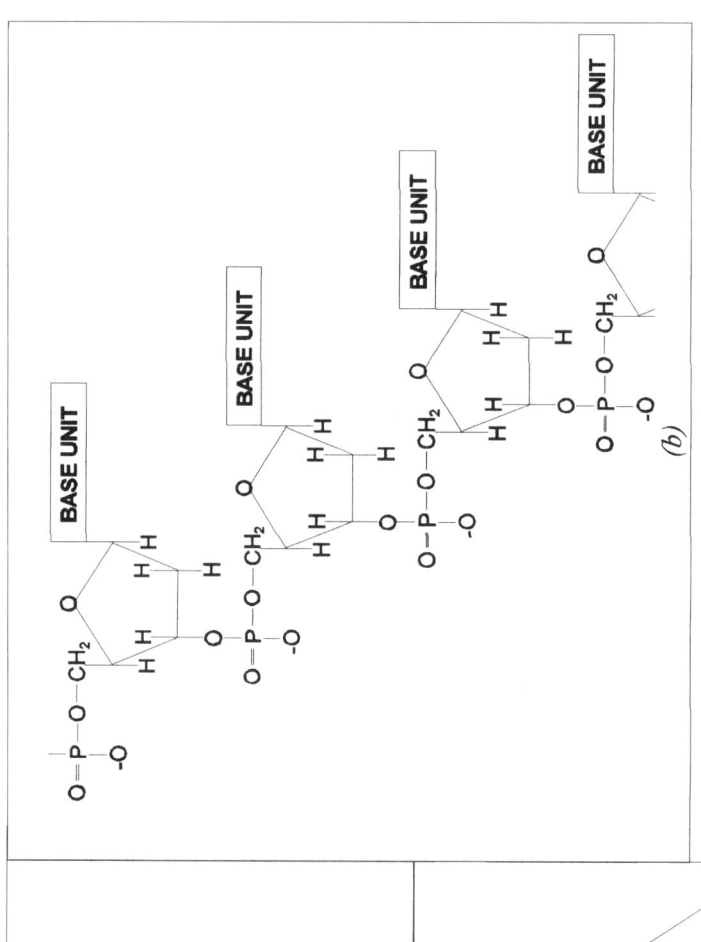

Figure 5–1. DNA structure. (a) The basic DNA nucleotide consists of a phosphate unit, a deoxyribose unit, and any one of four different base units. (b) The deoxyribose and phosphate units link together to form one strand of the DNA polynucleotide. (c) The double helix-structure is created by the bonds between the base pairs. As the arrows indicate, the strands run in opposite directions.

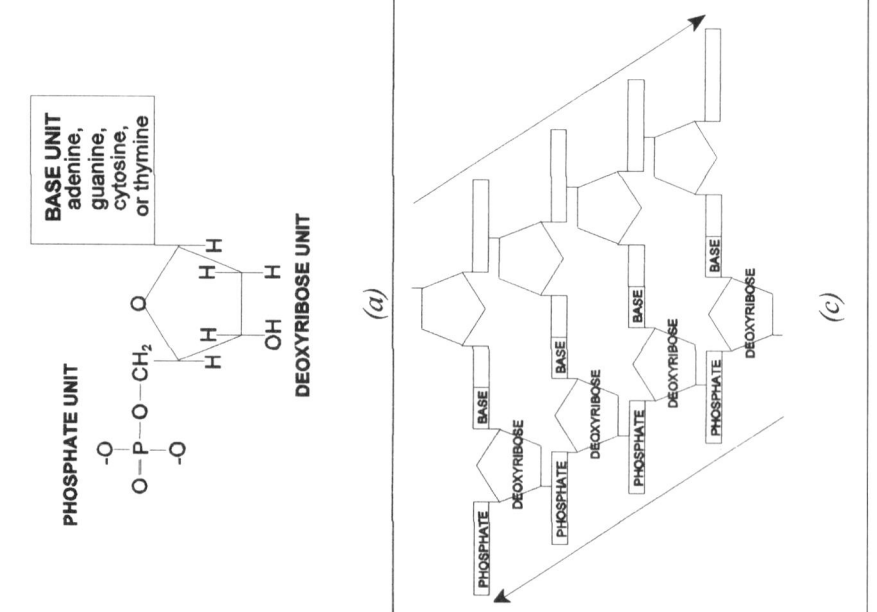

DNA—WHAT IS IT?

STRUCTURE

So, how can one say, on the one hand, that DNA is a "relatively" simple molecule but also say, on the other hand, that each chromosome is one molecule of DNA? Think of Leggo toys or (for an earlier generation) of Tinker toys. Beginning with some relatively simple pieces, incredibly intricate structures can be created by imaginative children. This conveys the principle though hardly the scope.

The beginning pieces for building a molecule of DNA are a type of molecule known as a *nucleotide*, which has three basic components: *(a)* a five-carbon sugar; *(b)* a phosphate; and *(c)* a base. The sugar part of DNA is always deoxyribose. The base portion of the nucleotide may be any one of following four: two—adenine (A) and guanine (G)—have the type of molecular structure called a pyramidine; the others—cytosine (C) and thymine (T)—have a structure called a purine. The structure of the phosphate varies a little, but we'll just call it the phosphate part. This gives us four basic nucleotides for building a molecule of DNA (we'll skip the long chemical names):

- deoxyribose, phosphate, and adenine
- deoxyribose, phosphate, and guanine
- deoxyribose, phosphate, and cytosine
- deoxyribose, phosphate, and thymine

The fact that DNA has only four different kinds of nucleotides may be why it was initially considered too simple to control heredity. The key lies in the way they always join together. The *rules* for putting them together are simple, the trick is in the execution.

The first rule of building a DNA *polynucleotide* (which means "many nucleotides") is that each phosphate unit must bond with a sugar unit, which bonds with a phosphate unit, and so forth. This leaves all of the bases aligned on one side, forming one strand of a DNA molecule. Because of variations of the phosphate units, it is a one-way chain that curls.

The base units pair off more selectively. The second rule is that adenine (A) must bond with thymine (T), and guanine (G) must bond with cytosine (C). Adenine and thymine have two points that bond together, like a two-pronged electrical plug that fits only in a two-pronged socket. Guanine and cystine have three points that bond together, like a three-pronged electrical plug that fits only in a three-pronged socket. Each adenine-thymine (A–T) and guanine-cytosine (G–C) unit is called a *base pair*.

Each unit of the base pair is linked with a deoxyribose unit, which in turn is linked with a phosphate unit. The final structure is the familiar long, twisted spiral of the double helix, with the chains of sugar and phosphate bridged by the base pairs, like rungs on a ladder.

There is apparently no limit to the number of nucleotides that can join together, and DNA polynucleotides can consist of several million nucleotide units.

DNA AND GENES

A *gene* is a segment of a DNA molecule. One gene may range from 75 to over 40,000 base pairs. In humans, if all the DNA nucleotides in the chromosomes were aligned in a single chain, it would be about three feet long.[2]

Genes may occur in groups or may be randomly spaced along the length of a DNA molecule. Some groups of genes are unrelated, but others form clusters called *multigene families*, which contain related units of biological information. In humans, for example, one multigene family contains the information for creating the globin proteins. Geneticists believe the clustering reflects evolutionary changes rather than a coordinated aid to gene expression.

A *marker* is a segment of DNA that occurs in a variety of forms and also occupies a known location on a chromosome. A *microsatellite* is a type of genetic marker that contains a repeating pattern that is highly genetically variable. Markers and microsatellites that have been identified during gene mapping are used as points of reference. Once markers have been mapped, laboratories can develop tests that identify their presence by the particular gene product or by some other means, and markers have become the basis for many DNA tests that identify hereditary disorders.

FUNCTIONS

DNA has two basic functions. The first is to create a copy of itself for cell division. The second is to provide a template (pattern) for gene products.

Genes provide directions for the assembly of either an RNA molecule or a protein (though some genes are nonfunctional). All living matter is based on proteins. Each protein consists of amino acids joined together in many different ways to create all the tissues in the body. Amino acids have been compared with the letters of the alphabet and proteins to complete sentences.

- *Contractile protein* produces muscles
- *Enzyme protein* acts as a catalyst to mediate biochemical reactions such as the storage and release of energy
- *Protective protein* provides immune and blood-clotting factors
- *Regulatory protein* coordinates biochemical reactions; for example, the regulatory protein insulin controls glucose metabolism
- *Storage protein* conserves materials for future use; for example, ferritin stockpiles iron in the liver
- *Structural protein* forms tendons, cartilage, and bone
- *Transport protein* conveys vital molecules to different parts of the body; for example, hemoglobin transports oxygen

GENE EXPRESSION

Gene expression is the process through which the gene's biological information is transmitted to the cell.

RNA—DNA'S PARTNER

DNA's partner in gene expression is *ribonucleic acid,* better known as RNA. Like DNA, the basic RNA unit is a nucleotide, with a sugar, a phosphate, and a base. However, RNA's sugar unit is ribose. Unlike DNA, RNA is a single polynucleotide chain. RNA also has four possible bases: three are the same as in DNA—adenine (A), guanine (G), and cytosine (C). The fourth base is uracil (U), which bonds with adenine.

THE GENETIC CODE

The *genetic code* is the set of biochemical instructions that directs the synthesis of

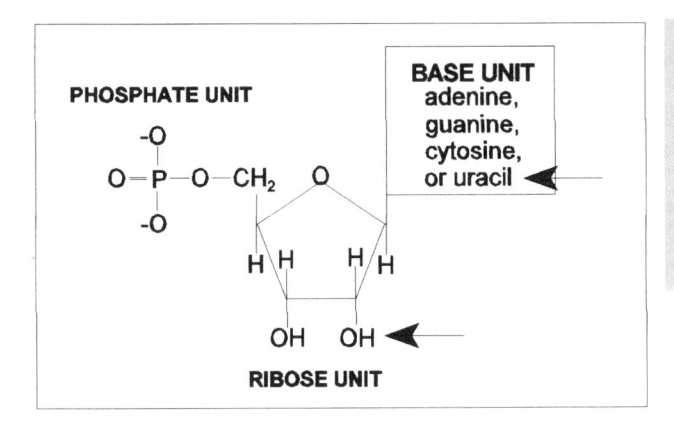

Figure 5-2. RNA structure. *Like DNA, the basic RNA unit is a nucleotide, with a sugar, a phosphate, and a base. The arrows indicate the components of RNA that differ from DNA.*

proteins. Because the information is first transferred to messenger RNA, the universal genetic code uses the initials of its four nucleotide bases—A, C, G, and U, representing adenine, cytosine, guanine, and uracil.

When arranged in groups of three (triplets), the four base units of RNA have sixty-four possible combinations. Each *codon*—that is, code unit—identifies either a specific amino acid or the end of a code sequence. Although there are sixty-four possible triplet codon sequences for the four RNA bases, there are only twenty different amino acids, so most amino acids have more than one codon. For example, the amino acid phenylalanine has two codons (UUU and UUC), and leucine has six (UUA, UUG, CUU, CUC, CUA, and CUG). Three codons (UAA, UAG, and UGA) signal the end of an amino acid sequence for the synthesis of proteins.

Each codon is like a word in a sentence: SEE THE DOG RUN END, though, of course, there is no space between each word. For example, the sequence UCU ACU UGG UAU GUU UAA would tell the cell to create a sequence consisting of the amino acids serine, threonine, tryptophan, tyrosine, valine, and stop. In this simple yet elegant way, genes direct the synthesis of complex proteins.

The genetic code is universal. Amazingly, the same basic amino acids and sequences are found in almost every organism on earth (though a handful of deviations have occurred over the millennia since life first began). Some sequences are conserved across all species. One sequence found in all life, for example, carries instructions for making ribosomes, which are the structures that actually manufacture proteins. Thus, life forms ranging from sulphur-eating bacteria in superheated volcanic fumaroles to yeasts, worms, dogs, and humans have this vital DNA sequence.

It is the universal genetic code that makes infectious disease possible. Viruses, which are "little more than a handful of genes, wrapped in a protein coat," conduct their nefarious molecular warfare by interacting directly with genes. They "take over molecular machinery of their hosts, forcing it to manufacture more viruses."[3]

Table 5-1. Comparison of DNA and RNA

	DNA	RNA
Sugar unit	Deoxyribose	Ribose
Structure	Double helix	Single chain
Bases	Adenine (A)	Adenine (A)
	Guanine (G)	Guanine (G)
	Cytosine (C)	Cytosine (C)
	Thymine (T)	Uracil (U)

Table 5–2. The Universal (Standard) Genetic Code

First Letter	Second Letter U	Second Letter C	Second Letter A	Second Letter G	Third Letter
U	UUU (phenylalanine)	UCU (serine)	UAU (tyrosine)	UGU (cysteine)	U
	UUC (phenylalanine)	UCC (serine)	UAC (tyrosine)	UGC (cysteine)	C
	UUA (leucine)	UCA (serine)	UAA (stop)	UGA (stop)	A
	UUG (leucine)	UCG (serine)	UAG (stop)	UGG (tryptophan)	G
C	CUU (leucine)	CCU (proline)	CAU (histidine)	CGU (arginine)	U
	CUC (leucine)	CCC (proline)	CAC (histidine)	CGC (arginine)	C
	CUA (leucine)	CCA (proline)	CAA (glutamine)	CGA (arginine)	A
	CUG (leucine)	CCG (proline)	CAG (glutamine)	CGG (arginine)	G
A	AUU (isoleucine)	ACU (threonine)	AAU (asparagine)	AGU (serine)	U
	AUC (isoleucine)	ACC (threonine)	AAC (asparagine)	AGC (serine)	C
	AUA (isoleucine)	ACA (threonine)	AAA (lysine)	AGA (arginine)	A
	AUG (isoleucine)	ACG (threonine)	AAG (lysine)	AGG (arginine)	G
G	GUU (valine)	GCU (alanine)	GAU (aspartate)	GGU (glycine)	U
	GUC (valine)	GCC (alanine)	GAC (aspartate)	GGC (glycine)	C
	GUA (valine)	GCA (alanine)	GAA (glutamate)	GGA (glycine)	A
	GUG (valine)	GCG (alanine)	GAG (glutamate)	GGG (glycine)	G

The 64 codons in messenger RNA (mRNA) either specify an amino acid or the end of a protein chain. The 20 amino acids are: alanine (Ala); arginine (Arg); aspargine (Asn); aspartic acid (Asp); cystine (Cys); glutamine (Gln); glutamic acid (Glu); glycine (Gly); histidine (His); isoleucine (Ile); leucine (Leu); lysine (Lys); methionine (Met); phenylalanine (Phe); proline (Pro); serine (Ser); threonine (Thr); tryptophan (Trp); tyrosine (Tyr); valine (Val).

TRANSCRIPTION AND TRANSLATION

The process of synthesizing proteins has two steps. In the first stage—*transcription*—DNA acts as a template (pattern) for the synthesis of an RNA molecule, which is called a *transcript*. In the second stage—*translation*—the RNA molecules assemble the components specified by the new *RNA transcript* to create a new protein molecule. All life transcribes and translates genetic material.

Errors in gene expression are minimized because the information flows in one direction.

DNA ➤ (TRANSCRIPTION) ➤ RNA ➤ (TRANSLATION) ➤ GENE PRODUCT

DNA transcribes its information to RNA, and RNA translates the information to protein. Proteins cannot direct the synthesis of RNA, and RNA cannot direct the synthesis of DNA—with the exception of retroviruses, which will be discussed later.

Not only does the information flow only from DNA to RNA but also only one strand (called the coding strand) of DNA participates in the transfer. The slight differences of the chemical structure at the ends of each DNA molecule ensures that the same strand always transcribes the information in the right direction.

There are actually three types of RNA, which are identified by their roles in protein synthesis: messenger RNA (mRNA); ribosomal RNA (rRNA); and transfer RNA (tRNA).

How does the DNA direct the creation of a new protein molecule? Within the cell's nucleus, the chromosome has uncoiled. An RNA enzyme (RNA polymerase) attaches to the DNA molecule at a specific point, which is the starting point of the segment to be copied. The enzyme forms a protective cover over the DNA segment, and the base pairs of that segment separate, exposing the ends of the bases. This is the coding strand or template for the synthesis that is to take place.

The enzyme travels along the DNA segment, unwinding the double helix, reading the information, and attaching the appropriate sequence of nucleotide units to the growing of strand of mRNA. Only a small area of the base pairs is separated at any one time, the base pairs rejoining as the new segment of RNA is complete.

Imagine that the exposed base triplets on the DNA are AGA TGA ACC ATA CAA ATT. This means that the matching base triplets of the new mRNA transcript must be UCU ACU UGG UAU GUU UAA, with the last triplet indicating stop. The enzyme separates from the DNA and releases the new transcript for finishing touches. Enzymes attach a "cap" (which promotes binding to a ribosome) to the beginning and a "tail" to the end of the mRNA transcript.

The new mRNA transcript, bearing the codon for the new protein, passes through the nuclear membrane into the cell's cytoplasm, where it moves to a ribosome. It is joined by a transfer RNA (tRNA), called the initiator. The tRNA has two important features. On one surface, it has a triplet of base units called an *anticodon,* which can bond with a codon unit on the mRNA. It also has a molecular "hook" that attaches to the specified amino acid.[4] Since the first triplet of our hypothetical mRNA transcript is UCU (the code for serine), the first tRNA to join it has the anticodon AGA and is bonded to a molecule of serine.

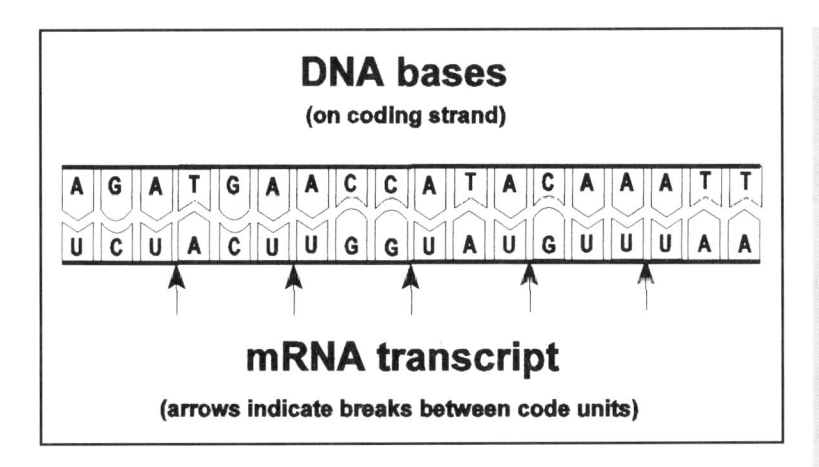

Figure 5–3. Transcription. *Here, the exposed bases on the DNA are AGA TGA ACC ATA CAA ATT. This means that the matching bases on the new mRNA transcript must be UCU ACU UGG UAU GUU UAA.*

72   GENETICS–AN INTRODUCTION FOR DOG BREEDERS

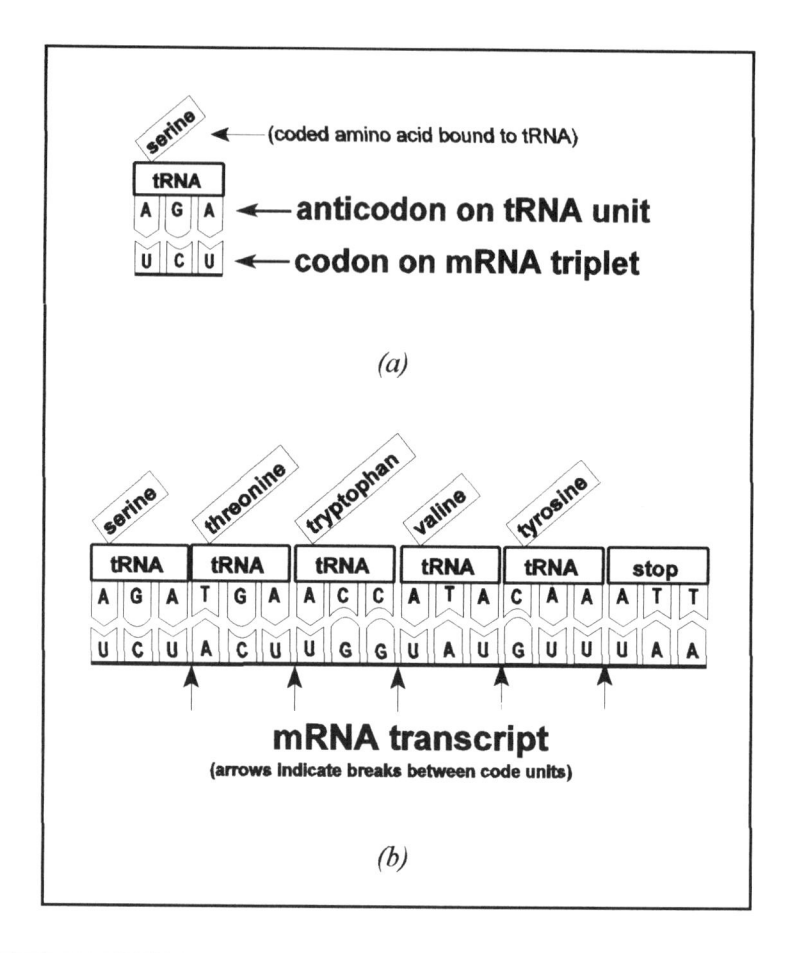

Figure 5–4. Translation. (a) A model of a codon triplet on an mRNA segment and the corresponding anticodon on a tRNA unit with its amino acid. (b) The base triplet sequence on the mRNA transcript is UCU ACU UGG UAU GUU UAA. The tRNA molecule's matching anticodons transfer the amino acids in the following sequence: serine, threonine, tryptophan, tyrosine, and valine. The final triplet, UAA, is a signal to cease transcription.

The mRNA and the tRNA are loaded onto the "platform" of a ribosome unit. A larger ribosome unit joins them. This has no platform but rather a tunnel through its interior. The two ribosomes come together.[5]

Other tRNA units arrive to join the coding surface of the mRNA, each transporting its appropriate amino acid. The amino acids pass through the tunnel, where ribosomal RNA (rRNA) bonds the amino acids together. With the "stop" codon, the new protein molecule emerges into the cytoplasm. The mRNA may proceed to other ribosomes and initiate a succession of protein units.[6]

All of this is a very simplistic overview of a highly complex process that occurs in the presence of special enzymes that facilitate the biochemical exchanges. The complete process of gene expression might be compared with manufacturing an automobile. In the first phase (transcription), a designer (coding strand of DNA) creates a

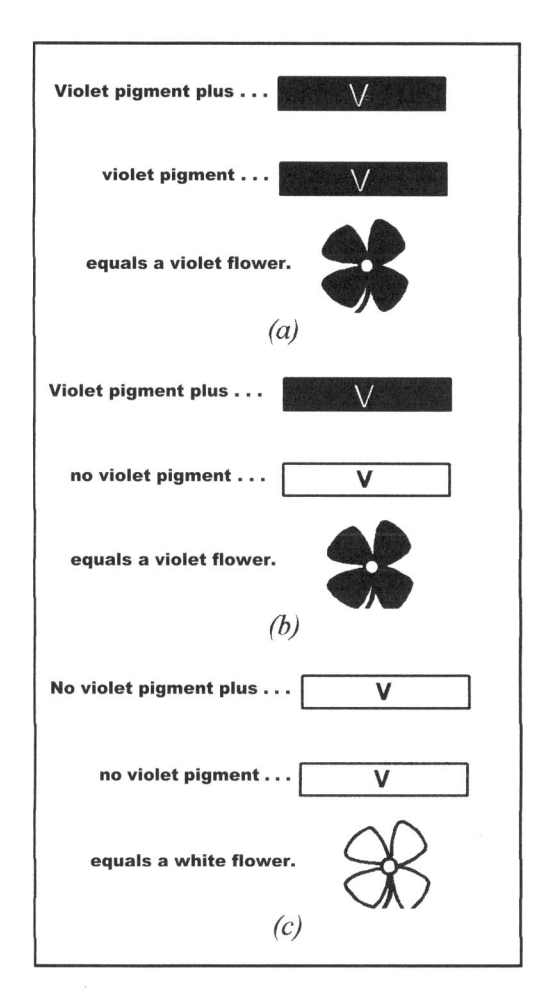

Figure 5–5. Complete dominance. *In violets, the allele for violet pigment (V) is a complete dominant over the allele for white (v). The dominant V allele produces an enzyme for violet pigment.*

(a) Homozygous dominant pair (VV). The phenotype is a violet flower.

(b) Heterozygous pair (Vv). With complete dominance, the V allele produces an abundance of enzyme, and a single V allele can mask the presence of the inactive r allele. The phenotype is a violet flower.

(c) Homozygous recessive pair (vv). The v allele produces no enzyme, and the phenotype is a white flower.

blueprint (mRNA transcript). Workers (tRNA) bring the parts to the assembly line. Along the assembly line inside the ribosome and facilitated by rRNA, the parts are joined together, and the finished product emerges. Furthermore, the product may be stored until needed.

The only exception to the flow of information from DNA to RNA occurs with retroviruses, which cause numerous deadly diseases including AIDS and some cancers. The genetic material in these viruses is RNA, and the flow of information is from RNA to DNA. When entering a host cell, the virus RNA instructs the cell to assemble a strand of DNA, which is then inserted into the host's own chromosomes, producing diseases that are virtually incurable.

Nevertheless, the retroviruses have made one priceless contribution to molecular genetics. Research on retroviruses led scientists to the discovery of *reverse transcriptase,* the enzyme that reverses the flow of information. "In researchers' hands, reverse transcriptase enables new manipulations of genes that make both genetic engineering and gene therapy possible."[7]

ANOTHER LOOK AT DOMINANCE

The concepts of gene expression and gene products clarify how the gene actions, introduced in Chapter 4, operate at the biochemical level. With heterozygous pairs, the dominant allele produces a functional gene product. Its partner may (*a*) be fully functional, (*b*) be functional to a lesser degree, (*c*) have altered function, or (*d*) have no function.

Figure 5–6. Incomplete dominance. *In carnations, the allele for red pigment (R) is an incomplete dominant over the allele for white (r). The R allele produces an enzyme for red pigment.*

(a) Homozygous dominant pair (RR). The phenotype is a red flower.

(b) Heterozygous pair (Rr). With incomplete dominance, a single R allele cannot produce sufficient enzyme to mask the presence of the inactive r allele. The phenotype is a pink flower.

(c) Homozygous recessive pair (rr). The r allele produces no enzyme, and the phenotype is a white flower.

With complete dominance, the dominant allele produces a sufficient amount of the gene product without the aid of its partner to express the phenotype even when paired with a partner that is not producing any share of the gene product. For example, Mendel observed that peas produce either white or violet flowers and that violet is dominant. The violet allele (V) produces an abundance of the enzyme that synthesizes violet pigment; the white allele (v) is biologically inactive (that is, has no function and produces no pigment), and a flower without any pigment is white.

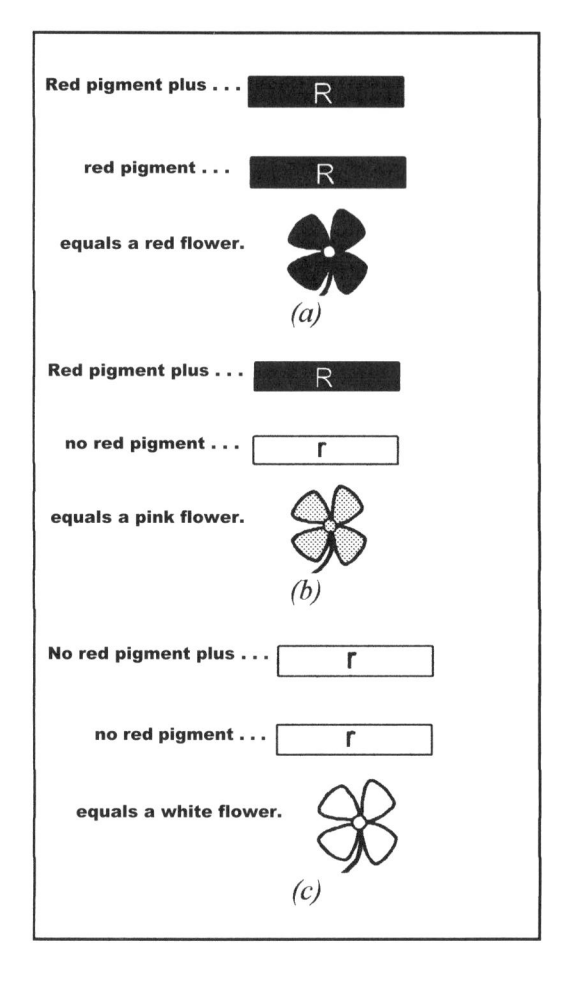

When dominance is incomplete, the heterozygote displays a phenotype that is intermediate between the homozygous dominant and recessive alleles. The dominant allele is biologically active, but without the help of an identical allele, it simply cannot produce enough gene product to hide the presence of a nonproductive partner. For example, the allele that produces the enzyme for the synthesis of red pigment in carnations only produces enough to do a halfway job, which results in pink color. There may be variation in the amount of enzyme that the gene can produce (variable dominance).

With codominance, both alleles are biologically active, each producing *different* gene products. In sickle cell anemia, for example, the heterozygous pair produces normal hemoglobin (Hb^A) and abnormal hemoglobin (Hb^S). The biological activity of both can be identified and measured through their gene products.

Molecular Genetics 75

Normal hemoglobin plus . . . Hb^A

normal hemoglobin . . . Hb^A

equals no sickled cell.

(a)

Normal hemoglobin plus . . . Hb^A

abnormal hemoglobin . . . Hb^S

equals rare sickled cell.

(b)

Abnormal hemoglobin plus . . . Hb^A

abnormal hemoglobin . . . Hb^S

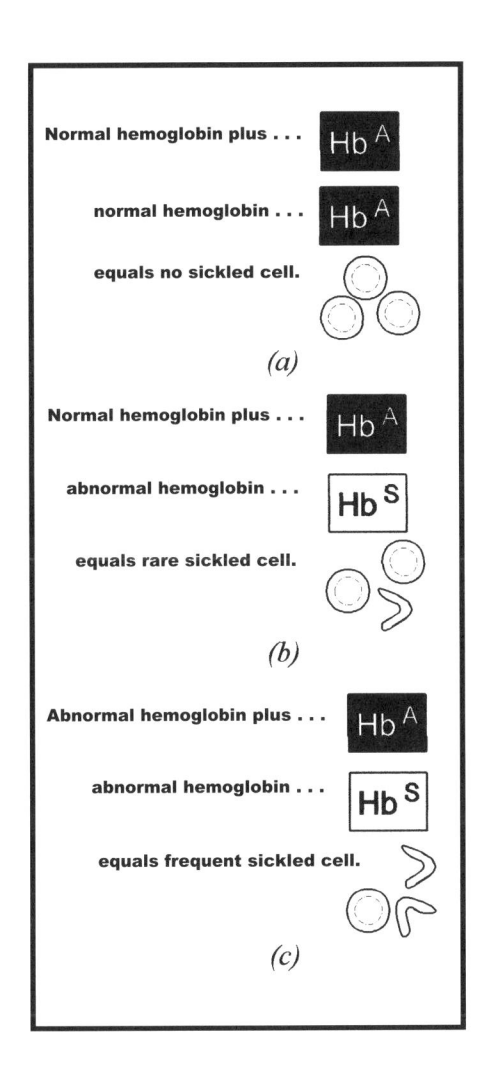

equals frequent sickled cell.

(c)

Figure 5–7. Codominance. *The alleles for normal hemoglobin (Hb^A) and for the abnormal hemoglobin of sickle cell anemia (Hb^S) are codominant.*

(a) Homozygous pair ($Hb^A Hb^A$). The phenotype is normal hemoglobin in a red blood cell that never sickles.

(b) Heterozygous pair ($Hb^A Hb^S$). The phenotype is both normal and abnormal hemoglobin in a red blood cell that rarely sickles.

(c) Homozygous recessive pair ($Hb^S Hb^S$). The phenotype is abnormal hemoglobin in a red blood cell that frequently sickles.

COPIES AND MISCOPIES

REPLICATION

The most unique feature of DNA is the molecule's ability to copy itself, a process called *replication*. Every time a cell divides (to grow additional cells, to replace worn-out cells, or to repair injured cells), it must make a complete copy of all genes. For example, the information stored in human DNA is found in every cell except mature red blood cells.[8]

Prompted and monitored by various enzymes, chromosomes begin replication with a separation (called a replication fork) between the bonds linking the base pairs of each strand. The separation progresses like an opening zipper along the length of the DNA molecule. Using the exposed bases as a pattern, an enzyme called *DNA polymerase* assembles a new strand by bonding free nucleotides to the exposed base units. Remember, the base pairs of each strand always bond in the same way—adenine (A) with thymine (T), and guanine (G) with cytosine (C). Therefore, if the sequence on the original strand is ACTCTATAC, the sequence created for the new strand must be TGAGATATG. Each new chromosome, containing one old strand and one new, twists into the characteristic double-helix shape as it forms.

Almost all DNA is located on the chromosomes within the cell's nucleus (*nuclear DNA*). In most multicelled organisms, however, a very small amount of DNA is found outside the nucleus (*extranuclear DNA*) as part of the complex cytoplasmic structures called mitochondria, which play a key role in the cell's energy cycle—their counterparts in the energy cycle of plants are called plasmids. Each cell has many mitochondria,

Figure 5–8. Replication. *Using the exposed bases as a pattern, enzyme called DNA polymerase assembles a new strand by bonding free nucleotides to the exposed base units. Each new chromosome, containing one old strand and one new, twists into the characteristic double-helix shape as it forms.*

sometimes several thousand. The *mitochondrial DNA* (mtDNA) carries the instruction for only 15 percent of its own structure as well as its own mitochondrial RNA (mtRNA) and ribosomes, and the balance is encoded by the chromosomes.

One theory suggests mtDNA originated as *symbiotic* (mutually beneficial) bacteria that invaded primitive one-celled life forms. This theory is based on similarities between mtDNA and bacterial systems such as a circular DNA molecule and asexual reproduction within the cytoplasm. The mitochondria appear to have their own version of the genetic code, which differs between organisms.

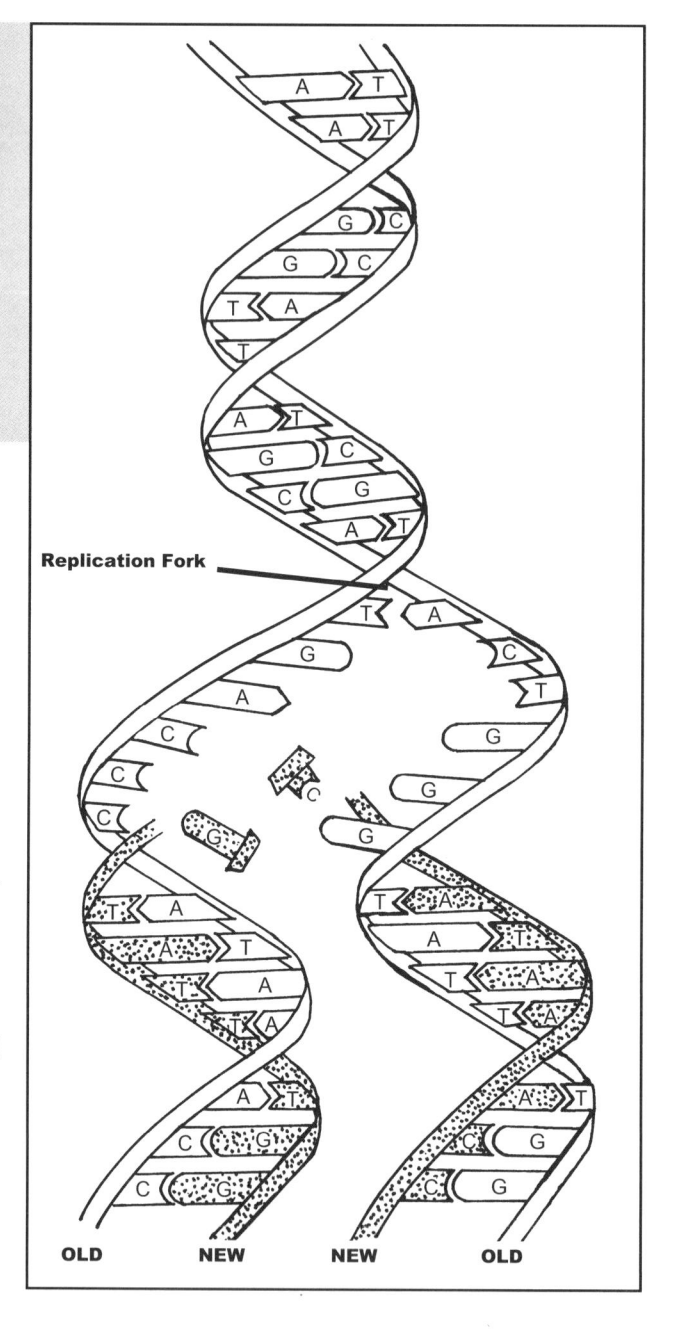

Within the cell's cytoplasm, mitochondria reproduce independently by simple fission—that is, by dividing into two parts. In other words, mtDNA cannot follow Mendelian inheritance, which requires paired genes. In almost all multicelled animals, mtDNA is transmitted to the next generation by way of the cytoplasm of the oocyte. Remember that during meiosis each oocyte produces one ovum containing almost all of its cytoplasm and three polar bodies with little or no cytoplasm. In this manner, most of the cytoplasm in each fertilized egg, along with its mtDNA, is inherited from the mother. With rare exceptions, any mitochondria in sperm do not survive.

Although many mysteries remain about the significance of mtDNA inheritance, it has helped geneticists trace the origins of some hybrids. In addition, two human disorders—Leber's optic atrophy and MERRF (myoclonus epilepsy with ragged red fibers)—have been linked with mtDNA.

MUTATIONS

A *mutation* is any alteration of the genome, chromosome, or gene. A gene mutation occurs through the gain, loss, or rearrangement of the nucleotide sequence of a DNA molecule.

During replication, a "proofreading" enzyme checks each newly assembled base pair and corrects any error it encounters. However, oversights—that is, mutations—occasionally slip through. For example, a base could be dropped from a sequence, or entire strings of bases may be inverted, repeated, omitted, or inserted in the wrong place. The substitution of a single base pair in the gene for hemoglobin that changes the code for glutamate to the code for valine produces the abnormal hemoglobin of sickle-cell anemia. Even one error per ten thousand nucleotides can lead to significant cumulative changes, and the wonder is that errors don't occur more often.

Mutations occur constantly as a result of environmental damage, and a *mutagen* is any physical or chemical agent that causes mutations. Willis states that "natural mutation rates are from 10^{-4} (one in ten thousand) to 10^{-8} (one in a hundred million) and thus rare enough to be safely ignored in most cases." According to Merrell, the estimated whole chromosome mutation rate for major deleterious mutations is "on the

---

AT THE DNA-SEQUENCE LEVELS
- *Point mutation*—the replacement of one nucleotide by another
- *Insertion or deletion*—addition of loss of a DNA segment
- *Inversion*—reversal of a DNA segment

AT THE GENE LEVEL
- *Silent mutation*—a point mutation within the gene with no change of the gene product
- *Missense mutation*—a point mutation with change of gene produce; usually causes mutant phenotype
- *Nonsense mutation*—a point mutation that changes the codon for an amino acid to a termination codon; usually causes mutant phenotype
- *Frameshift mutation*—an insert or deletion that alters the codon and usually causes a mutant phenotype

AT THE ORGANISM LEVEL
- *Lethal mutation*—a vital biological product is absent
- *Auxotrophic mutation*—failure of a gene product needed for the synthesis of a vital metabolite; some organisms survive if supplemented with the missing gene product
- *Conditional-lethal mutation*—some organisms survive only under limited environmental conditions

Source: T. A. Brown, *Genetics: A Molecular Approach* (London: Van Nostrand Reinhold, 1989), 171–174.

Figure 5–9. Types of mutations. *Mutations may be classified by the levels at which they occur.*

order of 1 percent per chromosome per generation."[9] Mutations that are not hereditary are also common. For example, many cancers are tissue mutations and, thus, not hereditary; however, the genetic instability and *potential for mutation* at the same site might be hereditary.

A *mutable gene* is one that has a significant rate of spontaneous mutation. The mutation rate of these inherently unstable genes may be affected by environmental conditions such as temperature. Although *retinoblastomas* (a type of retinal tumor) are inherited through an autosomal dominant gene, they also occur with no family history of the disorder and are thought to be a recurring spontaneous mutation. Another disorder that fits the definition is hemophilia, which occurs in many species, always as a sex-linked recessive.

Mutations are described in many different ways. The phenotype typical of the species is known as the *wild type,* and any other phenotype is known as the *mutant type.* Mutant phenotypes sometimes revert to the wild type. Rarely, a *back mutation* simply reverses the change at the same location. In a *second site reversion,* a second mutation at a different location produces a gene that synthesizes the same product as the wild type. *Suppression* is a new mutation on a different gene that restores the ability to synthesize the gene product.

CONTROL MECHANISMS

Clearly, all genes are not active at the same time, and some are active only at certain stages of life such as embryonic and fetal development, puberty, and pregnancy and lactation. The primary function of developmental control genes is the control of developmental decisions. *Anchor genes* are developmental control genes that act as on-off switches.

To insure the correct timing of gene expression, elaborate circuits of gene control have evolved, a regular pecking order, in fact. At the top are the master control genes. Then come regulator genes, which turn other (subsidiary) genes off and on; for example, the genes that produce fetal hemoglobin are turned off at birth, and the ones that produce normal hemoglobin are turned on. At the bottom of the hierarchy are ordinary genes that produce proteins for daily life—making hemoglobin, digestive enzymes, hormones, and so forth. In addition, the activation of gene expression is selective. For example, all cells contain the genes for producing thyroid hormone, but they are activated only in the thyroid gland.

Elaborate mechanisms control the timing of a gene's activity. Some control genes produce proteins called repressors, which bind to DNA just in front of the gene it controls. As long as the repressor is in place, it signals that the gene's protein is not to be produced. Another interesting type of control gene interrupts the synthesis of messenger RNA after a short portion of it has been made. Because the amino acid is already partially assembled, the cell can respond more quickly when it is needed.

An interesting example of how regulator genes work is found in *Escherichia coli,* a bacterium that geneticists have found very useful. When placed in an environment with lactose, a simple sugar, the bacteria begin producing a digestive enzyme encoded in a three-gene sequence. Between the promotor gene, which indicates the beginning of transcription, and the three-gene sequence lies "a stretch of DNA called a *control region* because it determines whether or not those genes are turned on." In this case, the control region is an "on" switch, and the information may be transcribed onto mRNA. A separate regulator gene produces a protein that turns off the digestive enzyme by binding to the "on" switch and interfering with transcription. However, lactose molecules combine with the "stop" protein, interfering with its message, and the production of the digestive enzyme continues until there are no more lactose molecules to neutralize the "stop" protein, thus turning off the digestive enzyme.[10]

Drlica points out that "since each regulatory protein has its own gene, one gene can influence the expression of another. Sometimes product of a gene influences expression of many other genes, including its own."[11] In this way, the alteration of a single regulatory gene can produce a cascade of changes affecting the entire organism.

GENETIC ENGINEERING

In its broadest definition, *genetic engineering* is the production of new genetic combinations. In this sense, humans have been practicing genetic engineering for thousands of years through selective breeding of plants and animals. Every time a human domesticates a plant or animal and alters natural selection, he or she acts as a genetic engineer.

CLONES

A *clone* is a group of genetically identical cells, all derived from the same ancestor, and modern cloning technology is an outgrowth of reproductive processes that began life on earth. *Primary reproductive cloning* occurs with species that reproduce asexually, such as all bacteria, most protozoa and algae, and some yeasts and higher plants. *Supplementary reproductive cloning* occurs with some species that can reproduce both asexually and sexually. Cancer cells are *tissue-level reproductive clones*.

A philodendron cutting is a clone of the parent plant. Among the earliest examples of cloning technology are the budding and grafting of plants. All naval oranges, which are seedless, are clones of the first seedless orange. Advances in technology have made it possible to develop *gene libraries,* collections of clones carrying a large number (sometimes all) of the genes from a particular organism. These libraries provide pure samples of genes for the study of recombinant DNA technology.

Cloning is less common in the animal kingdom. All identical twins are clones, and theoretically, artificial identical twins could be created by dividing early embryos and implanting the second in a surrogate mother. However, attempts to produce clones in mammals proved unsuccessful, and it was believed that as soon as the dividing embryonic cells become differentiated into skin, bone, nerves, and so forth, they lose the ability to develop into other tissues.

In 1996, Dr. Ian Wilmut and his colleagues at Scotland's Roslin Institute made history by cloning two lambs from a single ovum. Then, in early 1997, the news media erupted with the announcement that Wilmut and the institute had again made history by patenting a way of creating clones from the cells of adult animals. Their showcase was a sheep that had been cloned by implanting the DNA of a cell taken from an adult ewe's mammary gland, fusing it into an unfertilized egg from which all DNA had been removed, and implanting it into a surrogate mother. The breakthrough was a technique that reset the specialized DNA back to its full undifferentiated embryonic potential. This raised a worldwide furor about the ethics of cloning and visions of human clones a la Huxley's *Brave New World.*[12]

Genes have been cloned from bacteria in preserved tissues of human mummies and from extinct plants and animals. Will scientists be able to develop this to the point of restoring extinct species? It may happen sooner than anyone expects.

RECOMBINANT DNA TECHNOLOGY

To most people, genetic engineering means "gene splicing," which is the effect of what is more correctly termed *recombinant DNA technology*. The molecules resulting from the union of DNA derived from different sources is known as *recombinant DNA*.

Genetic engineering entered a new era with the discovery that some bacteria defend themselves from viruses by producing enzymes that sever the DNA bonds wherever the enzymes identified a specific sequence of bases. Furthermore, each of the DNA segments were left with "sticky" ends that were attracted to other segments. More than eighty of these *restriction enzymes* help researchers piece together new sequences of DNA.[13]

APPLICATIONS

The applications of genetic engineering seem to be limited only by the imagination. Microorganisms are being designed to decompose certain types of garbage, and one has already been developed to break down oil slicks. Other genetically engineered wonders include corn that is high in the amino acid tryptophan as well as cotton and tobacco with greater resistance to diseases and insects. A future hope is to transplant the nitrogen-fixing systems of legumes to other crop plants, eliminating the need for fertilizers. Through gene therapy, one or more normal genes are transferred into the body cells to overcome the effects of the defective gene.

REVIEW OF TERMS

anchor gene
clone
codon
DNA
gene expression
genetic code
marker
molecular genetics
mutation
mutant type
RNA
wild type

QUANTITATIVE GENETICS

Every dog breeder has been frustrated by the inconsistent hereditary patterns of traits such as leg length, chest circumference, and dentition that show a continuous range of expression and fail to follow any clear pattern from one generation to the next. The concepts discussed in this chapter will help breeders to understand the genetic basis and how to improve their chances of modifying such traits. The in-depth discussion of hip dysplasia in Chapter 13 is a practical example of how these concepts may be applied.

The study of traits that are characterized by continuous variation falls into the realm of *quantitative genetics*. Quantitative geneticists analyze continuous phenotypic variation; the analysis is based on the assumption that continuous variance is produced by the "combined action of many genes, each of small effect, at a number of loci, plus the effects of the environment, and takes into account the effects of dominance and epistasis and of genotypic x environmental interactions."[1]

CONTINUOUS AND DISCONTINUOUS VARIANCE

Quantitative traits are characterized by *continuous variance*—that is, the phenotype exhibits no abrupt changes but rather a smooth blending from one extreme to the other. In addition—

(a) most traits are affected by a number of loci
(b) the effects of alternate alleles at each locus are relatively small, and "identical phenotypes may be displayed by a great variety of genotypes"
(c) "the phenotypic expression ... is subject to considerable modification by environmental influences"[2]

These traits are characterized by a variable phenotype that is produced by the interaction of numerous genes and are referred to as *polygenic* (meaning many genes) or *multifactorial* (meaning many factors and implying an environmental influence). Although the terms are usually used synonymously, there is a slight difference of semantic emphasis.

The concept of major and minor genes arose to explain the differences between the *discontinuous variance*—that is, the either-or phenotypic difference produced by dominant-recessive pairs such as the alleles for black or brown coat color—typical of Mendelian traits and the continuous variance of quantitative traits. *Major genes* produce a readily identifiable effect on the phenotype and can be studied by Mendelian methods. *Minor genes* are those that produce such minor effects that their individual actions cannot be easily identified. They are, however, paired, and they are transmitted in a Mendelian fashion. Although the effect of each minor gene is small, they function in groups that have similar effects on the phenotype. Advances in molecular genetics have shown that the differences are more complex, and the terms major and minor are viewed as archaic. The concept of minor genes remains useful to breeders when trying to understand the dynamics underlying polygenic traits.

The term *polygenes* reflects the manner in which these genes function as a group to collectively control the expression of a trait. A *polygenic trait* is one with a variable phenotype that is produced by the interaction of numerous genes. *Modifiers* are polygenes that affect the expression of a specific, identifiable major gene.

ADDITIVE GENE ACTION

The cumulative contribution of polygenes at all loci toward the expression of a polygenic trait is described as *additive gene action,* and the averaging effects of substituting one polygene for another is known as *additive genetic variance*. Keeping in mind that additive variance does not necessarily mean that the genes are, in fact, exhibiting additive gene action, it is a useful *working hypothesis* and a way to develop a feeling for the expression of polygenic traits.

A good example of a polygenic trait is the effect of pigment dilution modifiers. All Weimaraners are gray, and the official shades are mouse-gray (very dark), deer-gray (very light), and silver-gray (medium). This implies that there are distinctive differences between them, but the reality is that the shades exhibit continuous variance. If these shades were determined by only one pair of major genes with incomplete dominance, the mating of two silver-gray parents would produce, on average, one dark-gray, one light-gray, and two medium-gray puppies. However, most puppies from two silver-gray parents are similar to the parents, and the extreme shades are very rare. This indicates that the genes controlling the different shades cannot be a single pair of major alleles.

There is no way to determine how many minor genes actually exist in the group of dilution modifiers, but it is possible to set up a hypothetical situation to illustrate additive gene action. First, assume there are three loci—*A*, *B*, and *C*—each with a dominant and recessive allele and all related to increasing or decreasing the amount of pigment. Second, assume that the darkest grays have the genotype *AABBCC,* and the lightest grays have the genotype *aabbcc*.

What happens if an extremely dark male with the genotype *AABBCC* is mated with an extremely light bitch with the genotype *aabbcc*? The offspring, of course, could only have the genotype *AaBbCc*, a shade of gray halfway between the parents. This averaging effect is typical of the mating of phenotypic extremes.

Genotypes produced by the mating of *AaBbCc* x *AaBbCc* (heterozygotes)

	ABC	ABc	Abc	AbC	aBC	aBc	abC	abc
ABC	AABBCC	AABBCc	AABbCc	AABbCC	AaBBCC	AaBBCc	AaBbCC	AaBbCc
ABc	AABBCc	AABBcc	AABbcc	AABbCc	AaBBCc	AaBBcc	AaBbCc	AaBbcc
Abc	AABbCc	AABbcc	AAbbcc	AAbbCc	AaBbCc	AaBbcc	AabbCc	Aabbcc
AbC	AABbCC	AABbCc	AAbbCc	AAbbCC	AaBbCC	AaBbCc	AabbCC	AabbCc
aBC	AaBBCC	AaBBCc	AaBbCc	AaBbCC	aaBBCC	aaBBCc	aaBbCC	aaBbCc
aBc	AaBBCc	AaBBcc	AaBbcc	AaBbCc	aaBBCc	aaBBcc	aaBbCc	aaBbcc
abC	AaBbCC	AaBbCc	AabbCc	AabbCC	aaBbCC	aaBbCc	aabbCC	aabbCc
abc	AaBbCc	AaBbcc	Aabbcc	AabbCc	aaBbCc	aaBbcc	aabbCc	aabbcc

Sorting the genotypes by frequency and plus-and-minus values

Scale	Frequency	Possible Combinations
+6	1	AABBCC (1)
+4	6	AaBBCC (2), AABbCC (2), AABBCc (2)
+2	15	AABBcc (1), aaBBCC (1), AAbbCC (1), AABbCc (4), AaBBCc (4), AaBbCC (4)
0	20	aaBbCC (2), aaBBCc (2), AaBBcc (2), AabbCC (2), AAbbCc (2), AAbbCc (2), AaBbCc (8)
-2	15	aaBBcc (1), aabbCC (1), AAbbcc (1), AabbCc (4), AaBbcc (4), aaBbCc (4)
-4	6	aaBbcc (2), aabbCc (2), Aabbcc (2)
-6	1	aabbcc (1)

Distribution of the genotype frequency

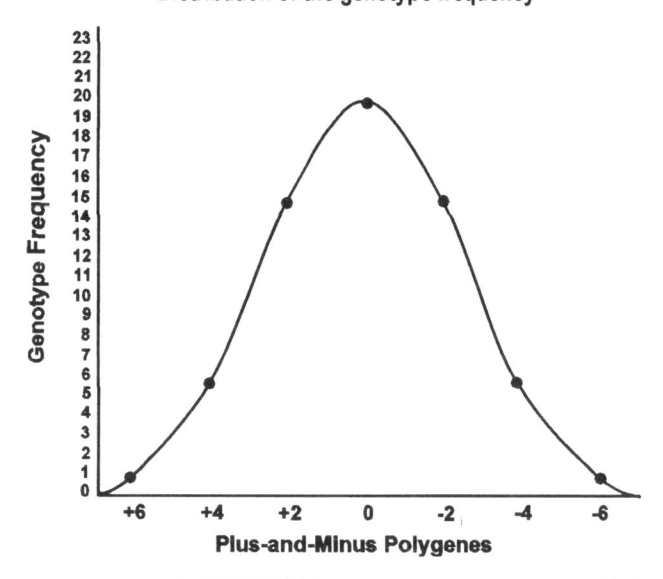

Figure 6-1. **Polygenic inheritance I.** *The offspring two dogs of like quality and similar appearance do not necessarily resemble parents that are not homozygous even with polygenic traits. Many genotypes are produced by the mating of AaBbCc and AaBbCc. The genotypes may be sorted out to determine the frequency of the plus-and-minus values. Finally, plotting the distribution of the genotype frequency on a bell chart illustrates that most of the offspring resemble the parents, some may fall at either end of the possible spectrum.*

Genotypes produced by the mating of *AaBbCc* x *AABBCC*
(the results are the same in each line, so it is not necessary to repeat the other seven)

	ABC	ABc	Abc	AbC	aBC	aBc	abC	abc
ABC	AABBCC	AABBCc	AABbCc	AABbCC	AaBBCC	AaBBCc	AaBbCCCC	AaBbCc

Sorting the genotypes by frequency and plus-and-minus values

Scale	Frequency	Possible Combinations
+6	8	AABBCC (8)
+4	24	AABBCc (8), AABbCC (8), AaBBCC (8)
+2	24	AABbCc (8), AaBBCc (8), AaBbCC (8)
0	8	AaBbCc (8)

Distribution of the genotype frequency

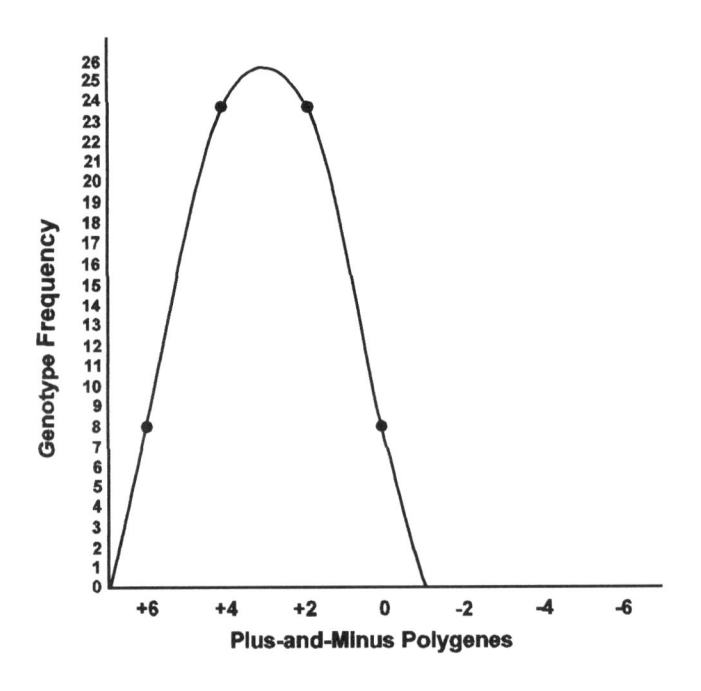

Figure 6–2. Polygenic inheritance II. *The mating of a homozygous dog with a heterozygous one reduces the possible genotypes of their offspring. In contrast with the seven genotypes of the first mating, only four different genotypes are produced by the mating of AaBbCc and AABBCC. The distribution frequency from AaBbCc and AABBCC produces less variation and reduces the distribution curve.*

Going to the next generation, what happens if those puppies with the genotype *AaBbCc* are mated? It is when the heterozygotes at the middle of the phenotype spectrum are mated that the continuous variance can be best observed. The checkerboards in Chapter 4 illustrated the possible combinations of one or two genes. A checkerboard for the three pairs in our example has sixty-four squares, and illustrates how dramatically the possible genotypes multiply.

It is conventional to regard polygenes as having plus-and-minus effects. The plus polygenes enhance or magnify the phenotypic effect, and minus polygenes reduce or totally inhibit the phenotypic effect. For our example, assume that the dominant genes *ABC* have a plus effect (increase the depth of gray color), and the recessive genes *abc* have a minus effect (decrease the depth of color). Because the effect of the individual genes cannot be measured, the only way to analyze their effects is to count the number of dominant and recessive genes in each genotype and assign a plus-and-minus value: six dominants (+6/ 0) would be +6; five dominants (+5/-1) would be +4; four dominants (+4/-2) would be +2; three dominants (+3/-3) would be 0; two dominants (+2/-4) would be -2; one dominant (+1/-5) would be -4; no dominants (0/-6) would be -6. Sorting out the genotypes according to the plus-and-minus values reveals genotypes covering the complete range of genotype, from extremely light to extremely dark, and continuous variance.

Figure 6–1 also illustrates that some genotype values occur more frequently than others. Counting the individual genotypes in each category from +6 to -6 shows a frequency distribution of 1, 6, 15, 20, 15, 6, 1. The distribution can be illustrated by applying the data to a graph, which reveals a bell-shaped curve. The same data can also be displayed using bars of different height.

Now imagine that a breeder decides the darker shades are more attractive and breeds his medium-gray bitch (*AaBbCc*) to a stud of the darkest shade (*AABBCC*). This too will produce a blending and continuous variance, though the distribution is a bit different. Sorting out the genotypes according to the plus-and-minus alleles gives a distribution of 8, 24, 24, 8. Applying the data to a graph again reveals a bell-shaped curve, though it is skewed to the left because there are so few minus polygenes.

This model of polygenic traits works with those that demonstrate additive genetic variance. Many traits that do probably have more than three genes, and it takes many generations to shift the distribution frequency. Piebald spotting appears to follow this pattern, and so does hip dysplasia. One or two breeders trying to shift toward an extreme phenotype have little impact, but when it becomes popular with judges, an entire breed can shift toward that extreme. Examples include the excessive leg furnishings of the American Cocker Spaniel and the Miniature Schnauzer. One word of warning—not all polygenic traits have additive genetic variance.

THRESHOLD EFFECTS

The term *threshold effect* describes a trait that develops only if the additive effects of the contributory alleles exceed a critical number. Dominant genes, additive genes, or even recessive genes can have thresholds for expression. The phenotype is characterized by discontinuous variance, which is why they are also known as all-or-none traits. With threshold traits, the concept of additive genetic action is usually (but not always) valid. In other words, when sufficient polygenes fall on either side of the critical threshold, they shift the expression to either phenotype A or phenotype B. There is, however, an underlying continuous variance. Most threshold traits are influenced by the environment, and the expression is determined by the interaction of genetic and environmental factors.

Initially, most threshold traits are identified as autosomal recessives because of the discontinuous variance and the lack of an identifiable dominance pattern. With recessive genes, however, the expression usually reveals a regular, predictable pattern and Mendelian ratios. Threshold traits exhibit no consistent ratio; normal parents sometimes produce abnormal puppies, but abnormal parents sometimes produce normal ones. Another indication of threshold heredity is a low incidence of the abnormality in one breed or strain and a high incidence in others.

Figure 6–3. Threshold traits.

A threshold trait with one threshold and two phenotypes

PHENOTYPE A ◄--► THRESHOLD ◄--► PHENOTYPE B
◄------UNDERLYING CONTINUOUS VARIANCE------►

A threshold trait with two thresholds and three phenotypes

PHENOTYPE A ◄--► THRESHOLD ◄--► PHENOTYPE B ◄--► THRESHOLD ◄--► PHENOTYPE C
◄--------------------UNDERLYING DISCONTINUOUS VARIANCE--------------------►

To complicate matters, some traits have two thresholds. Nicholas uses a cardiac abnormality as an example of a two-threshold trait. Before birth, a structure called the *ductus arteriosis* joins the aorta and the pulmonary artery. The function of the ductus arteriosis is to bypass circulation to the fetal lungs. The newborn's first breath expands the pulmonary blood vessels so that blood begins circulating through the lungs. This causes the great arteries shift their position in a way that clamps off the ductus arteriosis, which soon withers into a fibrous cord. Thus, after birth, an open or *patent ductus arteriosis* is abnormal. More rarely, the ductus closes partially, leaving a pouchlike structure called a *ductus diverticulum*. With this two-threshold trait, phenotype A is normal closure, phenotype B is ductus diverticulum, and phenotype C is patent ductus arteriosis.[3]

Unfortunately for this example, a 1993 report identified a single major gene defect that interferes with cardiac growth in a line of Keeshonds—after more than ten generations of selective inbreeding.[4] However, as pointed out above, dominant genes, additive genes, or even recessive genes can have thresholds for expression.

The concept of threshold traits is potentially useful for breeders when trying to identify the inheritance of some traits. Cryptorchidism (undescended testicles), for example, is generally discussed and studied as a single-gene trait. Robinson, however, suggests that cryptorchidism could be a polygenic threshold trait, and this possibility is discussed further on pages 158–159.[5]

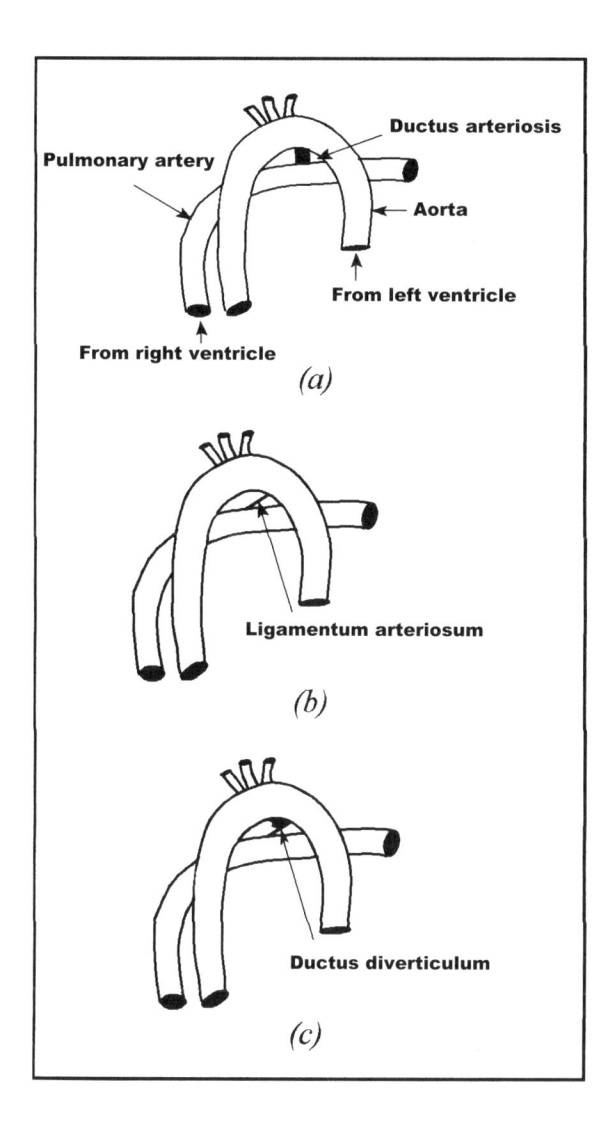

Figure 6–4. A two-threshold trait.

(a) In fetal circulation, the ductus arteriosis shunts blood from the pulmonary artery to the aorta, bypassing the lungs. When it persists after birth, it is known as a patent ductus arteriosis and must be closed surgically.

(b) With normal closure after birth, the ductus atrophies to a fibrous cord (the ligamentum arteriosum).

(c) Partial closure of the ductus arteriosis leaves a pocket in the aorta called a ductus diverticulum.

HERITABILITY

Webster defines *heritability* as capable of being inherited or of passing by inheritance. Geneticists use the term a bit differently.

Polygenic traits typically exhibit continuous variance, and part of this variation is produced by interaction with environmental factors. This raises the question of how much of the trait's expression can be attributed to the environment and how much to the underlying genetic structure. The answer is identified as the trait's *heritability*, which is the *percentage* of the variation that can be attributed to genetic factors; the value may also be given as a decimal number ranging from 0 to 1.

- A heritability value of 100 percent or 1.0 indicates that all of the variation is produced by genetic factors
- A heritability value of 0 indicates that all the variation is produced by environmental factors

- A heritability value of 40 percent or 0.4 indicates that 40 percent of the variation is produced by genetic factors and that the other 60 percent of the variation must be attributed to environmental factors

The analysis of heritability is very complex. Furthermore, *heritability values are not a constant; they apply only to a specific population at a specific time.* Selection or a different environment alters the value from one generation to the next.

Many studies of heritability are done with livestock, usually to determine the heritability of traits having commercial importance—such as growth rate, egg laying, butterfat yield—with the hope of improving the yield. With dogs, heritability studies have no commercial applications, and as a result, few have been done, though Verryn and Geerthsen reported a very comprehensive study of heritability in German Shepherds.[6] Being able to determine the heritability of structural traits such as leg length or chest circumference would provide important breeding guidelines, but unfortunately, the calculation requires a thorough understanding of mathematics and statistics that is beyond the ability of the average breeder.

It is also absolutely vital to distinguish between heritability and familiality. "Traits are familial if members of the same family share them, for whatever reason. Traits are heritable only if the similarity arises from shared genotypes." The occurrence of a disease in groups of related people or animals is all too often considered sufficient evidence of a genetic basis. For example, a 1910 report of pellagra (a vitamin deficiency disease) in the southern states concluded that pellagra was genetic because it ran in families.[7]

THE ENVIRONMENT AND PHENOTYPE

A major task of quantitative geneticists is to identify the ways in which genes interact with the environment to influence the phenotype. An *environmental factor* is defined as anything that causes a phenotypic effect that cannot be attributed to gene action. Nutrition is the most familiar example. Most breeders realize that good nutrition is vital to optimal growth and quality, and they conscientiously feed the best rations available. In doing so, they influence the puppy's adult phenotype by modifying the environment. Even something as seemingly unrelated as environmental temperature can have profound effects. In some reptiles, the environmental temperature during incubation determines the gender of the developing embryo by altering the product of a temperature-sensitive gene that regulates the development of the sex organs.[8]

The mother often has a profound effect on phenotype because of her impact on the *developmental environment.* This *maternal effect* includes everything affecting the progeny's phenotype that is directly attributable to the mother, such as the uterine environment, maternal antibodies, quantity and quality of milk, number of littermates, and transmission of worms and disease.

Geneticists have long been aware that the environment played a role in heredity. In fact, Darwin proposed that continuous variation of phenotype was produced by environmental factors. The problem that faced Darwin and his contemporaries was to prove that this was indeed the case.

The first concrete evidence of the environmental influence on phenotype came just after the turn of the century, when Wilhelm Johannsen began an experiment with nineteen strains of homozygous, self-pollinating beans. He observed a wide range of weight in individual beans within each strain as well as between strains; however, the *average* weight between strains was significantly different. Johannsen then selected the largest and smallest in each inbred strain in an attempt to separate the traits. However, the range of weights from the largest to smallest remained the same, as did the *average* weight. He concluded that the variance was caused by a difference in the individual environments—"number and position of beans in the pod, the number of pods, the time of seed set, and so on."[9] Dog breeders sometimes observe a similar range of variance within breeds and between litters, though the average size within a breed remains the same.

Johannsen's experiment showed that traits that are caused by the environment cannot be altered by selective breeding. For example, a dog that has skeletal deformities because of malnutrition will produce normal puppies; on the other hand, if the deformity is a simple dominant gene, ideal nutrition will not prevent the deformity in the offspring.

> Johannsen showed, unequivocally, that selection on environmental variation was futile; only if genetic variation was present was there a response to selection. Once the hereditary variation was exhausted, selection was no longer effective, for it could not create new variation.
> These results also led Johannsen to coin the words and draw the crucial distinction between genotype (the total hereditary constitution of an individual) and the phenotype (the sum of all the traits manifested by an individual and produced by its genotype interacting with the environment).[10]

Johannsen demonstrated that the relationship between genotype and phenotype is not absolute; rather the genes define the potential phenotype. If the environment fails to provide the combination of materials the gene needs to produce its particular gene product, the phenotype for that trait may be altered.

> Although a given phenotype is often equated with a particular genotype, this is overly simplistic. The genotype sets limits on the kinds of phenotypes that can develop, but one genotype can give rise to many phenotypes. The particular phenotype that develops is determined by the particular set of environmental conditions encountered by the developing embryo. The phenotypic modifications that occur in a developing organism are generally adaptive responses that enable the organism to cope better with its immediate environment. For example, tadpoles reared in ponds deficient in oxygen will have larger gills than controls reared in ponds with a more abundant oxygen supply, and are thus physiologically better adapted to obtain oxygen in their low O_2 environment.[11]

Adaptability means the alteration of phenotype without modification of the genotype. The tadpoles exhibited *developmental adaptability,* the environmental modification of a developing organism. Another example may be observed in dandelions: At low elevations and temperate climates, a dandelion is erect, with large leaves and flowers; if its seeds are planted at alpine elevations, the dandelions will be compact dwarfs.

Environmental variance is not consistent for all traits because some are more sensitive than others to environmental effects. Geneticists do not assume that the specific differences of the environment produce the same effects with all traits. For example, Strain A puppies may show more rapid growth than Strain B when fed the same high-quality product, and the assumption would be that they have a genotype for rapid growth. When both strains are raised on a poor-quality food, however, Strain B may show superior growth. Strain A, then, is the more sensitive to nutritional deficiency and is superior only when fed a high-quality diet.

Environmental changes are not necessarily fixed, and some traits change on daily, monthly, or yearly cycles. Yearly cycles are readily observed in birds, when the cocks may grow brilliant plumage to attract a mate, and the hens lay eggs and brood. A dog's coat not only exhibits seasonal variations but also responds to environmental variations of temperature; that is, a dog that spends the winter in an outdoor kennel develops a heavier coat than one that lives indoors.

With *environmental adaptability* the range of change is genetically limited. For example, all dogs respond to cold weather by growing a warmer coat, but the hair length and density (number of hairs per square inch) are limited by the genetic coat type.

Every breeder knows the frustration of selecting for traits related to size and shape, within the limits of the breed's basic structure. This is because "no major genes are known to affect either of these features." If all of the environmental factors (nutrition, exercise, health) are optimal, the dog's size and shape reflect the action of minor genes.[12]

REVIEW OF TERMS

adaptability
additive gene action
continuous variance
discontinuous variance
environmental factor
heritability
major genes
maternal effect
minor genes
modifiers
polygenes
quantitative genetics
threshold effect

Chapter 7

POPULATION GENETICS

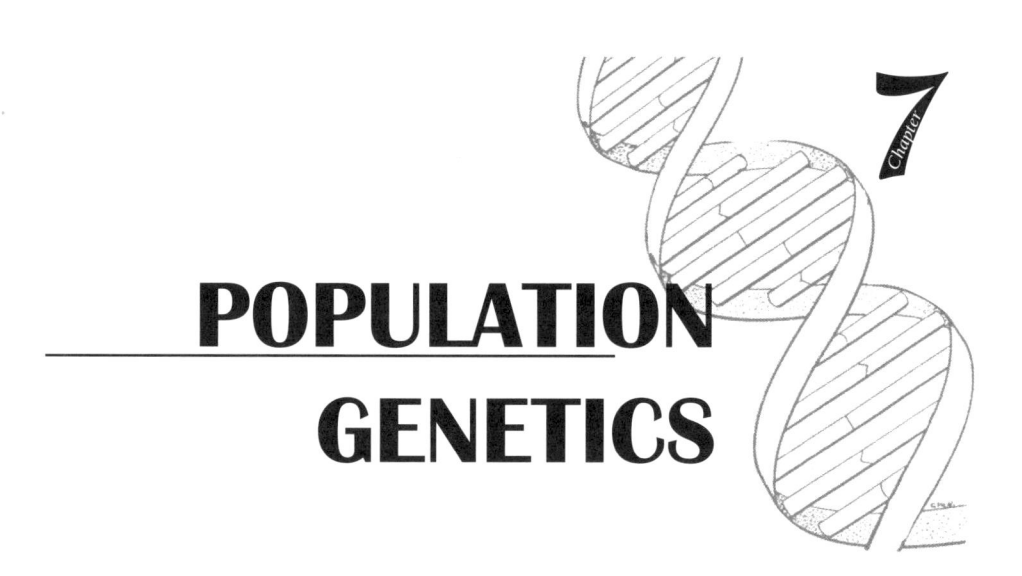

Have you ever considered your purebred dog as part of a population? A *population* is a breeding group with genes that have continuity from one generation to the next. Furthermore, your dog is part of a special population known as a *pure line*—that is, a population that breeds true for a particular trait or traits. Populations come in all sizes. The largest breed population would be the international one. Then would come the national, the state, the local, and the individual kennel population. Individual life spans are short, but a population persists for generations. All of the genes and their different allelic forms in a population are transferred from one generation to the next, giving the population a sort of immortality. The population's collective genes are known as its *gene pool,* a familiar term for most dog breeders.

Population genetics is the study of the genetic composition of populations, Mendelian gene frequencies, and factors that alter gene and genotype frequencies through the use of mathematical models to analyze the effects of mutation, selection, migration, and drift. There is some overlap with evolutionary genetics, which also studies these effects. The difference is that population geneticists try to reach generalizations about the evolutionary *process* through studying the effects at one or at a few loci. Although quantitative genetics also uses mathematical models, Merrell clarifies the difference: "Where the population geneticist deals with gene and genotype frequencies in natural populations, the quantitative geneticist deals with variances, covariances, and heritabilities in populations of domesticated plants and animals."[1]

GENE FREQUENCY

Gene frequency—the population's total number of different genes possible at any given locus—is a key concept of population genetics. Most of the time, the term makes the news when reporting the latest on endangered species. As more is learned about the canine genome and the alleles that produce hereditary diseases, gene frequency and estimates of the number of carriers within a breed will probably be mentioned more often in dog literature.

EQUILIBRIUM

The *Hardy-Weinberg law* states that in a large, random-mating population, the gene frequencies and genotype frequencies are constant—that is, in equilibrium. The ideal Hardy-Weinberg population is based on certain assumptions: (*a*) mating is random and all genotypes produce the same number of offspring; (*b*) there is no mutation; (*c*) there is no selective process that favors one genotype over another; (*d*) there is no addition from other populations or loss through departure; and (*e*) the population is infinitely large. In reality, no population meets all of these conditions, but these assumptions enable geneticists to measure, analyze, and describe populations and the ways they change.

It may be hard to visualize how *random mating*—each member of the population has an equal opportunity of mating with any individual of the opposite sex—applies to the breeding of purebred dogs, for unplanned matings are regarded as disasters. However, Nicholas points out that except for the particular traits that are being selected for, the genetic combinations for most traits are random.[2] In racing Greyhounds, for example, mating may be selective for speed but random for color, and within the Greyhound population, each generation produces a similar distribution of colors because the gene frequency for those traits is random. Thus, the Hardy-Weinberg law indeed applies to purebred dogs.

HOW DOES IT CHANGE?

In a large, random-mating population, changes of gene frequency are brought about by four factors: mutation, selection, migration, and random drift.

Mutation

"Natural mutation rates are from 10^{-4} (one in ten thousand) to 10^{-8} (one in a hundred million)."[3] Mutations of any type may eventually alter a population's gene frequency, especially if they confer a survival advantage. Mutations may be harmful, neutral, or beneficial. Nonrecurrent mutations occur once, and unless the mutation confers a *significant* survival advantage, they rarely have much effect on the population. Recurrent mutations, ones that occur repeatedly within the population, may produce a slow change if they are beneficial. "In effect, there is a pool of mutant alleles in any population, and this mutant gene pool constitutes an important portion of the total gene pool for the population."[4]

Mutations may be dominant or recessive or anything in between. Dominant mutations that are harmful tend to be eliminated from populations when the affected individuals fail to produce offspring. Harmful recessives, on the other hand, are virtually impossible to eliminate from a population because the undetectable heterozygotes preserve the genes from one generation to the next. Eventually, most harmful genes in a population are recessives.

Selection

Natural selection, often called survival of the fittest, is a primary way to alter a population's gene frequencies. The genes of individuals who survive long enough to reproduce remain part of the population's gene pool. Survival is often random, a matter of sheer luck—the good fortune of finding water in a drought, the bad luck of being snatched by the crocodile in the pool. Nevertheless, any trait that favors survival and that improves the chance of reproducing—greater tolerance for dehydration, faster reflexes to escape crocodiles—tends to increase the number of those genes within a population. If the environment changes so that a previously unimportant trait suddenly improves the chances of survival, then the frequency of that gene increases accordingly because those who don't have the trait don't live to reproduce.

Patterns of selection. Three patterns of natural selection have been identified: (a) stabilizing, (b) directional, and (c) disruptive.

Stabilizing selection favors the most common form of a trait. The alleles for less common traits tend to be eliminated, countering the effects of mutation, migration, and random drift.

In *directional selection,* the gene frequencies shift in a steady, consistent direction. This type of selection is favored when the environment alters, so that a trait at the extreme end of variance improves survival.

The classic example of directional selection is the English peppered moth. Like many insects, the peppered moth depends on color camouflage to escape the attention of predators, its gray color blending with the bark and lichens on tree trunks. Although both lighter and darker colors occurred, few of these escaped the predators. In the late 19th century industrial revolution, when pollution darkened the trunks with soot and killed the lichen, the darker color became a survival trait, and the gene frequency shifted in its favor. With the reduction of pollution, the tree bark recovered its former color, the medium color favored survival, and the gene frequency again shifted. The genotype of the typical peppered moth proved to be heterozygous *(Bb),* with an incompletely dominant allele for black pigment. The homozygotes were either lighter *(bb)* or darker *(BB).* Before the industrial revolution, most of the moths that survived to reproduce had the genotype *Bb,* insuring that both alleles persisted in the population. When the darker color favored survival, the gene frequency shifted, with the allele for *b* becoming rare. However, it is almost impossible to totally eliminate a recessive allele, and when the environment changed to again favor the heterozygote, the moth population quickly adapted to the new conditions.[5]

Disruptive selection occurs when the environment favors the survival of the extreme forms. The bills of the original finches that reached the Galapagos Islands were probably typical of all finches, and under normal circumstances any youngsters with different bills would be doomed. However, in the absence of other competing bird species, departure from the typical shape opened new sources of food to the finches. Those with thick, strong beaks to crush the hard cactus seeds survived and reproduced. Similarly, a long slender bill that could harvest nectar became a survival trait.

Heterozygous advantage. The peppered moths demonstrate one type of heterozygous advantage, but the classic example of a selective heterozygous advantage is that of sickle cell anemia. How can a recessive trait that is so deadly when homozygous contribute to survival when heterozygous?

About 10,000 years ago, the mutation of a bird microorganism enabled it to thrive in humans, causing the disease known as malaria. The organism eludes the immune system by taking up residence inside the red blood cells.

Humans also mutated. The substitution of a single base pair in the gene for hemoglobin changed the code for glutamate to that for valine, changing the gene product to hemoglobin-S—the abnormal hemoglobin responsible for sickle cell anemia. When the oxygen level in the blood around cells with hemoglobin-S drops below a certain level, the abnormal hemoglobin solidifies, and the red blood cells become sickled (form a crescent). The cells also sickle when attacked by malaria. The spleen removes and destroys sickled cells, and in the process, it also destroys malaria organisms.

When homozygous, with two alleles producing hemoglobin-S, the red blood cells have very little normal hemoglobin. Sickled cells tend to clump together, and when large numbers of cells are affected, the clumps obstruct the blood vessels, cutting off the blood supply to tissues, which then die.

The allele for hemoglobin-S is codominant with the one for normal hemoglobin, and heterozygous individuals produce both normal hemoglobin and hemoglobin-S. A balance exists between the protection of hemoglobin-S against malaria and the protection of normal hemoglobin against dangerously large clumps of sickled cells. In this way, people with one allele for hemoglobin-S have a better chance of surviving and having children.

It is believed that the mutation for hemoglobin-S probably occurred spontaneously in many human populations, but it remained rare or died out wherever it conferred no survival advantage. In addition to Africa, the hemoglobin-S allele is found in other populations where malaria occurs—the Middle East, Asia, Greece, Italy, Portugal. Thalassemia is another human blood disorder that arose in Mediterranean regions where malaria occurs; although the homozygote dies early in life, in this case also the heterozygote has a higher resistance to malaria.

Migration

The transfer of genes through the movement of individuals from one population to another is known as *migration,* and the spread of genes from one breeding population to others as the result of the migration is known as *gene flow.* The departing individuals take with them a portion of the population's *gene pool*—the population's collective genes—and new arrivals add to it. In this way, migration, which tends to be an ongoing process, reshuffles the population's collective genes and alters the gene frequencies.

Random Drift

The terms *random drift* and *genetic drift* refer to random changes of gene frequency produced by chance events.

Population size. A population's gene frequency changes randomly with each generation. Large populations are inherently stable, and the gene frequency is more or less constant (in equilibrium) from one generation to the next. The larger the population, the less impact random drift has on the overall equilibrium.

Small populations are especially sensitive to random drift. They typically begin as a splinter of a larger population that may, but usually does not, include all of the diverse genes that exist in the larger group. When the gene pool of the new population eventually reaches a new equilibrium, it differs from the parental population because of the changed gene frequency and reduced genetic diversity.

Founder effect. Random drift is profoundly altered by the *founder effect*, which is the change of gene frequency that occurs when a new population is based on a few individuals who carry only a small fraction of the genetic variation of the original population. The gene pool reaches a new equilibrium, with gene frequencies that are different than the parental population and with reduced genetic diversity. No matter how many descendants they have, no increase in numbers alters the gene frequency, and the gene pool is limited to those of the founding members unless altered by migration, mutation, natural selection, or further random drift.

In the early 18th century, about fifty Dunker (a religious sect) families from western Germany migrated to the United States. They did not marry outside their faith, and the genes of the founders reached a new equilibrium in which the gene frequency for neutral traits such as blood type is very different from both European and American populations.[6]

Bottleneck effect. Similar to the founder effect, a *bottleneck effect* is the fluctuation of gene frequency that occurs when a large population suffers devastating losses leading to an altered gene pool with reduced variability.

Purebred dogs. Random drift is an important consideration with purebred dogs because of the frequent splintering into smaller breeding populations.

Most modern dog breeds were founded in the late 19th century. The first step of founding a new breed is to begin a studbook and to register selected individuals considered good representatives of the desired breed phenotype. Then, studbooks are closed—that is, they no longer register individuals whose parents do not belong to the select population. The foundation of new breeds has continued into the 20th century. Although Bearded Collies are an ancient breed, the modern breed, which began in the 1940s, is primarily descended from Jeannie of Bothkennar and Bailie of Bothkennar, though other individuals were added selectively.

Splinter populations of purebreds are typically founded in different countries with the importation of only a few individuals. Additional splintering may occur with isolated local populations.

Bottleneck effects also occur in purebred dogs. An excellent example occurred in Weimaraners when fewer than a dozen survived the First World War. The Second World War created another bottleneck, though not as severe.

A variant of random drift occurs in purebred dogs when one sire becomes particularly popular and

Figure 7-1. Bearded Collie.

everyone races to use him. If the dog has "clean genes," the result can benefit the breed profoundly. On the other hand, it can be disastrous if the sire carries undesirable recessives, which spread rapidly through the breed population before breeders realize the problems. I once congratulated an acquaintance whose six-month-old bitch had gone best in show and commented about the overall good quality the breed seemed to have. He shook his head sadly and told me that the breed had been relatively free of genetic problems until an imported stud, which his puppy resembled, won a record number of bests in show and everyone promptly bred to him. "Now," he said gloomily, "everyone has monorchidism, bad bites, and bad temperaments."

GENETIC DIVERSITY

Most populations are dynamic, changing in cycles of expansion and increasing diversity, then dying off or splintering with decreasing diversity.

THE VALUE OF DIVERSITY

Role in Evolution

No evolution, no change is possible without genetic variability; alternatives must be available to adapt to a changing world.

In the past, many scientists believed that genetic variability in most species was low, with most individuals being homozygous for the wild-type alleles. The idea that all members of a species are homozygous for wild-type alleles has proven to be incorrect. Studies of genetic variation of more than 250 species found that anywhere from 10 to 60 percent of the genes are *polymorphic*—that is, have two or more alleles at the same locus. On the average, the number of heterozygous pairs ranged from 1 to 36 percent.[7]

When combined with sexual reproduction, there is a continuous generation of new genotypes. The number of potential combinations in species that reproduce sexually can actually exceed the number of individuals in the population. "Heterozygosity in the human has been estimated to occur in about 6.7% of the genetic loci. Assuming that there are 100,000 human loci, this indicates that a person is heterozygous at approximately 6,700 loci and could potentially produce 2^{6700} kinds of gametes."[8]

Geneticists now believe that "the variability within the gene pool may actually preadapt a population to cope with some environmental change in a later generation." Mutation is a rare event, but such changes—including lethal recessives—are preserved in the gene pool. Over millennia, species develop a reserve of mutations that in a changing environment become survival traits.[9]

Fruit fly studies that altered the food and space found in the environment discovered that strains with twice the genetic diversity adapted much faster than the less diverse strains. Consider also how rapidly insects developed resistance to DDT. A study of DDT resistance in *Drosophila* (fruit flies) used three different populations: inbred lines that had been developed for laboratory use and had no genetic diversity, noninbred laboratory strains with some diversity, and a wild population. None of the inbred lines demonstrated DDT resistance. The noninbred laboratory strains showed varying degrees of resistance as did wild *Drosophila*, and increasing DDT levels over time brought increasing resistance. Genetic analysis revealed a variety of mutations on different chromosomes and at different places on the same chromosome, but they all had produced the survival trait of resistance to DDT. When DDT was banned, resistance to it no longer served as a selective survival advantage, and DDT resistance is becoming less frequent in the populations.[10]

Fitness

The measures of fitness are survival, growth, fertility, and developmental stability, and in general, there is a positive correlation between heterozygosity and fitness. This phenomenon tends to preserve a variety of alleles in a population. Heterozygotes exhibit greater *homeostasis*—the ability to maintain physiological processes within normal limits despite varying external conditions. Natural selection favors heterozygotes, especially for traits related to vitality and fertility.

Heterosis

Heterosis is the marked vigor—characterized by greater survival, fertility, or capacity for growth—that is often shown by the offspring of genetically dissimilar parents. Also called *hybrid vigor,* heterosis is a fundamental genetic phenomenon; its opposite is inbreeding depression. *The degree of heterosis depends on differences of gene frequency in populations—the greater the difference, the more pronounced the response.*

One of the most important applications of heterosis is the practice of crossing two inbred lines of food crops, which increases the yield significantly. Because the heterosis effect wanes with succeeding generations, it is necessary to maintain separate inbred seed lines. British breeders of exhibition parakeets utilize heterosis to obtain their best show specimens. They use their top winners to found inbred lines. After about ten generations, inbred lines are crossed to obtain the superior size and vigor needed to win major exhibitions.

In purebred dogs, the spectacular success of imported sires and dams is usually attributed to the individuals. Although most undoubtedly deserve their laurels, it should be realized that hybrid vigor is also a significant factor. A classic example is found in the American Weimaraner, which began in 1939 with just one male and three bitches (two were full sisters). As a result of World War II, it was almost a decade before any more could be imported. After the war, crosses between these highly inbred dogs and German imports produced outstanding individuals whose show and performance records are only now being challenged.

THE LOSS OF DIVERSITY

The Natural Cycle

Inbreeding—the mating of individuals more closely related to one another than the average relationship within the population—is part of the natural population cycle; in fact, it is the norm for many species, particularly those of the plant kingdom.

The *degree* of inbreeding depends on the size of the population. All populations are inbred to some degree. The smaller the population, the closer the relationships, and in general, all small populations are regarded as inbred.

The question of whether the incest taboo has an instinctive basis is sometimes raised. Actually, kin recognition and avoidance of inbreeding have been occasionally identified in animals. For example, frogs that return to natal ponds produce significantly fewer sibling matings than random mating would produce. Kinship recognition has also been identified in Belding's ground squirrels, which engage in multiple matings resulting in multiple fathers; full sisters fought less and helped each other more than half-sisters. Among canines, observers of the highly inbred Isle Royale gray wolves report behavioral difficulties in pair bonding and speculate that it is caused by "recognition-triggered instinct for incestuous avoidance."[11] With few exceptions, such as the brother–sister marriages of the ancient Egyptian royal families, humans avoid inbreeding through the incest taboo. Sociologists point out that the avoidance of incest is not instinctive but probably arose from the need to avoid confusion within family relationships.

Inbreeding Depression

Inbreeding depression is the reduction of fertility and vigor associated with increased homozygosity; it is the opposite of heterosis. Of itself, inbreeding does not produce inbreeding depression. Inbreeding causes an increase of homozygosity; *if* the increased homozygosity leads to reduced fitness, it may be termed inbreeding depression. One theory is that this phenomenon is related to decreased developmental and physiological homeostasis owing to decreased genetic diversity.[12]

The most striking consequence of inbreeding is reduction of reproductive capability (fewer offspring born, fewer survivors) and physiological deterioration. High levels of abnormal sperm and diminished testosterone concentrations have been observed in strains of inbred mice and livestock. Inbreds are more sensitive to the environment and exhibit measurable environmental variance.[13]

Studies of Inbreeding

Pirchner points out that "in the 1910s and 1920s considerable hope was placed on the possibility of finding an ideal homozygote, i.e., an individual homozygous for all favorable alleles." By the "1930s, inbreeding was very much in vogue in animal breeding research. The reason was primarily the phenomenal success of hybrid corn. However, severe inbreeding depression, with the relatively low reproductive rate and the relatively high value of individual breeding animals, compared to corn, presented serious obstacles so that inbreeding as a tool for animal improvement has been relegated to a minor role."[14]

The high "cost" of inbreeding—both financial expense and viability loss—has been well established with agricultural and laboratory animals. Studies of inbreeding show a linear decrease of health and reproduction, and many lines become extinct. When the goal is to establish an inbred strain, it is necessary to begin with many lines to insure that some will survive inbreeding depression. One project with chickens began with 279 breeding lines; after three generations of inbreeding, only 30 lines survived; after fifteen generations, only 8 lines remained. Another project began with 20 pairs of mice; by the fourth generation, 10 lines remained, and after twelve generations, only 1 line remained. Different lines showed different responses to inbreeding, and surviving lines constitute a unique and select population. The egg production of 2 of the surviving chicken lines equalled that of commercial hybrids, and the line of surviving mice thrived until the study ended at the twentieth generation.[15]

The most serious consequence of inbreeding is that it increases the pairing of recessive traits—*and harmful genes tend to be recessive*. In 1946, Scott and Fuller began their behavioral research at the Jackson Laboratory at Bar Harbor with lines that were considered "good breeding stock." The nature of their studies required inbreeding, and each of the breeds (Basenji, Beagle, Cocker Spaniel, Shetland Sheepdog, Wire Fox Terrier) produced serious hereditary defects within the first or second generation. The average neonatal death rate among the purebreds at Bar Harbor was about 15 percent.[16]

Applications of Inbreeding

The most important application of inbreeding is the development of high-quality inbred strains that can be outcrossed to obtain a heterosis effect, and to achieve this, inbred strains must be maintained. This has been particularly effective with agricultural crops. However, as Pirchner pointed out, the technique has limited applications with livestock because the cost is considered too high in terms of the number of lines lost, and the rate of reproduction is too slow.[17]

As mentioned earlier, breeders of exhibition parakeets regularly develop inbred strains that can be crossed to obtain the heterosis effect. In their breeders lore, the rule of thumb for inbreeding is to expect serious recessives to cause a major "wipe out" at the fourth and fifth generations. The lines should begin to stabilize at the seventh generation, and the tenth generation produces the select individuals to cross with another inbred strain. This is the formula for producing best-in-show birds. Although these heterozygous winners won't breed true, they are used to found new inbred lines. The key to success here is that parakeets are extremely prolific as well as inexpensive to feed and maintain.

Inbreeding is used to produce populations of homozygous animals that are used for research. This has been particularly valuable with laboratory mice and rats used for medical and genetic research. In general, it has been found that after twenty generations of brother-sister matings, the mice are homozygous at 98 percent of their loci.[18]

Another recognized application of inbreeding is to fix a desired single-gene trait, particularly a recessive and commercially valuable one that might otherwise be lost. Prime examples of this are color mutations of fur-bearing animals and cage birds.

A GROWING CONCERN

Natural Populations

Endangered species. The loss of genetic diversity is a prevalent topic in literature about endangered species. The survival of some species that are being maintained by captive breeding programs is threatened by lack of genetic diversity. It is feared that species such as the California condor may have already passed the point of recovery even as captive breeding techniques are being perfected. The plight of endangered species and the many obstacles facing those trying to save them is movingly described in Jan DeBlieu's *Meant to be Wild: The Struggle to Save Endangered Species through Captive Breeding*.

The surviving Nene (Hawaiian goose) population stems from about six individuals—a population bottleneck. Attempts to reestablish them in the wild have not been succeeding because of a low hatching rate and failure of the goslings to thrive. Samples of DNA from museum birds collected almost one hundred years ago have one particular gene segment not found in any living birds. One survey of the ungulates (hoofed mammals) in zoos found that 49 percent of the inbred animals died before reaching six months old, whereas only 23 percent of the non-inbred offspring died.[19]

By the end of the 19th century, hunters had killed all but about twenty northern elephant seals. When hunting became illegal, the population grew rapidly. "Researchers who studied twenty-four genes found that the 30,000 members alive at the time carried the *same* alleles."[20] This species appears to be one of the fortunate ones that remained viable despite severe inbreeding.

Cheetahs. Concerned about the inbreeding among captive cheetahs, staff members of the National Zoo in Washington, D.C., obtained semen from a research center in South Africa in 1981. They hoped that the artificial insemination of the females in American zoos would increase the population's genetic diversity. Checking out samples, they were dismayed to discover that up to 70 percent of the sperm showed abnormalities, which is a characteristic sign of extreme inbreeding.[21]

Over the next two years, Stephen O'Brien, a geneticist with the National Cancer Institute, analyzed the blood from fifty-five cheetahs in American, European, and South African zoos for fifty-two proteins. Genetic diversity is evaluated by the analysis of blood proteins using a technique called gel electrophoresis. If a specific protein shows variation within a population, it indicates that there is also variation in the DNA codes for that protein. If there is no variation, the genetic codes are probably identical. O'Brien found absolutely no variation in the genetic material, no matter where the samples came from. He commented, "I have never seen a wild population with so little genetic variation."[22]

Expanding his search, O'Brien turned to museum specimens. There, he examined cheetah skulls in museums for symmetry. "The theory of genetic homeostasis, he explains, predicts that genetic diversity prevents physiological extremes and that species lacking diversity, such as inbred livestock, show greater skeletal dissimilarities than genetically diverse ones." The lack of symmetry in the cheetah skulls suggested that lack of diversity could be widespread.[23]

Cheetahs are so genetically uniform that skin from one can be grafted onto another, something previously found only with identical twins and highly inbred strains of laboratory mice.[24]

An epidemic of feline infectious peritonitis in 1982 killed 60 percent of the cheetahs in Oregon's Wildlife Safari Park's breeding program. The disease has a normal fatality of about 1 percent in domestic cats, and the park's lions showed few symptoms. Geneticists speculate that a virus acclimated initially to one cheetah's immune defenses and then proved equally successful against the immune defenses of others.[25]

The origin of the cheetah's lack of genetic diversity lies in the distant past. At the end of the last ice age, about 10,000 years ago, cheetahs and several closely related species roamed Europe, Asia, and North America as well as Africa. The drastic climatic change led to the extinction of 75 percent of the large mammal species of Europe, Asia, North America, and Australia. The African cheetahs survived as a species, but the population was reduced to so few individuals that the species lost its genetic diversity. Geographic separation, anywhere from 200 to 500 years ago, led to the development of the major subspecies, one in southern Africa and the other in eastern Africa. However, this was too recent to produce significant differences in their genetic constitution.[26]

Domesticated Populations

There is a growing concern over the loss of genetic diversity in domestic livestock and crop plants. The most successful crop plants have been cultivated worldwide, and the less successful ones are no longer cultivated. If all countries of the world cultivated X strain of wheat and a new disease wiped that strain out, what would happen?

A *gene bank* is a repository for the genes of living organisms, though the term is most commonly applied to repositories for plants. Preservation of the wild and less productive strains of crop plants insures that alternative genetic combinations are available for developing new strains that are resistant to that disease. Seeds are preserved at low temperature and humidity, and living plants are cultivated. The gene banks are also a source of genes being used to develop new and different plant varieties.

Animal genes are preserved in the form of frozen semen and embryos. For dog breeders, frozen semen preserves the genetic heritage of stud dogs long after their sterility or death. This is particularly valuable in breeds with small populations in which recessive disorders can quickly threaten the whole breed. If excessive inbreeding dangerously reduces a breed's genetic diversity, lost genes might be recovered through frozen semen.

Considerations for Dog Breeders

Dog breeders are concerned—or, if not, they should be—about genetic diversity. Most breeds began with a small but select group of individuals, experiencing the founder effect. Then, the populations underwent splintering as small groups spread around the world. At the same time, breeders consistently selected for uniformity, further reducing the genetic diversity. One result is the unfortunate fact that purebred dogs are notorious for genetic problems that are usually attributed to inbreeding. In *The Secret of Life,* Suzuki and Levine comment:

> You've probably heard of highly inbred dog breeds known for problems of one sort or another. Some, like golden retrievers, are prone to hip dysplasia and other debilitating ailments. There is also what animal breeders call inbreeding depression, a syndrome that includes low fertility, reproductive failure, and general failure to thrive.[27]

An article about hereditary blood and eye disorders of dogs points out the consequences of inbreeding:

> Inherited disorders are probably more common in purebred dogs than is generally realized, especially because of the selective inbreeding commonly practiced. These problems surface more often in rare breeds of dogs, which by necessity are inbred, and in breeds in which a particular animal (e.g., a major show winner) is popular and is used extensively for breeding. The inbreeding practices used to concentrate the desired characteristics also concentrate deleterious genes found in the line. Such genetic defects have become relatively widespread in selected lines of purebred dogs.[28]

It is important to place the inbreeding of purebred dogs in perspective. For breeds with large worldwide populations, inbreeding becomes the only way to consolidate highly valued traits. For breeds that originated or descended from a few twentieth-century individuals, inbreeding may be a luxury that the breed cannot afford.

Dog breeders should be alert for the warning signs of inbreeding depression, and this includes an awareness of trends *within the breed's population*. The onset is usually gradual, insidious and with little indication of the potential seriousness. Typically, only a few individuals are affected at first. The depression may progress in a variety of ways, affect only one aspect of health, or show a number of minor changes. Puppies and adults may be more susceptible to disease. Typically, reproduction is impaired, and males may exhibit a decline of libido over several generations, a growing loss of interest in females and reluctance to breed. Bitches may have increasingly irregular estrous cycles, fewer puppies per litter, and increasing need for cesarean deliveries. Maternal care may be indifferent. With all mammals, maternal traits are among the most sensitive to inbreeding depression. The maternal effects are influenced not only by the inbreeding of the mother but also on the degree of inbreeding of the developing embryos. For example, litter size is affected by degree of inbreeding of the mother (the more inbred, the less fertile) and inbreeding of young (the more inbred, the less viable).

The chapters on selection explore the choices available to breeders when considering their goals and the various ways to achieve them.

REVIEW OF TERMS

bottleneck effect
equilibrium
founder effect
gene frequency
gene pool
genetic drift
Hardy-Weinberg law
heterosis
hybrid vigor
inbreeding
inbreeding depression
population
population genetics
pure line
random drift
random mating

COAT COLORS AND MARKINGS

Color is the most easily identifiable of all hereditary traits, and it has been the key to the discovery of many genetic principles. The coat colors and markings of dogs offer a most rewarding way to practice the terms and concepts introduced in the chapter on Mendelian genetics. Two cautions must be given at the outset. First, the interactions between different loci demonstrate that even straight-forward dominant-recessive pairs are not always simple ones. Second, many aspects of canine color genetics are controversial and may change with future discoveries.

Clarence Little, a pioneer in canine color genetics (*The Inheritance of Coat Color in Dogs*), identified and described the loci and alleles that determine coat color. Research has clarified and modified various aspects of color since Little's work, and additional alleles have been identified.

COLOR ALLELES AND LOCI

The alphabetic letters that designate the color loci do not indicate the actual locations on chromosomes. Many mammals have color alleles that produce the same or similar gene products, and it is customary to identify them by the same letters, though the number of alleles may differ.

New alleles occur through mutation, creating alternative alleles—remember, an *allele* is any one of two-or-more alternative forms of a gene occupying the same position on a particular chromosome. Sometimes a species may have whole series of alternative alleles that may occupy a particular locus. In dogs, for example, four different alleles can occupy Locus *S*. However, no individual has more than two of the alleles—one on each chromosome. It may help to imagine a group of business suites in which each business is allotted only two reserved parking places for employees. Even if there are more than two employees, only two can park in the reserved places at any one time.

Table 8–1. Color Alleles, Effects, and Examples

Allele	Effects	Examples
Locus A Series: Dark-Pigment Pattern		
A^s	Dominant black	Labrador
A^y	Dominant yellow	Golden Retriever
A	Banded pigment in hair	Keeshond
a^{sa}	Saddle pattern	Airedale
a^t	Bicolored pattern	Doberman Pinscher
a	Recessive black	German Shepherd Dog
Locus B Pair: Black/Brown Pigment		
B	Black	Labrador
b	Brown	Sussex Spaniel
Locus C Series: Pigment Depth		
C	Full color pigmentation	Labrador
c^{ch}	Chinchilla dilution	Pug
c^e	Extreme dilution	West Highland White Terrier
c^b	Cornaz (blue-eyed albino)	Pekingese
c	Albino	Pekingese
Locus D Pair: Pigment Density		
D	Intense pigment density	Newfoundland
d	Dilute pigment density	Weimaraner
Locus E Series: Extension		
E^m	Black mask	Pug, Great Dane
E^{br}	Brindle	Greyhound
E	Extension	Sussex Spaniel
e	Restriction	Irish Setter
Locus G Pair: Progressive Graying		
G	Dark color lightens with age	Kerry Blue Terrier, Bedlington Terrier
g	Uniform color through life	Most breeds
Locus M Pair: Merle Pattern		
M	Merle or dapple pattern	Collie, Shetland Sheepdog, Dachshund
m	Uniform pigment	Most breeds
Locus S Series: White Pattern		
S	Solid color (self)	Weimaraner, Irish Setter
s^i	Irish-spotting pattern	Basenji, Boston Terrier, Brittany
s^p	Piebald spotting	Bull Terrier (white)
s^w	Extreme piebald spotting	Samoyed, West Highland White Terrier
Locus T Pair: Ticking		
T	Ticked coat	English Setter, German Shorthaired Pointer
t	No ticking	Most breeds

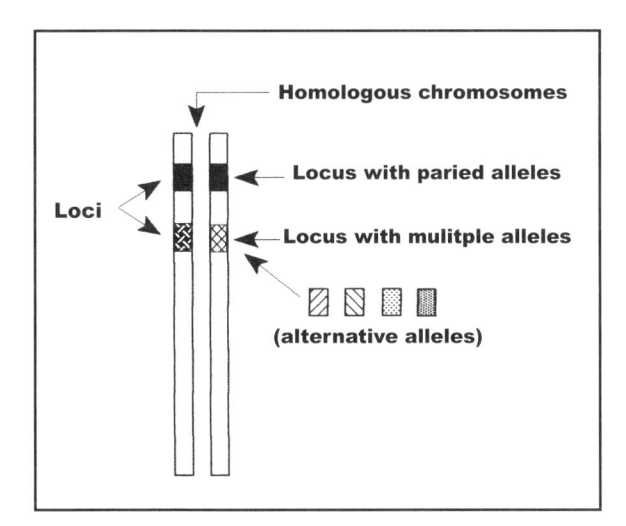

Figure 8–1. Alleles and loci.

What happens to those dominant-recessive relationships when there are more than two different alleles possible at one locus? The alleles in each series vary in dominance, and they are listed in order of their dominance, from the *most* dominant to the *least* dominant. Two terms describe the dominance relationship between two alleles in a series: *epistatic* (above) means more dominant, and *hypostatic* (below) means less dominant. In the Locus S series, for example, the S allele is epistatic to (more dominant than) all others in the series. The s^i allele is hypostatic to the S allele but epistatic to the s^p and the s^w alleles.

- S   solid-color
- s^i Irish spotting
- s^p piebald spotting
- s^w extreme piebald spotting[1]

The term *epistatic* should not be confused with *epistasis*, which refers to the genetic interaction whereby one gene alters or totally masks the phenotypic expression of another gene at a *different locus*. The gene for albinism (c), for example, totally masks the expression of all other genes at all other loci that affect the expression of pigment. The term is also used to refer any type of interaction between genes.

PIGMENT

It's hard to believe, but all colors are produced by only two pigments (areas with no pigment are white). All yellow shades (which include all reds) are produced by *phaeomelanin*—also called *light pigment*. All black and brown shades are produced by *eumelanin*—also called *dark pigment*. Remember the difference—

LIGHT PIGMENT = YELLOW/RED
DARK PIGMENT = BLACK OR BROWN

Some of the color alleles influence the expression of light pigment, some influence dark pigment, and some interact to modify both. So, remember the colors produced by each pigment!

LOCI WITH TWO ALLELES

For some reason, most literature about color discusses the loci in alphabetic sequence, beginning with Locus A, which is one of the most complex. It will be easier to begin with the most simple loci and work up to the more complex ones.

LOCUS *B* PAIR (BLACK/BROWN PIGMENT)

The Locus B pair (B and b), simple dominant-recessive alleles, modifies the shape of the granules of *dark pigment*. The dominant B allele produces elongated granules that appear black in color, whereas the paired *bb* alleles produce ovoid or spherical granules that appear brown. Same pigment, different colors! Dog fanciers often refer to brown as liver or chocolate, or in the case of Doberman Pinschers, as red.

In dogs that are red or yellow, the Locus B alleles are expressed in skin color, most visible on the nose and around the eye. A black nose indicates the genotype is B–, and a brown nose indicates the genotype is *bb*, though the colors may be lighter in the presence of genes that dilute pigment. A yellow Labrador Retriever with a black nose has the genotype B–, and one with a brown nose has the genotype *bb*. Remember that the dash after the B, by the way, merely indicates that the second allele is unknown or uncertain because it has no influence on the phenotype. In a series, it indicates that any one of the less dominant (hypostatic) alleles may be present.

LOCUS *D* PAIR (PIGMENT DENSITY)

The Locus D pair (D and d) modifies the density of pigment by changing the distribution of the granules within the hair follicle or skin cell. The dominant D distributes the pigment evenly to give full pigment density, except at the base of the hair where it is less intense. The recessive *dd* alleles dilute the color by clumping the pigment granules and distributing them irregularly.

When the dog's basic color is produced by dark pigment, the colors are either black (B–D–) or brown (bbD–). The genotype B–dd (dilute black pigment) yields the

Parents' genotype BbDd x BbDd

	BD	Bd	bD	bd
BD	BBDD black	BBDd black	BbDD black	BbDd black
Bd	BBDd black	BBdd blue	BbDd black	Bbdd blue
bD	BbDD black	BbDd black	bbDD red	bbDd red
bd	BbDd black	Bbdd blue	bbDd red	bbdd fawn

Figure 8–2. Locus B and Locus D interactions. *A mating between Doberman Pinschers with the genotypes* BbDd *and* BbDd *may produce black, red, blue, and fawn puppies.*

color known as *blue*. The genotype *bbdd* (dilute brown pigment) produces a silvery color known as *isabella* or *fawn*. In other species, such as cats, the color is called *lilac*—for example, the lilac-point Siamese cat. Oddly, most dog breeds that carry the *b* (brown) allele do not carry the *d* (dilution) allele. The Weimaraner is the only breed in which all individuals are homozygous *bbdd,* though the combination can also occur in Doberman Pinschers and several other breeds.

The dilution gene also affects light pigment, diluting red or yellow coats to cream, but the phenotypic difference is not as pronounced. The best example of the dilution can be observed in dogs with the bicolored (black-and-tan) pattern and the saddle pattern, in which the tan areas of blues and isabellas are also more dilute.

It is easy to see that interactions between two loci, each with only two alleles, quickly multiply the possible genotypes. The four alleles—*B, b, D, d*—produce the four typical Doberman Pinscher colors of black, red, blue, and fawn (isabella) from nine possible genotypes:

- *BBDD, BBDd, BbDD, BbDd*   black
- *BBdd, Bbdd*   blue
- *bbDD, bbDd*   red (brown)
- *bbdd*   fawn (isabella)

LOCUS *G* PAIR (PROGRESSIVE GRAYING)

The recognition of the Locus *G* alleles is based upon observation over time, and most breeds are homozygous for the recessive *g* allele. The dominant *G* allele produces a progressive silvering (graying) of the coat color. It occurs in some terrier breeds such as the Kerry Blue, the Bedlington, and the Dandie Dinmont as well as the Bearded Collie and Old English Sheepdog.

Puppies have full color at birth. Those that are homozygous (*GG*) begin silvering at a few weeks of age, reaching their mature color at about a year. When heterozygous (*Gg*), the silvering may begin almost as early, but it normally takes several years to complete the process.

Puppies with the genotype *ddG*– have dilute color at birth but also exhibit the progressive silvering.

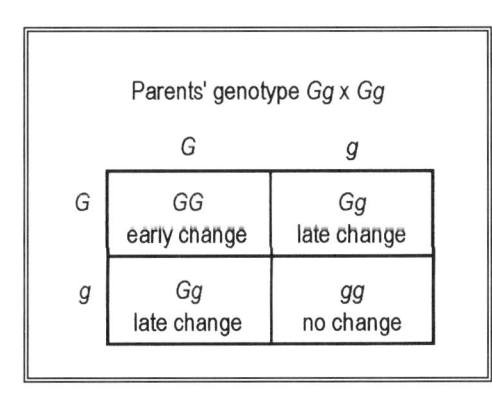

Parents' genotype *Gg* x *Gg*		
	G	g
G	GG early change	Gg late change
g	Gg late change	gg no change

Figure 8–3. Locus *G* alleles and phenotypes. *A mating between Kerry Blue Terriers with the genotypes Gg and Gg may produce puppies that change color early, late, or not at all.*

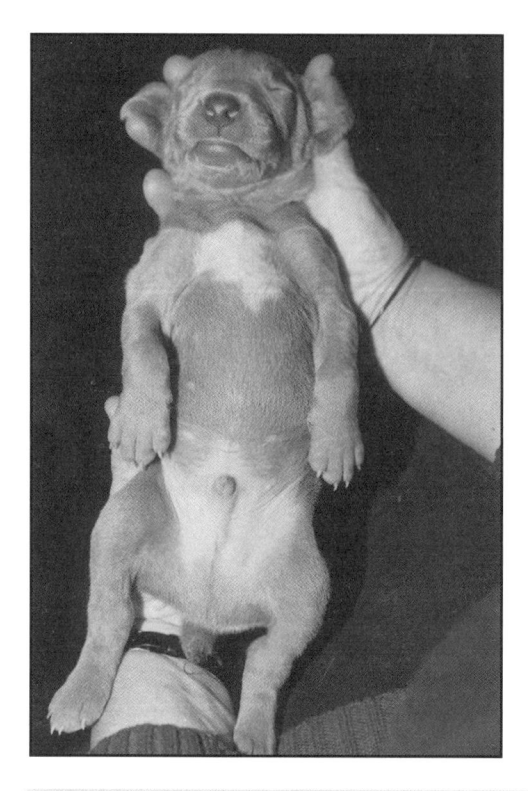

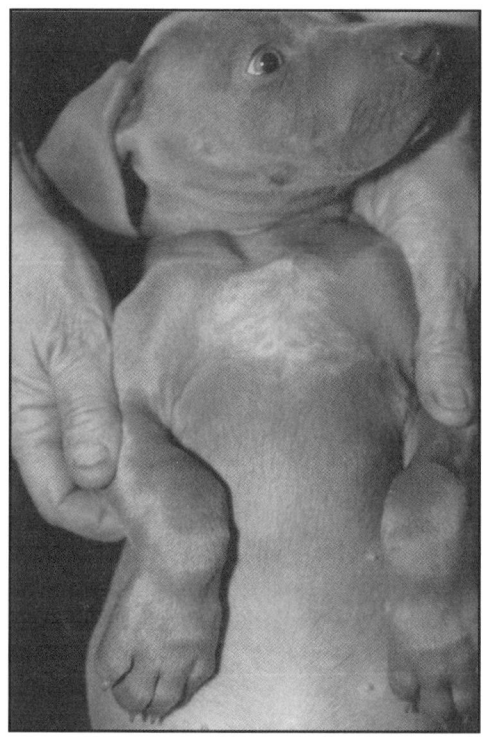

Figure 8–4. Ticking. *The T allele can only be expressed in white areas. This Weimaraner puppy with an unusually large white chest spot illustrates the presence of the allele in a typically solid-colored breed.*
  (a) The area is always clear white at birth.
  (b) By three months, the marking is no longer glaring, and by maturity, gray ticking almost completely camouflages the marking.
Reprinted, by permission, from Virginia Alexander and Jackie Isabell, Weimaraner Ways.

LOCUS *T* PAIR (TICKING)

At Locus *T*, the dominant *T* allele produces *ticking*—tiny flecks of pigmented hair—in otherwise nonpigmented (white) areas. The areas are white at birth, with ticking appearing within a few weeks. Ticking ranges from a few flecks to so many that the dog appears to be roan (a fairly even mixture of white and colored hairs); the roan effect is particularly evident in longhaired dogs. Most breeds are homozygous for the recessive *t* allele.

The *T* allele is typical of sporting breeds such as the English Setter and German Shorthaired Pointer as well as many hounds. Although ticking is associated with breeds that are primarily white with piebald spots, the allele also occurs in breeds that are typically solid in color. In the Weimaraner, for example, ticking has been observed in individuals that have relatively large white areas on the chest.

Dalmatian spotting, which is a special variant of ticking, is discussed under the Locus *S* alleles.

Figure 8–5. Ticking. *The Blue-ticked Hound is homozygous for the dominant T allele. Photo by Diane Calkins.*

LOCUS *M* PAIR (MERLE)

The most complex of all pairs, the M allele is incompletely dominant over the m allele. The locus is named for the *merle pattern* produced by the heterozygous alleles *(Mm)* and is characterized by irregular, dark patches against a lighter background that is a mixture of normal and pigment-deficient hairs. The classic expression is the *blue merle*, with irregular black patches against a blue background. The effect is clearest in dogs with dark (black or brown) pigment. With light pigment, the effect is not marked, producing indistinct golden patches, or it may be so minimal that it may not even be noticed.

Most breeds are homozygous for the *m* allele. The M allele is found in Collies, Shetland Sheepdogs, Australian Shepheds, Cardigan Welsh Corgis, Great Danes, and Dachshunds. In Dachshunds, the pattern is called *dapple*, because of the dappled effect of *Mm* on the solid-colored, shorthaired coat.

When homozygous *MM*, the coat is almost all white *(white merle)*. In Dachshunds, the coats range from dappled with some white markings to almost all white.

The M allele is an excellent example of *pleiotropy*—the phenomenon of a single allele causing a number of distinct and seemingly unrelated phenotypic effects. Even when heterozygous, the M allele is

Figure 8–6. Merle pattern. *The merle alleles, M and m, are an example of incomplete dominance. The mother and two puppies are blue merles (Mm), with patchwork pattern of light and dark gray. The puppy to the right is a white merle (MM), with a coat that is almost all white; this genotype is associated with small eyes with blue or partially blue irises and often has impaired hearing and fertility. Photo © Bonnie Nance.*

Figure 8–7. Locus M alleles and phenotypes. *A mating between merle Collies with the genotype Mm x Mm may produce blue merle, white merle, or normal-colored puppies.*

Parents' genotype Mm x Mm	M	m
M	MM white merle	Mm merle
m	Mm merle	mm normaL

associated with some deafness as well as occasional *wall eyes* (whitish irises) and other eye defects. When homozygous, the dogs usually have small eyes with blue or partially blue irises, and they often have impaired hearing and fertility.

The *harlequin pattern*—ragged black patches on a white background—is unique to the Great Dane. All other breeds are considered homozygous for the recessive h allele.

Geneticists have long associated the pattern with the merle allele, but only recently have the genetic factors have been identified. Although the harlequin allele (H) does not occur at Locus M, it can be expressed only in the presence of the merle allele, acting as a modifier, similar to the violet factor in parakeets. The action of the H allele is to eliminate the pigment-deficient hairs, leaving only the dark patches.

- *mmHh, mmhh*   normal color
- *Mmhh*   merle pattern
- *MmHh*   harlequin pattern
- *MMHh, Mmhh*   white merle

The genotype *MMHH* appears to be lethal to all embryos, and the combination of *MMHh* appears to be lethal to about half.[2]

Although the Great Dane standard disqualifies both whites and merles, blue merles and white merles are regularly produced by harlequin danes.

Unique to the Australian Shepherd, the *tweed pattern* displays the typical merle patchwork of dark spots on lighter areas. Although each light-colored area has a uniform color, there may be three or more patches, each of a different shade. Like the harlequin allele, the tweed

Figure 8–8. Harlequin pattern. *The unique harlequin markings are produced by a combination of the dominant merle allele and the harlequin allele at another locus. Photo © Kent and Donna Dannen.*

	MH	Mh	mH	mh
MH	MMHH (lethal)	MMHh white merle (semilethal)	MmHH (lethal)	MmHh harlequin
Mh	MMHh white merle (semilethal)	MMhh white merle	MmHH harlequin	Mmhh merle
mH	MmHH (lethal)	MmHh harlequin	mmHH (lethal)	mmHh normal
mh	MmHh harlequin	Mmhh merle	mmHh normal	mmhh normal

Parents' genotype MmHh x MmHh

Figure 8–9. Harlequin allele. *A mating between Great Danes with the genotype MmHh x MmHh may produce harlequin, blue merle, white merle, and normal-colored puppies. The litter may be small because the harlequin allele (H) is semilethal when heterozygous and lethal when homozygous.*

allele (Tw) is considered a modifier that is expressed only in the presence of the M allele.[3]

OTHER PAIRED LOCI

Clarence Little suggested two other color loci—R (roaning) and P (pink-eyed dilution). However, there is little evidence that these loci occur in dogs.[4]

LOCI WITH MULTIPLE ALLELES

LOCUS *C* SERIES (ALBINO)

The Locus C series controls the production of pigment throughout the coat, and each allele down the series leads to a progressive reduction of pigment expression. Although albinism is extremely rare in dogs, it is common in other mammals, especially in rodents, with each allele producing its characteristic phenotype.

- C full pigmentation
- c^{ch} chinchilla dilution
- c^e extreme dilution
- c^b cornaz
- c albino

In dogs, the expression of the Locus C alleles is based upon observations of phenotype rather than experimental studies. The presence of the last three alleles is highly speculative and controversial, being observed in only a very few dogs. Interactions with the dilution allele (*dd*) further complicate the identification of alleles.

Full Pigmentation

The *C* allele allows the full expression of color, both dark and light pigment.

Figure 8–10. Chinchilla allele. *A mating between dogs with the genotype Cc^{ch} and Cc^{ch} may produce puppies with pale shades, medium shades, or full color.*

Parents' genotype Cc^{ch} × Cc^{ch}

	C	c^{ch}
C	CC full color	Cc^{ch} medium shade
c^{ch}	Cc^{ch} medium shade	$c^{ch}c^{ch}$ pale shade

Chinchilla Dilution

The chinchilla or c^{ch} allele distinctly reduces the expression of light pigment, changing yellow to pale cream or near white. Robinson suggests that the rufus polygenes (discussed later) "can dilute yellow pigmentation to a cream, in essence mimicking the expected effects of c^{ch}." The c^{ch} allele has little, if any, effect on dark pigment. Little states: "Norwegian Elkhounds and Schnauzers in which the dark pigment is still plentiful but the yellow has been so reduced as to be almost, if not entirely absent, from the coat are good examples."[5]

Extreme Dilution

Little postulated the presence of a c^e allele in dogs to account for black-eyed whites. "A gene of this type might act upon tan-yellow dogs to produce pups which would be white at birth and which would remain so nearly white during increasing maturity that traces of very light-yellow pigment would be hard to find and/or would be definitely localized." The West Highland White Terrier, however, is the only breed he suggests as an example; both Willis and Robinson express skepticism.[6]

Cornaz

The possibility of a c^b allele is based on the 1929 report of Pearson and Usher. In their study of albinism with Pomeranians and Pekingese, they observed a pale, bluish-gray coat (called cornaz); the eyes were pale blue, with reddish pupils.

Albino

The c allele for complete albinism (red-eyed white) is widespread among rodents but very rare in dogs and cats. In fact, red-eyed white has been reported only in a few Pekingese.

LOCUS *S* SERIES (WHITE PATTERN)

The alleles of the Locus *S* (spotting) series determine the distribution and pattern of pigment. Little identified four alleles with the following sequence of dominance:
- *S*   solid-color
- s^i Irish spotting
- s^p piebald spotting
- s^w extreme piebald spotting[7]

The sequence reflects the decreasing areas of pigmented hairs. There is some question about the relative dominance of and interactions between the alleles when they are heterozygous. Because the expression is complicated by modifiers, which affect all of

Figure 8–11. Solid or self-colored. *The continuum of plus-and-minus modifiers with the S allele.*

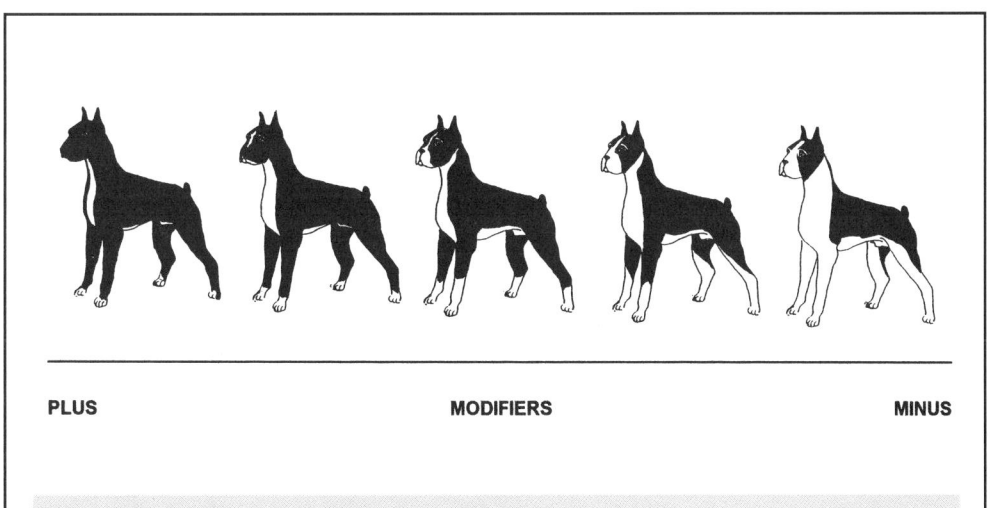

Figure 8–12. Irish spotting pattern. *The continuum of plus-and-minus modifiers with the s^i allele.*

the alleles, the discussion will be limited to the homozygous expression. In breeds that carry two or more of the S alleles, it is almost impossible to identify heterozygotes because of the plus-and-minus modifiers. Breeds such as the Greyhound that carry all four alleles exhibit a continuous range of phenotype, from solid colors to all white.

Plus-and-Minus Modifiers

All alleles at this locus are influenced by *genetic modifiers*—polygenes that affect the expression of alleles at an identifiable locus (see Chapter 6). The modifiers are designated as *plus* (more pigment, less white) or *minus* (less pigment, more white). With each allele, the extremes of homozygous expression resemble the extremes of the alleles above or below it in the series.

Solid Color

The homozygous S alleles produce a solid-colored coat, sometimes called *self-colored* by dog fanciers. The modifiers, however, produce occasional white markings on the throat, neck, chest, toes, abdomen, and penile sheathe. With homozygous S alleles, the most extreme expression of the minus modifiers—that is, the greatest amount of white—is known as the *pseudo-Irish pattern*. Weimaraners, Irish Setters, and most other solid-colored breeds do not carry the Irish spotting allele (s^i), and it is genetically impossible for them to have more extensive white than the pseudo-Irish pattern.

When breeders select against the white markings, they are actually trying to eliminate the minus modifiers. Selective breeding can reduce the incidence and area of white, but at best, it is a very slow process.

Irish Spotting

The *Irish spotting* allele, s^i (named for the Irish rats in which it was first described), produces a characteristic pattern of white on the muzzle, forehead, chest, abdomen, feet, and tail tip. The variable size of the white areas is determined by the plus-and-minus modifiers. Thus, homozygous s^i with extreme plus modifiers resembles the pseudo-Irish pattern produced by the homozygous S alleles with extreme minus modifiers. Basenjis and Collies are believed to be homozygous for the Irish spotting allele.

Piebald Spotting

The *piebald spotting* allele, s^p, produces widely variable areas of white. Breeds characterized by homozygous s^p alleles include Brittanies, Japanese Chins, and English Springer Spaniels.

Figure 8–13. Dalmatian spotting. *The unique spots are produced by a combination of the ticking allele and the flecking allele at another locus.* Photo © AKC, photo by Mary Bloom.

PLUS   **MODIFIERS**   **MINUS**

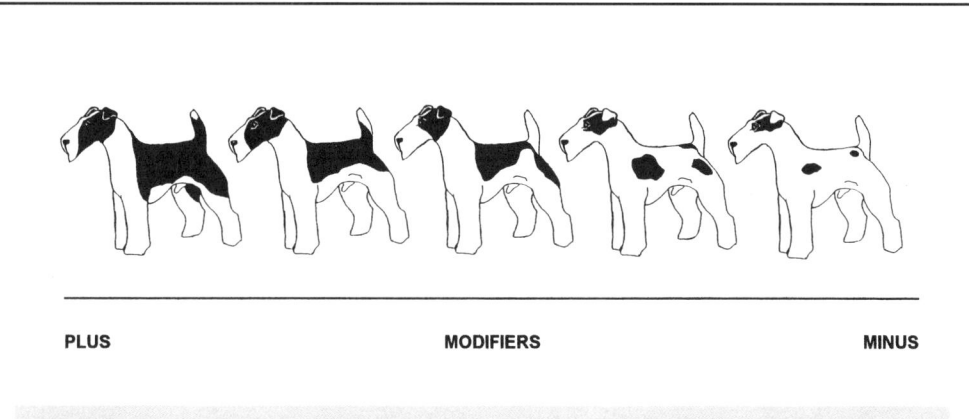

Figure 8–14. Piebald pattern. *The continuum of plus-and-minus modifiers with the s^p allele.*

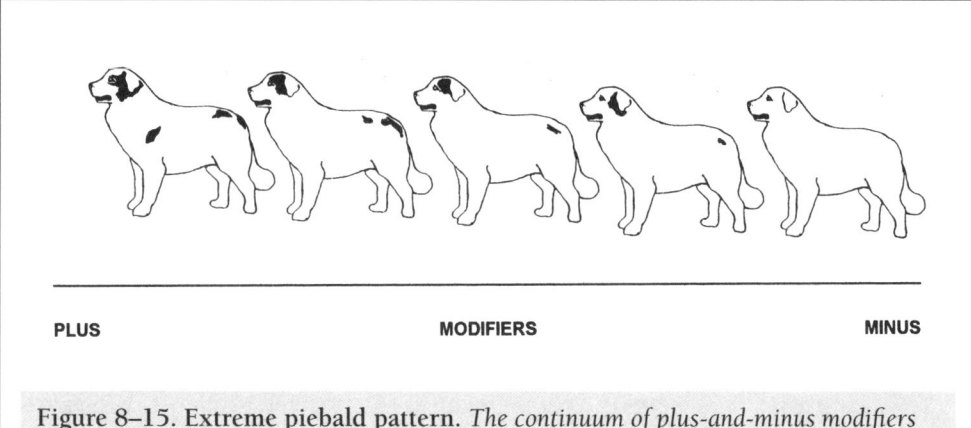

PLUS   **MODIFIERS**   **MINUS**

Figure 8–15. Extreme piebald pattern. *The continuum of plus-and-minus modifiers with the s^w allele.*

Extreme Piebald Spotting

The *extreme piebald* allele, s^w, further decreases the pigmented areas. Depending on the plus-and-minus modifiers present, the pattern ranges from solid white to white with spots of color on the ears, around the eyes, and in the tail area. Breeds that are considered homozygous for s^w include the Clumber Spaniel, the Samoyed, Great Pyrenees, and Maltese. Selective breeding has reduced the plus modifiers so that solid white has come to be considered typical of some breeds.

Little identified the Dalmatian genotype as $s^w s^w TT$, but he was unable to explain why the dark spots had no flecks of white hair. Schaible identified an interaction with a third allele that he designated the recessive *f*. The allele inhibits white flecking in the spots, and the Dalmatian genotype therefore, is $ff s^w s^w TT$. All other breeds are assumed to be homozygous for *F*.[8]

LOCUS *A* SERIES (DARK-PIGMENT PATTERN)

Locus A, named for the agouti (a rodent), is considered the most complex of all color loci. The four alleles described by Little have grown to six. The following is their *relative* dominance:
- A^s dominant black
- A^y dominant yellow
- A agouti (original wild allele)
- a^{sa} saddle pattern
- a^t bicolored pattern (black-and-tan)
- a recessive black

The *A* alleles are pattern factors that control the amount and regional distribution of dark pigment and light pigment. They act within the hair follicle, and their function is to switch pigment synthesis between light and dark. The alleles have intricate interactions within the series. Understanding the action of the alleles at this locus is complicated by two factors: (*a*) most breeds carry more than one *A* allele; and (*b*) all alleles at this locus interact with Locus *E* alleles.

Dominant Black

The A^s allele produces uniform distribution of dark pigment over the entire body, and its action is expressed in all dogs with black or brown coats. The allele is *almost* completely dominant over others in the *A* series. Examples of breeds that exhibit the homozygous A^s allele include the American Water Spaniel and the Curly-Coated Retriever.

The black color ranges from pure black to one with a brownish cast. So far, geneticists are uncertain whether the allele is unable to produce pure black without help from another locus or whether the brownish cast indicates the presence of a heterozygous allele.

Dominant Yellow

The A^y allele severely restricts dark pigment, producing yellow colors. When homozygous, the coat can be a clear gold, but it often has the black-tipped hairs called sable. Most A^y yellows have some black-tipped hairs, especially on the head and along the topline.

Agouti

The *agouti* allele is considered the normal or wild allele in this series. The *A* allele produces a band of light pigment on a shaft of dark hair. The location of the band varies; it may be terminal (end) or subterminal. The color of the back and sides of the coat is darker than that of the abdomen, extremities, and head, though the head often has darker markings. In dogs, the entire coat lightens very slightly from the puppy to the adult shade.

The homozygous *A* alleles occur in the Norwegian Elkhound, Keeshond, and Siberian Husky. Several schnauzer authorities mention that the correct salt-and-pepper color is produced by bands of white on black hair, noting that the facial mask is darker than the body color. When Donald Draper crossed Weimaraners with Norwegian Elkhounds and several other breeds in his studies of spinal dysraphism, he concluded that Weimaraners also carry the agouti allele, which would explain the breed's shimmering blend of silver shades.[9]

Figure 8–16. Agouti banding. *The agouti factor produces a terminal or subterminal band of light pigment in otherwise dark hairs.*
  (a) Normal hair.
  (b) Subterminal band of light pigment.
  (c) Terminal band of light pigment.
Reprinted, by permission, from Virginia Alexander and Jackie Isabell, Weimaraner Ways.

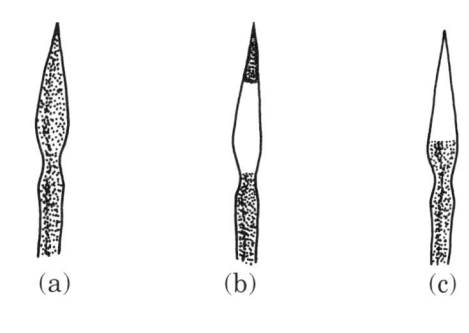

(a)   (b)   (c)

Saddle Pattern

The a^{sa} allele produces the *saddle pattern*, characterized by a V-shaped saddle of dark pigment over the back and sides, with areas of tan on the extremities and face. The saddle is typically darker at birth and lightens with maturity. The size of the area covered by dark pigment ranges considerably. The homozygous a^{sa} allele produces the typical pattern of the Airedale Terrier and German Shepherd.

Bicolored (Black-and-Tan) Pattern

The a^t allele produces the characteristic *bicolored pattern* of light and dark pigment typical of black-and-tan breeds such as the Rottweiler and Gordon Setter. (Willis prefers the term *bicolored* instead of black-and-tan, which implies that the pattern occurs only in black-and-tan dogs.[10]) The alleles are also homozygous in the Doberman Pinscher and may be observed in all of the breed's colors. The typical tan points are located as follows: above each eye; on each cheek; on the lips and lower jaw, extending under the throat; two spots on the forechest; below the tail; and from the feet to the pasterns and hocks, extending up the inner sides of the legs.

The pattern shows surprising variation. Even when homozygous, the depth of pigmentation

Figure 8–17. Agouti shading effect. *The agouti pattern of the Norwegian Elkhound is characterized by bands of light and dark pigment on most hairs, with scattered all-light hairs. In addition, some legs, top of the skull, and other body areas are often lighter. Photo © AKC, photo by Mary Bloom.*

Figure 8–18. Saddle pattern. *The saddle pattern of the German Shepherd Dog is characterized by a saddle of dark pigment with light pigment in other body areas. Photo by BJ McKinney.*

varies, the typical tan points are not always marked, and the color contrast is not always distinct. In some (such as Cocker Spaniels), the areas of tan are so reduced that without careful examination the animal might be classed as A^s.

Recessive Black

Carver confirmed a recessive black allele in the German Shepherd Dog. The allele has also been identified in Belgian Tervurens.[11]

Heterozygous Interactions

Interactions between heterozygous Locus A alleles are complex, with none in the series being completely dominant.
- $A^s A^y$ black/brown (black may have reddish cast)
- $A^s A$ black/brown (black may have reddish cast)
- $A^s a^{sa}$ black/brown (black may have reddish cast)
- $A^s a^t$ black/brown (black may have phantom reddish tinge at points)
- $A^y A$ yellow with banded hairs
- $A^y a^t$ shaded sable
- $A a^t$ lighter color, banded hairs

LOCUS *E* SERIES (EXTENSION)

The Locus E alleles affect the extension of dark pigment, and all of the alleles at this locus interact with those of Locus A.
- E^m black mask
- E^{br} brindle
- E extension of dark pigment (original wild allele)
- e restriction of dark pigment

Figure 8–19. Bicolored (black-and-tan) pattern. *The bicolored pattern of the Doberman Pinscher is characterized by dark pigment over most of the body with areas of light pigment above the eyes, cheeks, muzzle, perineum, under the tail, the lower legs, and the feet. Photo © Pets by Paulette.*

Black Mask

Little postulated an E^m allele for a black mask (also known as the superextension allele) that was dominant to all others in the series. The allele is expressed as a black mask on dogs that are not solid black. Robinson, however, considers the evidence that the black mask belongs in the E series unconvincing and treats it as a separate allele to which he assigns the symbol Ma.[12] Breeds with black masks include the Afghan Hound, the Belgian Tervuren, the Boxer, the German Shepherd, the Great Dane, and the Pug.

Brindle

The brindle allele, E^{br}, produces the *brindle pattern*, with stripes or bars of dark pigment, on a background of light pigment. It is dominant over the extension allele.[13] When combined with the A^s allele, which produces a solid coat of dark pigment (black or brown), the E^{br} is masked because there is no light pigment on which it can act. With all other A alleles, there is brindling in areas with light pigment.

- A^s–E^{br}–   black/brown
- A^y–E^{br}–   brindle
- $a^{sa}a^{sa}E^{br}$–   brindle in tan areas
- $a^t a^t E^{br}$–   black/brown, brindle points

In breeds such as the Greyhound and Whippet, interactions with alleles at the B and D loci produce a rich variety of brindle colors.

- A^y–B–D–E^{br}–   black brindle
- A^y–B–ddE^{br}–   blue brindle
- A^y–bbD–E^{br}–   brown brindle
- A^y–$bbddE^{br}$–   fawn (isabella) brindle

Figure 8–20. Brindle pattern. *The brindle allele acts on light pigment to produce bars of dark pigment. Photo © AKC, photo by Mary Bloom.*

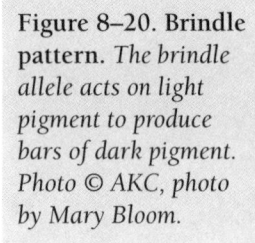

Extension

The E allele is considered the original, wild allele that produces normal extension or expression of dark pigment. It interacts with the Locus A alleles to produce a variety of effects.

- A^s–E–   black/brown
- A^y–E–   red/yellow or sable
- A–E–   agouti banding
- a^{sa}–E–   saddle
- $a^t a^t$E–   black/brown, tan points

Restriction

The homozygous ee alleles restrict the expression of dark pigment, producing the yellow shades expressed by light pigment. It does allow the expression of dark pigment

Figure 8–21. Locus A and Locus E interactions. *A mating between dogs with the genotype $A^s a^t E^{br} e$ and $A^y a^t Ee$ may produce puppies of a wide variety of colors and patterns.*

Parents' genotype $A^s a^t E^{br} e \times A^y a^t Ee$

	$A^s E^{br}$	$A^s e$	$a^t E^{br}$	$a^t e$
$A^y E$	$A^s A^y EE$ black/brown	$A^s A^y Ee$ black/brown	$A^y a^t E^{br} E$ brindle	$A^y a^t Ee$ yellow
$A^y e$	$A^s A^y Ee$ black/brown	$A^s A^y ee$ yellow	$A^y a^t E^{br} e$ brindle	$A^y a^t ee$ yellow
$a^t E$	$A^s a^t EE$ black/brown	$A^s a^t Ee$ black/brown	$a^t a^t E^{br} E$ black/brown with brindle points	$a^t a^t Ee$ black/brown with tan points
$a^t e$	$A^s a^t Ee$ black/brown	$A^s a^t ee$ yellow	$a^t a^t E^{br} e$ black/brown with brindle points	$a^t a^t ee$ yellow

on the nose, lips, and eye rims. Although recessive to all other alleles in the *E* series, homozygous *ee* alleles interfere with the expression of most Locus *A* alleles.
- A^s–*ee*   yellow
- a^{sa}–*ee*   yellow, lighter in tan areas
- $a^t a^t ee$ yellow, lighter shade at bicolored points

The expression of the A^y–*ee* genotype is uncertain.

The genotypes *ee* and A^y–*E*– both allow the expression of light pigment, and the various shades (fawn, orange, red, yellow, mahogany, lemon, and so forth) are determined by modifiers. It is difficult to identify which of the Locus *A* and *E* alleles are present in yellow dogs, though most breeds carry the alleles for either one or the other. In some breeds, the A^y–*E*– combination seems to allow some dark pigment on the tips of the hairs, giving the sooty appearance known as sable, which is more pronounced in longhaired breeds such as the Collie. In addition, a black mask can be expressed only in combination with A^y–*E*–. In contrast, the *ee* genotype is typically a uniform color. Breeds that are believed to have the *ee* genotype are the Beagle, Dalmatian, English Setter, Golden Retriever, Gordon Setter, Irish Setter, Labrador Retriever, Pointer, and Poodle.[14]

When the genotypes (A^s–*ee* and A^y–*E*–) are mated, some of the puppies have the genotype $A^s A^y Ee$, and the phenotype for that combination is black. Breeds that are thought to carry the alleles for both types of yellow are the Chow Chow, Cocker Spaniel (American and English), and the Field Spaniel. Irish Setters produce occasional black offspring, suggesting that a small number may have the A^y–*E*– genotype.[15]

OTHER COLOR FACTORS

Several other color factors that have been observed are not identified by a designated letter.

SADDLE VARIATION POLYGENES

The expression of the saddle pattern (a^{sa}) for the area covered and the intensity of color shows the continuous variance typical of polygenes. At one end of the spectrum, the dark pattern may be mixed with so many yellow hairs that it could be mistaken for a sable; at the other end, the dark hairs are so uniform and extensive that it approaches the black-and-tan pattern.[16]

UMBROUS (SABLE) POLYGENES

The *umbrous polygenes* influence the number of black-tipped hairs in the A^y–*E*– yellows, producing a range of shades from nearly gold to a dark, shaded sable. They appear to have no effect on the A^s–*ee* yellows. Examples of the action of the umbrous polygenes are found in the Collie and Shetland Sheepdog.[17]

RUFUS POLYGENES

The *rufus polygenes* influence the expression of light pigment, producing shades ranging from pale yellow to rich mahogany. They are expressed in the presence of both genotypes that produce yellow (A^s–*ee* and A^y–*E*–) as well as in the presence of the bicolored and the saddle patterns. The varying shades of Golden Retrievers and Irish Setters, for example, are attributed to the rufus polygenes.[18]

DILUTION MODIFIERS

The continuous variance of the expression of the recessive dilution alleles (*dd*) is produced by the *dilution modifiers*. Although the modifiers are not evident in black (*B–*) coats, they could be related to variations of the brown (*bb*, chocolate or liver) colors. Robinson suggests that they "may even be part of the rufus group," which affects the expression of light pigment.[19] A good example of the dilution modifiers may be observed in Weimaraners (*bbdd*), which range from very light (almost pewter color) to so dark that the color is sometimes confused with blue (*B–dd*), which also occurs in the breed and has a similar range of light to dark shades.

INTENSITY ALLELES

In his work with wolf hybrids, Iljin observed variation of the bands of light pigment in agouti hairs—gray-white, light-yellow, and rust—that appeared to function as an allelomorphic series. Iljin postulated the following sequence:

- *Int* dilutes the light band to a dirty white; overall color appears white or dirty gray
- int^m produces a yellowish-brown band; overall color appears wolf-gray
- *int* no dilution, broad bright yellow band; overall color appears reddish[20]

A dilution factor, the series differs from the Locus C alleles in that the dominance sequence is from the greatest dilution to the least dilution—that is, lightest to darkest. The presence of c^{ch} is difficult to confirm, and in most cases the intensity alleles are considered equally probable. Despite the similarities, there are enough subtle differences to support belief that two different loci are involved. Carver's data supported a dilution factor of this type in the German Shepherd, though it remains speculative in breeds that have not been as carefully studied.[21]

DARK-EYED WHITE

The genotype of dark-eyed white dogs is difficult to determine because several allelic combinations could eliminate pigment from the hair, which is what must be done to create white. Breeds that exhibit occasional spots near ears and base of the tail (Clumber Spaniel, white Bull Terrier, Great Pyrenees, and Samoyed) are believed to have the genotype $s^w s^w$. Carver's work with German Shepherd Dogs identified a simple recessive white, and he postulated an allelic pair with a dominant nonwhite (*Wh*) and a recessive white (*wh*).[22]

The genotype of other dark-eyed whites remains somewhat speculative. The first requirement would be to block the expression of dark pigment, which occurs with the genotypes *ee* and A^y–*E*–. The second requirement would be to inhibit the expression of light pigment, and the most likely genotype is believed to be the homozygous chinchilla alleles ($c^{ch}c^{ch}$). The A^y–*E*– genotype does not *always* remove all of the black, sometimes producing sable and allowing the expression of black masks. White dogs with black-tipped hairs or a mask are believed to have the genotype A^y– $c^{ch}c^{ch}E$–, though the genotype could also produce a clear white. The genotype A^s– $c^{ch}c^{ch}ee$ also produces white. Both combinations usually have a yellowish cast, though the latter genotype is believed to produce the clearest white.[23]

EYE COLOR

In general, brown dogs (those with paired *bb* alleles) have lighter eyes—that is, iris color—than black dogs (*B–*). Dogs with dilute pigment (*dd*) also typically have lighter eyes, usually shades of smoky gray. Robinson believes this range of color is produced by modifiers.[24]

Burns and Fraser suggest that the various shades are produced by a series of three alleles with incomplete dominance: *Ir*, for very dark; *ir^m*, for intermediate brown; and *ir^y* for yellow. Between them, the three could produce a range of colors from dark to very light brown.[25]

- *IrIr* very dark brown
- *Irir^m* dark brown
- *Irir^y* medium brown
- *ir^m ir^m* medium light brown
- *ir^m ir^y* light brown
- *ir^y ir^y* yellow

SUMMARY

In some ways, the genetics of coat color is very straightforward, but in other ways, many aspects remain mysteries. No attempt has yet been made to decipher the alleles that the coat color of quite a few breeds, and the alleles suggested for others are merely tentative. Many questions remain about the expression of the Locus C alleles. Is the black mask part of the Locus E series? What are the underlying alleles of black-eyed white dogs? The situation can really get confusing when the authorities disagree and use different symbols. Nevertheless, quite a bit of the knowledge presents clear applications of Mendelian genetics and offers an opportunity to study gene expression and the ways that the alleles interact at each locus and between the different loci.

In fact, it can be fun to sit at ringside and try to figure out the color alleles being expressed in breeds. Start with the simple ones and work up to complex ones such as Greyhounds and Cocker Spaniels.

REVIEW OF TERMS

agouti allele
bicolored pattern
black-and-tan pattern
blue merle
brindle pattern
chinchilla allele
dapple
dilution modifiers
epistatic
extreme piebald spotting
harlequin pattern
hypostatic
intensity
Irish spotting
isabella
light pigment
merle pattern
piebald spotting
rufus polygenes
saddle pattern
ticking
umbrous polygenes
white merle

Chapter 9

COAT TYPES AND QUALITIES

COAT TYPES

THE "BASIC" THREE

The three most common coat types show a consistent pattern of dominance within breeds that have all three as well as in breed crosses.
- *wirehair*—dominant over shorthair and longhair
- *shorthair*—recessive to wirehair, dominant over longhair
- *longhair*—recessive to wirehair and shorthair

Wirehaired

Wirehaired coats are typically double—that is, they have a short, soft, dense undercoat with a hard, straight, wiry topcoat. The undercoat, which ideally covers the whole body, keeps the dog warm, and its typical density may vary between breeds. The topcoat has a harsh appearance and stands slightly away from the body to protect

Figure 9–1. Miniature Schnauzer. *The smart appearance of this wirehaired coat is produced by stripping (hand plucking). Photo by Richard L. Holmes.*

125

the dog in all weather conditions; it is, to some extent, water repellent. A correct wirehaired coat requires minimal grooming.

The wirehaired coat sheds twice a year. The dead hairs tend to form mats unless removed by thorough brushing. The best way to remove the dead hair and stimulate the wiry texture of the topcoat is by *stripping*—a technique of plucking out the dead hair by hand. Pet owners who don't want to bother with this time-consuming and costly procedure often clip the coat. However, clipping inhibits growth of the wiry topcoat. After repeated clipping, more and more of the coat is composed of the softer and lighter undercoat, making the overall coat softer and lighter in color.

Shorthaired

Shorthaired coats show considerable variation in length and other qualities. The coat of the Whippet is certainly far shorter than those of the shorthaired German Shepherd and the Saint Bernard, both of which also have longhaired coats. In addition, minor differences in traits such as texture and density may be observed in the expression of shorthaired coats. Some shorthaired breeds always have undercoats, and some breeds never have undercoats. Yet another difference is that some individuals in a breed, such as German Shepherds and Weimaraners, have an undercoat, but others of the same breed do not.[1]

In shorthaired dogs without an undercoat, shedding may be prolonged, may not follow a seasonal pattern, and may even shed a little all year round.

Only a few standards describe shorthaired coats in detail. The Saint Bernard AKC breed standard is the only one that mentions the term *stockhaarig,* and it is used in reference to the shorthaired coat. The *Federation Cynologique International (FCI)* Weimaraner standard describes three types of recognized coats—shorthaired, longhaired, and *stockhaarig*. The shorthaired coat is very short and fine; the *stockhaarig* coat longer, coarser, and always has an undercoat. Dr. Hans Schmidt, a German breeder, has observed that the *stockhaarig* coat appears to be consistently recessive to the typical shorthaired coat but dominant to the longhaired coat, suggesting three alleles at the same locus, rather than modifiers or polygenes.[2]

Figure 9–2. Whippet. *A very short, smooth coat, rarely with an undercoat.*

Figure 9–3. Old English Sheepdog. *This breed is the archtypal "shaggy dog." Photo © AKC, photo by Mary Bloom.*

Figure 9–4. Collie (rough-coated vartiety). *The short hair on the legs and feet is a dramatic contrast to the lush coat of the neck, body, and tail. Photo © Robert and Eunice Pearcy.*

Longhaired

Longhaired coats show the greatest variety of all. Some, such as the Bearded Collie and Old English Sheepdog, have long hair all over, only slightly shorter on the face. Other breeds have areas of short hair in a typical pattern—the Shetland Sheepdog (face and feet) and the Afghan Hound (face, back, and tail). There seems to be no information about the heredity of these patterns.

Some aspects of longhaired coats show continuous variance and appear to be influenced by modifiers and to be altered by selective breeding. The American Cocker Spaniel evolved from the English Cocker, and the American breed's exaggerated leg furnishings are a recent development. The same effect can be achieved with wirehaired coats: American schnauzer breeders have also selected for fuller leg furnishings, which are more extensive than their European counterparts.

Most longhaired coats are double, with a short, soft, dense undercoat and a hard, straight topcoat. When the hairs die, they drop out of the follicles. The undercoat

Figure 9–5. Afghan Hound. *A striking combination of short and long hair in a unique pattern. Photo © Robert and Eunice Pearcy.*

usually sheds in the spring and the topcoat in the fall. There are, however, breed and individual differences as well as variations related to the climate.

Unlike most longhaired breeds, the Maltese and Yorkshire Terrier coats have no undercoat and do not shed seasonally. Instead, the coats grow continuously, like human hair, losing only occasional dead hairs. It takes from eighteen to twenty-four months to grow a ground-length coat. It takes even longer to grow the ground-sweeping coats of top show dogs, which are protected from breakage by wrapping and rolling small sections so that the hair won't drag on the ground.

UNUSUAL TYPES

Wooly and Corded

The Poodle's wooly coat comes in two distinctive types, both double. The "soft curly" coat feels both soft and dense. When unbrushed or wet, this type hangs in ringlets. If brushed, it is almost straight but slowly returns to curls. The thick undercoat helps to hold the shape when brushed. The soft curly coat easily develops cords. To start cording, owners comb out most of the undercoat so that the curling topcoat can begin

Figure 9–6. Maltese. *One of the few longhaired breeds with no undercoat, the exotic, ground-sweeping show coat is achieved by painstaking grooming and special care. Photo © Pets by Paulette*

Figure 9–7. Standard Poodle. *A wooly coat that is usually brushed.*

cording. Once started, the new undercoat adds body to the cords.

The Poodle's "steel wool" type has a dense, springy (never harsh or wiry) texture. The topcoat is shorter and coarser, with a tendency to form kinky curls instead of ringlets, and the undercoat is thick and wooly. The hairs are shorter and more brittle, and they do not develop satisfactory cords.

Although the corded coat is no longer fashionable for Poodles, the corded coats of the Puli and the Komondor have become the breeds' hallmarks. The Puli's coat ranges from slightly wavy to very curly, and some are so curly that they twist into cords within minutes after combing. The Puli may be shown with either a corded or a brushed

Figure 9–8. Komondor. *The corded wooly white coat is similar to the wool of sheep and enables this breed to mimic the animals that they are bred to guard. Photo © Tara Darling.*

coat. The Komondor coat is slightly coarser, and a noncorded coat after two years of age is a disqualification.

Cords that range from shoelace-type to one-half-inch ribbons are formed by the interweaving of the very curly outer coat and the undercoat. The dead hairs are not shed, and unless allowed to form cords or brushed with great determination to remove dead hair, the coats become hopelessly matted. The degree of topcoat waviness and amount of undercoat determines the width of the cords.

Hairlessness

The opposite of a coat, of course, is no coat at all. Unlike coat length, hairlessness exhibits different modes of inheritance in different breeds.

The Chinese Crested is hairless except for coarse hair on the crown (crest) of the head, the lower part of the legs, and the end of the tail; some have a line of coarse hair down the topline, which is undesirable. The trait is produced by an autosomal dominant gene that is lethal when homozygous, and all hairless Chinese Crested are heterozygotes. To perpetuate the breed, it is necessary to cross the hairless dogs with normal-coated ones, which are known as powderpuffs and may also be shown.

Although forward pointing canine teeth have been observed in some of the crested variety, the powderpuffs have normal dentition. No other abnormalities have been reported.

The hairless trait also occurs in several breeds that are not registered by the AKC—Inca Hairless Dog, Peruvian Inca Orchid, and Xoloitzcuintli (Mexican Hairless). The hairless varieties have sparse hair on the head and several other areas. In these breeds, the gene also is lethal when homozygous,

Figure 9–9. Chinese Crested. *(a) The dominant hairless gene is lethal when homozygous.*
(b) The powderpuff coat is recessive. Photo © Pets by Paulette.

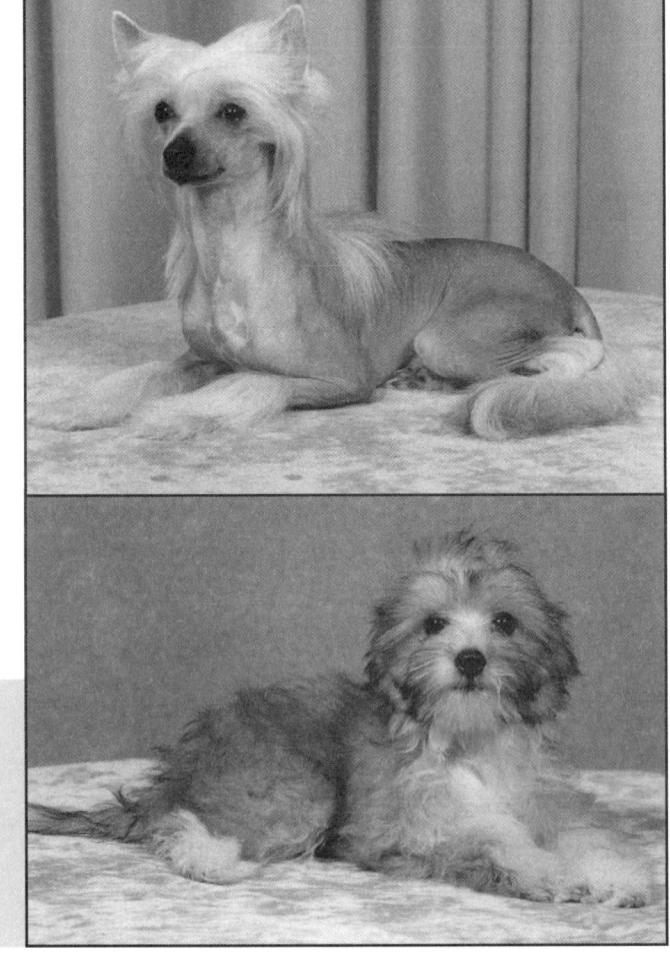

and all have powderpuff varieties, though the hair is shorter than that of the Chinese Crested.

In the American Hairless Terrier (a mutation of the American Rat Terrier) hairlessness is produced by an autosomal recessive gene. At birth, puppies have a sparse, downy coat, which is later shed and never regrown. Whiskers and eyebrows are normal. No other abnormalities are present.

COAT QUALITIES

In addition to length, coats have an incredible variety of other qualities. The inheritance of coat qualities such as density and texture appears to be inherited independently of basic type.

DENSITY

Although all coats become more dense—that is, have more hair per skin area—in cold weather, the variance of density is a hereditary trait. Whitney crossed a Norwegian Elkhound (which probably has the greatest density of all breeds) to a Bloodhound. The coat density of the progeny varied, and in general, the sparse coat appeared dominant over the dense coat. A brother-sister mating from the litter produced a range of coat density and no clear-cut segregation. Density, Whitney concluded, is a polygenic trait.[3]

TEXTURE

Crosses between the silky-haired setters and the coarse-haired hounds consistently produced rather coarse coats of all grades. In no case was the texture as fine as the setters. Whitney tentatively concluded that, in general, coarse is dominant over silky.[4]

UNDERCOAT

Some breeds have no undercoat at all. In other breeds, such as German Shepherds, some individuals have an undercoat whereas others have none. The same is true of Weimaraners, and breeders have noticed that puppies with an undercoat sometimes lose it completely and forever by the age of six to eighteen months.

Undercoat is a distinctly hereditary trait. Like their Bloodhound parent, the puppies from Whitney's Elkhound-Bloodhound cross had no undercoat. In general, undercoat appears to be recessive to the lack of undercoat.[5]

WAVY

In many breeds, the breeders have observed that straight-coated parents sometimes produce wavy-coated puppies. Whitney tried several crosses to determine the heredity of wavy versus straight. When he crossed a wavy-coated Borzoi to a Foxhound and a Bloodhound, the puppies had straight coats. Whitney also bred a wavy-coated Borzoi to a straight-coated Borzoi; half the puppies had wavy coats and half had straight coats. He concluded that wavy coats are indeterminate, but in general, straight tends to be dominant over wavy.[6]

Figure 9–10. Borzoi. *Many have a wavy coat. Photo © AKC, photo by Mary Bloom.*

KINKY

Whitney tried a number of crosses with the kinky-coated Irish Water Spaniel. Two litters from Cocker Spaniel crosses produced fourteen black, longhaired, straight-coated puppies; unlike the Irish Water Spaniel parent, all had tail feathering. A litter from an Irish Setter cross produced eight black puppies with straight coats. From a breeder who specialized in the latter cross, Whitney learned that it consistently produced black dogs with the setter-type coat, and he concluded that straight is dominant over kinky.[7]

CURLY

Burns and Fraser reported that all puppies from a breeding between a Curly-Coated Retriever and a Pointer had curly coats like the retriever parent. The curly trait also appears to be dominant in Poodles. Poodles bred to both Cocker Spaniels and Labrador Retrievers have been reported to consistently produce puppies with curly coats.[8]

FEATHERING

Whitney's Irish Water Spaniel crosses consistently produced feathering, suggesting that it is dominant to lack of feathering.[9]

The Saluki is an interesting shorthaired breed. The most common coat is short and silky, with feathering on the ears, legs, and tails. The smooth variety has a coarse texture and no feathering, and it appears to be recessive to the feathered coat.

Figure 9–11. Irish Water Spaniel. *A breed that is characterized by a kinky coat. Photo © Kent and Donna Dannen.*

Coat Types and Qualities 133

Figure 9–12. Curly-Coated Retriever. *A breed that is characterized by a curly coat. Photo © Tara Darling.*

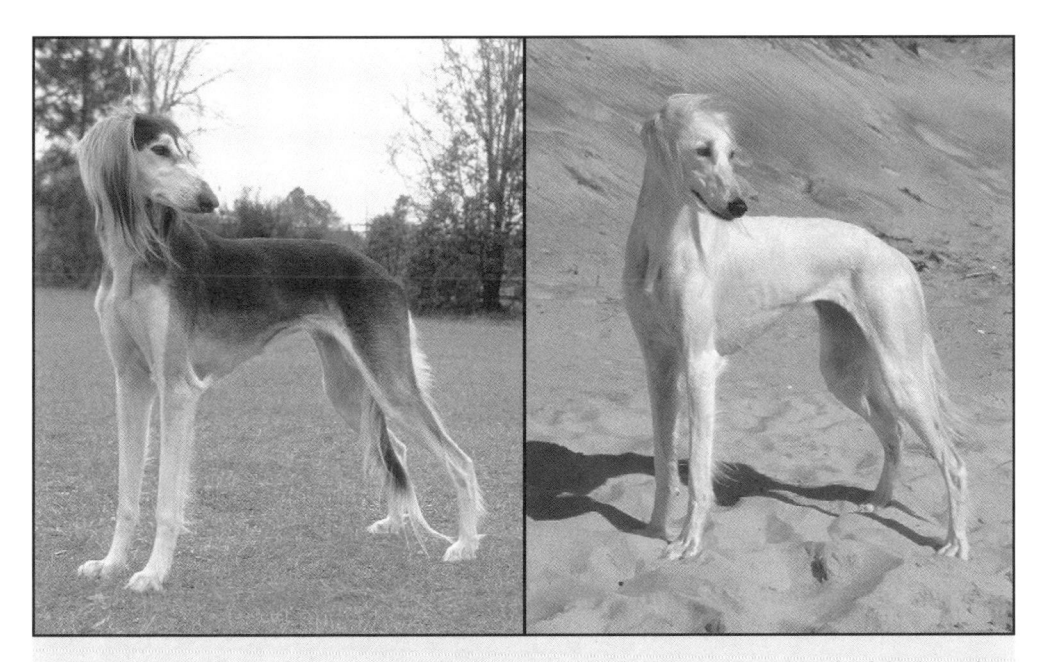

Figure 9–13. Saluki. *(a) Except for the feathering on the ears, tail, and back of the legs, the silky coat appears shorthaired. (b) The smooth variety has no feathering. Left photo © AKC, photo by Mary Bloom, and right photo © Tara Darling.*

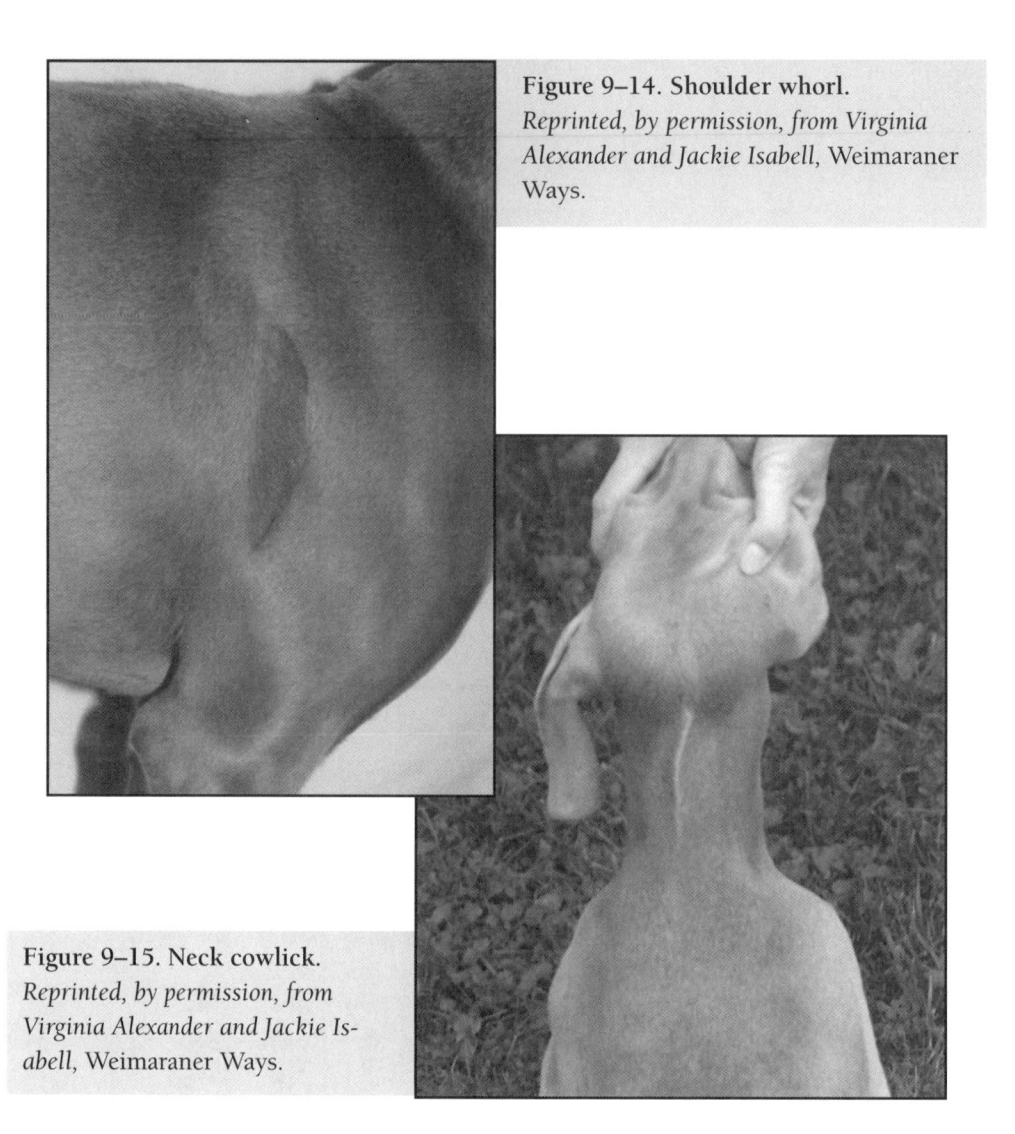

Figure 9–14. Shoulder whorl.
Reprinted, by permission, from Virginia Alexander and Jackie Isabell, Weimaraner Ways.

Figure 9–15. Neck cowlick.
Reprinted, by permission, from Virginia Alexander and Jackie Isabell, Weimaraner Ways.

WHORLS

Whorls or cowlicks are places in which the hair lies in a direction opposite to general hair direction. They range from circular or oval patches on the shoulder and flank to lines that run from the base of the skull to the withers. Pullig's study in Cocker Spaniels concluded that they are an autosomal recessive, though the location of the whorls varied.[10] Whorls have also been reported in Doberman Pinschers, Boxers, and Weimaraners.

RIPPLE COAT IN NEWBORNS

Whitney reported newborn puppies with long, regular ripples or stripes in their coats, which disappeared within a week, in Bloodhounds and Cocker Spaniels. Records of his Bloodhounds indicated that it is a recessive trait.[11]

Weimaraners are homozygous for the trait. There is considerable variation in the crispness of the ripple and the clarity of the stripes, which gradually fade in three to five days.

Figure 9–16. Ripple coat. *All newborn Weimaraners have ripple coats; they are homozygous for the simple genetic recessive trait, which occurs in many breeds. The zebralike stripes range from faint to crisp, but all disappear within three to five days. Reprinted, by permission, from Virginia Alexander and Jackie Isabell,* Weimaraner Ways.

Chapter 10
STRUCTURAL TRAITS

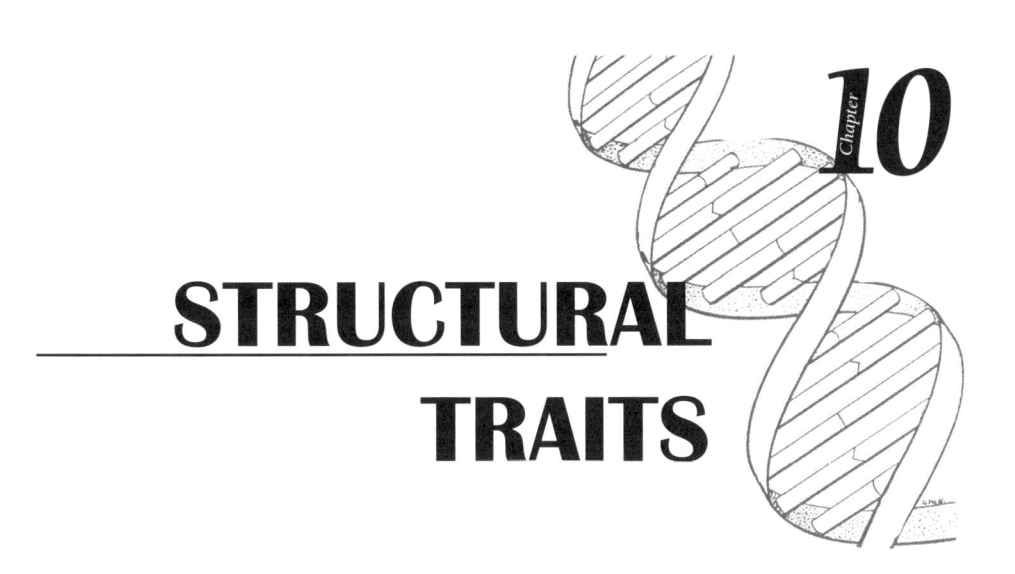

Data on the heredity of structural traits are, unfortunately, skimpy, and the brevity of this chapter reflects the scarcity of conclusive findings. As with coats, *clear* evidence of the mode of heredity is sparse. The primary difficulty is that most structural traits are polygenic, and clear-cut patterns of heredity cannot be identified. In addition, such traits are sensitive to environmental factors such as nutrition, exercise, and infectious disease.

THE HEAD

SKULL WIDTH

The skulls of dogs fall into three general types: (*a*) narrow skull base and great length (dolichocephalic)—Collie, Borzoi; (*b*) medium-wide skull base and length (mesoticephalic)—Pointer, Malamute; and (*c*) broad skull base and short length (brachycephalic)—Bulldog, Pekingese.

Whitney reported studies of crosses between breeds with different skull types that found the following:
- Greyhound with both the Bulldog and Pug produced long, narrow heads
- Dachshund with both French Bulldog and Boston Terrier produced intermediate-type heads
- English Bulldog with Basset Hound produced variable head types[1]

In his 1930 report, Marchlewski described the inheritance of several structural traits of Pointers and crosses with German Shorthaired Pointers. Within the breed, Pointers with fine, narrow skulls with little stop and snipy muzzles were dominant over skulls with the breed's characteristic broad skull with a deep muzzle and pronounced stop. The skulls of the German Shorthaired Pointers were broad and heavy, with less stop than the Pointers. When crossed with narrow-skulled Pointers, the

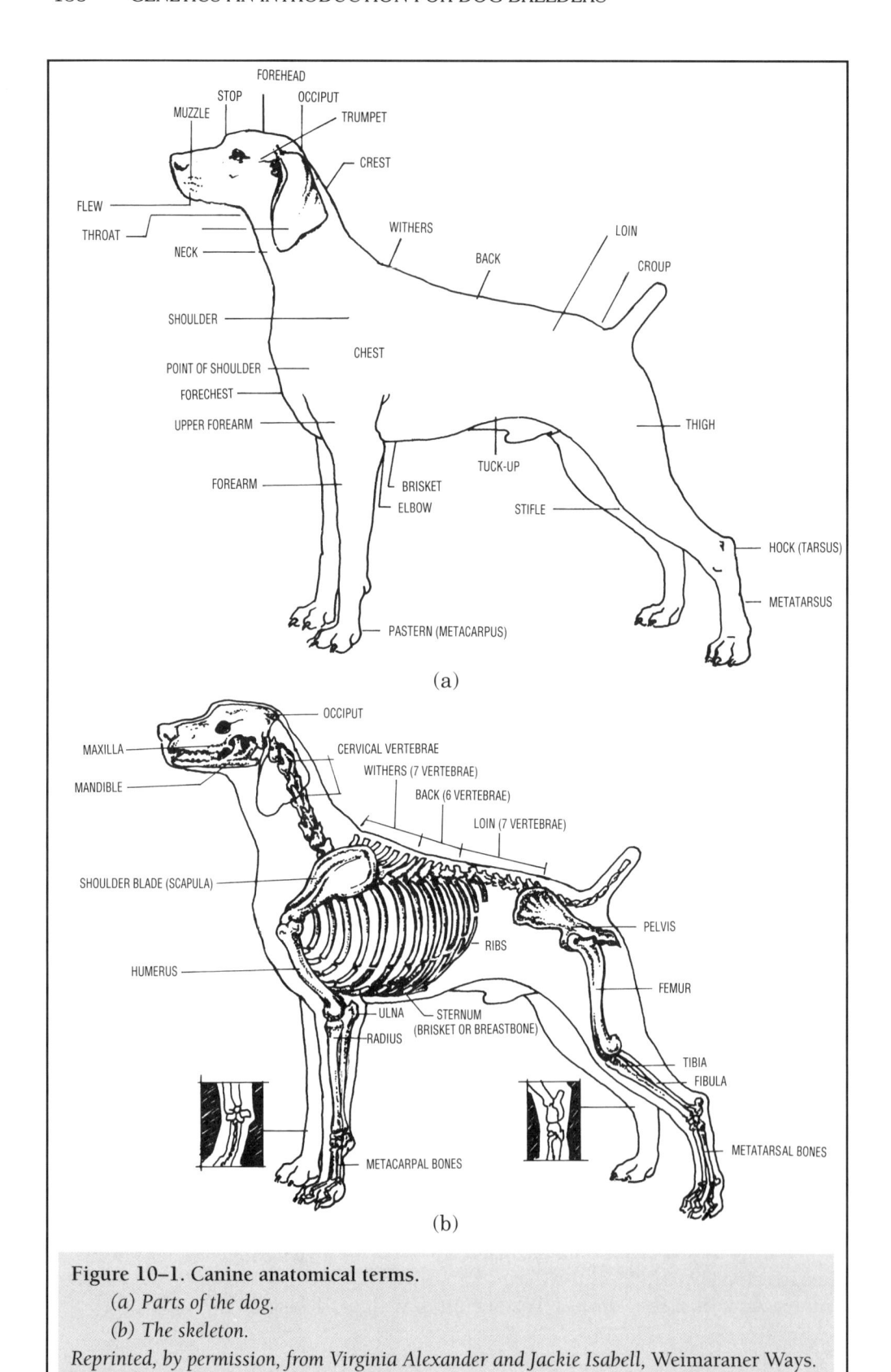

Figure 10–1. Canine anatomical terms.
   (a) Parts of the dog.
   (b) The skeleton.
Reprinted, by permission, from Virginia Alexander and Jackie Isabell, Weimaraner Ways.

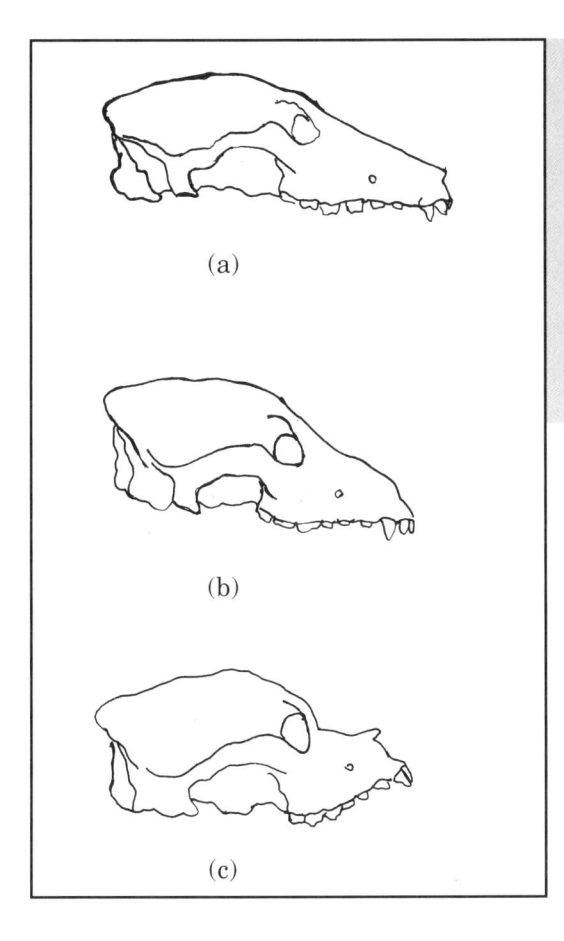

Figure 10–2. Basic skull types.
(a) Narrow skull base and great length (dolichocephalic)—Collie, Borzoi.
(b) Medium-wide skull base and length (mesoticephalic)—Pointer, Malamute.
(c) Broad skull base and short length (brachycephalic)—Bulldog, Pekingese.

narrow type was again dominant. Marchlewski concluded that the narrow-type skull behaved like a dominant, and that the genetic basis was relatively simple and showed clear-cut segregation. Willis observed a similar pattern of the narrow skull being dominant over the broader one in the descendants of a German Shepherd.[2]

EARS

As with skull width, some studies have been done of ears in crosses between breeds. The findings are almost as varied as the breeds crossed. Studies between breeds are complicated by the number of different traits related to ears: carriage, size, shape, thickness, placement on the skull, and so forth. All of these vary considerably within breeds.

In his study of ear carriage and size, Iljin suggested that three alleles determined the traits:

- H^a semierect (collies), completely dominant
- H lop ears (hounds), incompletely dominant
- h erect ears[3]

Other studies suggest that it is probably more complex.

Fox reported that in a study of coyote-Beagle hybrids, all of the F_1 generation had lop ears. Of the fourteen puppies in the F_2 generation, two had erect ears, four semierect, and eight lop ears.[4]

The ear of the German Shorthaired Pointer is larger and more rounded at the tip than the triangular ear of the Pointer. In his crosses of the breeds, Marchlewski observed that all of the offspring had the Pointer-type ear. From two accidental litters from Pointer bitches and an alsatian-type male, he reported that "small but hanging ears resulted showing some similarity to the type found in certain pastoral breeds and in the Mastiff."[5]

Whitney made many crosses between long-eared and short-eared breeds. He summed up the results: "The F_1s are never even halfway between the two extremes,

Figure 10–3. Ear types.
(a) Erect.
(b) Semierect (button).
(c) Lop or hanging.

and no F_2 pup has ever approximated the length of ear of the long-eared parent. Undoubtedly more than two factors are responsible."[6]

In his work with Border Collies, Kelley found that "both the dominant, semi-erect, and the prick-eared recessive occur." In crosses between collies homozygous for the semi-erect ear and prick-eared kelpies, the offspring generally have "ears at least less pricked than those of the kelpie parent. The progeny, when bred together, will leave some semi-erect- and some prick-eared pups."[7]

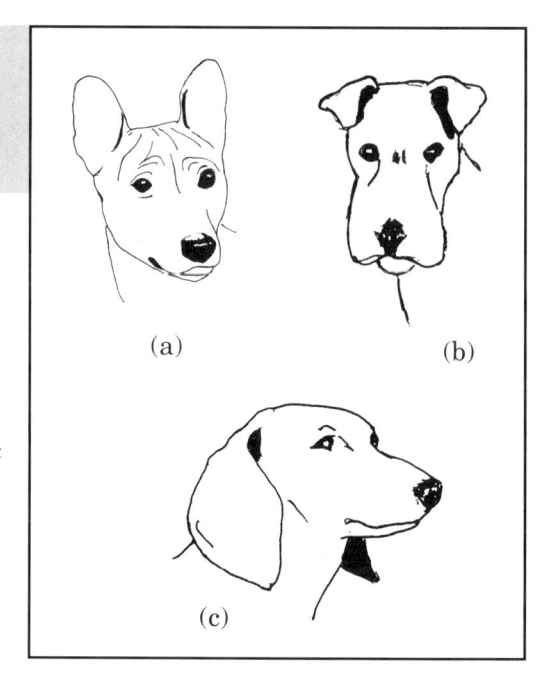

Willis observed that in German Shepherds, the erect ear is dominant or partially so over soft or dropped ears. There is a range in the age at which the ears become erect, and both ears do not always become erect at the same time.[8]

DENTITION

Many breed standards penalize incomplete dentition, but unfortunately, the heredity of missing teeth presents a confusing pattern.

One study of German Shepherds reported some interesting statistics. From matings of parents with complete dentition, 88 (44 percent) of 202 offspring had one or more missing teeth. From matings of parents with incomplete dentition, 17 (45 percent) of 38 had one or more missing teeth. Willis pointed out that "their data do not specify which teeth or the numbers per animal that were missing but almost certainly it would be premolars that were involved. The data are certainly not indicative of any simple mode of inheritance and do not conform to the view of Skrentny (1964) that missing teeth were an autosomal recessive in Dobermanns."[9]

Willis also commented that the difficulty of identifying the heredity of missing teeth is compounded by the fact that the apparently missing tooth is sometimes present below the gum rather than totally absent. In his opinion, fanaticism about faulting individuals for a trait with such a poorly understood inheritance may be dangerous in that their otherwise outstanding qualities may be discarded from a breeding program.[10]

Dogs with brachycephalic heads (Bulldogs, Boxers) frequently have imperfect dentition, and extra incisors have been reported. One study found that of 71 Bulldogs, 39.4 percent had one extra incisor. Other breeds had the following incidence: 26 percent of 140 Boxers; 8 percent of 36 Bullmastiffs; 4 percent of 101 Pugs; 1.3 percent of 74 Pekingese; and none of 23 Mastiffs.[11]

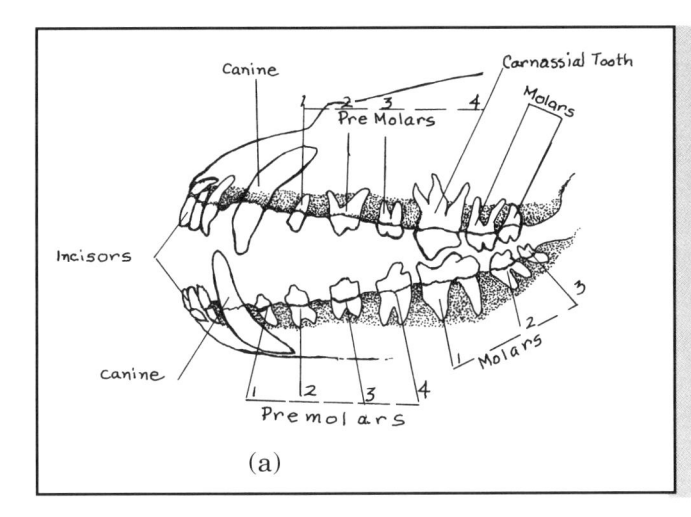

Figure 10–4. Dentition and bites.

(a) Complete dentition: each side of upper jaw—3 incisors, 1 canine, 3 premolars, 1 carnassial (4th premolar), and 2 molars; each side of lower jaw—3 incisors, 1 canine, 3 premolars, 1 carnassial, and 3 molars.

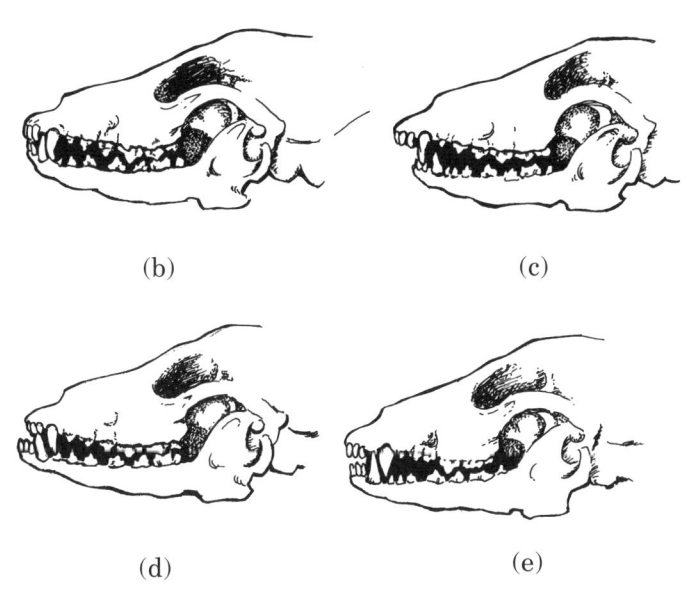

(b) Correct scissors bite.
(c) Overshot bite with upper incisors extending well beyond the lower ones. In very extreme cases, the upper canine can be in front of the lower one.
(d) An undershot bite with lower incisors extending beyond upper ones.
(e) A level or pincer bite.
(f) Wry mouth.

Reprinted, by permission, from Virginia Alexander and Jackie Isabell, Weimaraner Ways.

BITES

Abnormal bites range from very overshot to very undershot. Some breeds appear to have a higher incidence of bite faults than others. Within breeds, some strains or individuals do seem to produce more incorrect bites than the breed average.

Kelley suggested that an overshot bite in Border Collies might be produced by a recessive shortening of the lower jaw. Willis adds that "personal experiences in German Shepherds suggests that overshot bites in this breed are recessive. However this does not mean simple recessive inheritance nor does it imply a shortened lower jaw."[12]

Dogs with undershot bites usually have parents with scissors bites, suggesting that the trait is recessive. Nevertheless, when Whitney mated two Cocker Spaniels with undershot bites, all of the puppies had correct scissors bites.[13]

Upper and lower jaw structure appear to be independently inherited traits, and even the size of the incisors may play a role in the occlusion. The growth of the lower jaw may not parallel that of the rest of the head. The bite of one Weimaraner puppy kept his owner in a tizzy as it went back and forth from about one-quarter inch undershot to about one-quarter inch overshot before stabilizing into a scissors bite. The bite of his maternal grandsire went from scissors to slightly undershot at the age of two and one-half, after he finished his championship. The strangest that I've ever observed, however, was a male with abnormally short and vertical upper incisors that did not meet the lower incisors. Had the upper incisors been normal in length and at a forward angle, he would have had a scissors bite.

FLEWS AND NECKS

There appears to be some correlation between excessive *flews* (upper lips) and excessive neck skin. In general, *dewlaps*—loose, pendulous skin on the chin, throat, and neck—appear to be dominant over clean, tight-skinned necks. Marchlewski reported that in crosses between clean-necked English Pointers and German pointers with dewlaps, "the so called dewlap was present in every specimen of the F_1 generation."[14]

THE BODY

BODY TYPE

Marchlewski found that the inheritance of general body type paralleled that of skull type in Pointers. That is, the dogs with fine, narrow skulls had proportionally finer bone and substance than dogs with the broad skulls.[15]

In general, the German pointers had greater overall bone and substance than the English breed, "the chest rather wide than deep" and "the lumbar region rather long." Crosses between the English and German pointers produced offspring that resembled the English parent, *except* for the chest, which was intermediate between the two breeds.[16]

Within the German breed, Marchlewski mated two unusually lightly built individuals. Of their five puppies, two had the more typical heavy build.[17]

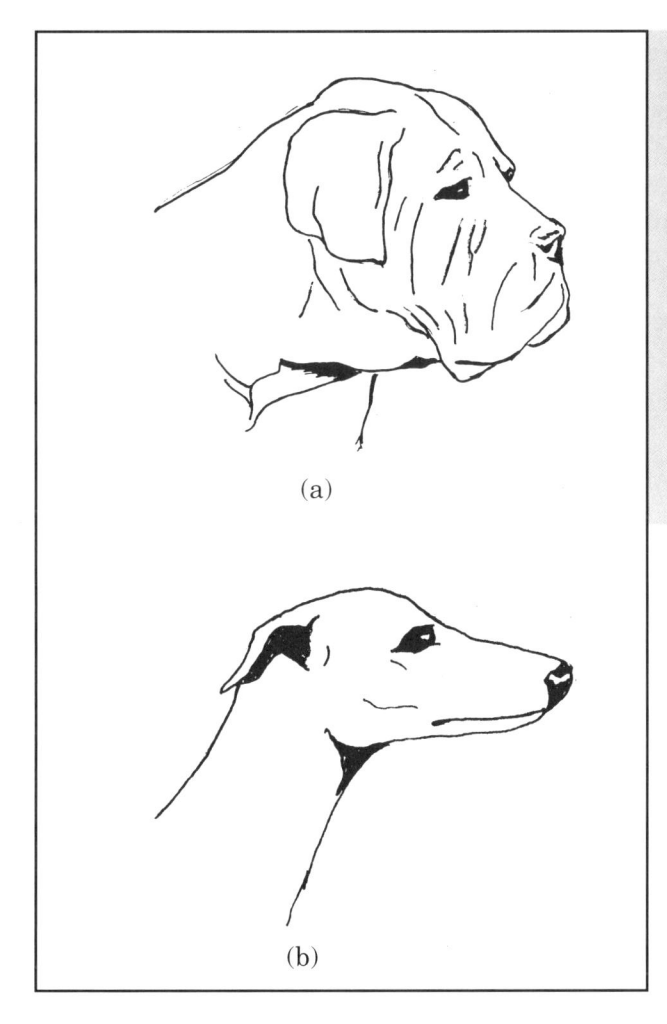

Figure 10–5. Neck and flew types. *Although extremes of neck and flew type are typical of some breeds, a wide range of type occurs within each breed. (a) Breeds like the Mastiff, with generous neck skin ("wet"), usually have pendulous flews as well. (b) Breeds like the Whippet, with a clean, tight-skinned ("dry") neck, usually have clean, tight flews as well.*

SIZE

Height

Overall size is a polygenic trait, and within a breed, size tends to drift toward the breed average. Tall plus tall does not produce taller puppies, and the offspring of two tall dogs may not be as tall as the parents. The best guide is to breed any animal that deviates from the desired height to one that is in the middle of the standard. Consistent selection for the breed's desired height eventually stabilizes the breed. Conversely, consistent selection for extremes can eventually alter the breed average; this can happen when judges show a strong preference for very tall or very short dogs for a prolonged period.

Every puppy's maximum size and general skeletal structure is set from the moment of conception. Few elements of structure, however, are more sensitive to the influence of nutrition, an environmental factor.

Leg length

In general, matings of between short-legged breeds and those with normal length legs consistently produced dogs with legs of intermediate length. One study reported short, intermediate, and normal length in the following generation, but another reported a greater range of length but no clear-cut differences.[18]

Whitney reported his observations of leg length in Bloodhounds. His cross of a short-legged bitch and a long-legged male produced four short- and five long-legged puppies. He then bred a short-legged bitch from that litter to four different long-legged studs; nineteen of her thirty-six puppies had short legs. A litter of eight from two short-legged parents, however, produced four short- and four long-legged puppies. Whitney concluded that, in general, short legs are dominant.[19] However, leg length does not consistently follow any clear dominant-recessive pattern.

Dwarfism

Achondroplasia (also called *chondrodystrophy*) is a hereditary dwarfism that appears to be a fairly common mutation in several species as well as in many breeds. It is typically a Mendelian dominant that is characterized by reduced growth of the long bones and abnormalities of other bones. The degree of abnormality ranges from very mild to gross defects but always produces some microscopic abnormalities of bony tissue. Whittick classifies the following breeds as achondroplastic:[20]

American Cocker Spaniel	Dachshund
Basset Hound	English Bulldog
Beagle	King Charles Spaniel
Boston Terrier	Pekingese
Boxer	Pug
Bullmastiff	

Clearly, the expression of achondroplasia is highly variable and can be modified by selective breeding. The real surprise is that some breeds have proportionally normal leg length, which Whittick calls "normal abnormals." He stresses, however, that they are all predisposed to some disorders related to the achondroplasia.[21]

Achondroplastic dwarfism has been reported in Alaskan Malamutes, Poodles, English Pointers, Samoyeds, and Weimaraners. In these breeds, the disorder is not "normal" and is often associated with other abnormalities.

Although the trait for abnormal dwarfism appears to follow a consistent Mendelian pattern within a breed, crosses between the achondroplastic breeds and those considered normal are inconsistent. Leg length is usually intermediate in the first generation, and ranges between short, medium, and long in the next. This is the pattern observed in Basset x Bloodhound, Dachshund x Fox Terrier, and Dachshund x Boston Terrier crosses.[22]

As with so many things in genetics, things that initially appear simple are far more complex when studied further.

DEWCLAWS

All breeds have *dewclaws* (vestigial toes not reaching the ground) on the front legs. In most breeds, rear dewclaws appear more or less regularly, though a few breeds—such as Poodles, Pekingese, and Weimaraners—never have rear dewclaws. In the Great Pyrenees, double rear dewclaws, which are not removed, are a prized

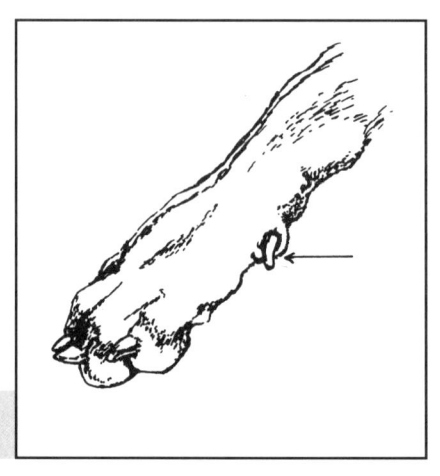

Figure 10–6. Dewclaw.

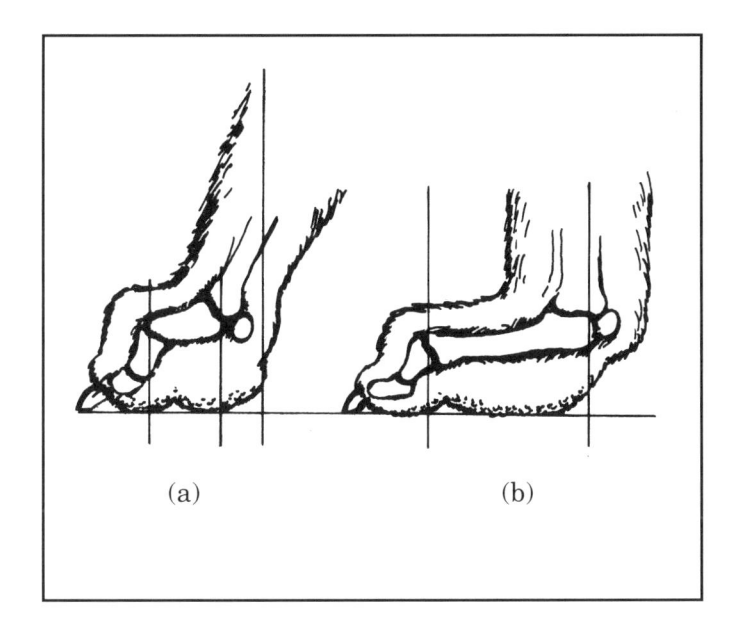

Figure 10–7. Feet.
(a) Cat.
(b) Hare.
Reprinted, by permission, from Virginia Alexander and Jackie Isabell, Weimaraner Ways.

breed trait. Double rear dewclaws have also been reported occasionally in Newfoundlands and Saint Bernards.[23]

In most studies, the presence of single dewclaws on the rear legs is dominant to lack of them. However, Kelley reported that in Border Collies dewclaw presence appears to be recessive. In a study of coyote-Beagle hybrids, in which none of the coyotes had rear dewclaws but four of the eight Beagles did, none of the F_1 generation had rear dewclaws. Of the fourteen puppies in the F_2 generation, only two had them.[24]

TAILS

About tails, Whitney comments: "If we inquire into the mode of inheritance of tail characteristics within any single breed, we seem to arrive nowhere so far as any definite Mendelian mode of inheritance is concerned."[25]

Popular Brittany lore holds that the short tail is lethal when homozygous, but there is no supportive evidence. Some Old English Sheepdogs are born with tail stubs, but most have natural tails. Cocker Spaniels carry hereditary factors for no tail (anury) and for short tail (brachyury).

In a study of coyote-Beagle hybrids, all of the F_1 generation had the bushy coyote tail. Of the fourteen puppies in the F_2 generation, twelve had bushy tails.[26]

Variable tail length occurs in German Shepherds.[27] Weimaraner breeders have observed variable tail lengths in puppies, which is the reason that removing a specific fraction of the tail when docking is an unreliable way to obtain the desired six-inch length at maturity; the best way to obtain the desired six-inch tail is to measure each one from the base of the tail to the end of the perineal area.

Figure 10–8. Tail length. *With some breeds, tails vary in the number of vertebrae, and each tail must be individually measured to determine the correct amount to remove.*

(a) Note the abrupt narrowing (typical of Weimaraners) of the tail on the right.

(b) Kinked tails are not uncommon.

(c) The amount docked varied in this litter, but the length remaining on the puppies was uniform.

Reprinted, by permission, from Virginia Alexander and Jackie Isabell, Weimaraner Ways.

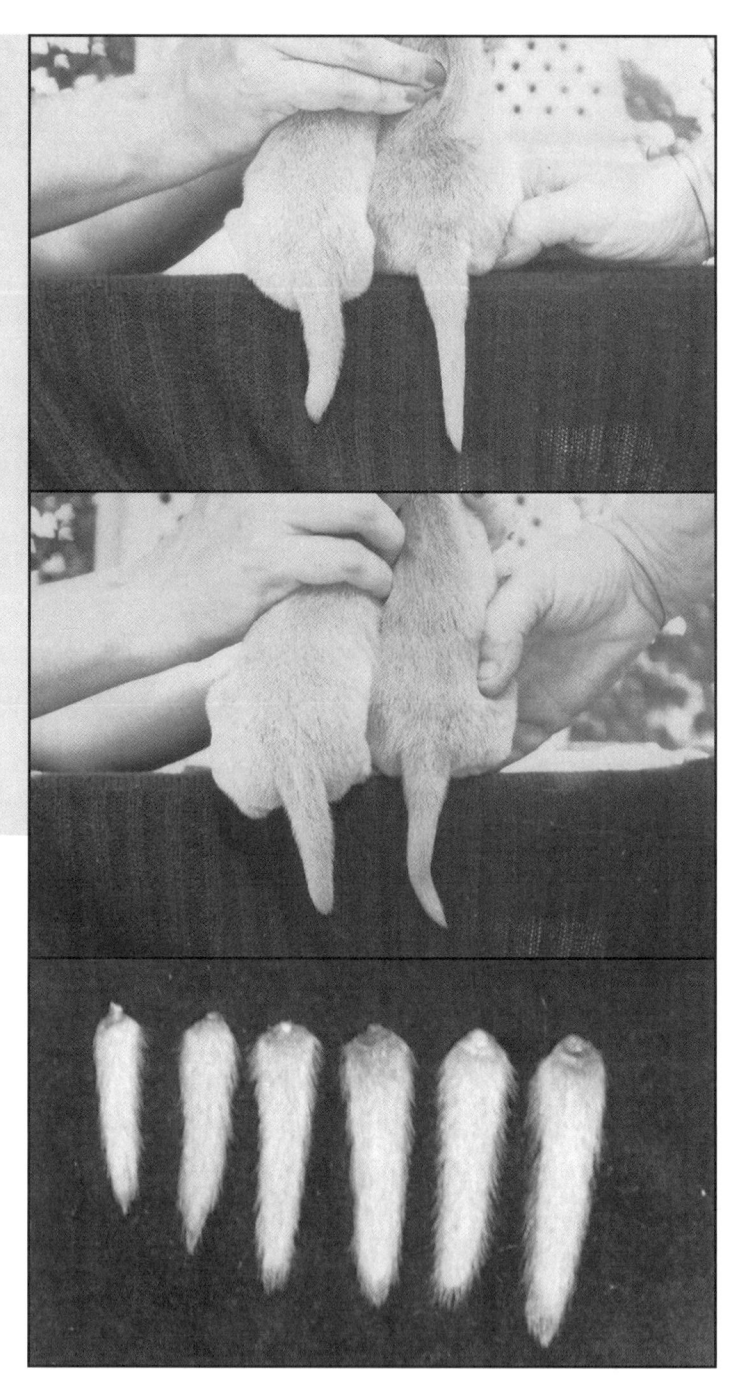

Chapter 11

CONTROL OF GENETIC DISORDERS

The control of genetic disorders begins with discovering the answers to four questions:
- Has the hereditary basis been confirmed?
- What is the incidence?
- What is the mode of inheritance?
- How can recessive carriers be identified?

VERIFYING A GENETIC BASIS

The diagnosis of many hereditary disorders can be complicated by nonhereditary problems that produce the same clinical presentation. The nonhereditary problems are known as *phenocopies*—that is, having a phenotype that resembles a genetic trait but is produced by environmental damage to the developing embryo or growing youngster. Differentiating between problems that are hereditary and those that are not is crucial to breeding plans. If hereditary, the question of whether or not to cull the parents and siblings must be considered; if a phenocopy, the environmental source must be identified and corrected if possible.

The term *teratology* stems from the Greek word *teras*, meaning monster of marvel, so it literally means the study of monstrosities. In modern usage, however, teratology is the study of congenital malformations and marked deviations from normal.

A *teratogen* is any substance, agent, or process that interferes with normal prenatal development. This broad term includes hereditary disorders and chromosomal anomalies. It also includes purely mechanical factors that interfere with normal development such as the restriction of fetal movement, which can be caused by uterine crowding or insufficient amniotic fluid, leading to the deformity of a limb.

One of the important concerns of teratology is the study of *teratogenic agents*, such as drugs, chemicals, and infections. Embryonic tissue is particularly vulnerable to teratogenic agents. (The embryonic period begins with the fertilized egg's first division; the fetal period begins when the basic structural features can be recognized.) The specific defect is determined by the point of embryonic development at which exposure occurs. Exposure when the tissues of the nervous system are differentiating into the brain, spinal cord, and nerves leads to abnormalities of that system. The dosage that produces defects has a relatively narrow range: a lower dosage causes no effect, and a higher one usually causes death (a 5 percent embryonic death with resorption is considered normal in canines, but little is known about specific causes).[1]

The table listing teratogenic agents (Table 11-1) includes an amazing number of common, everyday items that few breeders would view with appropriate alarm when their pregnant bitch is exposed to them. Who would guess that dehydration could cause cleft palates or that the antibiotic Acromycin could cause cryptorchidism? And what about those vitamins and minerals? The addition of such things as calcium, vitamins, eggs, and liver was once the only way to supplement the regular dog kibble during pregnancy, and breeders had to guess at the quantities. This contributed to the reasoning that if a little is good, more is better. Now, commercial preparations for the pregnant and lactating bitch are specially formulated to provide all caloric and nutritional needs. Many people cannot resist adding to even these, and a little liver or a few hard-boiled eggs are probably safe enough. However, *overdoses of vitamins and minerals during pregnancy are known to cause some congenital abnormalities*. Excess nutrients can produce defects of the aortic arch (calcium), cleft palate (vitamins A, D, or E), heart (vitamin D), or skeleton (vitamin D).

The key to preventing teratogenic disorders is careful prenatal care, which includes the following:
- Do not add vitamin and mineral supplements to any ration (except on veterinary prescription)
- Defer using pesticides or herbicides (some are absorbed directly through the skin or feet)
- Give antibiotics and other medications only when absolutely necessary, and whenever possible, use those rated as safe with pregnancy

Although the first clue that an abnormality has a genetic basis is the identification of a pattern among relatives, such patterns can be deceptive. A *familial trait* is one for which the incidence among relatives of affected individuals is higher than the general population because of (*a*) shared genes, (*b*) shared environment, or (*c*) combination of genes and environment. Relatives are often exposed to the same environment, and the familial pattern may reflect common environmental factors—climate, diet, stress, vaccinations, toxic plants and chemicals, and so forth. In 1910, the U.S. Public Health Commission came to the conclusion that pellagra (a disease caused by a deficiency of vitamin B_2) was hereditary because it exhibited a familial pattern.[2]

The first step, then, is to confirm that the disorder does indeed have a genetic basis, which is not always an easy task. Schneider recommends the following strategy for veterinarians:

> Clients should be asked for a careful history of treatments, illness, or unusual happenings during gestation, since causes may not be readily apparent. A breeding history of both sire and dam for three generations should also be obtained to determine the incidence of previous developmental defects. . . .

> Even with all the scientific data at one's disposal, the etiology may be difficult to determine, requiring a judgmental decision to be rendered.[3]

If congenital defects do occur, the knowledge that some can be caused by teratogenic agents as well as abnormalities of embryonic development helps the breeder sort out the possible reasons. Do some research and weigh the evidence before jumping to conclusions and blaming the parents or related bloodlines. On the other hand, don't go overboard and blame all congenital abnormalities on environmental causes. In every case, careful consideration of all possibilities is imperative.

On the bright side, eliminating genetic disorders by selective breeding is a difficult, long-term task, whereas eliminating disorders caused by teratogenic agents may be as simple as increasing or decreasing a vitamin. With confidence that the problem has a genetic basis, the breeder must turn to the more difficult task of learning more about it.

INCIDENCE

The actual incidence of a disorder within a breed's gene pool is very difficult to discover. For most disorders, the best a breeder can usually do is to discover whether it has occurred within his or her breed. Nevertheless, there are some resources that help with estimating the prevalence.

LISTS AND LIMITATIONS

Lists of the hereditary disorders that have been identified in each breed can be found in many veterinary textbooks and even in booklet form for dog fanciers; one is included in Appendix B. So many people regard such lists as the "gospel truth" that some limitations must be pointed out.

- The purpose of such lists is to document that a disorder has occurred in a specific breed; they give no clues to the incidence.
- The key phrase that is usually overlooked is *"thought to be genetic,"* which allows considerable latitude for an author's personal opinion. One booklet, the *Canine Consumer Report*, included things such as conjunctivitis, cystic ovaries, eclampsia, and sebaceous cysts, which really stretches credibility.[4]
- The best lists are compiled from veterinary literature. This means that someone must write an article mentioning the disorder, the breed, and the possibility that it is hereditary before it can be listed.
- Any disorder has only to be reported once for it to be included under the breed, and once on "the list," it's there forever.

Two examples from my own breed may illustrate the point. Distichiasis (an eyelash disorder) has been prevalent in Weimaraners for decades—everyone knew about it—but distichiasis was not listed under the breed until the early 1990s. Every list I've seen includes hemophilia as a breed problem. After almost thirty years of breeding and many years of trying to find someone who had even heard a rumor of a Weimaraner with hemophilia, I could not find one. I finally discovered a 1967 article that reported one litter in which the puppies from an accidental brother-sister mating died of a bleeding disorder, the mother died of metritis, and the father disappeared.[5] I haven't worried about hemophilia since then.

Table 11-1. Teratogenic Agents

Agent	Suspected Teratogenic Effects
NUTRIENTS	
Asparaginase (Pro-Zyme, K-Zyme)	Skeletal, brain, lung, kidney defects
Calcium Excess	Aortic arch defects
Niacin Deficiency	Fetal death
Riboflavin Deficiency	Cleft palate; short mandibles; skeletal defects; extra toes
Thiamin Deficiency	Fetal death
Vitamin A Excess	Skeletal, neural tube defects; cleft palate; no eyes; microcephaly
Vitamin A Deficiency	Cleft palate; diaphragmatic hernias; heart defects; hydrocephaly; fetal death
Vitamin C Deficiency	Fetal death; premature birth
Vitamin D Excess	Cleft palate; heart, skeletal, dental defects; mental retardation; increased fetal/neonatal death
Vitamin E Deficiency	Hydrocephaly
Vitamin E Excess	Cleft palate; growth retardation
Zinc Deficiency	Cleft palate; hydrocephaly; defects of skeleton, eyes, heart, lung, nervous system
ANTIBIOTICS	
Acromycin	Cryptorchidism
Antimycin A	Cardiac anomalies
Chloramphenicol (Chloromycetin)	Neural tube, diaphragm defects; cleft palate; defects; cryptorchidism
Chlorotetracycline (Aureomycin)	Skeletal defects; hypertension in offspring
Oxytetracycline (Terramycin)	Brownish discoloration of teeth; cryptorchidism
Penicillin	Rapid neonatal growth; no defects
Streptomycin	Hearing loss
Tetracycline	Stunting; skeletal anomalies; cleft palate; cataract
OTHER DRUGS	
Aspirin & Other Salicylates	Hydrocephaly; palate, facial clefts; eye, rib, vertebral defects; stillbirths; low birth weight
Corticosteroids	Cleft palate, lip; intrauterine death; umbilical hernias; decreased immunoglobulins
Dilantin	Cleft palate, lip; cardiac, digital anomalies
Phenothiazines	Neonatal respiratory distress; increased neonatal mortality
Phenylbutazone (Butazoladin)	Possible embryotoxicity
Sulfonamides	Skeletal, dental defects

Table 11-1. Teratogenic Agents (Continued)

Agent	Suspected Teratogenic Effects
ANTHELMINTICS (WORMING PREPARATIONS)	
Dichlorvos (Task)	Multiple abnormalities
Diethylcarbamazine (Caricide)	No established teratogenic effects (some suspected)
Telmintic	Embryotoxic, teratogenic effects
Piperazines	Safety not established
Nemex	No known teratogenic effects
Vercom Paste	Increased abortion; fetal abnormalities
Vermiplex	Cleft palate; growth retardation
PESTICIDES	
Captan	Crooked tails; hydrocephaly; open fontanelles
Carbaryl (Sevin)	Multiple skeletal, internal organ abnormalities; extra toes
Cyclodiene (Aldrin, Dieldrin)	Multiple defects; webbed feet; cleft palate
Diazinon	Enlarged fontanelles; missing teeth
Dichlorvos (flea collars, wormers)	Multiple abnormalities
Fenthion	Decreased birth weight
Mirex	Decreased litter size
Rotenone	Neural tube defects; growth inhibition
Warfarin	Skeletal anomalies; blindness; fetal death
MISCELLANEOUS	
Dehydration	Cleft palate (up to 28 percent of litter)
Hyperthermia (fever)	Central nervous system, skeletal, eye defects; microcephaly; mental retardation
Insufficient Oxygen	Structural, functional abnormalities
Parvoviruses	Locomotor incoordination; hydrocephaly; dwarfism; mental retardation; behavioral abnormalities; skeletal, dental defects
Pine Needles (ingestion)	Decreased birth weight; fetal death; abortion
Potato Blight	Neural tube defects
Vaccines	All modified-live viral vaccines potentially teratogenic

Source: Virginia Alexander and Jackie Isabell, *Weimaraner Ways*.

REGISTRIES

Registries for hereditary disorders monitor the frequency that a disorder occurs in a breed. Dogs that are found to be free of the disorder at the time of examination are given certification, which enables breeders to select individuals that show no indication of the disorder. (See Chapter 13 for additional information about these disorders.)

E. A. Corley, long-time director of the Orthopedic Foundation for Animals (OFA), pointed out one important limitation of registries: "OFA breed data represent information obtained from a select subset of the general canine population, and interpretation of the data is limited to this select population. This population primarily represents dogs used in breeding programs or potential breeding dogs."[6] Although there is no way of knowing the true incidence, such registries are a giant step forward.

Eye Disorders

A group of breeders organized the Canine Eye Registration Foundation (CERF) in 1974, and in 1988, it moved to the Veterinary Medical Data Base at Purdue University.

CERF maintains a registry of purebred dogs that have been examined by members of the American College of Veterinary Ophthalmologists (AVCO) for eye disorders proven *or suspected* to be hereditary in dogs. Owners register their dogs by sending CERF a copy of the examination form. Because of the variable age of onset of most disorders, CERF registration is good for only one year. Information from the computer-scannable CERF examination form becomes part of the growing volume of information about hereditary eye disorders. This is a tremendous aid to research as well as in tracking the incidence and trends in each breed. To spread the word and educate dog fanciers, CERF publishes a newsletter, books, and reports.

The AKC includes CERF certification information on litter registrations, on individual registration certificates, and on certified pedigrees. The letters CERF are followed by the dog's age in months. Because CERF certification is valid for only one year, *the AKC automatically deletes this information at the end of the following calendar year.*

Canine Hip Dysplasia

The oldest and best-known registry is for canine hip dysplasia. The Orthopedic Foundation for Animals (OFA) was founded in 1966 and evolved from a dysplasia-control program organized in 1960 by the Golden Retriever Club of America. Although OFA's objective is control and elimination of all orthopedic disorders in animals, it is best known for hip dysplasia, which has been identified in over one hundred breeds.

The OFA offered dog breeders a national registry and a way to rid dogdom of this hereditary scourge through evaluation of the *phenotype* of the hips by panels of three veterinary radiologists. From 1966 to 1973, the OFA examined and certified hip X-rays of dogs over twelve months old and classified them as normal, near normal, or dysplastic; in 1974, the age of examination and certification was raised to twenty-four months, and classifications changed to excellent, good, fair, borderline, mild dysplasia, moderate dysplasia, or severe dysplasia.

Initially, the OFA was a closed registry, and information on the certified dogs was released only with signed permission from the owner. Later, the information was released to national breed clubs for publication. The AKC includes OFA certification information on litter registrations, on individual registration certificates, and on certified pedigrees. The letters OFA are followed by the dog's age in months and a letter indicating the rating: E (excellent), G (good), or F (fair).

Elbow Dysplasia

The OFA offers a registry for elbow dysplasia, which has been identified in 47 of the 108 breeds evaluated.[7] The AKC also includes elbow certification information on litter registrations, on individual registration certificates, and on certified pedigrees.

The letters OFEL are followed by the dog's age in months, and there are no classifications.

Patellar Luxation

The Patellar Luxation Registry is also maintained by the OFA. The objectives of the registry are to identify those dogs that are phenotypically normal prior to use in a breeding program and to gather data on the genetic disease. The dogs must be twelve months or older when x-rayed, though preliminary evaluation is available. There are four grades of patellar luxation: Grade 1, intermittent luxation; Grade 2, frequent luxation; Grade 3, permanent luxation; and Grade 4, more severe permanent luxation.[8]

Hypothyroidism

In 1996, the OFA expanded its registries to include the non-orthopedic problems of thyroid and congenital heart disease. The objectives of the Canine Thyroid Registry are to identify those dogs that are phenotypically normal and to gather data on the genetic disease autoimmune thyroiditis. Annual testing is recommended until the age of four and then every other year. The registry classifications are (*a*) normal, (*b*) positive advanced autoimmune thyroiditis, (*c*) positive compensating autoimmune thyroiditis, and (*d*) positive idiopathic hypothyroidism.[9]

Congenital Heart Disease

The objectives of the Congenital Heart Disease Registry are "to gather data regarding congenital heart diseases in dogs and to identify dogs which are phenotypically normal prior to use in a breeding program. For the purposes of the registry, a *phenotypically normal* dog is currently defined as: 1) one without a cardiac murmur, or as 2) one with an innocent heart murmur that is found to be otherwise normal by virtue of an echocardiographic examination which includes Doppler studies." (An *innocent murmur*—also called physiologic or functional murmur—is most common in young, growing animals.) Dogs are not certified until at least a year old, though a preliminary certification can be obtained earlier.[10]

DNA Registry

The OFA also serves as the central repository of the DNA Based Genetic Registry. To enter a dog, the owner submits a copy of the DNA analysis by a recognized laboratory. Because the information on affected (homozygous) individuals is so important, there is no fee to register them. As the number of disorders that can be identified through DNA testing grows, this will become progressively more valuable to breeders.

OTHER RESOURCES

Once a breeder has identified the problems to be concerned about in his or her breed, a variety of additional sources of information is available. Information about the most prevalent disorders is frequently updated in all-breed publications, about breed-specific problems in breed publications, and about all of them in veterinary literature.

The newest source of information is the world wide web. One can browse for hours, and the number of sites for genetic disorders in dogs is rapidly growing. The only caution is that the quality, experience, and legitimacy of the source should be verified. Anyone can create a web site, and there an appalling amount of incorrect information about genetics on the web. The author, his or her credentials, and the sources of information should be clearly identified. Information that is contributed by reputable sources such as the AKC, universities, and most parent breed clubs is the most reliable.

MODE OF INHERITANCE

K. C. Barnett states: "The control and, or, eradication of inherited . . . disease in any species depends on two facts—the ability to diagnose the disease in question and a knowledge of its mode of inheritance."[11] Of the two, the mode of inheritance is far more elusive. The next time you look at one of those lists of hereditary disorders, notice how few include the mode of inheritance. In the veterinary literature reviewed for this book, a disturbing number of reports began with the presumption that the disorder was hereditary because it occurred in a small number (often less than ten) of related dogs. Only one study examined *both* genetic and environmental agents as potential causes and, rather ironically, it was one of the very few that later identified a definite hereditary mode.[12]

It is very difficult to develop an effective control program until it is known how a disorder is inherited. The expression of single-gene traits may be complicated by sex-linkage, codominance, variable penetrance, and variable expressivity. Autosomal dominants are the most responsive to selective measures, and mass screening could eliminate these disorders quickly. Unfortunately, most of the harmful autosomal genes are recessive, and control measures are only moderately effective unless there is a way to identify the heterozygous carriers. Whenever it *is* possible to identify the carriers, the recessive disorders are as responsive to selective breeding as dominant traits.

It is reasonable to assume that the gene that produces a hereditary disorder in one breed is the same gene that produces it in other breeds. After all, hemophilia is a sex-linked recessive in all of the species in which it has been identified.

The problem is that an identical phenotypic expression does not always indicate an identical mutation, and the mode of inheritance may differ with each. One clue is slight variations in the clinical presentation such as the age of onset. A good illustration of the difficulties involved may be seen with a form of early onset diabetes that has been linked with mutation of the gene that produces galactokinase, an enzyme related to glucose metabolism. This was first identified on human chromosome 7. A study of fifteen other families revealed fifteen *different* mutations of the same gene, making it an excellent example of a *mutable gene* (one that has a significant rate of spontaneous mutation). The next discovery was "evidence that a gene on chromosome number 20 is also associated with" the same form of diabetes.[13]

Further complicating identification is that some disorders that appear later in life may be acquired, rather than genetic. The ones encountered most often by breeders are the eyelid disorders (entropion, ectropion, distichiasis, and trichiasis) as well as some cardiac diseases, diaphragmatic hernia, and epilepsy. The best way to differentiate between acquired and genetic problems is to document that a disorder that can normally be identified at a specific age was not present at that time. If a puppy that had no heart murmur at six weeks develops one at the age of two years, it is probably an acquired problem. Similarly, a puppy that has two descended testicles when placed on a plane but has only one upon arrival is probably not a genetic cryptorchid. (The testicles are often retracted under stress and, if entangled with the spermatic cord, the retracted testicle will not descend again.)

SCREENING METHODS

The key to any control program is dependent on an effective method of identifying carriers of the defective gene and screening their offspring at a fairly early age. The ideal screening method identifies heterozygous as well as homozygous carriers.

DNA AND BIOCHEMICAL TESTS

Since the discovery of DNA, breeders have looked forward to the day when the genes for hereditary disorders could be identified. That day was heralded by the development of a test for copper toxicosis in Bedlington Terriers, using linkage with DNA markers.

VetGen, a molecular genetics company, specializes in the detection of canine genetic disorders as well as DNA profiling. By March 2002, VetGen offered direct DNA testing for the following disorders: *progressive retinal atrophy* (Irish Setter); *phosphofructokinase deficiency* (American Cocker Spaniel, Basenji, English Springer Spaniel); and *vonWillebrand's disease* (Bernese Mountain Dog, Doberman Pinscher, Manchester Terrier, Pembroke Welsh Corgi, all varieties of Poodle, Shetland Sheepdog, Scottish Terrier). DNA linkage testing was available for *copper toxicosis* (Bedlington Terrier); and *renal dysplasia* (Lhasa Apso, Shih Tzu, Wheaten Terrier). One of the best features of the tests is the simplicity of obtaining the DNA specimen, using a soft, nylon cheek brush to swab between the dog's cheek and gum. The report indicates whether the dog is clear of the specific disorder (no genes), a carrier (one gene), or affected (two genes) and gives a registration number and a card to apply for registration in the OFA's DNA Based Genetic Registry. In addition, there is information to assist with interpreting the test results and breeding strategies.

Biochemical tests are closely related to DNA tests. The heterozygotes of some single-gene disorders produce both normal and abnormal gene products that can be identified through biochemical screening, which is a variant of clinical screening. Examples of biochemical screening already being used with dogs are the tests for bleeding disorders—hemophilia A, hemophilia B, factor X deficiency, and von Willebrand's disease.

PHENOTYPE EVALUATION

Phenotype evaluation (also called clinical evaluation) is based on identifiable phenotypic traits. All of the registries—except the DNA registry, of course—are based on phenotype evaluation and certification of individuals that exhibit a normal phenotype. With widespread cooperation among breeders who use only dogs with a normal phenotype, it has been possible to significantly reduce the incidence of some disorders. The method is least effective with recessive traits in which the heterozygous carriers cannot be identified. One drawback is that most phenotypic evaluations cannot be done at an early age.

The methods of phenotype evaluation vary, ranging from X-rays for hip dysplasia to blood tests for hypothyroidism, electroretinography for progressive retinal atrophy, echocardiography for heart disease, and neurological reflexes for spinal dysraphia.

TEST BREEDING

With recessive traits, test breeding may be the only way to identify the carriers. The individual being tested is mated with a known producer of the recessive trait. If any progeny have the disorder, the one being tested is a carrier. Geneticists have calculated the probabilities: There is a 99 percent probability that the dog being tested is free of the trait if a minimum of six normal puppies occur with homozygous producer or a minimum of seventeen normal puppies with a heterozygous producer.[14] It is not, however, infallible, and several matings should be done. Remember, the occasional all-boy or all-girl litters do not indicate the lack of ability to produce both.

Test breeding is such a slow and costly process that many breeders only test promising stud dogs. Bitches for testing are usually difficult to locate, so if the breed has a control program to eliminate a particular problem, check with the national club before spaying a bitch that is a known producer of the trait.

Because one parent is a known producer of the trait, this means that *every puppy* produced by such a test mating is a potential carrier and should never be bred. In many cases, the puppies are suitable as pets, and being able to obtain limited AKC registration for such puppies has been a great help to breeders who utilize test breeding.

Chapter 12

CONGENITAL DISORDERS

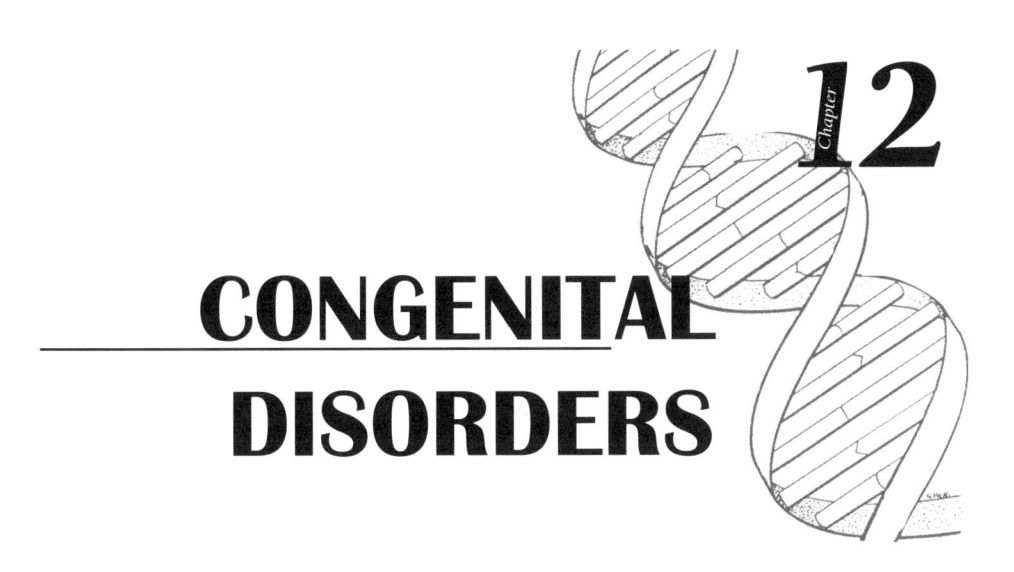

Congenital is defined as any character or trait that can be identified at birth *or* that is related to the constitution at birth. It is simply a descriptive term that neither includes all hereditary traits nor excludes those caused solely by environmental influences or by developmental accidents. The disorders described in this chapter can often be identified before puppies are seven weeks old and placed with new owners. They range from ones that are definitely hereditary with a known mode of transmission to those that are definitely not.

CLEFT PALATE

A *cleft palate* is the failure of the bony plates forming the roof of the mouth to close normally during embryonic development, usually leaving a fissure between the palate and the nasal passages. It is often accompanied by a cleft lip (harelip).

Cleft palates have long been considered a genetic disorder because they occur more frequently in families, but the incidence ratios do not conform to any hereditary mode. The genetic relationship was further confused by cases of Siamese twins in which only one twin had the abnormality. Human genetic studies clarified the difficulty of identifying the hereditary basis, and it turned out that cleft palates can be caused by autosomal genes, sex-linked genes, and chromosomal aberrations. Of the 153 different human syndromes associated with cleft palates and lips, 79 are caused by single-gene inheritance; the 79 syndromes account for only 5 percent of the total cases. Many environmental agents are linked with the defect, including vitamin A deficiency, vitamin A overdose, riboflavin and folic acid deficiency, aspirin, hypothermia, oxygen insufficiency, and cortisone.[1]

Occasional cleft palates occur in most breeds. Affected puppies can be identified shortly after birth because they cannot nurse properly; the fissure prevents effective suction on the nipple, and frothy bubbles appear at the nostrils. Studies of cleft palates in dogs variously conclude that it is an autosomal recessive or a dominant trait.[2] Overall, the incidence is so low that breeders should not be unduly concerned when one crops up, as most are probably accidents of embryonic development or exposure to teratogenic agents. Nevertheless, if cleft palates occur with any frequency or regularity, a genetic cause must be considered.

CRYPTORCHIDISM

Cryptorchidism is the failure of one or both testicles to descend into the scrotal sac—monolateral (unilateral) or bilateral cryptorchidism. *Monorchidism* is a contraction of monolateral cryptorchidism. The incidence of cryptorchidism is difficult to establish. It is considered "the most common disorder of sexual development, occurring in as many as 13 percent of male dogs presented to small animal clinics." Cryptorchidism is one of the American Kennel Club's all-breed disqualifications. The British Kennel Club declared cryptorchidism a disqualifying fault in the late 1950s but reversed this in 1969.[3]

The testes normally descend into the scrotum at about ten days, though they may be difficult to identify because of their small size and fat deposits in the area. If not descended by sixteen weeks, the probability of descent decreases sharply, though it has been reported as late as six months. Nevertheless, if they have not descended by eight weeks of age, the puppy should be considered genetically predisposed to producing the trait.[4] A cryptorchid puppy is basically healthy and makes an excellent pet, particularly for owners who prefer a neutered dog.

Although cryptorchidism is universally recognized as a hereditary trait, the specific mode of inheritance remains frustratingly elusive and controversial, and attempts to eliminate the trait through selective breeding have not been notably successful. Meyers-Wallen and Patterson commented that "the simplest model consistent with available evidence is sex-limited autosomal inheritance."[5]

Only Robinson suggests that cryptorchidism could be a polygenic threshold trait, but

Figure 12–1. *It is sometimes possible to palpate testicles in a newborn puppy. Reprinted, by permission, from Virginia Alexander and Jackie Isabell,* Weimaraner Ways.

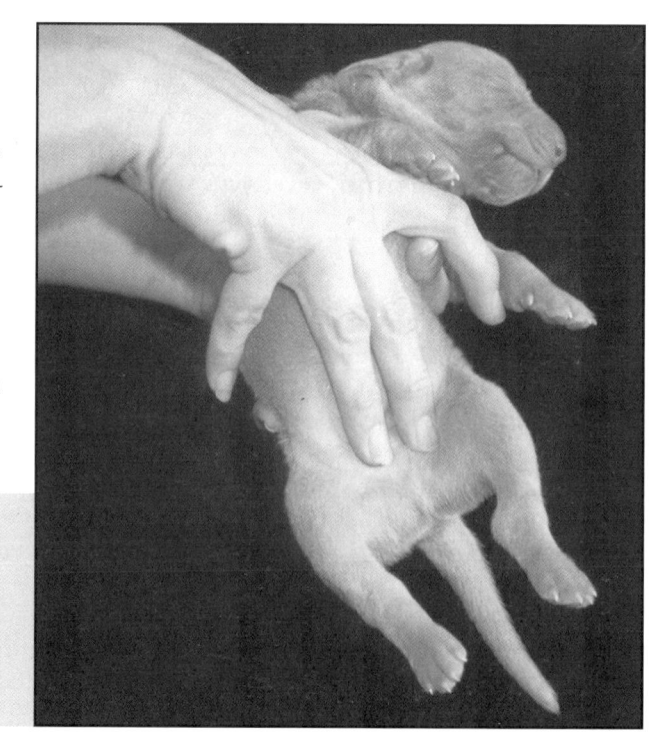

Figure 12–2. *The breeder palpates for testicles while the five-week-old puppy is happily distracted. Reprinted, by permission, from Virginia Alexander and Jackie Isabell,* Weimaraner Ways.

the idea merits consideration.[6] An acquaintance once quipped that delayed descent of the testicles is probably a form of cryptorchidism, an observation that made so much sense that I began noting the age of descent in my records. My first stud dog was one of seven males in the litter, of which two were monolateral cryptorchids and two were bilateral. His testicles, however, had descended at four weeks, and as a sire, he produced about one monolateral cryptorchid in about every third litter—a surprising improvement over his sire. A few years later I discovered that another Weimaraner breeder had started keeping records of the same trait at about the same time. We have both followed several generations of studs with confirmed early descent of testicles (no later than five weeks) and have observed a significant decrease of cryptorchidism in their descendants as well as an earlier age of descent. One of these studs sired a litter of one bitch and twelve males, and all testicles were descended by four weeks. Cryptorchism is a *sex-limited trait* (expression is limited to one gender even though the genes may be carried by both parents),

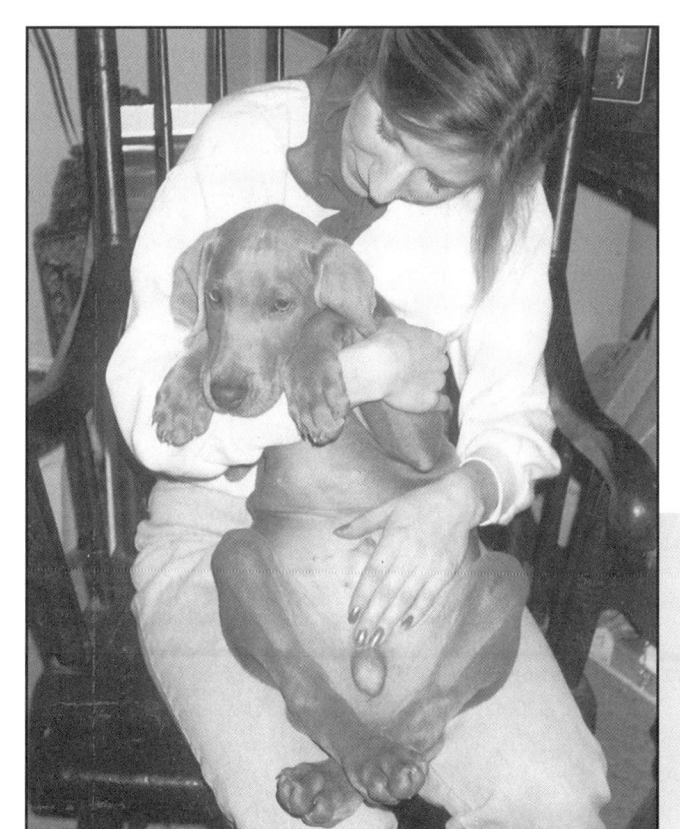

Figure 12–3. *Holding the puppy in a vertical position on the lap, apply gentle downward pressure to bring the testicles further into the scrotal sac.*
Reprinted, by permission, from Virginia Alexander and Jackie Isabell, Weimaraner Ways.

and another advantage of these sires is that their daughters produce few cryptorchids, even when bred to known producers of the problem. Unfortunately, our records are too casual for any valid research report—we didn't anticipate such phenomenal success. This age-related phenotype may be unique to our breed, but it is a promising and practical approach for other breeders to explore.

Almost every breeder has heard tales of "the disappearing testicle" in a male in which both testicles could be definitely palpated by the age of seven weeks but then one suddenly disappeared. This is often associated with being shipped by air or other similarly upsetting experience—the pick-of-litter male in my first litter lost one *after* his first match at the age of twelve weeks. Until the testes are too developed to pass through the inguinal ring, puppies can withdraw the testes from the scrotum, usually when excited or stressed. Occasionally, a retracted testicle becomes entangled with the spermatic cord, and it never appears again. If a testicle that has been clearly seen and palpated for several weeks disappears, and the "time of disappearance" is known, this is probably what has happened. In this situation, the problem is probably mechanical rather than genetic.

SWIMMERS' SYNDROME

A *swimmer* is a puppy that moves by sliding forward on a flattened sternum. Swimmers occur in many breeds and are openly discussed in most. The problem occurs most frequently in breeds characterized by short legs and wide chests such as the Bulldog, Basset Hound, and Pekingese. These breeds appear to be structurally predisposed, though the problem itself is not regarded as hereditary.

A hereditary quadriplegia resembling swimmers' syndrome has been reported in Irish Setters. The study followed eleven litters ranging in size from one to twelve puppies. The litters had an average inbreeding of 11.78 percent (half-sib inbreeding is 12.5 percent) and were from two different bloodlines. The pattern and distribution was consistent with that of an autosomal recessive.[7]

In long-legged breeds that typically have large litters, swimmers are associated with small litters. With an overabundance of food and no need to compete for a nipple, the puppies quickly become downright obese. Slight chest flattening of these roly-poly puppies may be observed within a few days after birth. The problem is progressive, and by ten to fourteen days, when they would normally start to support their weight and to take a few steps, the swimmer deformity is unmistakable. The wide, flat chest forces the forelegs outward, and the puppies can stand only with great difficulty. Without intervention, the puppies would be quite crippled.

The corrective measures are increased exercise and decreased food. At the first sign of flattened chests, experienced breeders immediately place a carpet or rubber mat in the whelping box. With better traction, the puppies can support their weight more easily, which in turn encourages greater activity. Other measures include cutting back the mother's food to reduce milk production and limiting the amount of time she spends with the puppies. If the problem is not noticed until the puppies are a few weeks old, taping the rear legs together for a few days usually gets them up on their feet.

The response is amazing, even if the puppies are as old as two weeks before an inexperienced breeder identifies the problem and learns how to correct it. Once puppies are on their feet and getting more exercise, the chests rapidly begin to recover a

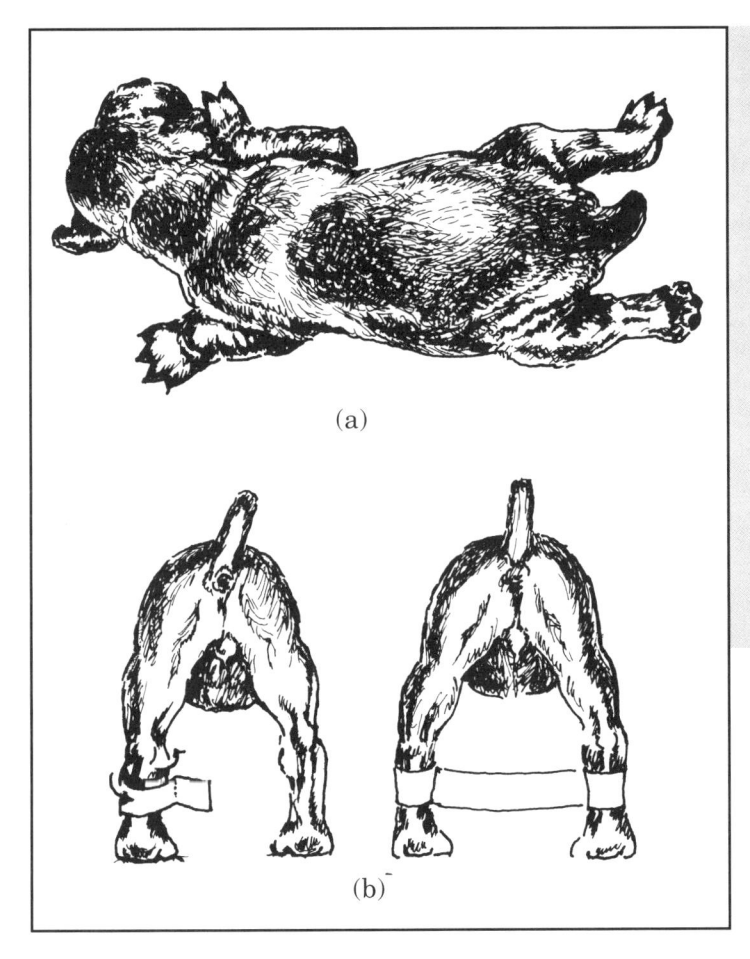

Figure 12–4. Swimmers.
(a) The characteristic pancake posture.
(b) In very severe cases, it is necessary to tape the rear legs for the puppy to stand up. After about forty-eight hours, cut the tape to see whether the puppy can stand by itself; if not, repair the cut tape. Most puppies can stand within three to four days. Reprinted, by permission, from Virginia Alexander and Jackie Isabell, Weimaraner Ways.

normal contour, and by the time their conformation is evaluated at seven weeks, it almost impossible to identify any abnormality. Because of this phenomenal recovery, swimmers are considered a simple overweight problem in the long-legged breeds. The only pattern identified is one of small litters with overfed puppies, and breeders usually do not consider swimmers a hereditary problem.

HERNIAS

UMBILICAL

An *umbilical hernia* is a soft, skin-covered protrusion of the intestine through a weakness in the abdominal wall at the umbilicus. Umbilical hernias range in severity from very minor ones that close without surgery to very severe ones.

The most massive type is an *omphalocele,* which is a herniation of the abdominal organs into the umbilical cord. Breeders sometimes report a puppy born with "a wide open hernia," which is probably a form of omphalocele, except that the internal organs are exposed. Omphaloceles must be surgically closed immediately after birth. The prognosis is poor because the hernias usually occur in conjunction with other congenital disorders such as a diaphragmatic hernia. The puppies are often vigorous, however, and breeders often try to save them—or at least have them humanely euthanized. Apply sterile gauze soaked in saline, wrap with an elastic bandage, and rush to the veterinarian.

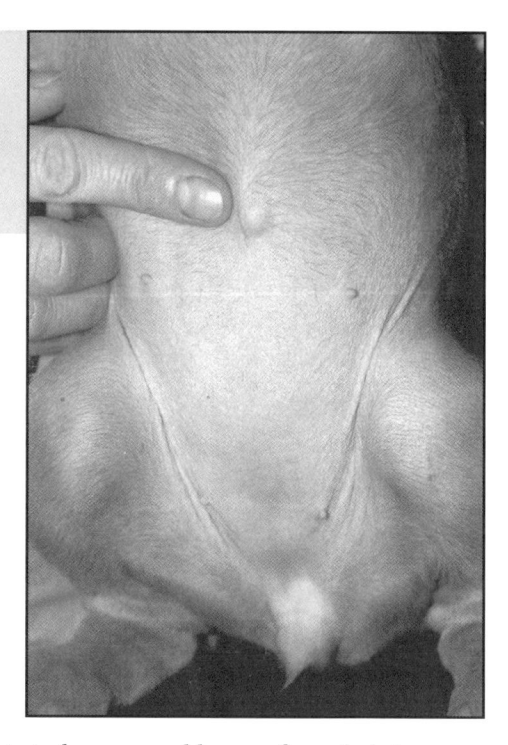

Figure 12-5. *Small umbilical bubbles that are often mistaken for hernias are caused by a minor subcutaneous accumulation of fluid from the cord. Reprinted, by permission, from Virginia Alexander and Jackie Isabell,* Weimaraner Ways.

A familial incidence has long been recognized, though the reported mode of inheritance varies from autosomal recessive to polygenic. However, umbilical hernias may also be caused by teratogenic agents such as corticosteroids. Further complicating identification of the hereditary mode is the fact that minor hernias may be caused by excessive traction (pulling force) on the umbilical cord at whelping. In addition, small umbilical bubbles that are often mistaken for hernias are caused by a minor subcutaneous accumulation of fluid from the cord; these can be minimized by tying the cord, even if this is done several hours after whelping.

The question of whether any dog with an umbilical hernia should be ever be bred is highly controversial. Purists would not breed any dog that had even a small hernia. At the other extreme, breeders have used dogs with hernias that required surgical repair but developed into significant producers, raising the question of where the breed would be if the breeders had been purists. This is one case in which the breeder's judgment (and ethics) is crucial.

In general, breeders use the following guideline: (a) unless the breeder is aware of a persistent pattern and a high incidence of hernias within the strain, the puppy is considered of breeding quality if the hernia closes without surgical intervention; (b) if the hernia

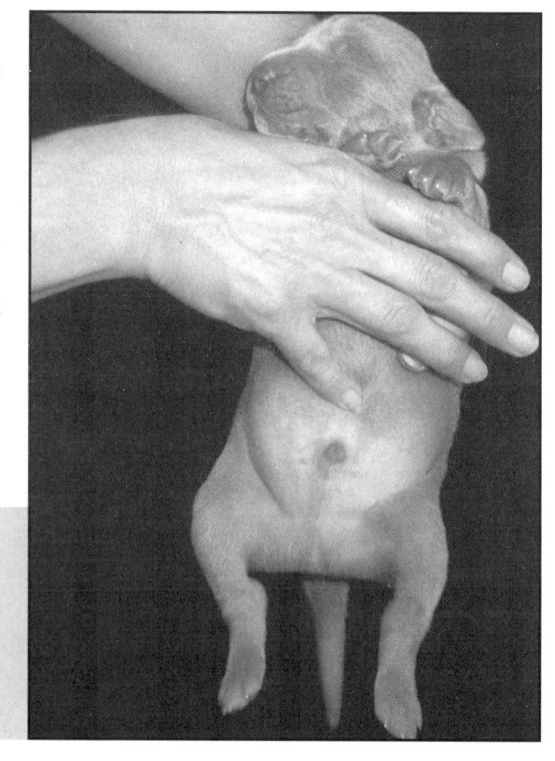

Figure 12-6. *If the tip of the little finger cannot be inserted into the hole, the hernia usually closes spontaneously, with no need for surgery. Reprinted, by permission, from Virginia Alexander and Jackie Isabell,* Weimaraner Ways.

requires surgical closure, the puppy should not be bred. Exceptions are made only if the puppy has outstanding merits and the owner (usually the breeder) is willing to do test breeding.

Surgery should be deferred until the puppy is over three months old; during surgery, the puppy should be checked for a diaphragmatic hernia, which sometimes occurs in conjunction with an umbilical hernia.

DIAPHRAGMATIC

A *diaphragmatic hernia* is an opening in the diaphragm, usually with the protrusion of the stomach and other abdominal organs into the thoracic cavity.

A genetic cause has been implicated in all species; however, studies have not identified the mode of heredity, and suggestions include a simple recessive, a polygenic recessive, and a dominant with incomplete penetrance. Teratogenic agents have also been implicated—quinine, phenmetrazine, vitamin A deficiency, and so forth. Diaphragmatic hernias diagnosed after puppies are a few months old are usually secondary to a traumatic abdominal injury, such as a fall or a kick (horse or human). Using a knee to correct jumping has also been implicated.[8]

Puppies with congenital diaphragmatic hernias are often stillborn or die shortly after birth, and without an autopsy, the death may be attributed to other causes such as the mother lying on the puppy. The symptoms are subtle, rarely noticed. Affected puppies sometimes have a soft spot in the abdominal muscle just below the rib that can be felt with gentle palpation. They may not nurse well, may always sleep with their heads propped up on something to help them breathe, or may exhibit excessive or persistent yawning. Veterinarians sometimes notice the characteristic, slightly different vocal quality at tail-docking time. Puppies with congenital diaphragmatic hernias rarely survive beyond seven weeks, though improved surgical techniques are increasing the survival rate. They should never, of course, be used for breeding.

CARDIAC ABNORMALITIES

About twenty-two different congenital cardiac abnormalities have been identified in canines. According to the OFA Congenital Heart Disease Registry, the most common defects are "(a) malformation of the atrioventricular valves, (b) malformations of ventricular outflow leading to obstruction of blood flow, (c) defects of the cardiac septa (shunting defects), (d) abnormal development of the great vessels or other vascular structures, and (e) complex, multiple, or other congenital disorders of the heart, pericardium, or blood vessels."[9]

The incidence ranges from 0.68 to 4.7 percent in different studies. The incidence is higher in purebred dogs than in crossbreds, and the incidence of specific disorders in some breeds (more than twenty-five breeds have an increased risk) is higher than in the general population of purebred dogs.[10]

Ductus diverticulum and patent ductus arteriosis were discussed in Chapter 6 as the classic example of a two-threshold polygenic trait. Conotruncal septum defects are another series of graded defects that appeared to conform to an additive polygenic model, but a 1993 report identified a single major gene in a line of Keeshonds—after more than ten generations of selective inbreeding.[11]

Cardiac defects have been produced in experimental animals by many teratogenic agents, including the following: aspirin and many other drugs or chemicals; too much vitamin A; too little oxygen, vitamin A, folic acid, riboflavin, and galactoflavin. So many teratogenic agents have been implicated that defects in littermates cannot be regarded as definitive evidence of hereditary factors.[12]

The symptoms of cardiac abnormalities depend on the severity of the defect. They range from sudden neonatal death to difficult breathing, slow growth, and lack of vigor. Puppies may show no signs at all until the demands of increased size or physical activity exceed the cardiac reserves. Most defects are first recognized when the heart is checked for murmurs. Puppies with serious cardiac disorders can be detected by a veterinarian, and this is an important reason for having all litters routinely examined at six or seven weeks of age. Even if this is not a problem in the breed or the bloodline, the examination is worthwhile because it will furnish a record that no murmur was identified at a specific age.[13]

There are too many disorders and potential causes to automatically condemn the parents of a puppy with a cardiac abnormality as carriers of a hereditary disorder. Analysis of prenatal health records and multigenerational pedigrees might provide clues but could not realistically include a large enough sample to be considered conclusive evidence. In general, one puppy with a cardiac defect is a warning but not a cause for immediate panic or condemnation of the parents, though it is prudent not to repeat the mating and, probably, to avoid crosses with similar bloodlines. Even several affected puppies in one litter could be caused by an environmental factor. A genetic cause must be acknowledged if (*a*) an individual produces puppies with cardiac defects from a different bloodline combination, (*b*) the defect appears in the offspring of siblings living in a different environment, or (*c*) the defect appears in the individual's descendants.

KEEP AN OPEN MIND

Breeders should assess every puppy for congenital disorders. Disorders such as cardiac abnormalities are not compatible with good health or longevity, and affected puppies should be put to sleep. Other disorders such as cryptorchidism and umbilical hernias are usually compatible with a long, healthy life with or without minor surgery.

When a congenital defect does occur, assess the things to which the bitch has been exposed while carrying the litter before blaming the stud or condemning the bitch. Most disorders are isolated cases with little hereditary significance. If however, the same disorder appears when the parent is bred to several dogs of varying bloodlines, or the same disorder appears in several generations, *then* a genetic linkage must be seriously considered.

The unthinking assumption that every congenital disorder has a hereditary basis is extremely dangerous. Priceless bloodlines (not to mention breeders' morale and reputations) can be destroyed while an unidentified teratogenic agent continues to prey on unsuspecting victims. Keep detailed records, watch for patterns, and consider the possibility of teratogenic agents as well as hereditary factors when congenital disorders occur.

Chapter 13

COMMON HEREDITARY PROBLEMS

This chapter focuses on the most common hereditary disorders, those that the *average* breeder is likely to either encounter or hear of over the years, plus some of the less common ones for which registries have been created.

BLEEDING DISORDERS

The *blood-clotting cascade* is a series of complex biochemical events that must occur before a blood clot can form. This is a fail-safe mechanism that prevents internal blood clots, which are normally fatal. Considering the many clotting factors required, it is not surprising that there are so many ways something can go wrong. The symptoms of bleeding disorders vary in severity, but all are characterized by abnormalities of a specific blood-clotting factor.

Most canine bleeding disorders also occur in humans and other mammals. This suggests that spontaneous mutation of these genes is not unusual and that the disorders can appear in any breed at any time.

Control programs have been quite effective in reducing the incidence of bleeding disorders. One notable success is the reduction of factor X deficiency in Cocker Spaniels from 20 percent in 1972 to less than 3 percent in 1981.[1]

THE HEMOPHILIAS

Hemophilia is a hereditary disorder characterized by excessive bleeding. Hemophilia A (classic hemophilia) is caused by a deficiency of clotting factor VIII, and it has been reported in most popular breeds as well as in mongrels, cats, horses, cattle, and humans. Hemophilia B (Christmas disease), caused by a deficiency of clotting factor IX, is less common, but it has been reported in humans, cats, and several dog breeds. It is interesting that both hemophilias are sex-linked genetic disorders of the X chromosome in all species. Robinson suggests that there is a mutational hot spot on the X chromosome.[2]

Symptoms of hemophilia A may be detected at whelping with the observation of prolonged bleeding from the umbilicus, or excessive bleeding may be noticed when tails are docked. Identification may be delayed, however, until the puppies are as old as three months. The first sign may be lameness, with or without swollen joints, caused by slow bleeding into the joints. Bleeding may occur at any time from any body area. The symptoms of hemophilia B are slightly less severe, and bleeding has been reported in heterozygous bitches.

With hemophilia A and B, biochemical screening tests for heterozygous females are over 90 percent accurate, and control programs have successfully eliminated the disorders in several breeds or families, though new mutations for the trait may occur at any time.

VON WILLEBRAND'S DISEASE

Von Willebrand's disease (vWD) is a hereditary disorder characterized by abnormally slow blood clotting owing to a deficiency of factor VIII, the same factor that causes hemophilia A. It differs from hemophilia A in that there is a decreased level of the von Willebrand factor (vWF) and low platelet retention (adhesiveness). The disorder has been identified in humans, cats, rabbits, and swine. In dogs, vWD was first identified in German Shepherd Dogs by Dodds in 1970. As of 1990, the disorder has been identified in fifty-four different breeds as well as in mongrels.[3]

VWD exhibits a wide variation of expression. In some breeds, bleeding occurs only in the homozygotes, with nonsymptomatic heterozygotes; in others, the heterozygotes are symptomatic and the homozygotes die before or shortly after birth. The symptoms may be mild—migratory lameness, tarry stools, blood-tinged urine, and so forth. Bitches may exhibit prolonged or excessive bleeding when in season or after whelping. The symptoms typically become less severe with age.[4]

The initial studies indicated that vWD is inherited as an incomplete dominant. The heterozygotes manifest a mild to moderate bleeding tendency that is usually severe to fatal in homozygotes. In some breeds, however, vWD appears to be inherited as an autosomal recessive with variable penetrance and expressivity.[5]

By the end of 1996, DNA testing for vWD was available for Doberman Pinschers, Shetland Sheepdogs, Scottish Terriers, and tests will probably be developed soon for other affected breeds. Until then, breeders can continue to use phenotypic screening.

The effectiveness of phenotypic screening for vWD varies, depending on whether or not the heterozygotes express clinical or subclinical clotting abnormalities. In breeds such as the German Shepherd Dog and others in which the heterozygotes can be identified, screening is quite effective; if only the homozygotes are symptomatic, however, the heterozygotes cannot be identified. The screening of seven different breeds for vWD from 1979 to 1981 decreased incidence significantly in three and showed improvement in the other four. Test matings of normal dogs have determined that the test method has over 90 percent accuracy.[6] Screening tests are most accurate when performed by coagulation laboratories that are experienced in testing animals. Puppies of large breeds can be tested at seven to eight weeks; sufficient blood cannot be obtained from smaller breeds until ten to twelve weeks of age. Bitches should not be tested when they are in season, pregnant, or nursing a litter. In addition, the dogs should be in good health and should not be tested within two weeks after worming, immunization, or taking any kind of medication.

EPILEPSY

Epilepsy is any of various disorders marked by disturbed electrical rhythms of the central nervous system and typically manifested by convulsions. Of itself, epilepsy is not a disease but rather a symptom of many different disorders and diseases that produce seizures.

Hippocrates observed the familial nature of epilepsy, and a great deal has been learned since then. Geneticists have identified over 100 genetic disorders with simple Mendelian inheritance that produce seizures in humans. About 85 percent of hereditary seizures, however, exhibit the familial pattern typical of polygenic traits.[7] In dogs, studies of the heredity of epilepsy tend to be inconclusive, contradictory, and confusing. This is probably because, as in humans, there are many different mutations.

Before assuming that a dog has a hereditary form of epilepsy, all nongenetic possibilities should be ruled out. For example, all of the following produce seizures:

brain tumor	infections
electric shock	kidney disease
encephalitis	liver disease
heavy metal ingestion	poisons/toxins
hypocalcemia	vitamin D overdose
hypoglycemia	trauma (including birth)
hypoxia	

Poisonous plants and herbicides are probably the most common cause of seizures in dogs because so many like to nibble on greenery. One of my friends planted yellow jasmine to shade a dog run, and the dog's seizures ended when this highly toxic vine was removed. Owners also may not always be aware when the dog has had an electrical shock. After one of my own dogs had two alarming seizures, my husband admitted that, earlier, the dog had laid down with his spine against an electric cattle prod that was accidentally switched on, producing an immediate grand mal seizure. The dog had no further seizures, but without knowing the cause, I would have always worried about a hereditary problem. Seizures are the most frequent and sometimes the only symptom of subclinical distemper encephalitis, which sometimes follows the immune-system stress of the so-called global vaccines that have as many as seven varieties of modified live viruses. Lead poisoning from old paint, old plumbing, or some imported crockery used for food or water could affect a whole kennel and present a grim picture of hereditary epilepsy. So, ask questions and look around for potential causes, because you might be able to do something to eliminate those.

EYE DISORDERS

THE RETINA

Progressive Retinal Atrophy

Progressive retinal atrophy (PRA) is a degenerative disease of the visual cells (rods and cones) of the retina that progresses to blindness. It is also known as peripheral or generalized PRA to distinguish it from centralized progressive retinal atrophy (CPRA). There are several forms of the disorder: "In rod/cone dysplasia, the visual cells fail to develop normally and degenerate within the first year of life, resulting in blindness. In rod/cone degeneration . . . , the visual cells develop normally and then undergo degeneration, with blindness occurring in the adult dog (age 5–7 years)."[8]

The symptoms of PRA were first described in Sweden by Magnusson in 1909 in Gordon Setters. It is characterized by gradual loss of night vision, slowly progressing to total bilateral blindness. Differential diagnosis is important because some nongenetic disorders have similar symptoms.[9]

The disorder came to public attention in the 1950s when it was identified in Irish Setters. Now, there are *few breeds in which PRA has not been detected.* So far, PRA appears to be recessive in all breeds in which it has been identified. Because of the great variation in the age of onset, however, there is some question whether the same locus or even the same chromosome is affected in different breeds.

One of the most disturbing aspects of PRA is the late onset, often after the affected dogs have produced offspring. The typical age of onset varies in different breeds. For example, symptoms may begin as early as twelve months in longhaired Dachshunds, at about two years in Norwegian Elkhounds, and as late as six to nine years in Toy Poodles. In addition to the recent tests using DNA analysis, electroretinograms can now identify incipient PRA at latest by ten weeks of age, years before the clinical onset.[10]

Control programs for PRA have been successful only with breed-wide effort and cooperation. British breeders of Irish Setters embarked on a control program in 1947, hoping to eradicate the disorder in five years; it actually took thirteen years. Because of the relatively early onset in Irish Setters, the program was feasible. An attempt to expand the program to other affected breeds in Britain proved less successful.[11] DNA analysis has recently become available for Irish Setters, and it will probably be developed for other breeds in the near future.

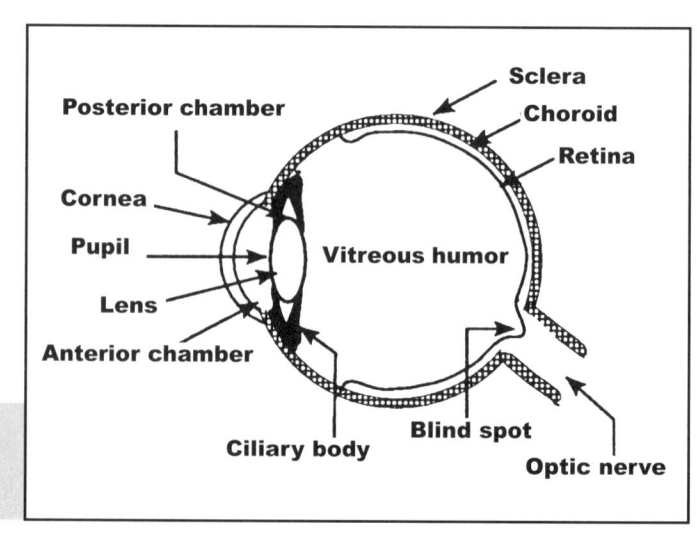

Figure 13–1. Parts of the eye.

Central Progressive Retinal Atrophy

Central progressive retinal atrophy (CPRA) is a progressive degeneration of the retina's photoreceptor cells that is secondary to disease of the underlying pigment epithelium. Degeneration of the central area of the retina is slow and does not always progress to total blindness. The characteristic scattered spots of brown pigment on the *tapetum* (retinal layer producing "eye shine") are similar to retinitis pigmentosa in humans. In advanced stages, the spots decline in number and gradually disappear. Parry first described the symptoms in 1954. There is no night blindness; if anything, night vision appears to be enhanced. The dogs have good peripheral vision but trip over obstacles directly in their paths. The age of onset ranges from two to ten years, though changes may be identified as early as eighteen to twenty-four months.[12]

CPRA is most frequent in sporting and working breeds in England (especially collies and retrievers); it is not common in other countries.[13]

The inheritance of CPRA is uncertain, but it is suspected to be a dominant with variable penetrance. In Labrador Retrievers, the mode of inheritance appears to be a dominant with about 80 percent penetrance. In Briards, however, CPRA appears to be an autosomal recessive.[14]

With CPRA, the outlook for control programs is more promising, as with most dominant traits. The International Sheepdog Society (Britain) examined all Border Collies attending trials in 1965, finding an incidence of 12 percent in 500 dogs. The society decreed compulsory examination of all breeding stock and certification at two years. By 1973, the incidence dropped to under 2 percent, showing the rapid decline typical of a dominant trait.[15]

Retinal Dysplasia

Retinal dysplasia is an abnormality leading to retinal detachment at birth or shortly afterward, causing blindness. Breeds in which the disorder has been identified include Bedlington Terriers, Labrador Retrievers, Sealyham Terriers, and Yorkshire Terriers. So far, retinal dysplasia appears to be an autosomal recessive in these breeds.[16]

Other abnormalities may be related to retinal dysplasia. Affected puppies have abnormal behavior, suggesting brain damage—a similar disorder in humans is associated with central nervous system and cardiovascular abnormalities. Matings of two affected dogs have had a high neonatal mortality.[17]

Initially, *multifocal retinal dysplasia* (identified in Beagles and Cocker Spaniels) was considered a variant of retinal dysplasia but is now classified as a separate disorder. It is characterized by multiple retinal folds with minimal effect on vision. The heredity is uncertain but probably recessive.[18]

CATARACTS

A *cataract* is the dull whitish cloudiness of the lens or capsule in one or both eyes that may eventually lead to blindness. Cataracts are classified by the age of onset (congenital, juvenile, senile), location, cause (primary, secondary), degree of opacity (incipient, immature, mature, hypermature), and shape. Cloudiness caused by cataracts must be differentiated from *nuclear sclerosis*—normal clouding caused by increased nuclear density with old age. A primary cataract is associated with no other eye or systemic abnormality. Most cataracts are secondary to age or to other disorders (diabetes, malnutrition, trauma, infections, and other inflammatory disorders).

Cataracts are widespread and can occur in any breed at any time. In most breeds with a high incidence, hereditary factors are suspected, though the mode of inheritance has not been identified.

GLAUCOMA

Glaucoma is the elevation of pressure within the eye that leads to damage of the optic disk and gradual loss of vision. The age of onset varies, but it typically develops in middle-aged and older dogs. The two types of primary glaucoma—open-angle and angle-closure—are considered hereditary.

Glaucoma is widespread. Although the mode of inheritance has not been identified in many breeds, it varies in the breeds in which it has been identified. Open-angle glaucoma in Beagles is caused by an autosomal dominant. In the Welsh Springer Spaniel, angle-closure glaucoma is caused by a dominant and occurs twice as often in bitches. Angle-closure glaucoma has also been reported in the Basset Hound, Beagle, Cocker Spaniel, English Cocker Spaniel, English Springer Spaniel, Miniature Poodle, Norwegian Elkhound, Samoyed, and Siberian Husky.[19]

THE EYELIDS

Entropion and Ectropion

Entropion is an inward rotation of the eyelid that is characterized by watery eyes, blinking, conjunctivitis, sensitivity to sunlight, pain, and inflammation. *Ectropion* is the drooping or sagging of the lower eyelid (sometimes called *haw*) that is characterized by excessive drying of the cornea with overflow of tears. Chronic conjunctivitis aggravates the problems, and surgical correction is necessary if the symptoms are severe and persistent.

Both disorders may be either a congenital genetic trait or an acquired problem, secondary to injuries or chronic conjunctivitis. Several reports state that entropion appears to be inherited as a dominant with complete penetrance; others suggest a dominant with incomplete penetrance or a recessive. No specific mode of inheritance is reported in literature on ectropion. The American College of Veterinary Ophthalmologists suggests that it is polygenic, influenced by genes that influence the eyelids, the eye socket, and other traits associated with skull structure.[20]

Trichiasis and Distichiasis

Trichiasis is the term for normal eyelashes that curve inward, irritating the cornea and causing chronic eye inflammation. It is considered a probable genetic disorder because of the high incidence in some breeds, though

Figure 13–2. Eyelash abnormalities. *Reprinted, by permission, from Virginia Alexander and Jackie Isabell, Weimaraner Ways.*

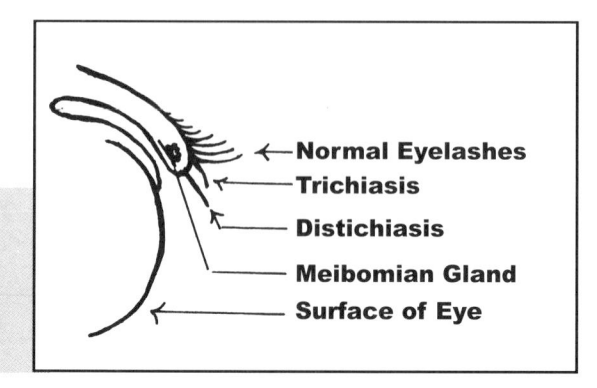

the mode of inheritance is not reported in the literature. However, trichiasis can also be acquired through chronic irritation.

Distichiasis is the term for extra eyelashes that emerge from the meibomian glands along the margin of the eyelid—from one to ten hairs may emerge from a single gland. The number of affected glands varies, ranging from a few extra eyelashes to what appears to be a complete second row. Most of these lashes lack pigmentation, which makes detection difficult. The lashes themselves vary from soft fine hairs that cause little or no irritation to stiff bristles that cause considerable damage.

The symptoms include eye irritation, sensitivity to light, excessive tearing, and corneal ulcers, though it may be nonsymptomatic. If the lashes cause corneal irritation, they may be removed by electrolysis or by surgical removal of the affected glands.

Distichiasis may be either congenital or acquired through chronic eye irritation, and the age of onset ranges from a few weeks to ten years. The disorder has been reported to be a dominant with incomplete penetrance.[21]

Weimaraner breeders have observed eyelashes of both textures and patterns that suggest two modes of heredity. Recently, several breeders have been studying and comparing the pedigrees and litter records of affected dogs in which the presence of soft, fine lashes was observed *before twelve weeks of age*. In most cases, they could identify a parent or a sibling of a parent that also had distichiasis at an early age, a pattern that suggests a dominant with incomplete penetrance. Interestingly, the lashes sometimes disappear later. The hard, bristly lashes, on the other hand, are quite rare, and only a general familial relationship could be identified, suggesting that it is an entirely separate trait that is recessive. These lashes are usually white, and if more than a few are present, they can be seen without magnification shortly after the eyes open.

All puppies should be carefully examined by a veterinarian at six weeks and again by the breeder in the final litter evaluation. The fine, almost colorless eyelashes of trichiasis

Figure 13–3. *Check puppies very carefully for the fine, almost colorless lashes characteristic of distichiasis. Reprinted, by permission, from Virginia Alexander and Jackie Isabell,* Weimaraner Ways.

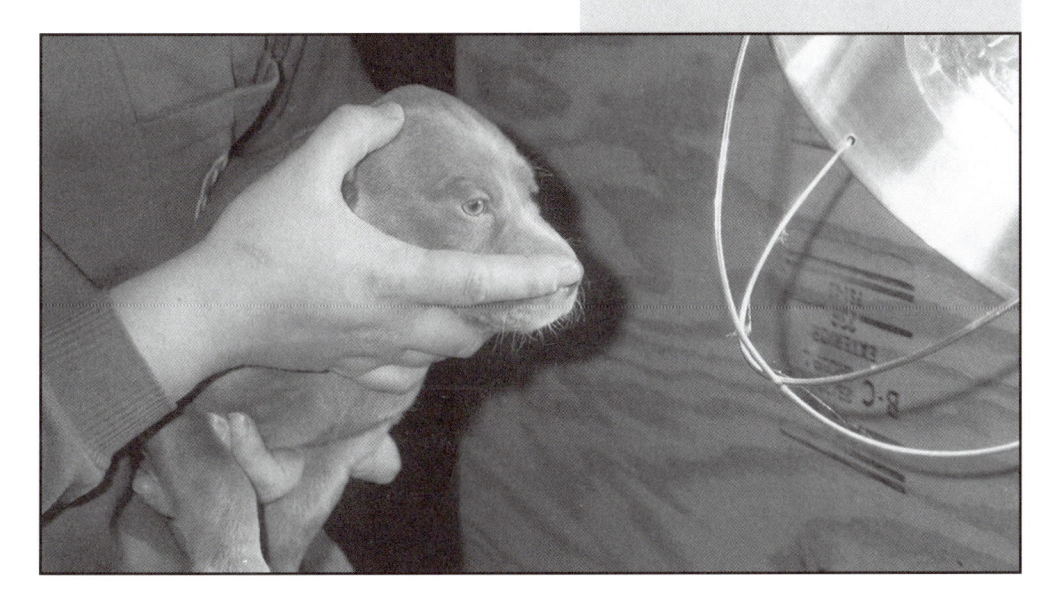

and distichiasis can be seen with a magnifying glass only in very bright light. Although sunlight is best, a bright, white reflective light works almost as well.

HYPOTHYROIDISM

Hypothyroidism simply means a deficiency of the thyroid hormones. Screening tests can identify two types of hypothyroidism—idiopathic and autoimmune (Hashimoto's thyroiditis)—both with a variable age of onset. The term *idiopathic* simply means that the cause is unknown, and an idiopathic disease means that although there is a recognizable pattern of symptoms and sometimes even a cure, the cause is unknown. Dodds defines *autoimmune thyroiditis* as "an immune-mediated process that develops in genetically susceptible individuals and is characterized by the presence of antithyroid antibodies in the blood or tissues." About 90 percent of hypothyroidism is of the autoimmune type.[22]

Because thyroid hormones play a role in the metabolic function of all cells, the symptoms affect all systems—blood, neuromuscular, skin, circulatory, gastrointestinal, reproductive system, and so forth. Early in the disease, the disorder can be identified only through blood tests; the symptoms do not appear until the thyroid gland loses its reserves and can no longer compensate for the thyroid antibodies. Dodds estimates that from 50 to 70 percent of the thyroid tissue is damaged or destroyed before the reserves are depleted and symptoms appear. The disorder can be easily treated with thyroid hormone.[23]

A marked familial pattern is associated with all immune-related disorders in both humans and dogs, though the specific mode of inheritance has not been identified in any. In humans, the immune-mediated disorders include scleroderma, autoimmune thyroiditis, lupus erythematosis, and rheumatoid arthritis. Although several family members may have the same disorder, the more typical pattern is for members to have different disorders within the group of immune-mediated diseases, suggesting that there is an underlying common abnormality of the immune system.Dodds recommends testing bitches before breeding because a "bitch with antithyroid antibodies in her blood may pass these along to her puppies in her colostral milk," though the significance of this is unknown.[24]

Autoimmune thyroiditis has now been identified in more than fifty breeds. Breeds considered to be at high risk include Doberman Pinschers, Golden Retrievers, Dachshunds, Miniature Schnauzers, Irish Setters, Cocker Spaniels, Airedales, Great Danes, Boxers, Poodles, Shetland Sheepdogs, and Old English Sheepdogs.[25]

SKELETAL DISORDERS

HIP DYSPLASIA

Canine hip dysplasia (HD), first described by Schnelle in 1935, has been identified in more than one hundred breeds. Hip dysplasia has been diagnosed in humans as well as cats, horses, and most other domesticated animals.[26]

Hip dysplasia is usually defined as the malformation of the hip joint of variable severity: *Subluxation* is the slight displacement of the joint; *luxation* is the total dislocation of the joint. Wayne H. Riser, one of the early authorities on the disorder, describes HD as "not one disease, but many diseases that result in common degenerative lesions of the hip joints," and that "many genetic and environmental factors can secondarily trigger events that bring about the condition." Therefore he defines hip dysplasia as "a concentration of factors from a pool of genetic weakness and environmental stresses that falls into a programmed pattern of progressive remodelling and degenerative joint disease. The degree of involvement varies from minute changes in the bone structure to total destruction of the hip joint."[27]

The symptoms range from none at all to severe, crippling lameness. The hip is a ball-and-socket-type joint, with the head of the femur (ball) fitting snugly into the acetabulum (socket). A shallow or deformed socket does not allow a snug fit, which leads to abnormal friction and secondary damage to the joint with wearing away of the bones—degenerative joint disease (DJD). The hip structures, from best to worst, are described as follows:

- *Normal.* The well-rounded femoral heads fit snugly into the (acetabulums) sockets
- *Near-normal.* The femoral heads fall away slightly from the sockets
- *Borderline.* There is a mild degree of displacement between the femoral heads and sockets
- *Dysplastic.* There is marked separation between the femoral heads and sockets, with structural changes of both heads and sockets
- *Severely dysplastic.* The femoral heads are out of the sockets (seven luxation), with structural changes of both heads and sockets.

History

Control programs. All control programs have been based on the phenotype evaluation of hip X-rays. Control programs in many countries and with many breeds are based on the principle that selection for normal phenotype perpetuates the normal genes. It has been proven that using Normal x Normal or Normal x Near Normal matings significantly increases the percentage of normal hips in the offspring. The more severely the parents are affected, the higher the frequency and severity in the offspring; the higher the proportion of normal ancestors and siblings of parents, the higher the proportion of normal offspring. Riser points out: "In our work with breeders where small numbers of subjects were involved, every report, without exception, has indicated a decline in the number of affected generations when only dogs and bitches with normal hips were mated."[28]

In 1966, the Orthopedic Foundation for Animals (OFA) offered the first national, all-breed registry for dysplasia-free dogs through evaluation of the *phenotype* of the hips. This was the first large-scale attempt to control a hereditary problem, and in a nationwide frenzy of enthusiasm to rid dogdom of this hereditary scourge, breeders jumped on the bandwagon with a wave of wholesale euthanasia of animals that failed to receive OFA certification. Progress was slow, however, and enthusiasm was followed by a high degree of breeder frustration.

From 1966 to 1973, OFA examined and certified hip X-rays of dogs over twelve months old and classified them as normal, near normal, or dysplastic; in 1974, the age of examination and certification was raised to twenty-four months, and classifications were changed to excellent, good, fair, borderline, mild dysplasia, moderate dysplasia, and severe dysplasia.

Some early theories. When the initial belief that HD was a recessive trait fell before evidence that it did not respond to selective breeding as rapidly as expected, new theories of the cause popped up with regularity. The theory that HD was a neuromuscular disorder of the pectineus muscle attracted a substantial following.

For a while, many breeders gave megadoses of vitamin C in the belief that it could prevent HD. "A variety of nutritional and mineral supplements have been used in attempts to alter or prevent the course of hip dysplasia in the dog. Diet has not affected the occurrence or course of the disease other than the mechanical effect of increased or decreased weight upon the hip joint."[29]

Studies of ovarian hormone effects were initially promising. In high doses, ovarian hormones increased the incidence of HD. Even Greyhounds, which had been considered free of HD at the time, developed the disorder. The flaw in the theory was that the hormone levels required to produce HD do not occur naturally, and it was eventually concluded that estrogens had nothing to do with *spontaneously occurring hip dysplasia*.[30]

There was no easy way out! Hip dysplasia is indeed a polygenic trait, but dedicated breeders have slowly reduced the incidence with generations of painstaking selection.

Incidence and trends. The incidence and severity of HD is difficult to estimate because the OFA's records reflect a select subset of the population. However, these records do reflect trends, especially with the percentage of hips that are rated as excellent. Dr. G. Gregory Keller points out, "The reason we look at excellent hips as a barometer of progress is the argument that the decreasing percentage of dysplastic hips can be due to prior screening. There is prior screening, and radiographs of hips that obviously are dysplastic may not be submitted."[31]

> The data show that the rate of excellent hips more than doubled in 19 breeds from 1980 to 1993–1994: Akita, Airedale Terrier, Bouvier des Flandres, Bloodhound, Bernese Mountain Dog, Bullmastiff, Chesapeake Bay Retriever, Chow Chow, Collie, English Setter, Great Dane, Great Pyrenees, Golden Retriever, Giant Schnauzer, Gordon Setter, Irish Setter, Newfoundland, Puli and Rottweiler.
>
> The incidence of excellent hips grew by more than 50 percent in nine additional breeds: Alaskan Malamute, Bearded Collie, Belgian Tervuren, Labrador Retriever, Norwegian Elkhound, Rhodesian Ridgeback, Old English Sheepdog, Weimaraner and West Highland White Terrier.
>
> The statistics were developed from a base of 127,315 submissions of dogs born in or before 1980 and 61,322 dogs born in 1993–1994.
>
> "In the 1980s we reported about two and a half dysplastic hip reports for every excellent report. Currently our data show that there is an excellent hip reported for almost every dysplastic report. There are more normal dogs, and more of the normals are excellent," Keller said.[32]

Genetic and Environmental Interactions

Heritability. It is now well established that HD is a polygenic trait, and the expression of polygenic traits is influenced by a combination of many genetic and environmental factors. Heritability refers to the *percentage* of the variation of the expression of a character or trait that can be attributed to genetic factors. In other words, the

Table 13–1. Trends in Hip Dysplasia

BREED	RATING TOTAL DOGS	≥1980	1986–87	1993–94	CHANGE ≤1980 to 1993–94
Afghan Hound	% Excellent	24.3	34.4	30.3	+24.7
	% Dysplastic	5.5	8.3	4.1	-25.5
	Total Dogs	2,768	314	122	
Airedale Terrier	% Excellent	4.4	7.1	9.5	+115.9
	% Dysplastic	14.6	14.8	9.5	-34.9
	Total Dogs	521	350	305	
Akita	% Excellent	7.5	15.9	20.5	+173.3
	% Dysplastic	17.5	17.2	10.1	-42.3
	Total Dogs	2,208	1,242	975	
Alaskan Malamute	% Excellent	10.4	18.2	20.0	+92.3
	% Dysplastic	14.1	12.3	8.1	-42.6
	Total Dogs	3,816	863	581	
Australian Shepherd	% Excellent	10.5	14.0	14.5	+38.1
	% Dysplastic	8.6	6.9	4.8	-44.2
	Total Dogs	2,248	1,158	1,678	
Bearded Collie	% Excellent	9.7	12.9	15.4	+58.8
	% Dysplastic	9.8	7.6	3.2	-67.3
	Total Dogs	474	264	246	
Belgian Sheepdog	% Excellent	23.8	30.6	34.9	+46.6
	% Dysplastic	2.9	3.4	1.5	-48.3
	Total Dogs	525	206	209	
Belgian Tervuren	% Excellent	14.5	18.7	24.3	+67.6
	% Dysplastic	5.3	4.2	3.9	-26.4
	Total Dogs	640	284	259	
Bernese Mountain Dog	% Excellent	2.8	5.9	10.3	+267.9
	% Dysplastic	32.8	23.4	12.6	-61.6
	Total Dogs	566	622	842	
Bloodhound	% Excellent	0.5	0.7	3.5	+600.0
	% Dysplastic	25.9	33.1	22.1	-14.7
	Total Dogs	564	136	113	
Bouvier Des Flanders	% Excellent	3.0	6.0	7.5	+150.0
	% Dysplastic	19.5	19.1	11.5	-41.0
	Total Dogs	853	554	522	
Brittany Spaniel	% Excellent	5.7	6.8	7.7	+35.1
	% Dysplastic	20.3	18.7	10.3	-49.3
	Total Dogs	2,824	926	845	
Bullmastiff	% Excellent	1.7	1.7	3.9	+129.4
	% Dysplastic	30.6	27.0	21.6	-29.4
	Total Dogs	421	167	437	
Chesapeake Bay Retriever	% Excellent	5.9	10.1	12.3	+108.5
	% Dysplastic	25.5	24.1	18.4	-27.8
	Total Dogs	1,783	663	665	

Table 13–1. Trends in Hip Dysplasia (Continued)

Breed	Rating Total Dogs	≥ 1980	1986–87	1993–94	Change ≤1980 to 1993–94
Chow Chow	% Excellent	4.2	7.9	10.0	+138.1
	% Dysplastic	22.8	24.0	14.3	-37.3
	Total Dogs	737	516	210	
Cocker Spaniel	% Excellent	12.5	10.6	9.2	-26.4
	% Dysplastic	8.4	7.6	3.1	-63.1
	Total Dogs	553	677	618	
Collie	% Excellent	11.2	14.6	30.2	169.6
	% Dysplastic	4.3	3.5	0.9	-79.1
	Total Dogs	419	144	116	
Dalmatian	% Excellent	9.7	8.9	9.9	+2.1
	% Dysplastic	7.0	4.0	3.1	-55.7
	Total Dogs	485	179	191	
Doberman Pinscher	% Excellent	12.5	19.9	17.9	+43.2
	% Dysplastic	8.2	6.3	4.5	-45.1
	Total Dogs	2,415	797	702	
English Cocker	% Excellent	11.9	17.3	16.6	+39.5
	% Dysplastic	7.3	6.0	4.8	-34.2
	Total Dogs	757	416	337	
English Setter	% Excellent	3.3	8.2	8.9	+169.7
	% Dysplastic	28.5	15.6	11.6	-59.3
	Total Dogs	1,605	548	473	
English Springer Spaniel	% Excellent	7.0	7.3	7.8	+11.4
	% Dysplastic	20.2	16.3	9.6	-52.5
	Total Dogs	1,914	687	651	
German Wirehaired Pointer	% Excellent	13.8	16.1	17.1	+23.9
	% Dysplastic	9.9	9.8	9.4	-5.1
	Total Dogs	556	192	181	
German Shorthaired Pointer	% Excellent	19.6	21.9	24.4	+24.5
	% Dysplastic	7.5	6.0	2.6	-65.3
	Total Dogs	1,449	640	706	
German Shepherd Dog	% Excellent	2.5	3.1	3.3	+32.0
	% Dysplastic	20.7	22.8	16.8	-18.8
	Total Dogs	12,810	6,284	6,453	
Giant Schnauzer	% Excellent	4.4	7.1	13.9	+215.9
	% Dysplastic	24.3	21.4	16.0	-34.2
	Total Dogs	963	253	194	
Golden Retriever	% Excellent	1.8	3.2	4.7	+161.1
	% Dysplastic	23.4	23.8	16.6	-29.1
	Total Dogs	18,170	7,784	6,918	
Gordon Setter	% Excellent	3.8	8.9	9.8	+157.9
	% Dysplastic	25.9	21.4	19.2	-25.9
	Total Dogs	1,142	439	256	

Common Hereditary Problems   177

Table 13–1. Trends in Hip Dysplasia (Continued)

Breed	Rating Total Dogs	≥1980	1986–87	1993–94	Change ≤1980 to 1993–94
Great Pyrenees	% Excellent	8.8	13.1	18.3	+108.0
	% Dysplastic	9.9	12.4	8.7	-12.1
	Total Dogs	851	367	311	
Great Dane	% Excellent	6.2	11.3	13.9	+124.7
	% Dysplastic	13.4	12.3	9.5	-29.1
	Total Dogs	2,219	495	490	
Irish Setter	% Excellent	5.0	9.0	12.1	+142.0
	% Dysplastic	15.1	12.8	9.2	-39.1
	Total Dogs	3,954	534	371	
Keeshond	% Excellent	5.7	10.8	6.9	+21.1
	% Dysplastic	7.9	9.2	3.4	-57.0
	Total Dogs	812	249	204	
Labrador Retriever	% Excellent	10.4	16.0	17.7	+70.2
	% Dysplastic	14.5	13.6	11.5	-20.7
	Total Dogs	15,342	9,861	12,331	
Newfoundland	% Excellent	3.3	6.5	9.8	+197.0
	% Dysplastic	32.4	25.0	17.8	-45.1
	Total Dogs	1,888	928	732	
Norwegian Elkhound	% Excellent	5.4	4.0	8.1	+50.0
	% Dysplastic	24.8	26.6	10.9	-56.0
	Total Dogs	1,031	248	148	
Old English Sheepdog	% Excellent	7.4	14.6	14.5	+95.9
	% Dysplastic	23.6	20.4	8.4	-64.4
	Total Dogs	4,876	553	332	
Poodle	% Excellent	7.7	9.0	10.7	+39.0
	% Dysplastic	17.3	15.8	8.7	-49.7
	Total Dogs	2,404	893	903	
Puli	% Excellent	13.0	24.3	26.2	+101.5
	% Dysplastic	12.4	7.8	3.1	-75.0
	Total Dogs	508	103	65	
Rhodesian Ridgeback	% Excellent	13.9	19.4	22.2	+59.7
	% Dysplastic	12.2	7.0	2.4	-80.3
	Total Dogs	1,198	527	603	
Rottweiler	% Excellent	4.0%	7.6	10.4	+160.0
	% Dysplastic	24.0	23.5	17.0	-29.2
	Total Dogs	6,869	10,057	7,247	
Saint Bernard	% Excellent	4.5	2.5	3.9	-13.3
	% Dysplastic	47.8	51.9	44.2	-7.5
	Total Dogs	843	79	102	
Samoyed	% Excellent	8.1	7.9	11.9	+46.9
	% Dysplastic	13.8	11.0	9.2	-33.3
	Total Dogs	4,182	1,051	564	

Table 13–1. Trends in Hip Dysplasia (Continued)

Breed	Rating Total Dogs	≥ 1980	1986–87	1993–94	Change ≤1980 to 1993–94
Shetland Sheepdog	% Excellent	26.0	27.5	27.7	+6.5
	% Dysplastic	6.0	9.1	4.0	-33.3
	Total Dogs	550	586	1,075	
Siberian Husky	% Excellent	24.2	38.0	35.0	+44.6
	% Dysplastic	2.7	2.1	0.9	-66.7
	Total Dogs	4,689	972	571	
Standard Schnauzer	% Excellent	7.5	9.3	6.0	-20.0
	% Dysplastic	11.5	10.2	6.5	-43.5
	Total Dogs	799	236	199	
Vizsla	% Excellent	12.1	16.0	17.0	+40.5
	% Dysplastic	10.4	8.3	3.8	-63.5
	Total Dogs	1,646	486	607	
Weimaraner	% Excellent	12.7	20.9	22.4	+76.4
	% Dysplastic	12.1	10.5	5.3	-56.2
	Total Dogs	1,680	526	700	
West Highland White Terrier	% Excellent	11.4	17.4	17.2	+50.9
	% Dysplastic	6.7	4.9	3.4	-49.3
	Total Dogs	570	386	296	
Total of all Breeds	% Excellent	7.8	10.5	12.2	+56.4
	% Dysplastic	17.4	17.6	12.3	-29.3
	Total Dogs	127,315	62,653	61,322	

Breeds with more than 400 dogs evaluated in or before 1980 compared to dogs born in 1986–1987 and 1993–94.
Source: Orthopedic Foundation of America, "30 Years of Progress: OFA Data Confirm Dramatic Improvements in Dogs Hips," Letter, July 1, 1997.

percentage indicates the genetic expression, and the balance is attributed to the environment. Remember, *heritability values are not a constant; they apply only to a specific population at a specific time.*

After reviewing the literature on the heritability of HD in German Shepherds, Willis commented: "All these estimates were made on German Shepherd Dogs and are the best available. They suggest that between 25 and 40% of the variation seen in hip structure is due to additive genetic factors and the remaining 75–60% is caused by non-additive genetic factors or by environmental aspects."[33]

A biomechanical disorder. Despite the significant reduction of hip dysplasia in many breeds, little progress has been made in identifying the specific system or biomechanism being affected by the genes. The best analysis of this question is still Riser's classic 1975 paper—"The Dog as a Model for the Study of Hip Dysplasia: Growth, Form, and Development of the Normal and Dysplastic Hip Joint"—which includes an excellent review of the early literature plus Riser's own research. Although the material is not recent, the lengthy paper (over 100 pages) explores aspects of HD that cannot be found elsewhere.

Riser's most startling point is that the genes that produce HD are not related to the structure of the hip itself. In studies of both dogs and humans, the hip joints are *always normal at birth,* when the acetabulum and femoral head are composed of soft cartilage. "The changes in bone merely reflect changes that occur in the cartilage, supporting connective tissue and muscles."[34]

This led Riser to describe HD as "a biomechanical disease representing a disparity between primary muscle mass and disproportionately rapid skeletal growth. . . . The lag or failure of the muscle to develop and reach functional maturity at the same rate as the skeleton results in joint instability. Abnormal development is induced when the acetabulum and femoral head pull apart and trigger a series of events that end in hip dysplasia and degenerative joint disease." In other words, the genes that are critical to the development of HD are not related to the structure of the hip itself but rather to traits that interfere with the hip's normal growth and development. Stress begins when the puppy pushes itself to nurse. The most critical period of development of HD is from birth to sixty days. The newborn's hip joints are soft and elastic, and "any changes in biomechanical balance, stress, compression, traction, muscle pull, lubrication or congruity [that is, harmony between the parts] between the femoral head and acetabulum affect the programmed pattern of normal hip joint development."[35]

Riser points out that *"dysplasia can be increased, decreased, or prevented by controlling the degree of joint instability."*[36] He explains:

> The changes that occur seem to correlate with the degree and length of time of the biomechanical imbalance. If the imbalance is corrected and congruity [harmony] is reestablished before a certain stage in the development of the hip, progression of the dysplasia stops and the hip returns to normal development.
>
> If full congruity can be maintained until the muscles and nerves are fully functional, muscle power is sufficient to maintain biomechanical balance so that full congruity between the parts is maintained.[37]

In children, development of HD can be stopped and even reversed if discovered early enough. The treatment is to apply a Frejka splint, consisting of a pillow that is belted between the legs to maintain continuous contact between the acetabulum and hip joint until the acetabulum deepens. The importance of mechanical congruity is further demonstrated by the effect of cultural variations of the ways of carrying infants on the incidence of HD in the population. In cultures where the mothers carry infants bound to their waists, with the legs in abduction (like the Frejka splint), HD is almost unknown; in cultures that bind infants to cradleboards, which prevent abduction and congruity, the incidence is very high. When one group of Navajo mothers began using diapers, which hold the legs in abduction, instead of cradleboards, the incidence of HD dropped dramatically, far more than would be consistent with a purely genetic disorder.[38]

In one study, newborn pigs were placed in casts that extended their legs like humans in cradleboards. Dysplastic changes developed immediately. When the casts were removed, the changes stopped and the shape of joint improved.[39]

What about dogs? Yes, dysplasia can be prevented in a congenitally predisposed young dog by confinement in small cage that forces the puppy to sit on its haunches most of the time.[40] Of course, this usually ruins the puppy's temperament and does nothing to improve the breed, but it is possible.

Riser concludes that (a) HD "occurs only if hip joint instability and joint incongruity are present in the young child or animal" and that (b) HD "can be prevented if hip joint congruity can be maintained until ossification [bone formation] makes the acetabulum less elastic and the abductor muscles and supporting soft tissues become sufficiently strong and functional to prevent femoral head subluxation."[41]

Identifying the multiple traits. Riser explored the multiple hereditary traits that affect biomechanical stability. The incidence of HD is about the same in breeds with similar physical structure *even though there is no genetic exchange between the breeds.* Riser ranked thirty-eight medium to giant breeds according to the prevalence of HD, which ranged from 43.2 to 4.2 percent. The six breeds with the highest percentage and nine with the lowest were compared. Although the groups varied widely in appearance, similarities emerged when compared for body size, body type, and growth pattern. The incidence was highest in breeds characterized by poor muscles and coordination and lowest in breeds characterized by good muscles and coordination.[42]

Height and weight are clearly related to the development of HD. Breeds with the lowest rates of dysplasia tend to be closer to the size of the ancestral dog than those with higher rates. Riser points out that, again, this is a biomechanical function; engineers knew that "when the height of a structure was doubled, the bracing had to be tripled or the structure would fall of its own weight." HD rarely occurs in dogs less than 30.5 cm (9.26 inches) tall and weighing less than 11.3 kg (24.91 pounds). At least half of dogs that are over 50.8 cm (15.43 inches) tall and weigh 34 kg (74.95 pounds) or more have HD.[43]

Growth patterns that predispose puppies to HD appear to be a combination of several factors: "growth, weight gain, and nursing aggressiveness" appear to be related to risk.[44]

Overweight puppies run a high risk of stressing and injuring the muscles that maintain correct contact within the joint. In general, the age of onset and severity of symptoms is higher in heavier, more rapidly growing puppies. More than weight alone is involved. Males typically weigh more than bitches, and within each gender group, the heaviest pups are at greater risk for developing HD.[45]

Nicholas comments that "restricted feeding during the growth phase can reduce the liability to hip dysplasia." Kasström's fascinating study analyzed the effects of varying nutrition and weight gain in five litters with a high parental frequency of hip dysplasia. In each litter, half was fed a high-caloric diet and the other a low-caloric diet. Their hips were palpated before the age of twelve weeks. The study "found that hip dysplasia was more frequent, occurred earlier, and became more severe in the dogs with a rapid weight gain caused by increased caloric intake than in the dogs which had a low weight gain because of restricted feeding." Furthermore, the final diagnosis showed a closer correlation between feeding and weight gain than for tightness or laxity of the hip joints before twelve weeks of age.[46]

Temperament, too, plays a role. The first stress on hips occurs when a puppy supports itself to nurse, hind legs pushing hard. Riser observed that the heaviest pups were "more aggressive, worked the hardest while nursing, and spent the most time feeding."[47]

Table 13–2 Relationship Between Phenotype and Hip Dysplasia

Trait	Low Incidence	High Incidence
BODY SIZE		
Size and weight	Near that of the ancestral dog	Giant, weight 2–3 times that of ancestral dog
Bone	Trim, small in diameter	Coarse, large in diameter
Head	Narrow and long	Broad and oversized
Feet	Small and well arched	Oversized and splayed
BODY TYPE		
General	Slender racing, hunting, fighting type	Stocky type
Thorax	Deep and narrow	Barrel shaped
Skin	Trim and tight	Loose, thick, wrinkled
Body fat	Limited	Excess
Muscles	Well-developed, hard	Deficient in quantity and tone
Joints	Stable, well-developed ligaments and tendons	Unstable, weak ligaments and tendons
Gait	Well-coordinated, fleet, light-footed	Poorly coordinated, slow, awkward, heavy-footed
GROWTH		
Birth	Small at birth	Fat and heavy for age
Growth	Slow	Early rapid
Maturation	Late physical and sexual	Early physical and sexual
Appetite	Good but self-limiting	Indulgent

Source: W. H. Riser, "The Dog as a Model for the Study of Hip Dysplasia," *Veterinary Pathology* 12(1975): 244.

The positive correlation between the pelvic muscle index and the incidence of HD further substantiates the importance of the relationship between height, weight, and muscle. The index is determined by the following formula:

$$\frac{\text{WEIGHT OF PELVIC MUSCLES (KG)}}{\text{TOTAL BODY WEIGHT (KG)}} \times 100 = \text{PELVIC MUSCLE INDEX}$$

Riser found that the probability of HD could be predicted by this index: HD rarely occurs in dogs with an index over 10.89 and always occurs in dogs with an index below 9.0. Furthermore, he also determined that the pelvic muscle mass is more dependent on heredity than on exercise.[48]

The relationship between joint laxity and the development of HD has long been recognized. Riser writes: "There is evidence that the wide range of acetabular and femoral changes occurring in hip dysplasia are the consequences of joint laxity. The possibility that this may be associated with or influenced by the rate of muscle maturation has not been explored."[49]

Riser concludes that hip dysplasia is related to the

> genetic transmission and heritability of certain body size, type, conformation, movement, growth pattern, and temperament. This conclusion is based on the facts that the prevalence of hip dysplasia is approximately the same in a number of breeds with similar body characteristics and there is no gene flow between these purebred breeds. Since these facts must be respected, biomechanical and environmental factors associated with certain body conformation and size must be considered as the causes.[50]

Another environmental factor in the development of hip dysplasia is excessive exercise during the growing phase, when it produces injury and stress to vulnerable, rapidly growing hips, especially between the ages of four and six months. Although studies have shown that extreme confinement of puppies substantially reduces the incidence of HD, the early social deprivation produces adverse effects on temperament and trainability.[51]

Riser suggests that the reason that HD is so rare in wolves are that they grow slowly, remain relatively underweight, and do not begin hunting until between six and ten months old, all of which minimize stress and injury to their immature joints.[52]

Additive genetic action and variance. The cumulative contribution of polygenes at all loci toward the expression of a polygenic trait is described as *additive gene action*, and the averaging effects of substituting one polygene for another is known as *additive genetic variance*. Although additive variance does not always indicate that the genes are, in fact, exhibiting additive gene action, it is a useful working concept for dog breeders. These concepts were introduced in Chapter 6 and are repeated here to clarify how they may be interacting with hip dysplasia.

The phenotypic traits that appear to predispose dogs to hip dysplasia are related to body size, body type, growth rate, weight, temperament, pelvic muscle mass, and joint laxity. The relative importance of each may differ in each breed, and all may not be factors in every breed. To visualize their interaction, consider each as a distinct allele that controls the expression of the following specific traits:

a = body size
b = body type
c = growth rate
d = weight
e = temperament
f = pelvic muscle mass
g = joint laxity

The diagrams and tables illustrating polygenic interactions (pages 83–84) illustrate the interaction of just three alleles, and we have identified seven that may be related to HD. By selecting the normal hip phenotype for many generations, the additive effect of these many genes may be shifted toward the desired range of expression.

Diagnostic Concerns

Breeder resistance and dissatisfaction with the identification of HD through the traditional X-ray evaluation of hip phenotype is based on a number of interrelated factors.

Table 13–3. Relationship Between Pelvic Muscle Mass and Hip Dysplasia

Index	Expected Incidence
14.20	All dogs have normal hips, and the disease was unreported
12.17	All dogs have normal hips, but the disease was reported in some siblings
11.63	Probability 94% that dogs would have normal hips
10.89	Probability 86% that dogs would have normal hips
9.00	All dogs have some degree of dysplasia
8.00	All dogs have badly dysplastic hips
5.60	All dogs have luxated hips

Source: W. H. Riser, "The Dog as a Model for the Study of Hip Dysplasia," *Veterinary Pathology* 12 (1975): 254.

Radiographic versus clinical hip dysplasia. There may be little correlation between a radiographic diagnosis of HD and the expression of symptomatic (clinical) HD; in fact, dogs with amazingly severe radiographic dysplasia may never have any clinical symptoms.

F. W. Nicholas, the author of *Veterinary Genetics*, discusses the problem:

> One of the causes of the controversy is that HD is traditionally diagnosed not on clinical signs but by subjective evaluation of a radiograph. . . . The problem with this is that in most populations, the incidence of abnormal hips as diagnosed by radiography is much higher than the incidence of clinical hip dysplasia (CHD). This immediately creates a credibility gap between veterinarians and breeders, because all too often a dog that can jump a fence six feet high is diagnosed as being dysplastic according to its radiograph. The solution to this problem is for breeders and veterinarians to realize that there is a difference between *selection criteria and selection objectives.*[53]

In other words, the objective is the elimination of symptomatic clinical hip dysplasia. The criteria, however, is the subjective assessment of the hip's phenotype to identify radiographic hip dysplasia, which is not necessarily associated with any physical impairment.

Nicholas continues:

> The failure to distinguish between selection objectives and selection criteria has led to much confusion in relation to HD control programs. The problem is that most articles and papers on HD discuss radiographic diagnosis as if it were clinical diagnosis. Thus, when people talk about the incidence of HD being altered as a result of a selection programme, they are almost always referring to the incidence of RHD and not CHD.[54]

All OFA statistics are based on radiographic HD, and unfortunately, there are no statistics for clinical HD. In addition, the statistics are based on a select population.

Breed variance. Willis points out another source of dissatisfaction: "One problem frequently overlooked in the development of radiographic standards for hip joints is the variability between breeds. There is a tendency to assume that normality is a constant feature identical in all breeds."[55] Developing standards for each breed might reduce the gap between radiographic and clinical HD.

Phenotypic variance. Phenotypic variation can be produced by a number of factors that affect the evaluation of X-rays. E. A. Corley, long-time head of the OFA states: "Anesthesia, estrus, level of physical activity, and age are factors that may affect the magnitude of radiographic subluxation." He recommends taking X-rays one month before or after estrus. In addition, "differences in positioning, such as pelvic rotation, femurs not placed parallel, or stifles not rotated inwardly, is a major cause of phenotypic variation within a population."[56]

Experienced breeders have learned that the veterinarian's skill in positioning dogs for X-rays is of critical importance. The appearance of hip depth and fit depends on correct positioning and often makes a critical difference in the OFA classification. If the depth, shape, and tightness in the socket appear questionable, it may be a matter of incorrect position, and it is usually worthwhile to have a second X-ray taken by another veterinarian. If the X-ray shows clear evidence of bony spurs or arthritis, however, better positioning cannot alter the diagnosis.

Early diagnosis. Naturally, breeders hope for a reliable way to identify HD in puppies. Palpation of the hips under anesthesia between the ages of eight and twelve weeks identified varying degrees of joint laxity, which was thought to predict the quality of the hips at maturity. During the heyday of hip palpation, conscientious breeders put down many puppies, even entire litters, before the correlation was found to be inconsistent. Willis pooled the results of three palpation studies. Puppies were palpated at about two months and later x-rayed. From 90 puppies diagnosed as normal on palpation, 25.6 percent were diagnosed as dysplastic when x-rayed, and from 108 puppies diagnosed as dysplastic on palpation, only 66.7 percent were diagnosed as dysplastic when x-rayed.[57]

To meet the need for earlier identification of HD, the OFA has been evaluating the X-rays of younger dogs. In the preliminary evaluations done for dogs ranging from four to twenty-three months old, the mean age was eleven months. Repeat studies at twenty-four months by the same veterinary radiologists showed reliability ranging from 71.4 percent in Chesapeake Bay Retrievers to 100 percent in Welsh Springer Spaniels. Overall, of the dogs rated dysplastic on the preliminary evaluation, 2.58 percent received normal ratings at twenty-four months. Of those rated normal, 8.49 percent received dysplastic ratings at twenty-four months; of those rated borderline, 56.9 percent received normal ratings at twenty-four months.[58]

Like palpation, the most recent method of early diagnosis, PennHIP (University of Pennsylvania Hip Improvement Program) is based on identifying joint laxity. Its objective is "to provide an improved method of determination in a relatively young dog, of the later development of CHD." It is a radiographic procedure based on positioning the dog to measure passive hip laxity (the degree of joint looseness when the dog's muscles are completely relaxed). The procedure is performed by veterinarians who have been trained and certified and who can be contacted through ICG (International Canine Genetics). The results are presented as a percentile that compares the amount of laxity with others of the same breed rather than a on pass/fail basis. Dittmann describes the method as "acceptably accurate," adding, "as with all diagnostic tests, PennHIP's accuracy is not 100%, but in direct comparisons it is far superior to any other available diagnostic methods."[59]

(a)   (b)

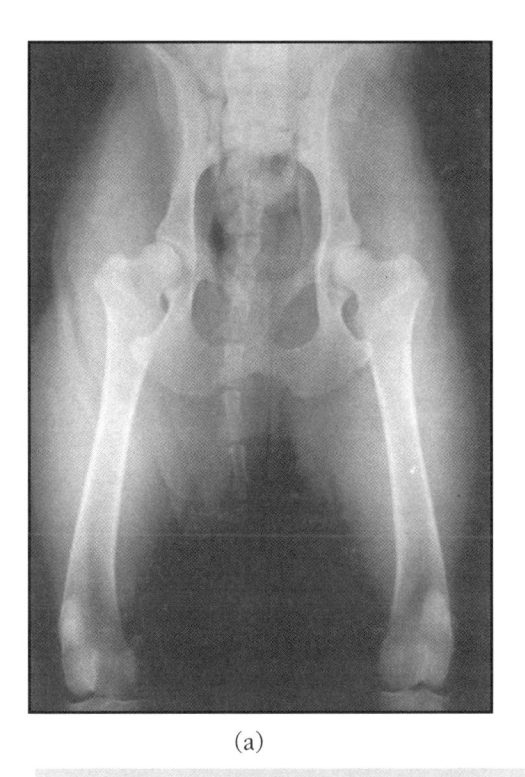

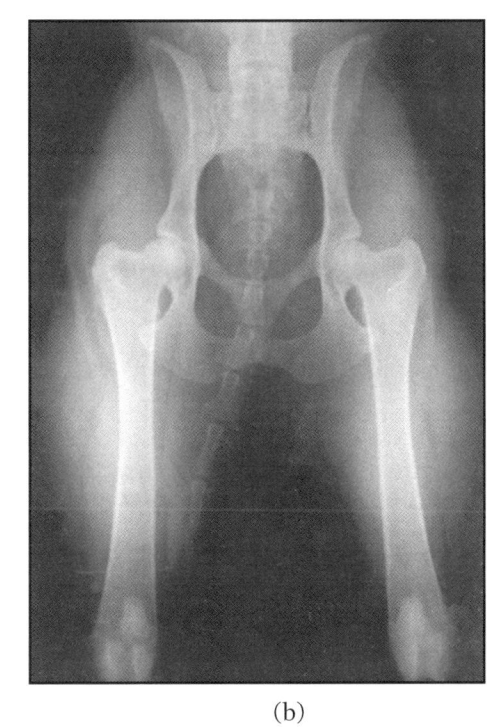

Figure 13–4. Positioning for hip X-rays. *Correct positioning is vital for correct OFA evaluations of hip X-rays.*

(a) Poor positioning. The first thing that stands out is that the femurs are not parallel. Looking closer, it can be seen that the patellas are not centered, indicating that the femurs have too much outward rotation and contributing to the shallow appearance of the hip sockets. Notice the flattened area on the hip to the left, which might be mistaken for dysplasia. This is the place that a tendon attaches to the femoral head, and it is visible only because of the extreme outward rotation. The slight tilt of the pelvis makes the hips appear asymmetrical and of uneven depth.

(b) Correct positioning. When correctly positioned, the hips appear entirely different, and the X-ray received an OFA rating of good. The hips are symmetrical, with deep sockets and smoothly rounded femoral heads.

Corley summarizes the concern of some radiologists and breeders about early diagnosis based on joint laxity:

> Virtually all dogs appear to have some degree of joint laxity; at what point this becomes abnormal in a given breed is yet to be determined. Some young and some mature dogs with joint laxity develop radiographically normal hips, and at necropsy, their hips are also normal. Others with relatively tight hips may develop radiographic and necropsy changes associated with CHD. The issues of joint laxity and stress radiography were raised in the 1960s, and a number of recent reports on these issues provide some answers and raise other questions. Therefore, the OFA recommends caution in diagnosis of CHD based solely on joint laxity unless the joint laxity is extreme.[60]

A Commonsense Approach

How many breeders and owners take great pride in feeding puppies well to speed their growth or to make them appear more mature in the show ring? How many jog with their puppies or condition them for early stamina in the field?

Genetic purists proclaim that dogs that are not genetically predisposed to HD cannot develop it and advocate stressing hips through excess weight and exercise. The problem with that approach is that it is not very realistic. Most breeders select for a multitude of traits such as correct breed temperament, working aptitude, structural balance and soundness, and type. It is not practical to keep large numbers of growing puppies until they are full grown, then euthanize those with less than perfect hips. Is it any more ethical to sell puppies to loving families on the condition that they follow such a program than it is to produce puppies from parents that have not been x-rayed at all?

As with most things, moderation and common sense suggest a reasonable approach.

Do not try to force rapid growth and early maturity by overfeeding puppies. If the ribs can be seen when the puppy stretches or turns and there is no palpable layer of fat over the ribs, the puppy's weight is about right. The best indication of good nutrition is a healthy, shining coat. Hip dysplasia is not only more frequent but also occurs earlier and is more severe in puppies that gain weight rapidly.

Give the puppy access to a large yard to run and play as desired. With self-exercise, the puppy limits his or her own activity with the onset of fatigue or stress, which the puppy cannot do when accompanying someone taking a long walk, jogging, or horseback riding. Exercise can be gradually increased *after* the thigh muscles show good development and hold the head of the femur firmly in the socket.

Using only dogs that have been x-rayed for breeding has been proven to have a cumulative beneficial effect over the generations. If it is occasionally desirable to use an exceptional individual that has radiographic (but not clinical) dysplasia to reinforce some of the other desired breed traits, make full disclosure to buyers and be sure that the puppies are certified before being bred to insure that the mating produces no ongoing setbacks in hip quality.

ELBOW DYSPLASIA

The complex elbow joint consists of three bones—the humerus, the radius, and the ulna. According to the *Merck Veterinary Manual*, "There are 3 conditions that affect the canine elbow joint that can be regarded as *elbow dysplasia*: the ununited anconeal process (UAP), the fragmented coronoid process (FCP), and OCD [osteochondritis dissecans] of the medial humeral condyle; all of which are manifestations of osteochondrosis." E. A. Corley of the OFA and his associates gave the following definition: "Canine elbow dysplasia is a developmental anomaly of the elbow joint that is manifested as early osteoarthritis with or without an ununited anconeal process. It may occur bilaterally or unilaterally, with varying degrees of severity."[61]

All three conditions produce the same general symptoms of lameness, pain elicited by flexing and extending the elbow, and crepitation (cracking noise). All lead to early secondary degenerative changes—that is, osteoarthritis. Surgery to remove bone fragments and minimize the severity of degenerative changes is moderately successful. There are some important differences in the breeds affected, however, as well as other factors.

Ununited Anconeal Process

The anconeal process is one of the protruding bony structures on the ulna that articulates with the humerus. The anconeal process develops separately from other bone-growth points. The developmental point appears at about 91 days, and the anconeal process normally unites with the ulna at about 124 days.[62]

The specific cause is unknown. Although trauma has been suggested, the prevalence in some breeds suggests a hereditary disorder. UAP is reported in many breeds, but it is most common in German Shepherd Dogs, Basset Hounds, and Saint Bernards. It is also reported in Irish Wolfhounds, Newfoundlands, Bloodhounds, Labrador Retrievers, Afghan Hounds, and Great Danes.[63]

Fragmented Coronoid Process

The coronoid process is the second protruding bony structure on the ulna that articulates with the humerus. FCP can occur alone or in conjunction with osteochondritis dissecans.

Again, the prevalence of FCP in some breeds suggests a hereditary disorder. It is most common in German Shepherd Dogs, Labrador Retrievers, Golden Retrievers, Newfoundlands, and Saint Bernards.

Osteochondritis Dissecans

Osteochondritis dissecans (OCD) is osteochondrosis of any moving joint cartilage.

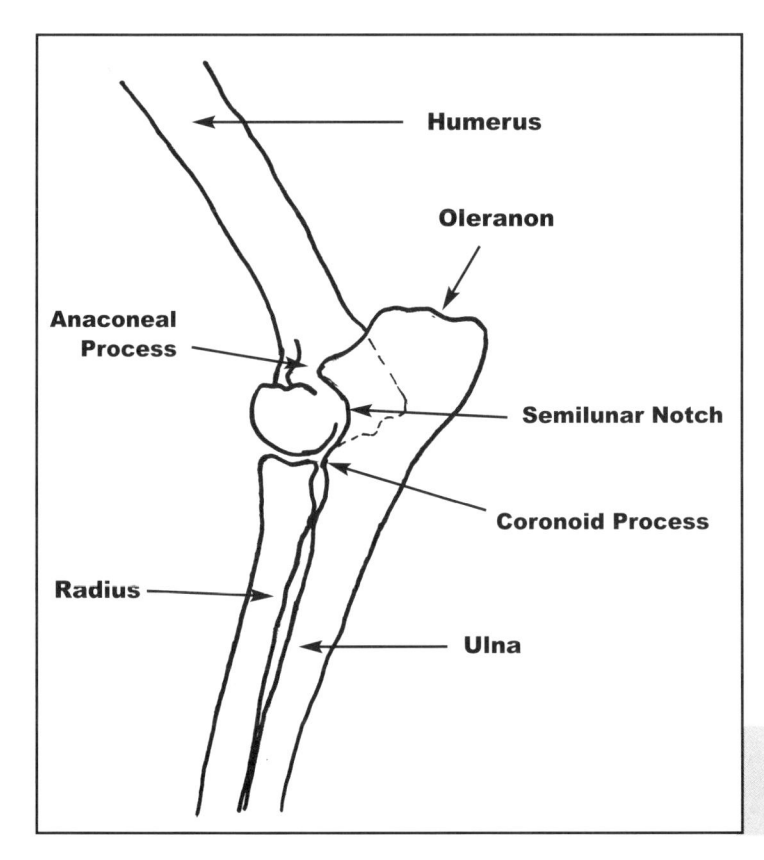

Figure 13–5. The elbow joint.

The definitions of *osteochondrosis* vary:
- *Merck Veterinary Manual.* A "disturbance in endochondral ossification that may involve the articular cartilage (osteochondritis dissecans), the physis (retained cartilage cores, Osgood-Slatter disease), or the area of fusion of periarticular ossification centers (ununited anconeal process, fragmented coronoid process)."
- *Encyclopedia of Animal Care.* A "condition in which there is destruction of bone and cartilage."
- *Leonard's Orthopedic Surgery of the Dog and Cat.* A "disease of immature joints characterized by separation of the cartilage from the underlying bone, lameness, and degeneration of the joint. Occurs most often in the shoulder, it also occurs in the distal humerus (elbow), stifle, and hock."[64]

A 1990 report of the dogs (mostly Labrador Retrievers and Golden Retrievers) owned by the Guide Dogs for the Blind in Great Britain concluded that OCD had a high heritability, was significantly higher in males than in females, and was multifactorial. A 1991 report of a dog guide Labrador Retriever colony in Australia concluded: "The incidence in progeny varied between different sires and dams and was associated with the severity of radiographic evidence of elbow arthritis in sires and dams with dams contributing significantly more than sires, suggesting a 'maternal' effect." Surgical treatment produced a recovery rate of 84 percent. The report closed with: "It is now important to investigate how dams are producing this effect. If it turns out to be non-genetic, incidence may be reduced by appropriate husbandry and management of the breeding females."[65]

PATELLAR LUXATION

Patellar luxation is the dislocation of the patella, the bone in the stifle joint that corresponds with the human knee, and it may affect either one or both rear legs. Like elbow dysplasia, the term is applied to three distinct disorders.

Medial Luxation (Toy, Miniature, and Large Breeds)

Found in toy, miniature, and large breeds, medial luxation is considered hereditary, though the mode of heredity is unknown. The age of onset ranges from shortly after birth to old age, and the symptoms vary with severity. In small breeds, from 75 to 80 percent of patellar luxation is of the medial type. The affected leg typically rotates inward (out at hock, feet pointed inward), with most weight shifted to the forelegs.

Lateral Luxation (Toy and Miniature Breeds)

The heritability of lateral luxation in toy and miniature breeds is unknown. The usual age of onset is from five to eight years. The symptoms may develop suddenly, sometimes following minor trauma. This type is associated more with soft tissue damage than with skeletal abnormalities. The position of the affected legs is described as knock-kneed.

Lateral Luxation (Large and Giant Breeds)

Lateral luxation is most common in Saint Bernards, Great Danes, and Irish Wolfhounds, and heredity is suspected. The typical age of onset is about five or six months, and it usually affects both legs.

THE ROLE OF NUTRITION

With skeletal disorders, identification of the hereditary mode is particularly difficult because nutrition—an environmental factor—seems to play a particularly critical role in their development. The papers presented at the Waltham International Symposium on Nutrition of Small Companion Animals and published in a 1991 supplement of the *Journal of Nutrition* explore the relationship between nutrition and skeletal growth disturbances. Dämmrich gave the best overview:

> The incidence of growth disturbance in the skeletons of the large and giant breeds is continuously increasing. There is disagreement among investigators regarding the nomenclature and causes of these disturbances. There is concern whether all or only some of these growth disturbances are osteochondroses, and there is lack of agreement as to the roles that nutrition, genetics and biomechanics play in their pathogenesis [source of abnormalities]. . . .
>
> Currently, the osteochondrosis syndrome is considered by some to be a biomechanical disease. Lesion development requires two essential elements: rapid skeletal growth and an overloading of the growing skeleton due to increasing muscle mass and body weight. Some observations support this theory. Rapidly growing males are more frequently affected than female dogs. The incidence of osteochondrosis increases with preferential selection for increased body size.[66]

Dämmrich describes a study of Great Danes puppies in which one group was fed as much as they wanted and the other was fed 20–30 percent less through the age of six months. The free-fed puppies had accelerated bone growth, but the bone was of relatively low density and had less resistance to biomechanical lesions. "Overnutrition in the growing puppy creates a mismatch between the rates of body weight increase and skeletal growth, and this eventually leads to overloading skeletal structures." He concludes that overnutrition predisposes puppies to the development of osteochondrosis.[67]

Most breeders are aware that insufficient calcium, phosphorus, and vitamin D produce the skeletal deformities of rickets, and some believe that it is important to provide growing puppies with extra calcium to be certain their growth is not stunted. With modern balanced puppy rations, this is not only unnecessary but also very dangerous, especially if only calcium is added.

Studies of the effect of chronic excess calcium in growing puppies have shown that oversupplementation with calcium can produce *stunted growth,* osteochondritis dissecans, canine wobbler syndrome, and other skeletal disorders.[68]

The NRC recommended daily allowance of calcium is 120 mg per pound of body weight (265 mg per kg); the recommended daily allowance of phosphorus is 100 mg per pound of body weight (220 mg per kg). In dry kibble, this would be about 1.1 percent of calcium and 0.9 percent of phosphorus.[69] These amounts are actually exceeded in some puppy rations.

Clearly, there is a great deal more to be learned about skeletal disorders, both in regard to heredity and nutrition. Meanwhile, common sense may prevent the development of some problems.

- Begin with a good quality puppy ration, but be careful not to overfeed the puppy; the "right" food and amount is whatever keeps the coat glossy but the ribs *slightly* showing until at least ten months old.
- Never let a puppy leap for a Frisbee and minimize any activities that stimulate jumping.
- Limit the puppy to self-initiated exercise in a fenced yard until at least six months old—older if the breed has the structure associated with a high incidence of CHD.

Such simple measures minimize risks and may contribute substantially to a long, healthy life for your dog.

SELECTION—THE THEORIES

Chapter 14

*S*election is the differential reproduction that changes a population's gene frequencies. With natural selection, the gene frequency is influenced by traits that improve the probability of survival and reproduction. Natural selection occurs in a random-mating population because individuals differ in fertility and viability, and the genes for traits that favor survival and reproduction tend to increase in frequency. The survival of fertilized eggs is random, however, and the transfer of genes to the next generation is not necessarily uniform. Artificial selection, of course, is the differential reproduction caused by human intervention.

Although all breeding implies artificial selection, definitions vary. One defines *animal breeding* as "the practical application of genetic analysis for development of lines of domestic animals suited to human purposes." Another definition is that *breeding* is a combination of selection procedures and systems of mating.[1]

EFFECTS OF SELECTION

Artificial selection alters a population's gene frequency, increasing the frequency for selected traits. The phenotype of the selected parents differs from that of the population average for either one or for multiple traits. The difference between the average of the parental population and the average of their offspring is known as the *selection response*.

The selection response diminishes as the trait becomes widespread in the population, until there is no further response to selection. For example, all Rottweilers are black and tan. There is also a limit to the response for traits such as speed and size. Greyhounds can go no faster because of the underlying structural limitations, and Great Danes can grow no taller.

Theoretically, phenotypic variance should disappear when genotypic variance is eliminated by selective breeding. Surprisingly, many studies have shown that there is a

limit to the selection response and reduction of variance (that is, inbreeding); variance may persist even after inbreeding for over thirty generations.[2] The selection limit occurs for several reasons:
- Inbred homozygotes are more sensitive to environmental variations than heterozygotes
- A purebred population may already be near the selection limits
- The trait being selected for may be opposed by natural selection—that is, fertility and viability—and the heterozygotes may be superior; natural selection resists inbreeding because homozygotes are less fit to survive[3]

Selection to eliminate undesirable single-gene traits that are complete dominants is highly effective. Because the phenotype expresses the dominant gene, one might say that what you see is what you get. It is extremely difficult, however, to entirely eliminate a recessive trait from a population. Although selection can reduce frequency of a recessive gene, the response to selection decreases as the frequency of the gene decreases because of the difficulty of identifying heterozygotes. The development of screening methods that identify heterozygotes, of course, makes recessive traits as responsive to selection as dominant traits.

To illustrate the effect of gene frequency and difficulty of eliminating recessive genes, imagine that a commercial parakeet breeder with an aviary containing 1,000 randomly mating birds—900 green (*GG* or *Gg*) and 100 blue (*gg*)—decides to develop pure color strains. A pure strain of blues, of course, can be created immediately simply by separating them from the greens, but what about the greens? A calculation of the gene frequency would predict that of the remaining 900 green birds, 400 are homozygous *GG*, and 500 are heterozygous *Gg*. Removing the homozygous blues shifts the gene frequency, and the next generation would have about about 540 homozygous greens (*GG*), 480 heterozygous greens (*Gg*), and 60 homozygous blues (*gg*). Further culling will reduce the number of blue birds in successive generations, but with random mating, it is unlikely that the trait could be entirely eliminated.

SELECTION PROCEDURES

The standard selection procedures are very general. Keep in mind that they were developed for working with large populations, often with species that reproduce rapidly, such as mice, which first reproduce at nine weeks, then every four weeks thereafter. These procedures have been widely applied to domestic animals, often with the objective of improving traits of economic importance such as the amount of milk or the number of eggs.

SINGLE TRAITS

Individual Selection

Individual selection for a single trait is also called *mass selection* and *performance selection*. The selection of breeding animals solely for one trait has been spectacularly successful with traits such as egg laying and milk production. The procedure produces a rapid change of gene frequency, which diminishes as the trait becomes widespread in the population.

The method has had some applications for dog breeding. For example, traits such as coat or color were given priority during the developmental stages of some breeds. Breeds used as guide dogs for the blind showed a marked increase in the number that successfully completed training when selected for this single quality of guiding. Most breeders, however, must select for such a variety of traits that individual selection is simply not practical.

Tandem Selection

Similar to individual selection, *tandem selection* focuses on one trait and, after improvement, then moves on to another. The sequence of traits is determined by the breeder's priorities.

This procedure has very limited practical application, working best with traits that have a definite economic value. With dairy cattle, for example, the breeder might decide to focus first on improving milk volume and then on altering its fat content.

MULTIPLE TRAITS

Independent Culling Levels

Setting a minimum standard for a spectrum of traits and discarding all animals that are below the minimum for all characters is known as *independent culling levels*. This is probably the oldest form of selection used by animal breeders. Farmers have always tried to retain the best animals to be used for breeding—sheep that produce the best wool, swine with the best weight gain, leanest meat, and so forth.

The advantage is that the procedure considers many traits simultaneously, which forces the breeder to identify the most important ones. In addition, the culling may be an ongoing process: some may be culled at weaning, some at a year, and some at breeding age. The disadvantage of independent culling levels is the lack of flexibility and the difficulty of defining realistic criteria. Unless the scale is very carefully planned, there is danger of culling otherwise outstanding animals for relatively trivial traits. Dog breeders tend to discard smashing individuals for mismarks or excessive size and to keep mediocre ones that have no glaring faults but no special merits. The table illustrating independent culling levels (Table 14-1) is an example of what might be developed for adult Whippets.

Total Score Index

A variation of independent culling levels, the *total score index* (also called *selection index*) assigns each trait a numerical value. Quantitative geneticists have developed this procedure to a sophisticated science for livestock breeders, using elaborate equations to measure the heritability of traits as well as their genetic correlation and economic value.

The advantage of the procedure is that there is no limit to the number of different traits graded, and an index systematcially identifies the relative importance of each trait. Mating the highest-scoring individuals has been remarkably successful with livestock; in fact, the total score index is considered the most effective of all selection procedures.

The application of the total score index for dog breeding presents several obstacles. The first problem is the population size—what is practical for several hundred

Table 14–1. Independent Culling Levels (Whippet Adult)

Trait	Minimum Level	\multicolumn{6}{c}{Dogs Evaluated}
		1	2	3	4	5	6
1 Breed type & balance	Very Good	EX	VG	G	G	VG	EX
2 Sound front	Very Good	EX	VG	VG	EX	VG	EX
3 Sound rear	Very Good	EX	VG	EX	EX	VG	VG
4 Head	Very Good	VG	VG	VG	VG	VG	G
5 Ears	Correct	OK	OK	OK	prick	OK	OK
6 Bite	Scissors	OK	OK	OK	OK	OK	OK
7 Eye color	Brown or hazel	OK	OK	OK	blue	OK	OK
8 Eye rim	Full pigment	inc.	OK	OK	OK	OK	OK
9 Height	19–22 in.	22	23	20	21	22	21
10 Movement	Very Good	EX	VG	G	VG	VG	EX
11 Temperament	Correct	EX	G	VG	VG	EX	EX
12 Racing desire	Very Good	EX	VG	G	EX	EX	EX
Final Decision	Reason rejected	8	—	10,12	5,7	—	3

Key: EX = Excellent; VG = Very Good; G = Good; inc. = incomplete pigmentation

cattle or several thousand chickens is difficult with even twenty purebred dogs. The other obstacle is that the dramatic success with livestock is based on mathematical values of quantitative traits. Remember, selection alters gene frequency, which in turn alters heritability values, and the information must be determined for each population as well as updated for each generation. Few breeders would have the knowledge of quantitative genetics or mathematical skill to implement them.

Some dog breeders find it of value to use a modified form of the total score index that identifies specific traits and weights them. Even trying to develop one is useful because such an index requires a breeder to identify specific traits and to assign them relative values. Its usefulness depends entirely on the breeder's (*a*) ability to select traits that contribute to an ideal individual, (*b*) skill in weighting traits in order of relative importance, and (*c*) ability to evaluate the traits consistently and objectively. When creating an index for my own breed, I found it necessary to make a separate one for bitches to give due consideration to maternal qualities. Fertility is usually assumed in such indexes, but natural whelping, a generous supply of milk, and skills that insure the survival of puppies during the critical first weeks are factors to consider. Even if the implementation proves to be impractical, it is helpful to develop an index and review it every few years because priorities change with experience.

Table 14–2. Total Score Index—Individual Weimaraners (Bitches)

Desired Traits	Rating	Value	Score	Totals
CONFORMATION (30 PERCENT)				
Head and ears: balanced; high-set ears		x 1		
Neck: medium length; clean throat		x 1		
Tail set: high		x 2		
Topline: straight, strong		x 2		
Dentition: complete; scissors bite		x 3		
Feet: compact, high arch, thick pads		x 3		
Chest: brisket to elbows, good width & forechest		x 3		
Front angulation: 45-degree angle		x 3		
Front: straight		x 4		
Rear: straight and strong		x 4		
Rear angulation: balanced with front		x 4		
Subtotal				
MOVEMENT (10 PERCENT)				
Coming: moves true when approaching		x 3		
Going: moves true when going away		x 3		
Side: strong drive and reach		x 4		
Subtotal				
TEMPERAMENT (30 PERCENT)				
Field aptitude		x 15		
Trainability: eager, responsive		x 5		
Boldness: confident in any situation		x 5		
Friendliness: protective only when appropriate		x 5		
Subtotal				
HEALTH (30 PERCENT)				
Hip x-rays: OFA certified		x 10		
Natural vigor: never sick		x 10		
Maternal qualities		x 10		
Subtotal				
Total Score:				

Ratings: 0 = unacceptable; 1 = poor; 2 = fair; 3 = average; 4 = good; 5 = outstanding

Table 14–3. Total Score Index—Comparisons (Bitches)

Name (Maximum Points)	Conformation (150)	Movement (50)	Temperament (150)	Health (150)	Total (500)
Amy	136	42	130	130	448
Bessie	150	46	135	140	471
Cora	148	46	125	130	449
Daisy	150	46	90	50	336
Ellie	114	35	125	110	384

Family Selection

Geneticists define *family* as the progeny from full-sib or half-sib matings. There are two different forms of family selection:
- *Family.* The quality of the offspring (family) from two or more litters is evaluated; all individuals from the highest-scoring litter are retained for breeding, and the other litters are discarded.
- *Within family.* The quality of the offspring (family) from two or more matings is evaluated; the best individuals from each litter are retained for breeding.

Family selection is most effective with large-scale breeding operations, especially for the development of inbred strains. The limitation of applying family selection to dog breeding is it requires more than one litter for comparison.

SYSTEMS OF MATING

GRADING UP

Breeding the females on hand to a male of better quality is known as *grading up*. The best females in each generation are retained and again bred to a top sire. This is an old and widely practiced system and is an effective way to improve the quality of cattle and other commercial livestock.

When applied on an individual basis, the best example is found with racing thoroughbreds. Mares are usually bred to the best stallion that the owner can afford. The sale value of thoroughbred yearlings is strongly influenced by the performance success of the dam. Sale catalogs include a record of the dam's racing performance as well as that of her own dam and grand dam, and it also includes the performance records of their offspring. If sired by the same stallion, the yearling produced by a stakes-winning mare from a line of excellent producers will bring a far higher price than the one from a mare that never won a race from a dam line that failed to produce winners. The reason is based on the statistical evidence that the yearling produced by the stakes winner has a far greater chance earning significantly more money. Occasionally, a very average mare, known as a *blue hen*, produces several exceptional foals. The reason may be a fortuitous *nick*—a genetically complementary mating that produces superior offspring—with the stud, or it may be that chance has endowed the mare herself a better combination of genes than suggested by her own performance and bloodlines.

Grading up is a common practice among dog owners. Many breeders have started out with a very average bitch that they bred to a champion, and as their experience grew, they refined their criteria. The results tend to be unpredictable, though occasionally lucky breeders have enjoyed spectacular results with canine blue hens. As with thoroughbreds, the results of grading up are largely dependent on the genetic quality of the dam plus a lucky nick with an excellent stud.

DEGREES OF RELATIONSHIP

The degrees of relationship are dependent on and relative to the size of the population and diversity of the gene pool. Small populations that originated with a few individuals are more closely related than larger, more genetically diverse ones.

Inbreeding

When discussing systems of mating, *inbreeding* is usually defined as the mating of full siblings or parent-progeny matings, though the mating of half-siblings is also considered inbreeding. *Backcrossing*—a specific type of inbreeding—is mating to a parent or grandparent.

The goal of inbreeding is to fix and preserve desirable traits by increasing homozygosity. With dogs, the goal is to increase *prepotency*—the ability to consistently and predictably transmit specific traits to progeny—for desirable traits, which is typical of inbred strains. Homozygous traits are predictably transmitted to every offspring; heterozygous traits are transmitted randomly. In the ideal prepotent individual, therefore, the phenotype would be the same as the genotype, homozygous for all desired traits.

The *inbreeding coefficient* is defined as the probability of homozygosity by descent, and it is expressed as a percentage. In every generation, each parent transmits only half of his or her genes, and each subsequent generation again reduces the genes from an individual by half—in other words, 50 percent in first generation, 25 percent in the second, and 12.5 percent in the third. When the same ancestor appears in the pedigree of both sire and dam, it increases the probability that the same genes will be duplicated in the progeny and that they will be homozygous.

In dogs, the popularity of inbreeding varies among breeds. It is rare among Whippets, for example, and rather common among Weimaraners. The most consistently successful combination that I know of is the mating of an outstanding bitch to her top-producing grandsire. One reason for success, perhaps, is that grandpa's genetic qualities are better understood by the time he is a senior citizen. In the past, this technique has rarely been among the breeder's options because of the grandparent's age, sterility, or death. With the recent development of frozen canine semen, more breeders will be able to include backcrossing as a way to achieve their long-term goals.

The danger of inbreeding is that it also fixes undesired structural, internal, and temperamental traits. As one writer commented, inbreeding "leads to random fixation of genes, increased homozygosity and, for some traits, inbreeding depression."[4] One line known for its smashing toplines, superb balance, and solid rears used half-brother–half-sister matings with great success for about four generations, until the occasional bad bites, missing teeth, and splayed feet also became fixed in the line.

For dog breeders, then, inbreeding is a mixed bag, a system best used to achieve specific goals and to enhance desired traits while being carefully alert for developing problems. I wince every time I overhear a ringside novice say, "Inbreeding is the only way I can develop my own strain." Willis warns that inbreeding is "dangerous in the wrong hands. The novice with a fair sort of animal who imagines he must inbreed her to one of her close relatives is likely to run into more trouble than success. If one is going to inbreed one must have good sound stock and a good knowledge of what was behind them."[5]

Before embarking on a program of inbreeding, consider the following questions:
- Is the breed's gene pool diverse enough that inbreeding is desirable?
- How inbred are your own dogs?
- Are you sure that your dogs are free of hereditary recessive disorders?
- What breed faults might you be concentrating by inbreeding?
- What do you expect to achieve by inbreeding?

Judicious inbreeding is often of great value to individual kennels and occasionally to an entire breed. It is most successful when the breeder has in-depth knowledge of the dogs' genetic background and intends to fix specific desirable traits.

Linebreeding

A rather loose term, *linebreeding* is the mating of related individuals. The closeness of the relationship is highly variable, falling somewhere between inbreeding and outcrossing, depending on the population size. For dog breeders, linebreeding offers a compromise, and in many ways, it is a good one. Although linebreeding is a slower and less direct way to fix desirable traits, it offers more options than inbreeding with fewer risks.

Outcrossing

Outcrossing is the mating of *relatively* unrelated individuals. It increases heterozygosity and creates new genetic combinations by bringing together genes from diverse sources.

The primary reason for the unpopularity of outcrossing among dog breeders is the fact that it does introduce unknown and sometimes undesirable traits. A line that has consistently produced strong toplines and good feet may lose this consistency. On the other hand, the line may lack strong rears and good bites.

Used judiciously, outcrossing is a very useful tool, and sometimes, it is the only way to achieve certain goals. The most common reasons for outcrossing are (a) to acquire desired traits that do not exist in a line and (b) to dilute undesirable recessives. Outcrossing is imperative when a line shows signs of inbreeding depression, such as a decline of vigor, disease resistance, and fertility. Inbreeding depression can develop insidiously in an entire breed through the extensive use of only a few popular successful sires for several generations, in which case it is necessary to turn to lines from another country.

ASSORTIVE MATING

Assortive mating is based on selection for specific phenotypes and is often combined with mating systems based on relationships.

Like Begets Like

The mating of animals of similar phenotypes tends to produce offspring that resemble them and is known as *like-to-like, type-to-type,* or *positive assortive mating.* It is obvious, of course, that the mating of individuals with similar faults should be avoided.

With polygenic traits, consistent type-to-type matings gradually shift the gene frequency to the desired end of the phenotype spectrum. The most familiar example of positive assortive mating is the practice of breeding only dogs that are free of hip dysplasia, and the effectiveness is borne out by the remarkable improvement that has been achieved in some breeds. The system has also been an effective way to improve behavioral traits such as the aptitude for hunting and guide-dog training.

Because it alters the gene frequency within a population, type-to-type breeding is one of the most successful of all systems for achieving a consistently desirable overall phenotype. Since the inbreeding required to reestablish the population after World War II, the German Weimaraner Club has relied on type-to-type mating for successfully developing and maintaining the desired, uniform breed phenotype. The German Shepherd Club in Germany appears to have a similar policy.

Willis, a British German Shepherd breeder, points out that when German imports are crossed with inbred English strains, the German dogs fail to reproduce their phenotype except when bred to individuals with similar phenotypes.[6] This is a good example of how difficult it is to overcome the prepotency established by inbreeding. Once a trait is fixed by inbreeding, it is very resistant to change.

When outcrossing is needed to overcome traits that have become fixed in a line or for inbreeding depression, type-to-type mating offers the best way to maintain desired phenotype. All in all, it is a safe way for novices to get started and an effective way for breeders with only a few bitches to produce consistently good quality over the years.

Attractive Opposites

Negative assortive mating—the mating of dissimilar phenotypes—is also known as *unlike-to-unlike*. In general, this system tends to cancel out undesired traits and is sometimes called *compensatory mating*.

This is probably the most common mating system of all, because most breeders avoid breeding individuals with identical faults. It is quite effective with polygenic traits because they do tend to cancel each other out. With traits determined by one or two alleles, however, the puppies are usually like one parent or the other, rather than in between.

GATHERING DATA

Unlike livestock breeders, who can utilize measurable data and quantitative genetic equations, dog breeders must gather less concrete information in other ways.

PEDIGREE ANALYSIS

For novices, a dog's pedigree is usually a meaningless piece of paper; for experienced fanciers, it is a profile of genetic potential, often containing a surprising amount of information. AKC conformation and performance titles document that certain phenotype standards have been achieved, and the inclusion of OFA numbers and CERF certification offers easier access to that information. The other advantage to title holders in a pedigree is that it is easier to compile detailed information about the individuals. Pictures of many appear in books and other breed literature. Records of the breed's top producers are another source of material. Best of all is that those with a high public profile have been seen and touched by many breed fanciers, who can give first-hand descriptions of their best and poorest traits.

Pedigree analysis is vital and should be ongoing. Study the prepotency of both families and individuals. Familial prepotency is evaluated by in-depth study of the pedigree, noting traits (both good and bad) that occur with regularity in individuals and littermates. The patterns are easier to identify with popular stud dogs, though some kennels are known for outstanding bitches.

Sometimes a stud nicks well with bitches of a particular strain, producing offspring superior to either parent. If you identify a special nick, take advantage of it if your dogs are related.

PROGENY TESTING

Rating the genetic value of individuals according to the quality of their offspring from several different mates—the more offspring, the better—is known as *progeny testing*. Usually, this cannot be done with bitches because of the limited number of combinations that can be tried, though patterns may be identified over several generations.

When comparing the merits of the offspring of two studs, be sure to notice how many of the dams are champions. A top-winning stud that has been bred only to champion bitches is bound to have a high percentage of winners. When puppies from a less well-known dog who has attracted only pet-quality bitches begin winning consistently, it is a pretty safe bet that his genetic qualities are sound.

Stud-dog classes, though informative, exhibit only the best of the dog's progeny. Whenever possible, try to see whole litters. The puppies that show up at local matches are usually a more representative cross section of what the stud is producing, though again, they are usually the ones of better quality. Inexperienced owners are easily discouraged when their puppy loses. Sometimes the puppies are slow to mature, sometimes they are simply beaten by better handling, and sometimes the competition is exceptional. I selected one stud dog after seeing seven outstanding sons (from three unrelated non-champion bitches) lined up in the nine-to-twelve month class and looking like an open class at a major. On the other hand, "closet cases" from big-name studs have provided some useful insights. Occasionally, I have seen undershot bites in puppies sired by a stud whose owner continued to proclaim that he had never produced the fault.

Another situation in which progeny testing is the only way to determine an individual's genetic value is when the phenotype has been altered by an environmental factor. The conformation of a German bitch imported just after the war, for example, was considered "unimpressive," but her owners suspected that her faults might have been caused by severe, early malnutrition. Her progeny proved her genetic merit. If a puppy has been kicked in the face by a horse and had a broken jaw, the wry mouth will probably not be hereditary.

One promising six-month-old bitch that I owned was hit by a car and dislocated her hip. She finished her championship easily, winning a best of breed and a futurity as well. Although I submitted the X-ray of the dislocated hip along with her OFA X-ray, she was diagnosed as dysplastic. Riser states: "Traumatic coxofemoral luxation is followed by remodeling and degenerative joint disease. When healed, these changes are generally indistinguishable from spontaneous canine hip dysplasia." The joint capsule is ruptured as well as the teres ligament, and the joint never regains its former congruity and stability because supporting tissues were torn.[7] Because of her strong ancestry of OFA certified individuals and her own outstanding quality (a best of breed and futurity winner), I decided to breed her anyway. I took two important precautions: (a) she was bred to two unrelated sires from lines that were well known for good hips; (b) copies of the OFA report and correspondence were given to each puppy buyer, who understood progeny testing. Her offspring had good hips, and several of her puppies became outstanding producers.

RISK ASSESSMENT

Risk assessment can be defined as an estimation of the chance of success or failure before deciding on a particular action. With the development of reliable ways to identify harmful genetic traits, especially if evaluations can be made at an early age through DNA testing, breeders can apply risk assessment for eliminating those traits. Table 14–4 shows the probabilities of passing on an autosomal recessive trait with different combinations of clear, carrier, and affected individuals.

When there is a way to to identify genetic carriers of a trait, it is not always necessary to eliminate the carriers from a breeding program. It may, in fact, even be desirable to keep some carriers if the trait is prevalent in the breed and eliminating all carriers in one generation would decimate the breed population and quality. The alternative is a multigenerational plan with testing all progeny. Important factors are (a) whether the merits of the dog or bitch are sufficiently outstanding to justify the expense of testing the entire litter and (b) what the odds are that some of the puppies will be free of the disorder.

The best choice for a carrier bitch is a mating with a stud that has tested free of the undesired gene. On average, half of the puppies should be free of the gene, and the other half would be carriers. A fifty-fifty chance of getting a puppy that can be certified free of the problem isn't too bad, especially if the parents are free of problems that could eliminate the clear puppies—hip dysplasia, bad bites, cryptorchidism, and

Table 14–4   **Risk Assessment for Autosomal Recessive Traits**

Combinations	Clear male	Carrier male	Affected male
Clear female	100% clear	50% clear, 50% carriers	100% carriers
Carrier female	50% clear, 50% carriers	25% clear, 50% carriers, 25% affected	50% carrier, 50% affected
Affected female	100% carriers	50% carrier, 50% affected	100% affected

Key

Ideal: no puppies will carry the gene.

Safe: half of the puppies be clear, and half will carry the gene.

Safe: all of the puppies will carry the gene, but none will be affected.

Serious risk: one fourth of the puppies will be clear, half will carry the gene, and one-fourth will be affected.

High risk: half of the puppies will be carriers, and helf will be affected.

Not recommended: all of the puppies will be affected.

so forth. The carriers could be placed with spay-neuter contracts and limited (non-breeding) registration.

Suppose that the stud that is most complementary to the bitch's traits is also a carrier? In this case, the odds drop to only a fourth of the puppies testing clear, half of them being carriers, and the other fourth, being homozygous for the disorder, would need to be euthanized. In breeds with large litters, it may still be a feasible mating. The odds, however, are only approximate, and the smaller the litter the higher the risk that none of the puppies will be clear.

One benefit of DNA screening of entire litters is that any puppies that are free of the disorder have a much higher potential breeding value than untested puppies. Once a test has been developed and is available, any buyer who plans to breed would be foolish to consider a puppy that has not been tested.

CHOICES

Selection procedures and systems of mating should be regarded as a breeder's tools, not as ironclad rules. Dog fanciers discuss the merits of inbreeding, linebreeding, and outcrossing as if they were mutually exclusive systems. A more productive approach is to regard them as tools that breeders employ to achieve the desired results. Each breed and each breeder has different goals and problems to overcome, and what works with one may not work for others.

Be as flexible as the artist who chooses between tools—a fine-pointed detail brush, a soft fan-shaped blender, or sometimes, even a palette knife—to achieve certain effects. Perhaps this is why breeding is considered an art as well as a science—there are no hard and fast rules to guide breeders in choosing the right tool for each task.

Chapter 15

SELECTION— THE ART

WHY AN ART?

There is an undeniable element of *art* (skill acquired by experience, study, or observation) to dog breeding, though it is difficult to define. Dr. James Edwards (head of AKC Judges Education and Research Department) commented: "The best geneticists in the world can't predict what will happen when a particular dog and bitch are mated."[1] The best breeders, however, seem to achieve success more often than others with comparable knowledge, experience, and quality bloodlines.

Just think of all of the factors the serious dog breeder must take into consideration. There is selection for positive traits such as sound physical structure, breed type, temperament, and breed aptitude. This is juggled with selection against negative traits such as hip dysplasia. Add to this the need to develop prepotency for desired traits and the fact that factors change with each generation. One breeder, who happens to be a trained geneticist, described the process as "knitting and purling."

When asked about why a particular mating was spectacularly successful, breeders always have a rational explanation. However, when asked why the litter was better than others, most admit they did nothing different. The one common factor is that the matings were often preceded by an intuitive confidence that the particular mating would be exceptional and the success was more a confirmation of belief than a surprise.

The art, therefore, also includes some *intuition,* which is defined as the power or faculty of attaining direct knowledge without evident rational thought and inference, *or* simply as quick and ready insight. As usual, experience helps. It often brings a subconscious knack of perceiving many diverse factors, and the ability to weave all of them together, envisioning the results.

So why study genetics? I don't know any successful, ethical breeder who doesn't believe that knowing more about genetics would improve the quality of their breeding. The breeder who understands genetics can judiciously "knit and purl" with polygenic traits. With hip dysplasia, for example, one can tip the scales through consistent selection for the additive effects, weighing the environmental factors, and even risking the occasional use of dogs that have radiographic dysplasia but are exceptional in every other way.

GETTING ACQUAINTED WITH A BREED

How does one go about getting started as a breeder and minimizing 20/20 hindsight? The typical dog breeder starts by buying a bitch and breeding a litter, with attention to quality development later. Only a minority do some homework and comparative shopping. Nevertheless, most wish they had known more before starting.

The obvious first step is to read everything that has been published on the breed, starting with breed books and articles in *Dog Fancy* and *Dog World*.

Actually, the best way to quickly become acquainted with a breed is by attending meetings and activities of the local breed club before even buying a puppy. It's often the only way to meet a variety of dogs and develop a feeling for the breed's unique character and temperament. Face it: Some are yappy, others snappy; some are lazy, others bounce off walls. After being around them for a while, you may decide to try another breed. Weimaraners, for example, want to touch someone all the time—the owner of one that came into the rescue program said she couldn't stand it and would not have bought one if she had known. The club is also a way to meet owners and breeders and to discover breed activities—such as field events, herding, schutzhund work, or coursing as well as dog shows and obedience trials.

Join the national breed club in order to receive its publications. The content is current. Who is doing what in shows, obedience, and field? What hereditary problems are of concern, and what is being done about them? This is also where breeders advertise their winners and litters.

A FIRM FOUNDATION

A lot has been written about selecting the foundation dogs for breeding, but none seem to consider the novice's dilemma. It is almost impossible to make the best possible choice without experience, but you can't get the experience until you begin breeding. Once you've bred a litter or two, other breeders are more willing to share their own experiences and also more willing to trust you with their more special puppies. Therefore, although it is best to base a breeding program on the best you can get, there are some advantages to breeding your nice but average bitch to a good-quality stud (grading up). One old acquaintance did everything right when she bought and developed her foundation bitch only to discover with the first litter that breeding was *not* her thing.

THE FOUNDATION BITCH

The brood bitch is the heart of the kennel and the breeding program, a foundation on which to build; the AKC even defines *breeder* as the owner of the bitch. It is not unusual for breeders who have only one or two brood bitches at a time to develop a distinctive strain that has a significant impact on a breed.

Through the brood bitch, the breeder can select the stud dog that is most likely to produce the desired traits, whereas the stud dog can only hope for discovery by the owner of that "just-right bitch." The only limitation with a bitch is the potential number of litters she can produce, which allows less room for experimentation and testing—every litter must count.

Get off to a flying start with the best you can find. Why waste years and generations to achieve a level of quality that could have been obtained at the beginning? Just think! What if you could get a puppy from a top-winning show dog, from a futurity winner, or from a top-producing dam? Buying a bitch with exceptional breeding potential places the buyer on the same level as her breeder. Where you go from there is entirely a matter of judgment (and luck), but buying from an experienced breeder usually carries the added bonus of experienced advice.

When selecting foundation breeding stock, the competitive records of individuals are a less reliable guide than the overall records of the family and progeny. How many great champions of the past have progeny of comparable merit? Great winners come from great families, so focus on the family; evaluate the bad traits as well as the good ones—look at all aspects (including fertility) of the family. With sound quality in the foundation dogs, progeny quality should be consistent.

The ideal situation is to begin with a bitch that is already a champion, OFA certified, and screened for genetic problems. Naturally, these are rarely available, but don't pass up the opportunity if you find one. Next down the list of choices would be a young adult that is of obvious show quality but has not yet been shown. Many breeders keep the two best bitches in a litter and make a final choice after they've grown up.

Because the foundation bitch is usually acquired as a puppy, she must be objectively evaluated when she reaches maturity. There is a limit to how accurately potential can be assessed at seven weeks, and a promising puppy doesn't always develop into the desired quality. Finishing a conformation or performance title is always an advantage but not always possible. In some breeds, it is extremely difficult to finish a championship, and injuries can ruin a promising youngster's chances. For overall qualities, seek (and carefully weigh) the opinions of experienced breed authorities—breeders, judges, handlers. For strengths and weaknesses of specific traits such as topline or shoulder layback, the bitch's breeder, if experienced, is usually the best source of information. Take advantage of every genetic screening test that is available. When starting out, it is easier to buy another bitch than to eliminate the hereditary disorders such as hip dysplasia and PRA from a line.

Despite all precautions, there is always a chance that the bitch may not produce quality puppies. If the quality of the first litter is disappointing, it could be merely an unfortunate combination with the stud; select another stud (preferably from different bloodlines) for her second litter. If the same traits show up again, it may be better to spay the bitch and begin again than to embark on generations of compensatory selection to eliminate multiple problems. The need to do unlike-to-unlike matings to overcome faults is a negative approach and to be avoided whenever possible.

THE STUD DOG

The first question is, do you *need* a stud? Unless your goal is just to create puppies rather than breed quality, the answer is don't bother, especially when new to a breed.

Most top studs are developed by their breeders. They begin to develop a reputation through competitive success and advertising, which they must follow up with quality progeny. Unless the dog is a top winner, only studs from well-known kennels will be used by breeders. Few breeders can afford to keep enough bitches to develop a breeding program around one or more studs. If you want to try anyway, it means breeding, leasing, or buying compatible bitches to prove the stud's reproductive potential. An impatient owner can ruin a promising stud career by breeding to an inferior bitch just to see what happens. Any faults in his puppies are usually blamed on the sire and will haunt the stud for years to come unless the puppies are sold with limited registration papers.

Top-quality studs are even harder to find than good bitches. If one is available, he may not be suitable for the kennel's bitches. I bought one stud dog that became available when the owners divorced. Not only was he a champion and proven sire but also had *already* nicked well with my bitches.

CHARTING A COURSE

BLOODLINES

Bloodlines are an indicator—*not a guarantee*—of individual genetic quality. The key is to maximize the odds of striking gold when starting out.

Begin to gather data for pedigree analysis immediately. Some breed clubs publish yearbooks with pedigrees and records of individual dogs. Study lists of the breed's top producers.

Don't overlook oral sources of information. There is no better source than people who have themselves seen the breed greats. It takes time to seek them out and even more time to establish your own credentials. But what rewards! The positive ones—"that dog was a showman"; the negative ones—"that dog was lame until the sun warmed his hips." All such tidbits contribute to knowledge of the breed.

It is also worthwhile to discover more about the nonchampions in the pedigree, as well as littermates that never appeared in competition, though this requires some detective skill. Although lack of a title may mean that the individual lacked quality, consider some of the following I discovered with a little sleuthing in my breed:

- A male who won two 5-point majors at his first two shows was killed by a car after he sired one litter
- A pick-of-litter bitch was kicked in the head by a horse, causing loss of an eye and a deformed jaw
- A multiple best-of-breed winner from the classes never finished a championship because of the owner's divorce

No lack of quality here!

From time to time people bring me pedigrees of local dogs, usually a pet bitch that they want to breed. Sometimes I spot individuals from litters that I helped to grade (or that I bred) and can recall just why some of the puppies were sold as pets. The most interesting was a sire from a litter in which all males were cryptorchid.

Astute breeders study the progeny that studs are producing, watching for the ones that are consistently transmitting the traits they wish to acquire or reinforce in their own dogs. The most prepotent sires, though always of good quality, are not always the biggest winners; however, they often *produce* the biggest winners.

STATE OF THE BREED

Evaluation of Breed Quality

A great deal may be learned by studying the breed's greatest individuals of the past—competitive records, pedigrees, photographs, breed literature (written and oral)—to identify traits that made them outstanding. However, do not hold great dogs of the past in unrealistic reverence, for the legend may surpass the reality. Purebred dogs are genetically dynamic, and changes can take place within a decade; in addition, fashion—what the ideal dog should look like—also alters breeds.

Study the breed's dogs of ten or twenty years ago, and develop an overview of the breed by asking questions:

- Are the dogs of the current generation better or worse than their ancestors?
- What qualities have improved or declined?
- Is the incidence of undesirable traits increasing or decreasing, or have totally different problems emerged?
- Has the popularity of a particular sire drastically altered the breed gene pool?

Be aware of the state of the breed, as this will affect breeding decisions. This is the only way to identify problems that are affecting the entire breed, and breed-wide problems are the most difficult to overcome. What hereditary disorders must be avoided at all costs?

What are the breed's strengths and weaknesses? Common problems in a breed must be taken into consideration, behavioral as well as structural. After all, breeds do not acquire a reputation for viciousness without reason. If most dogs in the show ring have poor toplines, this is obviously a trait of greater concern than in a breed with uniformly good toplines.

Breed type is another consideration. In some breeds there is such a variation of type that a dog may be unbeatable in one part of the country but never place in another, even under the same judges. A dog that is at the top of the standard in height may tower over all others in some areas. A well-built, stocky dog may look like a tank in a class of fine-boned ones. In general, a dog that is closest to the median can win in any part of the country, especially when combined with overall balance and soundness. In other words, be cautious about extremes.

Breed Population

One obvious factor that is often overlooked when developing a breeding program is the breed's population. Remember all that stuff about populations, gene frequencies, and genetic drift? The smaller the breed population, the greater the consequences of *genetic drift*, the random change of a population's gene frequency.

In 1995, for example, the AKC registered 132,052 Labrador Retrievers and 93,656 Rottweilers. These are large populations! In these breeds, inbreeding is vital to fix genetic traits, but if a breeder gets into trouble, there is a large population from which to find solutions.

Going down the AKC registration list (Table 15-1), breed populations drop rapidly. From number 36 to 81, the numbers registered range from less than 10,000 to just above 1,000. These breeds might not be classified as small populations, but they are not very large.

In breeds in which less than 1,000 puppies are registered each year, breeders may observe genetic drift within a decade, and there is a greater risk that undesired traits may become widespread. If they do, eliminating them would be more difficult. Migration—that is, importing dogs—may be necessary to overcome problems. The last-ranked breed, number 140, registered only 25 puppies, and inbreeding, obviously, is a primary concern.

Table 15–1. 1995 AKC Registrations

Rank	Breed	Reg.
10	Yorkshire Terrier	36,881
20	Rottweiler	17,722
30	Bulldog	12,092
40	Australian Shepherd	5,940
50	Keeshond	3,119
60	Whippet	1,952
70	American Staffordshire Terrier	1,443
80	Japanese Chin	1,084
90	Border Terrier	663
100	Standard Schnauzer	500
110	American Water Spaniel	323
	Petit Basset Griffon Vendeen	323
120	English Toy Spaniel	182
130	Pharaoh Hound	110
140	Harrier	25

Genetic Diversity

The major factor to consider when assessing a breed's genetic diversity is how recently it underwent a founder effect or a bottleneck. For example, most Bearded Collies trace their descent from a very few dogs in the 1940s, and less than a dozen Weimaraners in Germany survived World War I.[2]

Even if all undesirable recessives could be eliminated, geneticists warn that a gradual loss of vitality and fertility is cumulative with continued reduction of genetic diversity. Thus, the periodic infusion of totally new bloodlines is not only beneficial but also vital when the genetic base of a breed becomes so limited there is no other way to avoid combinations that produce undesired recessive traits.

To evaluate the breed's genetic diversity, try laying out a twelve-generation pedigree. In many American breeds, this provides a graphic demonstration of their limited genetic diversity. Never underestimate the power of the *patterning effect* when the same ancestor appears many times in a pedigree. *Faults* from the distant past are just as likely to crop up as the virtues. Sheer distance in generations does not always dilute. An unpleasant surprise is sometimes explained when that twelve-generation pedigree reveals twenty crosses to old Ch. Eat 'Em Alive, Ch. Gimpy-in-the-Morning, or Ch. Long-as-a-Freight Train in the tenth, eleventh, and twelfth generations. Written history records their glory; only oral history from old-timers recalls their faults.

IDENTIFYING GOALS

Identifying priorities is vital. Without some direction, it is easy to get lost between improving one trait, avoiding faults, making sure of breed aptitude, and maintaining correct temperament. While focusing on these, many breeders overlook health and reproductive traits—remember, sterility is ultimately fatal to any breeding program.

Because there is no *perfect* dog or bitch of any breed, each breeder must create an imaginary picture of the ideal dog. This image of the long-term goal is so personal that it is doubtful that any two fanciers imagine the same dog. In a similar way, desirable and undesirable traits are essentially a subjective, personal value judgment. When developing a breeding plan, this image of the perfect dog must be sharpened to identify and define the step-by-step short-term goals that help to make the ideal dog a reality.

Although the purpose of competition is to identify individuals worthy of perpetuating the breed, maintain a commonsense perspective about competitive success; remember that winning is merely the exterior gauge of progress, and success is fleeting unless the winning individuals reproduce their good traits. Keep an open mind, and make every effort to consistently strive for something a little bit better with each generation. The breeder of sound, balanced individuals with good breed type, temperament, and showmanship as well as sound aptitude for the breed's functional talent is bound to be successful over the years. The key is to maintain objective breeding goals and flexibility.

A breeder strives for genetic reliability and consistency, for quality inside and out. Competitive success is primarily recognition of outstanding phenotype—that is, the visible qualities that provide clues to the dog's genotype. The breeder is equally concerned about traits that cannot be observed. In their quest for winners, breeders tend to overlook important traits. Males should be virile and fertile into their senior years. Bitches should have regular estrus, mate willingly, whelp easily, display good maternal instincts, and produce ample milk. Robinson points out that there "is no point in creating a superlative strain only to find that it is held in low esteem because of poor health or reproductive capability."[3] Temperament is ultimately the most important trait of all, because who wants any dog that isn't a pleasure to live with? Realistic breeding goals, then, focus on a dog's ability to reproduce desired traits such as longevity with good health, a long reproductive life, performance aptitude, and biddable temperament as well as the exterior structure.

Realistic goals also consider the number of dogs it is possible to keep. Obviously, it is easier to maintain a larger number of small dogs than big ones, but breeds also vary in the amount of individual attention they require and whether or not they become neurotic without it. To how many dogs can you give enough training, grooming, health care, and love? How many puppies that you don't plan to keep can you care for until they can be placed in good homes? These realities influence (or should influence) breeding goals.

MATCHMAKING

Set at least one major and several minor objectives for each litter. Although the long-term goals are to eliminate undesired traits and to strengthen desirable ones, this is not always possible in one generation. Choose practical, achievable, short-term objectives (such as better hips, stronger topline, or more stylish point) for each mating.

Selecting the stud dog is, obviously, a vital decision. The best-winning dog in show or field is not necessarily the optimum, complementary mate for your bitch. However, the stud should be proven in competition, preferably a champion and a proven sire.

When looking for the stud that is most likely to accomplish the major objectives, consider all males in the United States as potential mates—and do not overlook

Canadian-owned males that are accessible. Analyze their individual qualities, their bloodlines, and their progeny. See as many studs as possible in person, or obtain videotapes. Talk with people who know the studs and have seen their ancestors. Study their progeny. Consider the big winner's champion litter brother, who may produce the desired traits more consistently, or perhaps it would be better to go back to their sire.

After identifying studs that appear promising, shipping and other factors may then be taken into consideration. The last place to economize is by limiting the choice of stud to one that is local, because the merit of the sire is reflected in the quality of the litter and the salability of the puppies; surprisingly, puppies sired by faraway studs are often in greater demand than those sired by local studs. Occasionally, however, *after* all factors are studied and carefully weighed, the stud most likely to fulfill the objectives may turn out to be the champion in the breeder's backyard; because all possibilities have been considered, such a mating would not be labeled "backyard breeding."

Chapter 16

EVALUATION AND RECORDS

After selection (and puppies) comes evaluation of the results, which provides the basis for future selection. The bitch's next litter must be planned, deciding whether to repeat a successful mating or use a different stud; the stud's merit must be weighed. In addition, the breeder must decide which, if any, of the puppies to keep for the next generation. Evaluation of the results begins with the birth of the first litter, and it never really ends.

PUPPIES

Over many generations, it is possible to identify patterns, so detailed observations and records—gender, color, weight, development, and behavior—data that grow more valuable over the years. Details fade quickly, so keep an informal diary to jot down anything and everything observed. Later, a more formal format can be developed, but it is surprising how helpful even the crudest notes can be.

SOME OBVIOUS DECISIONS

When the goal is to select the best puppies to produce the next generation, it helps to identify as early as possible the ones that won't make the cut. Some faults can be identified immediately or within the first few weeks. A puppy's color or coat may be a breed disqualification. Physical faults that do not impair life expectancy may make the puppy unsuitable for breeding. A puppy with a hernia that requires surgical repair can lead a long, healthy life as someone's pet. The cryptorchid males are perfect for people who want a neutered male.

HEALTH

Birth Through Seven Weeks

It is always a good idea to have an autopsy done on any stillborn puppies. It may reveal cardiac abnormalities, diaphragmatic hernias, and other internal problems that are important to have on record. One or two over several generations do not always indicate a genetic problem, but it is always a cause for concern and should be monitored.

Veterinary Examination

A formal veterinary examination at the age of seven weeks documents each puppy's health, and a copy of the signed certificate can be given to each new owner. Even if all are in perfect health, it is important to document the problems that did *not* occur in the litter.

Figure 16–1. Veterinary examination record. *A formal veterinary examination given at the age of seven weeks documents each puppy's health, and a copy of the signed certificate can be given to each new owner.*

Veterinary Examination Record

PUPPY	DATE OF BIRTH:
SIRE:	DAM:
DESCRIPTION:	

FINDINGS

EYES:

BITE:

HEART:

HERNIA:

GENITALIA:

OTHER COMMENTS:

VETERINARIAN:

ADDRESS:

SIGNATURE: DATE:

An examination is the only way to identify some cardiac problems, which may be undetected unless a puppy is examined for a shipping health certificate. The breeder-owner of a lovely bitch had made all of the arrangements to ship her for breeding when the veterinarian detected a heart murmur; it could have been a recently acquired problem, but the breeder couldn't be sure. Regardless, a pregnancy was clearly too risky. A few years later another owner discovered that a puppy to be shipped, the picture of health, had no wall between the heart ventricles and would soon have died. I realized that I had no records either and that it might be important to know when and where a potentially hereditary cardiac defect first occurred, and my puppies have been screened since then.

The information has been useful for other reasons. Those disappearing testicles mentioned earlier? The signed record proved they were there before the puppy was shipped. If the puppy has a hernia, the veterinarian states whether surgical repair is definitely indicated or whether there is a chance it may close without intervention. Documenting the absence of problems that can develop after the time of sale protects the breeder's reputation for integrity. We have found this particularly helpful with distichiasis, which may be either hereditary or acquired. Most cases may be detected by seven weeks, and with later onset, the acquired form becomes increasingly probable. Curiously, this routine screening of all puppies has revealed that occasionally a few extra eyelashes sometimes disappear spontaneously.

TEMPERAMENT AND APTITUDE

Puppies Under Foot

Begin keeping notes about each puppy's behavior immediately. There are surprising variations between individuals and between litters. Some newborns are immediately vigorous, greedy eaters, and scramble immediately back to the mother when removed from the teat. Some puppies (and litters) are noisy and active, whereas others are quiet. Occasional puppies resist cuddling and need extra handling.

Behavioral notes become increasingly valuable over generations as certain puppy behavior can be correlated with traits at maturity. For example, the first puppy out of the whelping box exhibits both boldness and problem-solving aptitude, which is strongly correlated with good hunting ability.

One advantage of being a small breeder is that it is so much fun to have the puppies in the kitchen or family room. They are under constant observation, and the breeder becomes familiar with each little personality.

The value of early socialization and handling is well established in the dog fancy; the geneticist would describe it as the environmental influence on innate behavioral traits. Frequent handling and socialization enhances the puppies' temperament stability. They become accustomed to household noises and to the voices of men, women, and children (keep the television turned on if necessary).

Testing

The earliest tests for aptitude were developed for guide dogs. These tests are very effective with breeds that need similar working aptitudes, but they have not been notably helpful with sporting breeds. Imaginative breeders can create their own breed-specific tests.

Different breeds sometimes respond in different ways to the same situation. Virginia Alexander developed a series of tests with Weimaraners and has tried them with other sporting breeds. She discovered that there was a difference even between sporting breeds. When testing the puppy's response to a strange object, she used an open umbrella, and when the puppy approached, the assistant hiding behind the umbrella gave it a twitch. The ideal response, and typical of Weimaraners, was for the puppy to show no fear and to approach the umbrella. The test didn't work very well for other sporting breeds: The retrievers consistently tried to carry the umbrella away, and many of the setters showed frightened aggression, with raised hackles and barking before running off.[1]

The most important feature of aptitude testing is that it provides each puppy with an opportunity to learn. Regardless of the score, each puppy that was tested showed improved boldness and a more outgoing personality.

ONE BY ONE—INDIVIDUAL EVALUATION

The objective of individual evaluation is to discover which traits that are observed in puppies have a positive or negative correlation with the traits they will have at maturity. Which traits improve, stay the same, or get worse? The ability to identify puppies of potential breeding quality early and accurately is a definite advantage.

Age

At some point, the puppies of many breeds pass through a stage in which their body proportions approximate those they will have at maturity, and this is the ideal time to evaluate them. The age at which this occurs varies between strains within a breed, and it certainly varies between breeds. In Weimaraners, for example, the ideal age for most is about seven to eight weeks, though some lines are better at nine weeks. When starting out *and* when outcrossing, it is important to evaluate the litter weekly to determine the optimal age.

Figure 16–2. Photographic Record. *At about seven weeks, most Weimaraner puppies have the approximate height-length proportions they will have at maturity. Photographs like this are reassuring during the months that follow as puppies go through awkward stages of growth. (This picture was taken with a black cloth tacked to the wall, and the handlers wore black gloves.)*

Picture Perfect

A good picture is worth a thousand words, and photography is a priceless aid in the assessment of each puppy's physical structure. Profile photographs of stacked puppies provide a permanent record of traits such as the balance, topline, neck length and placement, croup angle, and front and rear angulation.

Polaroid pictures are a boon to record keeping because the breeder knows immediately whether the puppy is correctly posed. In addition, problems with lighting, camera angle, and other environmental features can be identified and corrected.

Hands-on Evaluation

The photographic records should be supplemented by *detailed* notes about each puppy's structure. Weekly evaluations and notes are the best way to gain experience and to become familiar with the breed's and the line's developmental pattern.

Table 16–1. Example of a Chart-Style Examination Record

Sire: Ch. Midnight Special   Dam: Ch. Day in the Sun

Puppy	Bite	Feet	Front	Shoulders Ang.	Shoulders Width	Top-line	Loin	Rear Ang	Rear Str.	Comments
Male 1	1	1	2	2	2	2	1	1	2	Small white spot on chest. Right pastern out slightly.
Male 2	1	1	1	1	2	1	1	1	1	Very narrow stripe on chest. Excellent overall balance.
Male 3	1	1	2	1	2	2	1	1	1	No white. Pasterns slightly loose. Very large.
Bitch 1	1	1	1	1	1	1	1	1	1	White hairs on chest. Excellent overall
Bitch 2	1	1	1	1	1	1	1	1	1	Large white patch on chest. Otherwise excellent.

Key

Bite	1 scissors with good overbite 2 tight scissors 3 even 4 undershot	**Shoulder width** (between blades)	1 1–2 fingertips between 2 3-4 fingertips between 3 more
Feet	1 very tight 2 moderately tight 3 loose 4 splayed	**Loin**	1 3–4 fingers 2 more than 3–4 fingers
		Topline	1 straight, even when relaxed 2 straight, softens when relaxed 3 soft
Front	1 drops straight, no flexion at pasterns 2 drops straight, slight looseness at pasterns 3 poor	**Rear angulation**	1 excellent 2 moderate 3 poor
Shoulder angulation	1 excellent 2 moderate 3 poor	**Rear strength**	1 excellent 2 moderate 3 poor

Puppy Evaluation Record

LITTER: G   SEX: Male
NAME: Gunner   IDENTIFICATION: Green collar

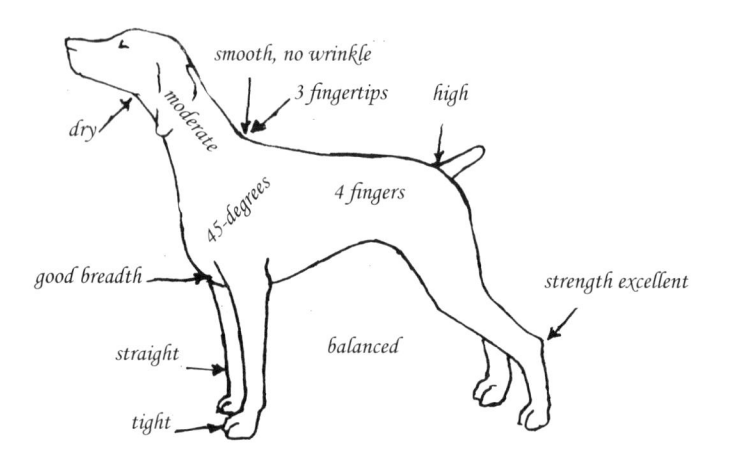

(Profile drawing of dog with annotations:)
- smooth, no wrinkle
- 3 fingertips
- high
- dry
- moderate
- 45-degrees
- 4 fingers
- good breadth
- strength excellent
- straight
- balanced
- tight

COMMENTS: Angulation very balanced. Good overbite. White—dot on chest, both pasterns. Movement—excellent drive and reach, slightly out at the elbows. Testicles down at 4½ weeks. Temperament—most vocal and assertive male. Bird response—strong, immediate response; first to grab bird; growled and ran off.

Figure 16–3. Chart-style individual puppy evaluation record. *An individual puppy evaluation record allows more detailed notes. With a profile drawing, it is simple to add comments with lines to each structural feature.*

The form in which the records are kept are not as important as being certain there is some comment about each trait on each puppy's record. I've used several formats over the years, starting with a simple written description that is still useful. Then, I tried a chart-type format for several years. The format that *I* settled on in the end, because I find it the easiest to use is a profile drawing with handwritten comments and lines to each structural feature. The advantage over the chart is that I can make more detailed notes. The important point is that the information is always written down, and the more detailed the better. If the information is there, early records can be converted to whatever format the breeder adopts later.

The structural correlations vary within each breed, so only broad generalizations can be made within the breed and within each line. Nevertheless, the observations of

other breeders are always helpful, and most are happy to share their knowledge. For example, the following axioms are true for most Weimaraners:
- Fronts are usually stable—what you see in the puppy is what you get in the adult—but may fall apart before stabilizing again at maturity
- Rear strength usually improves, especially if the puppy has lots of angulation
- Croup angle is usually stable but may change up to twelve months; if it changes, the angle always becomes steeper
- Toplines sometimes improve
- Short necks stay short
- Shoulders can be evaluated at seven weeks, except with a few lines that develop late and cannot be evaluated until nine weeks

MOVEMENT

Evaluation of movement is complicated by the varying age at which puppies attain sufficient coordination. In general, movement that is good tends to be just as good at maturity, no matter what happens while the puppy goes through awkward growth stages. Nevertheless, notes about movement—coming, going, and side—are the only way to discover any correlation between puppy and adult.

OBSERVATION

Although breeders utilize it all the time, surprisingly few realize that observation is an important evaluation tool. Most breeder observations are made at a subconscious level, and when these observations are confirmed later, they may be ascribed to ESP or instinct. It is not unusual for first-time breeders to identify the best puppy in the litter, especially if there is a range of quality. After all, they have lovingly observed the litter over many weeks, watched their movement at play, and seen a puppy pause in a show stance. Observation works best with small groups of three to five puppies, especially if divided by gender. In litters of uniform color, brightly colored collars are the secret to identifying individual puppies in a group at play.

Observation is not only a valid evaluation tool but also often the most important one for identifying exceptional quality. Watch for eye-catching balance, attitude, grace, and coordination. Puppies that have pleasing balance at an early age tend to have that quality as adults. Observation of natural movement, stance, and attitude remains the best way to identify puppies with specials potential (group winner and best in show)—the rare ones with great style, charisma, and showmanship. It is also a good way to identify puppies that may have obvious conformation flaws but sometimes finish more quickly than sounder siblings because of their "look-at-me, I'm the best!" attitude.

PUTTING IT ALL TOGETHER

The time has come for decisions. The qualities of each puppy have been studied from many perspectives. The breeder has come to know the individual character through temperament and aptitude testing. The veterinary examination has identified any puppies with undesirable hereditary traits that can be detected at an early age. Conformation has been analyzed in many ways. The hands-on evaluation of each part (head, shoulders, and so forth) has identified specific structural strengths and weaknesses. Photographic analysis has shown how the parts fit together when standing

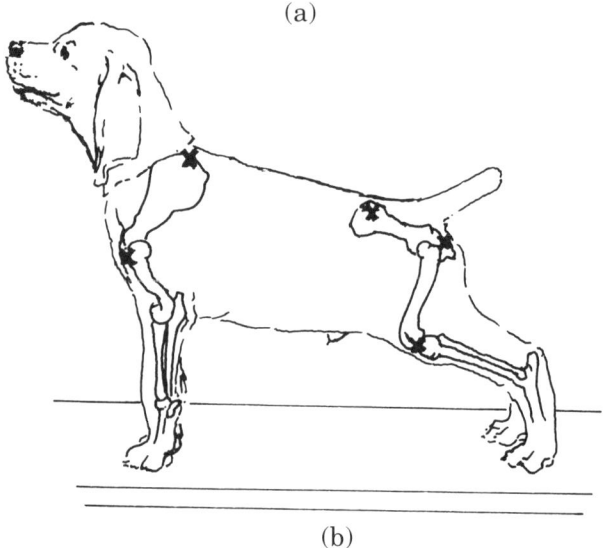

Figure 16–4. Evaluating shoulder structure. *This is a useful technique, especially when there is some question about the length of the upper forearm or balance between the front and rear angulation.*

(a) Palpate the puppy's shoulder bones, and mark guide points on the photograph.

(b) Using tracing paper, trace the puppy's profile in pencil, then draw over them in ink. Sketching in the bone placement clearly illustrates the shoulder structure. Height is measured from the withers to the heel; length is measured from the point of the shoulder to the tip of the pelvis. The first line below the puppy is its length and the second is its height. The height-length proportions of this puppy are good, and the line of the shoulder appears to be in fairly good balance with the rear. The sketch, however, reveals that the upper forearm is too short and the shoulders far from ideal.

Reprinted, by permission, from Virginia Alexander and Jackie Isabell, Weimaraner Ways.

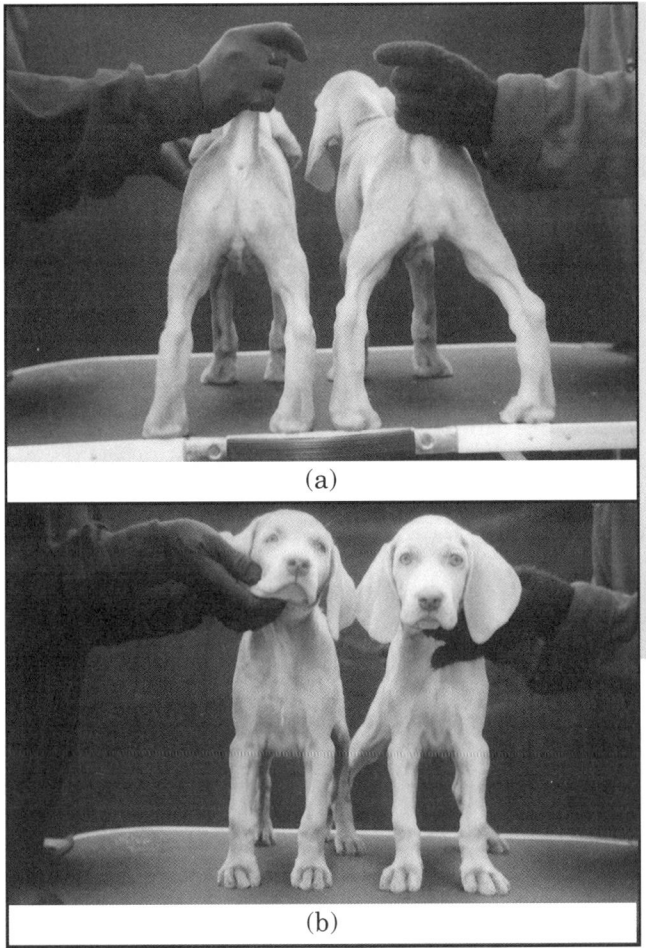

Figure 16–5. Comparisons. *When ranking the conformation of puppies in a litter of uniformly good quality (always a joy), the breeder can be reduced to nitpicking. In this situation, extra help is needed to stack the finalists on the table at the same time. Who has the best front, the best rear, the best topline, or the best feet? These pictures were posed to exaggerate the faults, but there are always some minor differences. (a) Compare the rears. (b) Compare the fronts. Reprinted, by permission, from Virginia Alexander and Jackie Isabell,* Weimaraner Ways.

still, and movement analysis has indicated how they fit when in motion. Finally, observation has revealed the puppy with exceptional dynamic balance, natural poise, and charisma.

Evaluate the litter as a whole for traits that appear in most, whether faults or virtues. If you observe a trend toward moderate or too-little angulation, for example, one of the traits to consider in potential mates for these puppies would be prepotency for greater angulation. On the other hand, if all have straight, strong toplines, they will probably be prepotent for strong toplines, and this trait would not be a concern when selecting a mate.

Finally, it is time to evaluate the litter in terms of the goals of the breeding. It is time to ask some questions: Which puppy fulfills the goals of this particular mating? Which puppy comes closest to my visualization of the standard? Which puppy do I want to keep?

A variety of things can occur. Imagine that the breeder's goal for the mating was to improve shoulder layback without compromising soundness.

1. *Significant success.* The entire litter has better shoulders than the dam and is uniformly sound. In this case, the breeder may want to keep the two best puppies for at least a few more months, preferably until they are adults.
2. *No improvement of the trait.* If all of the puppies have adequate shoulder angulation like the dam but none are an improvement over her, the breeder has two choices: (a) keep the best puppy and hope for improvement in the next generation, or (b) face the fact that if no progress is shown, it may be

best not to keep any of the puppies and to try the mother with a different stud. A good compromise in this situation might be to place the two best puppy bitches on co-ownerships, with the option of choosing the sire for a breeding and a puppy from that litter.

Sometimes, the choices are rough. What if the puppy that has exactly the hoped-for shoulders also has the worst topline in generations? In terms of show-ring success, this would not be the breeder's pick of litter; in terms of improving the long-term quality of the line and breeding the perfect breed specimen, that puppy may be a key producer. If good toplines are typical of the bloodlines of both parents, with luck, the bad topline may be a fluke.

Assessing puppies is, at best, an educated guess at what the puppy will grow into. Experience with preceding generations is invaluable, which is why photographs and detailed records become more valuable over the years. In other words, experience helps.

ONGOING EVALUATION

PERIODIC OBSERVATION

To identify developmental patterns, the puppies should be evaluated again at six, twelve, and twenty-four months. Growth patterns vary between strains and even within strains. Some puppies mature early, others take years. Some develop evenly, whereas others grow one body part at a time. Detailed records enable the breeder to identify which ones are worth waiting for.

ALL GROWN UP

By the time the litter reaches three years, each puppy's record, ideally, has a great deal of additional information, both good and bad. Pictures, show, obedience, and working accomplishments are always a pleasure to record. Notes about reasons for lack of achievement are often equally valuable, however.

Information about genetic quality is priceless. The importance of the results of screening tests for hip dysplasia and other hereditary disorders is obvious, but many other tidbits contribute to the total picture. What about temperament? Are problems such as shyness, dog aggressiveness, or biting showing up in enough puppies to warn of an underlying genetic tendency? Don't overlook general health, fertility, vitality, and longevity.

PRODUCE RECORDS

The final part of the dog's total record would include reproductive qualities, because this is what it's all about. In addition to the number of champions, keep track of other details.

For males, try to identify prepotency for specific traits, both good and bad. What traits do they consistently pass on to their offspring? What faults are they unable to overcome in a bitch? Don't overlook reproductive traits such as low libido or early infertility.

Reproductive qualities are particularly important in bitches. For example, the bitches in some families may be known to have "silent seasons"—that is, their discharge is too scant to be certain of the day on which they came in heat—which makes it very difficult to know when to breed. Ease of whelping is important. Occasional cesareans

Figure 16–6. Adult Breeding Evaluation Record. *This type of record becomes progressively more valuable when planning matings for descendents.*

NAME: Ch. DayStar's Nordic Spirit, CD, JH, CGC   **CALL NAME:** Katie   **REG.:** SE 324787

SIRE: Ch. Starfire's Silver Challenge, UDT, MH

DAM: Ch. DayStar's Southern Comfort, CD, TD

BREEDER: Owen Richter

DATE OF BIRTH: 11/7/93

OFA NO.: WE-1798 Excellent   **CERF:** Not done

SIBLINGS: 3 males (1 cryptorchid), 2 bitches. None with white markings. 1 male 28+ inches at 11 months, others within standard.

EVALUATION

AGE AT EVALUATION: 14 months   **DATE:** 1/15/94

EVALUATED BY: Cindy Jennings (judge)

GENERAL IMPRESSION: Large-boned bitch with clean lines, appears elegant despite substance. Very sound, stands square without twisting legs. Great ring attitude. May have specials potential.

MOVEMENT: COMING: Slightly out at the elbows
GOING: Strong, moves close but no crossing over
SIDE: Good drive, smooth, topline steady

TEMPERAMENT: Thinks she's hot stuff, but eager to please. Easy to handle. Doing well in obedience.

HEIGHT / WEIGHT: 26 inches, holds at about 65 pounds

BITE / DENTITION: Scissors bite. No missing teeth

HEAD: TOP SKULL: Feminine, in proportion
STOP: Moderate
MUZZLE: Clean, tight flews, planes parallel to top skull
EYES: Amber, oval shaped
NOSE: Good pigment

NECK: Long, clean throat

CHEST: Well sprung, slight herring gut mars balance

FORECHEST / BRISKET: Well developed, brisket almost to elbows

BACK: Straight and solid, no bounce when moving

LOIN: About four fingers, looks longer

TAIL: LENGTH: About six inches, light
TAILSET: High, flat croup
CARRIAGE: High but not straight up

SHOULDER: ANGULATION: About 40 degrees
UPPER ARM: Slightly short, could be problem
WIDTH: About one inch between shoulder blades

FORELEGS / PASTERNS: Legs straight. Pasterns, slight forward slope, no sideways twist

FEET: Tight, cat feet, thick pads, nails short

REAR: ANGULATION: Balanced with shoulders
STRENGTH: Hocks resist movement in or out when stacked

COAT: COLOR: Medium-gray
MARKINGS: No white anywhere
TEXTURE: Slightly coarse

Figure 16-6 (Continued)

Ch. DayStar's Nordic Spirit, CD, JH, CGC		
Ch. Starfire's Silver Challenge, UDT, MH OFA Excellent	Ch. Graymar's Majestic Prince OFA Good	Ch. Graymar's Captain Nemo OFA Good
		Frosty's Esta, UDT OFA No record
	Ch. Sassafras Silver Celebrity OFA Excellent	Ch. Debonaire's Gray Knight, CDX OFA Normal
		Ch. Sassafras Silver Jubilee, CDX, TD OFA Good
Ch. DayStar's Southern Comfort, CD, TD OFA Good	Ch. Moonrock Field Marshall OFA Excellent	Ch. Greif v. d. Jagdheim (Import) OFA Excellent
		Ch. Moonrock Cameo, CD OFA Excellent
	Ch. Graymar's Shooting Star OFA Good	Ch. Graymar's Majestic Prince OFA Good
		Graymar's Leading Lady OFA Fair

for malpositioned puppies are one thing, but multigeneration cesareans for *uterine dystocia* (abnormal labor) should be alarming. Volume of milk and maternal instincts are also hereditary and should be evaluated.

SOME FINAL THOUGHTS

Dog breeding is fascinating, even addictive, and sometimes breeders, in their quest for success, begin to forget the reasons they became interested in dogs in the first place—their love for a wonderful companion. It doesn't take many years for a kennel population to explode into an unmanageable size, and the pensioners are too often neglected, even put to sleep. Before starting a breeding program, before breeding another litter, before keeping another puppy, ask yourself if you have enough time to be a good owner to those you already own.

Sooner or later every breeder will have some puppies that must be put to sleep, and this requires considerable fortitude for most dog owners. Dog breeding does not allow much room for experimentation, for consummating a risky mating just to see what will happen or for breeding individuals that have serious, undesirable hereditary traits.

According to AKC statistics, the average dog breeder stays in the game for about five years. Those who stay around for a decade or so genuinely appreciate and understand that there is no formula for success. Every generation is different and presents unique problems to resolve. A saying from the Talmud offers some good advice: "A man stays wise as long as he searches for wisdom; as soon as he has found it, he becomes a fool."

APPENDIX A
BREED COLORS AND ALLELES

The color descriptions are based on AKC breed standards in effect in 1992, though most are simplified to focus on the aspects that are related to color.[1] For example, all breeds with solid colors have occasional white markings produced by the minus modifiers, and it would be redundant to include here the amount that is permissible. The color alleles of some breeds have not been studied and no summaries are possible.

The lack of uniform adjectives for color leads to confusion. The genotype of gray and silver, for example, could be either B–dd, $bbdd$, or even A– (agouti), and the terms *brown*, *liver*, and *chocolate* are all used to describe the genotype bb. Remember, a dash (–) indicates that the allele at that locus is masked.

Little, Willis, and Robinson give the most complete descriptions of breed color alleles, but there are some differences between even these experts. The symbols here are those used by Robinson. The alleles and dominance sequence in each series are also Robinson's except for the inclusion of the black mask extension in the Locus E series.

Affenpinscher

Black, gray, silver, red, and black-and-tan, and other mixtures are permissible.

Little suggests that the darker grays have the genotype $A^y a^t$.[2] None of the authorities suggest the alleles that might produce the gray or silver.

$A^s/A^y/a^t$, B, C, D, E^m/E, g, m, S, t

black	A^s–
black-and-tan	$a^t a^t$
red	A^y–

Afghan Hound

All colors, but combinations should be pleasing.
$A^s/A^y/a^t$, B, C/c^{ch}, D/d, $E^m/E/e$, g, m, S, t

Airedale Terrier

Black or dark-grizzle saddle (some red mixed with the black is not objectionable); head, neck, and rest of body tan.
a^{sa}, B, C, D, E, g, m, S, t

Table A-1. Color Alleles and Effects

Allele	Effects
LOCUS A SERIES: DARK-PIGMENT PATTERN	
A^s	Dominant black
A^y	Dominant yellow
A	Banded pigment in hair
a^{sa}	Saddle pattern
a^t	Bicolored pattern
a	Recessive black
LOCUS B PAIR: BLACK/BROWN PIGMENT	
B	Black
b	Brown
LOCUS C SERIES: PIGMENT DEPTH	
C	Full color pigmentation
c^{ch}	Chinchilla dilution
c^e	Extreme dilution
c^b	Cornaz (blue-eyed albino)
c	Albino
LOCUS D PAIR: PIGMENT DENSITY	
D	Intense pigment density
d	Dilute pigment density
LOCUS E SERIES: EXTENSION	
E^m	Black mask
E^{br}	Brindle
E	Extension
e	Restriction
LOCUS G PAIR: PROGRESSIVE GRAYING	
G	Dark color lightens with age
g	Uniform color through life
LOCUS M PAIR: MERLE PATTERN	
M	Merle or dapple pattern
m	Uniform pigment
LOCUS S SERIES: WHITE PATTERN	
S	Solid color (self)
s^i	Irish-spotting pattern
s^p	Piebald spotting
s^w	Extreme piebald spotting
LOCUS T PAIR: TICKING	
T	Ticked coat
t	No ticking

Akita

Any color, including white, brindle, and pinto. The colors range from almost cream-white through reds, browns, and black, and no more than one-third of the color can be white.

The breed color has not been studied, and no summary of the alleles has been suggested.

Alaskan Malamute

Light-gray through intermediate shades to black, always with white on underbodies, parts of legs, feet, and part of mask markings. Face markings should be either caplike or mask-like. A white blaze on forehead and/or collar or spot on nape is acceptable, but broken color extending over the body is undesirable. White is the only acceptable solid color.

The breed color has not been studied, though Robinson suggests that A (agouti) or a^{sa} occurs in the breed.[3]

American Foxhound

Any color.

The colors and patterns are similar to the Beagle. Variations of shade are attributed to the c^{ch} allele.

$A^y/a^{sa}/a^t$, B, C/c^{ch}, D, E/e, g, m, $S/s^i/s^p/s^w$, T/t

American Staffordshire Terrier

Any color—solid, particolor, patched—permissible; more than 80 percent white, all white, liver, or black-and-tan is discouraged.

$A^s/A^y/a^t$, B/b, C, D/d, $E^{br}/E/e$, g, m, $S/s^i/s^p/s^w$, t

black	A^s–D–E–
blue	A^s–ddE–
black-and-tan	$a^t a^t D$–E–
red	A^y–D–E–
fawn	A^y–ddE–
brindle	A^y–D–E^{br}–
blue brindle	A^y–ddE^{br}–

American Water Spaniel

Solid liver, dark-chocolate.
Variations of shade are attributed to the c^{ch} allele.
A^s, b, C/c^{ch}, D, E, g, m, S, t

Anatolian Shepherd Dog

Fawn (usually with black mask), tricolor, and white as well as brindle and black.

Robinson identifies the genotype for fawn (A^y), tricolor (actually fawn plus piebald spotting, A^y–$s^p s^p$), and white (A^y–c^{ch}–).[4]

Australian Cattle Dog

Blue: Blue or blue mottled with or without other markings; blue with tan markings; head markings are black, blue, or tan. *Red speckle:* Even red speckle all over, including undercoat, with or without darker red markings on the head.

The breed color has not been studied, and no summary of the alleles has been suggested.

Australian Kelpie

Black, red, blue, or fawn, with or without tan.

The breed color has not been studied, and no summary of the alleles has been suggested.

Australian Shepherd

Blue merle, red (liver) merle, black, liver, and red, with or without white or tan markings.

The breed color has not been studied, and no summary of the alleles has been suggested. The combinations mentioned under Collies and Shetland Sheepdogs offer some possibilities.

Australian Terrier

Sandy, red, and blue-and-tan.

The breed color has not been studied, and no summary of the alleles has been suggested.

Basenji

Chestnut-red, pure-black, brindle, and tricolor (black, tan, and white); white markings in the Irish pattern (white feet, chest, and tail tip, white legs, blaze, and collar optional).[5]

$A^s/A^y/a^t$, B, C, D/d, E^{br}/E, g, m, s^i, t

red	A^y–D–EE
black	A^s–D–EE
brindle	A^y–D–E^{br}–
black-and-tan	$a^t a^t$D–EE
blue	A^s–ddEE
cream	A^y–ddEE

Basset Hound

Any recognized hound color; distribution of color and markings of no importance.

Variations of shade are attributed to the c^{ch} and the *Intensity* alleles.

$A^y/a^{sa}/a^t$, B, C/c^{ch}, D, E, g, m, S/s^i/s^p, T/t

Beagle

Any true hound color.

Dogs with no more white than the pseudo-Irish pattern are *S*; those with more extensive white are Ss^p, Ss^w, $s^p s^w$, or $s^w s^w$. Variations of shade are attributed to the c^{ch}

and the *Intensity* alleles. The *b, d,* and *e* alleles are rare.

a^{sa}/a^t, B/b, C/c^{ch}, D/d, E/e, g, m, S/s^p/s^w, T/t

Bearded Collie

All are born black, blue, brown or fawn, with or without white markings. With maturity, the coat color may lighten. Tan markings occasionally appear and are acceptable.

Color that lightens with age indicates the presence of the *G* allele. The breed color has not been well studied, and the Locus *A* and *E* alleles are uncertain. Tan markings would be produced by a^t. The fawns could be either A^s–*ee* or A^yA^yE–. Willis suggests that the breed's origin favors the latter combination. He also mentions that some have black masks, which would indicate the presence of E^m.[6]

—, B/b, C, D/d, —, G/g, m, S/s^i/s^w, t

Bedlington Terrier

Blue, sandy, liver, blue-and-tan, sandy-and-tan, liver-and-tan.
Except for creams, all are born dark and lighten at maturity.
$A^s/A^y/a^t$, B/b, C/c^{ch}, D/d, E/e, G, m, S, t

blue	A^s–B–C–D–
blue-and-tan	a^ta^tB–C–D–
liver	A^s–bbC–D–
liver-and-tan	a^ta^tbbC–D–
sandy	A^y–bbC–D–
cream	A^y–bb$c^{ch}c^{ch}$dd

Belgian Malinois

Rich-fawn to mahogany, with black overlay, black mask and ears; underparts, tail, and breeches lighter. (Shorthaired.)

A^y, B, C, D, E^m, g, m, S, t

Belgian Sheepdog

Black. (Longhaired.)[7] *Disqualification:* Any color other than black.

A^s, B, C, D, E^m, g, m, S, t

Belgian Tervuren

Rich-fawn to mahogany, with black overlay; underparts of body, tail, and breeches cream, gray, or light-beige; face has black mask (complete absence is a serious fault); ears mostly black; chest normally black but may be mixture of black and gray; washed out predominant color severely penalized. *Disqualifications:* Solid black, solid liver, white except on tips of toes, chin, and muzzle. (Longhaired.)

Tervurens have produced black puppies, and the recessive black (*a*) allele may occur in the breed.[8]

A^y, B, C/c^{ch}, D, E^m/E, g, m, S, t

red	A^y–B–C–
gray	A^y–B–$c^{ch}c^{ch}$

Bernese Mountain Dog

Tricolor—jet-black ground color, rich rusty points, clear white markings on legs, chest, and face; white legs or collar are serious faults. *Disqualification:* Any ground color other than black.

Solid-colored, extreme white, and russet-brown dogs have been reported. The extreme white could be $s^w s^w$, and the brown could be bb—both recessives that could be carried for many generations.[9]

a^t, B, C, D, E, g, m, s^i, t

Bichon Frise

White. May have shading of buff, cream, or apricot around the ears or on body but more than 10 percent color is penalized.

The breed color has not been studied, and no summary of the alleles has been suggested.

Black and Tan Coonhound

Coal-black with rich tan points in the bicolored pattern. *Disqualification:* Solid patch of white that extends more than one inch in any direction.

a^t, B, C, D, E, g, m, S, t

Bloodhound

Black-and-tan, red-and-tan, and tawny.

In addition to c^{ch}, the *Intensity* alleles have been suggested to explain the different shades of color.

$A^y/a^{sa}/a^t$, B/b, C/c^{ch}, D/d, E, g, m, S, t

Border Collie

Black-and-tan, tricolor, sable-and-white, black-and-white.

The breed color has not been studied, and no summary of the alleles has been suggested. Robinson comments that the most common color is black with white markings and suggests the presence of A^s and s^i.[10]

Border Terrier

Red, grizzle-and-tan, blue-and-tan, wheaten.

All are born dark; those with the *G* allele lighten at maturity. The *A* and *E* alleles are tentative. Variations of shade are attributed to the c^{ch} and the *Intensity* alleles.

$A^y/a^{sa}/a^t$, B, C/c^{ch}, D, E^{br}/E/e, G/g, m, S, t

Borzoi

Any color or combination of colors.

The brindle effect is believed to be produced by the mixture of shades with the long coat rather than the brindle allele. Willis suggests that the s^i may be present, though rare. Variations of shade are attributed to the c^{ch} and the *Intensity* alleles.[11]

$A^s/A^y/a^t$, B, C/c^{ch}, D, E/e, g, m, S/s^p/s^w, t

Boston Terrier

Brindle, seal (black, with reddish cast in bright light), or black with white markings. *Disqualifications:* Solid brindle, seal, or black; gray or liver colors.

All-white dogs may be extreme piebald (s^w). The disqualifications suggest that the b or d alleles may occur in the breed.

A^s/A^y, B, C, D, E^{br}/E, g, m, s^i/s^p, t

black	A^s–EE
brindle	$A^yA^yE^{br}$–

Bouvier des Flandres

From fawn to black; pepper-and-salt, gray, and brindle. Chocolate-brown, white, and particolors to be penalized.

The breed color has not been studied, and no summary of the alleles has been suggested.

Boxer

Fawn (from light-tan to mahogany) and brindle; black mask; when present, white markings must not exceed one-third of the ground color. *Disqualifications:* Any color other than fawn and brindle; white exceeding one-third of the entire coat.

A^y, B, C, D, $E^m/E^{br}/E$, g, m, $S/s^i/s^w$, t

brindle	E^{br}–S–
red/fawn	E–S–
brindle-and-white	E^{br}–s^i–
red/fawn-and-white	E–s^i–
white	—s^ws^w

Briard

All uniform colors except white; black, shades of gray and tawny, deeper shades preferred; combinations of two colors allowed as long as none are spots and the transition is gradual and symmetrical. *Disqualifications:* White coat or spotted coat; white on chest exceeding a one-inch diameter.

The breed color has not been well studied, and the Locus A and E alleles are uncertain. The occasional tan markings would be produced by a^t. The fawns could be either A^s–ee or A^yA^yE–.[12]

Brittany

Orange-and-white or liver-and-white in standard particolor or piebald patterns; clear or roan patterns; some ticking desirable. *Disqualification:* Black in coat.

A^s, b, C, D, E/e, g, m, s^p, T/t

liver-and-white	E–
orange-and-white	ee

Brussels Griffon

Red: Red-brown with a little black at whiskers and chin. *Beige:* Mixture of black and reddish-brown, usually with black mask. *Black-and-tan:* Black with uniform red-brown markings. *Black:* Solid black. *Disqualification:* White spot or blaze anywhere on coat.

$A^s/A^y/a^t$, B, C, D, E^m/E, g, m, S, t
red A^y-
black A^s-
black-and-tan $a^t a^t$

Bull Terrier
Colored: Any color other than white or any color with white markings; brindle preferred. *Disqualification:* Predominantly white dogs. *White:* Markings on head permissible but severely faulted elsewhere.

Blues (*dd*) occurred in the past, but the allele is believed to be eliminated.[13]
$A^s/A^y/a^t$, B, C, D, E^{br}/E, g, m, $S/s^i/s^w$, t

Bulldog
Colors are preferred in the following order: (*a*) red-brindle; (*b*) all other brindles; (*c*) white; (*d*) solid red, fawn, fallow; (*e*) piebald.

The fawn shade known as fallow may be produced by $c^{ch}c^{ch}$.
$A^s/A^y/a^t$, B, C/c^{ch}, D, $E^m/E^{br}/E$, g, m, $S/s^i/s^p/s^w$, T/t

Bullmastiff
Red, fawn, brindle.
A^y, B, C, D, $E^m/E^{br}/E$, g, m, S, t

Cairn Terrier
Any color except white; dark ears, muzzle, and tail tip desired.
All are born dark; those with the *G* allele lighten at maturity.
A^y/a^t, B, C/c^{ch}, D, $E^m/E^{br}/E$, G/g, m, S, t

Canaan Dog
Black and brown, solid and with white markings (some piebald).
The breed color has not been studied, and no summary of the alleles has been suggested.

Cavalier King Charles Spaniel
See English Toy Spaniels.

Chesapeake Bay Retriever
Any shade from dark-brown to faded-tan or deadgrass. *Disqualifications:* Black; white except on chest, abdomen, or spots on feet.

Variations of shade are attributed to the c^{ch} and the *Intensity* alleles.
A^s, b, C/c^{ch}, D, E, g, m, S, t

Chihuahua
Any color—solid, marked, or splashed.
The c^{ch} allele, the *Intensity* allele, and the rufus polygenes have been suggested to account for the different shades of color.
$A^s/A^y/a^{sa}/a^t$, B/b, C/c^{ch}, D/d, $E^m/E^{br}/E/e$, g, m, $S/s^i/s^p/s^w$, t
black A^s–B–D–

black-and-tan	$a^t a^t B$–D–
blue	A^s–B–dd
blue-and-tan	$a^t a^t B$–dd
liver	A^s–bbD–
liver-and-tan	$a^t a^t bbD$–
liver sable	A^y–bbD–
red (black nose)	A^y–B–D–
red (brown nose)	A^y–bbD–

Chinese Crested

Any color or combination of colors.

The skin is dark with piebald markings; the light piebald areas are usually dotted with darker spots. Skin colors include black, mahogany, blue, copper, lavender. The breed color has not been studied, and no summary of the alleles has been suggested other than the alleles for solid (S) and piebald (s^p).

Chinese Shar-Pei

Any solid color. *Disqualification:* Not a solid color (albino, brindle, bicolored or saddle pattern, etc.).

The breed color has not been studied, and no summary of the alleles has been suggested.

Chow Chow

Solid red (light golden to deep mahogany), black, blue, cinnamon (light fawn to deep cinnamon), and cream. Solid color with lighter shading on ruff, tail, and breeches.

Variations of shade are attributed to the c^{ch} and the *Intensity* alleles.

$A^s/A^y/a^t$, B, C/c^{ch}, D/d, E/e, g, m, S, t

Clumber Spaniel

White with lemon or orange markings, the fewer body markings the better.

Willis and Little suggest believe that the Locus B allele is B (black). Robinson disagrees, pointing out that the nose leather is usually liver or flesh, indicating the presence of b. Dogs with more extensive markings might be s^p.[14]

A^s, B/b, C, D, e, g, m, s^w, T/t

Cocker Spaniel

Black: Jet-black, black and tan. *ASCOB (any solid color other than black):* Any solid color except black *and* any such color with tan points. *Particolor:* Two or more clearly defined colors, one of which shall be white; roans of accepted roaning patterns or alternating hair colors throughout coat. *Disqualifications:* Solid and tan pointed colors with white other than on the chest and throat; tan points in excess of 10 percent; particolors more than 90 percent primary color.

The roan pattern is believed to be $s^p s^p$ or $s^p s^w$ with ticking. Rare blues (dd) have been reported in the breed. Both genotypes for red can occur in the breed, but A^y–E– is rare. The c^{ch} allele and the rufus polygenes have both been suggested to account for the different shades of color.

$A^s/A^y/a^t$, B/b, C/c^{ch}, D, E/e, g, m, S/s^p/s^w, T/t

black	A^s–B–E–S——
black-and-white	A^s–B–E–s^ps^ptt
black-and-white ticked	A^s–B–E–s^ps^pT–
black-and-tan	a^ta^tB–E–S——
tricolor (black)	a^ta^tB–E–s^ps^ptt
liver	A^s–bbE–S——
liver-and-white	A^s–bbE–s^ps^ptt
liver-and-tan	a^ta^tbbE–S——
red (black nose)	A^s–B–eeS——
red (brown nose)	A^s–bbeeS——
red-and-white (black nose)	A^s–B–ees^ps^ptt
red-and-white (brown nose)	A^s–bbees^ps^ptt

Collie

Sable (light-gold to dark-mahogany) and white, tricolor (black, white, tan), blue merle, and white (may have sable or tricolor markings).

A^y/a^t, B, C, D/d, E, g, M/m, $s^i/s^p/s^w$, t

sable	A^y–D–mm
blue sable	A^y–ddmm
sable-and-merle	A^y–D–Mm
blue-sable merle	A^y–ddMm
tricolor (black)	a^ta^tD–mm
tricolor (blue)	a^ta^tddmm
black-and-tan merle	a^ta^tD–Mm
blue-and-tan merle	a^ta^tddMm
white merle	——MM

Curly-Coated Retriever

Black or liver.

A^s, B/b, C, D, E, g, m, S, t

black	B–
liver	bb

Dachshund

Solid colors: Red and cream. *Two colors (bicolored pattern):* Black, chocolate, wild boar, gray (blue), and fawn (isabella)—all with tan points. *Brindle:* Black or dark stripes. *Dapples:* Clear brownish, grayish, or white ground color, with irregular patches of dark-gray, red-yellow, or black.

The occasional wolf-gray or grizzle could be A or a^{sa}. Rare brindles (E^{br}) have been reported. Variations of shade are attributed to the c^{ch} and the *Intensity* alleles.

A^y/a^t, B/b, C/c^{ch}, D, E^{br}/E, g, M/m, S, t

black-and-tan	a^ta^tB–mm
liver-and-tan	a^ta^tbbmm
red or sable (black nose)	A^y–B–mm

red or sable (brown nose)	A^y–bbmm
dappled black (bluish-gray)	$a^t a^t$B–Mm
dappled liver (beige)	$a^t a^t$bbMm
dappled red (light-red)	A^y–B–Mm

Dalmatian

Ground color always pure white; black or liver spots should be round and well defined, from the size of a dime to a half-dollar. *Disqualifications:* Patches (sharply defined mass of color appreciably larger than other markings, but spots that meet are not patches), tricolor, or color markings other than black and liver.

This is the only breed believed to carry and be homozygous for the recessive flecking (*f*) allele that, in combination with paired s^w alleles, produces the distinctive spots.[15]

A^s/a^t, B/b, C, D, E, *f*, g, m, s^w, T

black	A^s–B–E–
liver	A^s–bbE–
black-and-tan	$a^t a^t$B–E–

Dandie Dinmont Terrier

Pepper or mustard, with muzzle darker than shade of topknot; pepper ranges from dark blue-black to light silver-gray; mustard ranges from red-brown to pale-fawn, head being creamy white.

All are born dark and lighten at maturity. The mustards are dark sable at birth, and the peppers are black-and-tan.

A^y/a^t, B, C, D, E, G, m, S, t

pepper	A^y–
mustard	$a^t a^t$

Doberman Pinscher

Black, red, blue, and fawn (isabella) with sharply defined tan markings. *Disqualification:* Any other color.

a^t, B/b, C, D/d, E, g, m, S, t

black	B–D–
blue	B–dd
red	bbD–
fawn	bbdd

English Cocker Spaniel

Solid colors (black, liver, or shades of red), particolors (clearly marked, ticked, or roaned), and tan pointed.

The roan pattern is believed to be $s^p s^p$ or $s^p s^w$ with ticking. Both genotypes for red can occur in the breed, but A^y–ee is rare. Variations of shade are attributed to the c^{ch} and the rufus polygenes.

$A^s/A^y/a^t$, B/b, C/c^{ch}, D, E/e, g, m, S/s^p/s^w, T/t

black	A^s–B–E–S—
black-and-white	A^s–B–E–$s^p s^p$tt
black-and-white ticked	A^s–B–E–$s^p s^p$T–

black-and-tan	$a^ta^tB-E-S--$
tricolor (black)	$a^ta^tB-E-s^ps^ptt$
liver	$A^s-bbE-S--$
liver-and-white	$A^s-bbE-s^ps^ptt$
liver-and-tan	$a^ta^tbbE-S--$
red (black nose)	$A^s-B-eeS--$
red (brown nose)	$A^s-bbeeS--$
red-and-white (black nose)	$A^s-B-ees^ps^ptt$
red-and-white (brown nose)	$A^s-bbees^ps^ptt$

English Foxhound

Any good hound color—black, tan, white—or any combination of those three. The colors and patterns are similar to the Beagle.

$A^y/a^{sa}/a^t$, B, C/c^{ch}, D, E/e, g, m, $S/s^i/s^p/s^w$, T/t

English Setter

Orange belton, blue belton, tricolor (blue belton with tan markings), lemon belton, and liver belton.

Belton means flecked; *blue belton*, for example, is a flecked black. Solid whites are probably s^ws^w. Show lines primarily descend from the Lavarack strain and are typically ticked. The clear colors are typical of the Llewellen strain used for field.

A^s/a^t, B/b, C, D, E/e, g, m, s^p/s^w, T/t

orange belton (brown nose)	$A^s-bbees^p-T-$
blue belton (flecked black)	$A^s-B-E-s^p-T-$
tricolor	$a^ta^tB-E-s^p-T-$
lemon belton (black nose)	$A^s-B-ees^p-T-$
liver belton	$A^s-bbE-s^p-T-$

English Springer Spaniel

Liver or black with white markings or predominantly white with black or liver markings; tricolor; liver-and-white or black-and-white with tan markings; blue- or liver-roan. Off colors such as lemon, red, or orange not to place.

A^s/a^t, B/b, C, D, E/e, g, m, s^p/s^w, T/t

black-and-white	$A^s-B-E-s^p-$
tricolor (black)	$a^ta^tB-E-s^p-$
liver-and-white	$A^s-bbE-s^p-$

English Toy Spaniel

The solid variety colors are called *Ruby* (red) and *King Charles* (black-and-tan); the particolors are called *Blenheim* (red-and-white) and *Prince Charles* (tricolor).

The Cavalier King Charles Spaniel is a larger, racier variety, weighing from eight to ten pounds. It comes in all four colors, but red-and-white is the most common.[16]

A^s/a^t, B, C, D, E/e, g, m, $S/s^i/s^p$, t

Ruby (red)	A^s-eeS-
Blenheim (red-and-white)	$A^s-ees^ps^p$
King Charles (black-and-tan)	a^ta^tE-S-
Prince Charles (tricolor)	$a^ta^tE-s^ps^p$

Field Spaniel

Black, liver, golden-liver, or any of these with tan markings; particolors are undesirable.

The colors are similar to the English Cocker Spaniel. Variations of shade are attributed to the c^{ch} allele.

A^s/a^t, B/b, C/c^{ch}, D, E/e, g, m, s^i/s^p/s^w, T/t

Finnish Spitz

Golden red, from pale honey to deep auburn. Black hairs along topline and in tail permitted.

The breed color has not been studied, though Robinson attributes the color to A^y–E–.[17]

Flat-Coated Retriever

Solid black or liver. *Disqualifications:* Yellow, cream, or any other color than black or liver.

A^s, B/b, C, D, E, g, m, S, t

black	B–
liver	bb

Fox Terrier

White should predominate; brindle, red, or liver markings are objectionable, otherwise color is of no importance.

A^y/a^{sa}/a^t, B/b, C, D, E, g, m, s^p/s^w, T/t

French Bulldog

All brindle colors, fawn, white, brindle-and-white, and any other except those disqualified. *Disqualifications:* Black-and-white, black-and-tan, liver, mouse, and solid black (no trace of brindle).

A^y, B, C, D, E^{br}/E, g, m, S/s^i/s^p/s^w, T/t

fawn	E–S–
fawn-and-white	E–s^i–
brindle	E^{br}–S–
brindle-and-white	E^{br}–s^i–

German Shepherd Dog

Varies in color, and most are allowed; pale colors, blues, and livers are serious faults. *Disqualification:* White.

The breed has been extensively studied but still presents a somewhat confusing picture. Black (a) is recessive. Factors producing black-eyed whites are not understood. In addition to c^{ch}, both the *Intensity* alleles and the rufus polygenes have been suggested to explain the different shades of color. The E^{br} allele has almost disappeared from the modern breed.[18]

A^y/A/a^{sa}/a^t/a, B/b, C/c^{ch}, D/d, E^m/E/e, g, m, S, t

sable	A^y–C–
gray-sable	A^y–$c^{ch}c^{ch}$
saddle	a^{sa}–C–

black-and-tan	a^t–C–
black-and-cream	a^t–$c^{ch}c^{ch}$
black	aaC–

German Shorthaired Pointer

Solid liver or any combination of liver-and-white such as liver-and-white ticked, liver-spotted and white ticked, or liver-roan. *Disqualifications:* Solid white or any area of black, red, orange, lemon, or tan.

A^s, b, C, D, E, g, m, S/s^p/s^w, T/t

liver	S——
liver-and-white	s^p–tt
liver-and-white ticked	s^p–T–
liver roan	$s^w s^w$T–

German Wirehaired Pointer

Liver-and-white, usually either liver-and-white spotted, liver roan, liver-and-white spotted with ticking and roaning, or solid liver.

A^s, b, C, D, E, g, m, S/s^p/s^w, T/t

Giant Schnauzer

Solid black or pepper-and-salt.
See Miniature Schnauzer.

Golden Retriever

Various shades of rich gold; extremely light and dark shades are undesirable.
In addition to c^{ch}, both the *Intensity* alleles and the rufus polygenes have been suggested to explain the differences of color.

A^s, B, C/c^{ch}, D, e, g, m, S, t

Gordon Setter

Black with clearly defined tan (bicolored pattern) markings of either chestnut or mahogany. *Disqualifications:* Predominantly tan, red, or buff, or lacking typical pattern.

Variations of shade in the tan markings are attributed to the c^{ch} allele and the rufus polygenes.

a^t, B, C/c^{ch}, D, E/e, g, m, S, t

black-and-tan	E–
red	ee

Great Dane

Brindle: Yellow with black stripes, black mask preferred. *Fawn:* Yellow-gold with a black mask. *Blue:* Steel blue. *Black:* Glossy black. *Harlequin:* White base with black patches. *Disqualification:* Any other color.[19]

A^s/A^y, B, C, D/d, E^m/E^{br}/E, g, H/h, M/m, S/s^p/s^w, t

fawn	$A^y A^y$D–EEhhmm
brindle	$A^y A^y$D–E^{br}–hhmm
black	A^s–D–EEhhmm
black-harlequin	A^s–D–EEHhMm

blue	A^s–ddEEhhmm
blue-brindle	$A^yA^yddE^{br}$–hhmm
blue-harlequin	A^s–ddEEHhMm
merle	A^s–D–EEhhMm

Great Pyrenees
All-white or white with markings of badger, gray, reddish-brown, or varying shades of tan.

Other suggested alleles are A^s and e.

A^y/a^{sa}, B, c^{ch}, D, E, g, m, s^w, t

Greater Swiss Mountain Dog
Black and white with tan markings. Red tricolors occur but are not acceptable.

The breed color has not been studied, but the color and pattern is similar to that of the Bernese Mountain Dog.

Greyhound
Color immaterial.

The c^{ch} and *Intensity* alleles as well as the rufus polygenes have been suggested to account for the different shades of color.

A^s/A^y, B, C, D/d, $E^{br}/E/e$, g, m, $S/s^i/s^p/s^w$, t

red	A^yA^yD–E–S–
red-and-white	A^yA^yD–E–s^p–
fawn	A^yA^yddE–S–
fawn-and-white	A^yA^yddE–s^p–
black	A^s–D–E–S–
black brindle	A^s–D–E^{br}–S–
black-and-white	A^s–D–E–s^p–
blue	A^s–ddE–S–
blue brindle	A^s–ddE^{br}–S–
blue-and-white	A^s–ddE–s^p–

Harrier
Same as the English Foxhound (any good hound color—black, tan, white—or any combination of these).

See English Foxhound.

Havanese
A wide variety of colors and color combinations.

The breed color has not been studied, and no summary of the alleles has been suggested.

Ibizan Hound
White or red (from light, yellowish red called lion to deep red), solid or in any combination. *Disqualification:* Any color other than red or white.

The breed color has not been studied, though Robinson suggests that the critical alleles are A^y and s^p, and that the liver nose indicates bb.[20]

Irish Setter

Mahogany or rich chestnut-red with no black.

Rare black, black-and-tan, and black-and-sable dogs have been reported, suggesting that some reds may be produced by the A^y–E– alleles and that the breed also carries the a^t allele. The variations of color are attributed to the rufus polygenes.

A^s, B, C, D, e, g, m, s, t

Irish Terrier

Solid shades of bright-red, golden-red, red-wheaten, or wheaten.

The c^{ch} and the rufus polygenes have both been suggested to account for variations of color.

A^y, B, C/c^{ch}, D, E, g, m, S, t

Irish Water Spaniel

Solid liver.

Rare bicolors have been reported, indicating the presence of a^t. The c^{ch} allele is believed to produce the range of color.

A^s/a^t, b, C/c^{ch}, D, E, g, m, S, t

Irish Wolfhound

Gray, brindle, red, black, pure white, fawn, or any other color that appears in the deerhound.

In addition to c^{ch}, both the *Intensity* alleles and the rufus polygenes have been suggested to account for the differences of color.

A^y, B, C/c^{ch}, D, E^{br}/e, g, m, S, t

Italian Greyhound

Any color and markings except brindle and black-and-tan. *Disqualifications*: Brindle and black-and-tan.

Variations of shade are attributed to the c^{ch} allele.

$A^s/A^y/a^t$, B, C/c^{ch}, D/d, $E/e/E^{br}$, g, m, $S/s^i/s^p/s^w$, t

Japanese Chin

All particolors—black-and-white or red-and-white; bright, clear red preferred, but red includes all shades of sable, brindle, lemon, and orange.

A^s/A^y, B, C, D, E/e, g, m, s^p, t

Keeshond

Mixture of black and gray, with an outer coat of black-tipped hair and undercoat of pale-gray or cream; any solid color or deviation is faulty.

The c^{ch} and the rufus polygenes have both been suggested to account for the different shades of color. Robinson suggests that the color could be a^{sa} with minus rufus polygenes. Willis attributes the rare orange sables (sometimes called tawny) to A^y.[21]

A, B, C/c^{ch}, D, E, g, m, S, t

Kerry Blue Terrier

Born black; should show graying by eighteen months; mature color any shade of blue-gray ranging from deep-slate to light blue-gray. *Disqualifications:* Solid black.

All are born dark; those with the *G* allele lighten at maturity.

A^s, B, C, D, E, G/g, m, S, t

Komondor

White. *Disqualification:* Any other color.

As in most all-white breeds, the color alleles are difficult to identify, and none have been suggested.

Kuvasz

White. Occasional dogs with yellow saddle are faulty.

As in most all-white breeds, the color alleles are difficult to identify, and none have been suggested.

Labrador Retriever

Black, yellow, or chocolate.

A^s, B/b, C/c^{ch}, D, E/e, g, m, S, t

yellow (black nose)	B–ee
yellow (brown nose)	bbee
chocolate	bbE–
black	B–E–

Lakeland Terrier

Solid colors include blue, black, liver, red, red grizzle, and wheaten. In saddle-marked dogs, the saddle may be blue, black, liver, or varying shades of grizzle; tan is wheaten or golden tan.

Variations of shade are attributed to the c^{ch} and the *Intensity* alleles.

$A^s/a^{sa}/a^t$, B, C/c^{ch}, D/d, E/e, g, m, S, t

blue	A^s–B–ddE–
black	A^s–B–D–E–
liver	A^s–bbD–E–
red	A^s–B–D–ee
wheaten	A^s–B–ddee
black saddle	a^{sa}–B–D–E–
blue saddle	a^{sa}–B–ddE–
red saddle	a^{sa}–B–D–ee

Lhasa Apso

All colors, with or without dark tips on ears and beard.

The breed color has not been studied, and no summary of the alleles has been suggested.

Lowchen

Any color or combination of colors.

Maltese
White; light-tan or lemon ears allowed but undesirable.
A^s, B, c^{ch}, D, e, g, m, s^w, t

Manchester Terrier
Jet-black with clearly defined mahogany-red points. *Disqualification:* Any other color.
a^t, B, C, D, E, g, m, S, t

Mastiff
Fawn, apricot, or brindle with black muzzle, ears, and nose.
In addition to c^{ch}, the *Intensity* alleles have been suggested to account for the different shades of color.
A^y, B, C/c^{ch}, D, $E^m/E^{br}/E$, g, m, S, t

Miniature Bull Terrier
White: White, markings on head not to be penalized. *Colored:* Any color to predominate.
See Bull Terrier.

Miniature Pinscher
Solid clear-red, stag-red (intermingling black hairs), black with clearly defined tan points, chocolate-and-tan. *Disqualification:* Any other color.[22]
A^y/a^t, B/b, C, D/d, E, g, M/m, S, t

Miniature Poodle
Any solid color, with an even color at the skin. Blue, gray, silver, brown, cafe-au-lait, apricot, and cream may show varying shades of the same color on different parts of the body. *Disqualification:* Particolors.

Those that are born dark and lighten at maturity have the G allele; those born light and stay about the same shade are dd.

A^s/a^t, B/b, C/c^{ch}, D/d, E/e, G/g, m, S, t

(BLACK NOSES)

black	B–C–D–E–gg
gray (born black)	B–C–D–E–G–
light-red	B–C–D–$eegg$
silvery-red	B–C–D–eeG–
maltese (born blue)	B–C–ddE–gg
silver (born black)	B–C–ddE–G–
dull smoky-red	B–C–$ddeegg$
very pale silvery-red	B–C–$ddeeG$–
cream to white	B–$c^{ch}c^{ch}D$–$eegg$
cream to white	B–$c^{ch}c^{ch}D$–eeG–
cream to white	B–$c^{ch}c^{ch}ddeegg$

white	B–$c^{ch}c^{ch}ddeeG$–
(BROWN NOSES)	
liver	bbC–D–E–gg
grayish-brown	bbC–D–E–G–
silver-beige	bbC–D–$eegg$
pale silver-beige	bbC–D–eeG–
dull bluish-brown	bbC–ddE–gg
silvery-brown	bbC–ddE–G–
dull-cream	bbC–$ddeegg$
pale cream-white	bbC–$ddeeG$–
beige-brown	$bbc^{ch}c^{ch}D$–E–gg
silver-beige	$bbc^{ch}c^{ch}D$–E–G–
cream to white	$bbc^{ch}c^{ch}D$–$eegg$
white	$bbc^{ch}c^{ch}D$–eeG–
white, off-white	$bbc^{ch}c^{ch}ddE$–gg
pale smoky-beige	$bbc^{ch}c^{ch}ddE$–G–
white	$bbc^{ch}c^{ch}ddeegg$
white	$bbc^{ch}c^{ch}ddeeG$–

Miniature Schnauzer

Salt-and-pepper: A combination of black-and-white banded hairs with unbanded black and white hairs; light-gray or silver-white at typical bicolored points. *Black-and-silver:* Black with silver at the typical bicolored pattern points. *Black:* Rich, glossy black. *Disqualifications:* Solid white or white other than a small white chest marking.

The colors in of the schnauzer breeds are poorly understood. The salt-and-peppers are nearly black at birth, often with cream at the bicolored pattern points. The overall silvery color is attributed to the banded hairs expressed by the agouti allele, with the c^{ch} alleles reducing the expression of light pigment throughout the coat. The black-and-silvers would be $a^t a^t$, but the silver color of the points are difficult to explain. Although $c^{ch}c^{ch}$ would be expected to produce a very light color, Little suggests the possibility that the c^e allele (extreme dilution) also occurs in the breed, which would account for the silvery points. Whites, which are a recognized variety in Germany, occasionally occur in American litters, and the color appears to be consistently recessive.[23]

$A^s/A/a^t$, B, $C/c^{ch}/c^e$, D, E, g, m, S, t

black	A^s–
salt-and-pepper	A–
black-and-silver	$a^t a^t$

Newfoundland

Solid: Black, brown, and gray in solid colors or with white at any, some, or all of the following locations: chin, chest, toes, and tip of tail. *Landseer:* White with black markings. *Disqualification:* Any other color.[24]

A^s, B/b, C, D/d, E, g, m, S/s^p, T/t

black	B–D–S–
blue	B–ddS–

brown $bbD-S-$
Landseer $B-D-s^p s^p$

Norfolk Terrier

All shades of red, wheaten, grizzle, and black-and-tan.

A^y/a^t, B, C, D/d, E, g, m, S, t

Norwegian Elkhound

Medium-gray, variations in shade determined by length of black tips and quantity of guard hairs; undercoat, stomach, buttocks, and thighs of light-silver. Black muzzle, ears, and tail tip. *Disqualification:* An overall color other than gray.

All are born black with scattered gray hairs, which is considered typical of the *A* allele. Originally the breed occurred in many colors, and occasional reds and browns (*bb*) still occur.[25]

A, B/b, c^{ch}, D, E^m/E, g, m, S, t

Norwich Terrier

All shades of red, wheaten, grizzle, and black-and-tan.

A^y/a^t, B, C, D/d, E, g, m, S, t

Old English Sheepdog

Any shade of gray, grizzle, blue, or blue merle, with or without white markings or in reverse; any shade of brown or fawn objectionable.

All are born dark; those with the *G* allele lighten at maturity.

A^s, B, C, D, E, G/g, M/m, $S/s^i/s^p$, t

Otterhound

Any color or combination of colors is acceptable.

The breed color has not been studied, and no summary of the alleles has been suggested.

Papillon

White with patches of any color. *Disqualifications:* Solid white or no white.

A^y/a^t, B, D, E/e, g, m, $s^i/s^p/s^w$, t

Pekingese

All colors—solid, brindle, particolor—allowed; black mask and spectacles desirable.

Variations of shade are attributed to the c^{ch} allele. The c^b (cornaz) allele produces blue-eyed pale-gray; the *c* (albino) allele produces red-eyed white.

$A^s/A^y/a^t$, B, $C/c^{ch}/c^b/c$, D/d, $E^m/E/e$, g, m, $S/s^i/s^p/s^w$, t

Petit Basset Griffon Vendeen

White with any combination of lemon, orange, black, tricolor, or grizzle markings.

The breed color has not been studied, and no summary of the alleles has been suggested.

Pharaoh Hound

Range from tan to rich-chestnut with white on chest, toes, tail tip, and snip on face. *Disqualification:* Any solid white spot on the back of neck, shoulder, or any part of the back or sides.

The breed color has not been studied, and no summary of the alleles has been suggested.

Pointer

Liver, lemon, black, orange; either in combination with white or solid colored.

A^s/a^t, B/b, C, D, E/e, g, m, s^p/s^w, T/t

black-and-white	A^s–B–E–s^p–
liver-and-white	A^s–bbE–s^p–
lemon-and-white (black nose)	A^s–B–ees^p–
orange-and-white (brown nose)	A^s–$bbees^p$–

Pomeranian

Any solid color, any solid color with lighter or darker shadings of the same color, any solid color with sable or black shadings, particolor, sable, and black-and-tan.

Particolors (s^p), blues (dd), and masks (E^m) are now rare in the breed. The c^b (cornaz) allele produces blue-eyed pale-gray. Variations of shade are attributed to the c^{ch} and the *Intensity* alleles.

$A^s/A^y/a^t$, B/b, $C/c^{ch}/c^b$, D/d, E^m/E, g, m, S/s^p, t

Portuguese Water Dog

Black, white, and various shades of brown; black-and-white; brown-and-white.

The breed color has not been studied, and no summary of the alleles has been suggested.

Pug

Silver, apricot-fawn, and black; black mask.

In addition to c^{ch}, both the *Intensity* alleles and the rufus polygenes have been suggested to explain the differences of color.

A^s/A^y, B, C/c^{ch}, D, E^m/E, g, m, S, t

silver	$A^yA^yc^{ch}c^{ch}$
apricot-fawn	A^yA^yC–
black	A^s–C–

Puli

Solid colors or black, rusty-black, all shades of gray, and white.

The breed color has not been studied, and no summary of the alleles has been suggested. Benis comments that, in general, darker colors appear to be dominant over lighter and white appears to be recessive.[26]

Rhodesian Ridgeback

Light-wheaten to red-wheaten.

The breed color has not been studied, though Robinson suggests that the color is produced by the A^y and E alleles.[27]

Rottweiler

Black with clearly defined markings of rust to mahogany. *Disqualification:* Base color other than black.

a^t, B, C, D, E, g, m, S, t

Saint Bernard

White-and-red, red-with-white, or brindle-with-white; black mask.

The brindle effect is attributed to varying sable shading rather than the brindle allele. In addition to c^{ch}, the *Intensity* alleles have been suggested to account for the different shades of color.

A^y, B, C/c^{ch}, D, E^m/E, g, m, $s^i/s^p/s^w$, T/t

Saluki

White, cream, fawn, golden, red, grizzle-and-tan, black-and-tan, and tricolor.

$A^s/A^y/a^t$, B, C/c^{ch}, D, E^m/e, g, m, $S/s^i/s^p/s^w$, T/t

Samoyed

Pure white, cream, biscuit, and white-and-biscuit. *Disqualification:* Any other color.

As in all white breeds, the underlying alleles are difficult to identify; the A^s–ee combination has also been suggested.[28]

A^y, B, c^{ch}, D, E, g, m, s^w, t

Schipperke

Solid black. *Disqualification:* Any other color.

Reds, fawns, chocolates, and blues occur in the breed.

A^s/A^y, B/b, C, D/d, E, g, m, S, t

black	A^s–B–D–
blue	A^s–B–dd
chocolate	A^s–bbD–
red	$A^y A^y$B–D–

Scottish Deerhound

Dark blue-gray preferred; light- to dark-gray, brindle, yellow, sandy-red, red-fawn.

The all-white dogs may be s^w. Variations of shade are attributed to the c^{ch} allele. Records of the late nineteenth- and early twentieth-centuries report black-and-tans and masks, but the alleles have apparently been eliminated from the breed.[29]

A^s/A^y, B, C/c^{ch}, D, $E^m/E^{br}/E/e$, g, m, S, t

Scottish Terrier

Steel- or iron-gray, brindle, grizzle, black, sandy, wheaten.

In blacks, the A^s allele would mask the E alleles, which could be either E or E^{br}. Variations of shade have been attributed to the c^{ch} allele, the *Intensity* alleles, and the rufus polygenes.

A^s/A^y, B, C/c^{ch}, D, E^{br}/E, g, m, S, t

black	A^s——
brindle	$A^y A^y$C–E^{br}–
wheaten	$A^y A^y c^{ch} c^{ch}$EE

Sealyham Terrier

Solid white or with lemon, tan, or badger markings on head and ears.

A^y, B, C, D, E, g, m, s^p/s^w, t

Shetland Sheepdog

Black, blue merle, and sable, marked with varying amounts of white and/or tan. *Disqualifications:* Brindle.

Basically the same alleles as the Collie, except that the disqualification suggests that the E^{br} allele also occurs in the breed. *See* Collie.

A^y/a^t, B, C, D/d, E, g, M/m, $s^i/s^p/s^w$, t

Shiba Inu

Red (dark to light), red sesame (red with black hairs), black-and-tan, black sesame (black with red hairs), white, brindle; white markings.

The breed color has not been studied, and no summary of the alleles has been suggested.

Shih Tzu

All colors allowed.

The breed color has not been studied, and no summary of the alleles has been suggested.

Siberian Husky

All colors from pure black to pure white.

The breed color has not been studied, and no summary of the alleles has been suggested.

Silky Terrier

Blue-and-tan in saddle pattern; the blue may be silver, pigeon, or slate shades, with deep, rich tan.

The breed color has not been studied, and no summary of the alleles has been suggested. The breed was developed through crosses of the Australian Terrier and the Yorkshire Terrier, so the alleles are probably similar.

Skye Terrier

Full (adult) coat has varying shades of the same color; colors are black, blue, dark- or light-gray, silver-platinum, fawn, and cream; black ears, muzzle, and tip of tail.

All are born dark; those with the G allele lighten at maturity. Variations of shade are attributed to the c^{ch} and the *Intensity* alleles.

A^y/a^t, B, C/c^{ch}, D, $E^m/E^{br}/e$, G/g, m, S, t

Soft Coated Wheaten Terrier

Any shade of wheaten.

The breed color has not been studied, and no summary of the alleles has been suggested.

Spinoni Italiani
White, orange roan, chestnut roan, orange-and-white, and chestnut-and-white.
The breed color has not been studied, and no summary of the alleles has been suggested.

Staffordshire Bull Terrier
Red, fawn, white, black, blue, and any shade of brindle as well as any of these colors with white. *Disqualifications:* Liver and black-and-tan.
The *b* allele occurred in the past but is unlikely in the modern breed.
$A^s/A^y/a^t$, B, C, D/d, E^{br}/E, g, m, $S/s^i/s^p/s^w$, t

black	A^s–D–E–
blue	A^s–ddE–
black-and-tan	$a^t a^t$ D–E–
red	A^y–D–E–
fawn	A^y–ddE–
brindle	A^y–D–E^{br}–
blue brindle	A^y–ddE^{br}–

Standard Poodle
Any solid color; coat is an even color at the skin but may show varying shades of the same color on different parts of the body. *Disqualification:* Particolors.
See Miniature Poodle.

Standard Schnauzer
Pepper-and-salt, solid black.
See Miniature Schnauzer.

Sussex Spaniel
Rich golden liver.
A^s, b, C, D, E, g, m, S, t

Tibetan Spaniel
All colors and mixtures of colors.
The breed color has not been studied, and no summary of the alleles has been suggested.

Tibetan Terrier
Any color or combination of colors.
The breed color has not been studied, and no summary of the alleles has been suggested.

Toy Manchester Terrier
Jet-black with clearly defined mahogany-red points. *Disqualification:* Any other color.
See Manchester Terrier.

Toy Poodle

Any solid color; coat is an even color at the skin but may show varying shades of the same color on different parts of the body. *Disqualification:* Particolors.

See Miniature Poodle.

Vizsla

Solid golden rust in different shadings. *Disqualifications:* Massive areas of white on chest; white anywhere else on the body; solid white extending above the toes.

The breed color has not been studied, and no summary of the alleles has been suggested, though Robinson suggests that the color is produced by the combination of A^y–E– and b.[30]

Weimaraner

Shades of mouse-gray to silver-gray. *Disqualification:* Blue.

The varying shades of the head and body are produced by the A (agouti) allele. Ticking may occur in white markings. The shades exhibit the continuous variance consistent with the dilution modifiers.[31]

A/a^t, B/b, C, d, E, g, m, S, T/t

gray (isabella)	A–bb
blue	A–B–
"dobe" marked	$a^t a^t bb$

Welsh Corgi (Cardigan)

All shades of red, sable, and brindle; black with or without tan or brindle points; blue merle. *Disqualifications:* Body color predominantly white; any other color.

A^y/a^t, B, C, D, E^{br}/E, g, M/m, $S/s^i/s^p$, t

Welsh Corgi (Pembroke)

Red, sable, fawn, black-and-tan, with or without white markings; very serious faults are white body color with red or dark markings, white on back, black-and-white with no tan, and blue.

A^y/a^t, B, C, D, E, g, m, S/s^i, t

Welsh Springer Spaniel

Rich dark-red and white.

A^s, b, C, D, e, g, m, s^p, T/t

Welsh Terrier

Black or grizzle saddle, spreading up onto neck, down onto the tail and upper thighs; tan is deep reddish-brown or slightly lighter.

a^{sa}, B, C, D/d, E/e, g, m, S, t

West Highland White Terrier

White.

As in all white breeds, the underlying alleles are difficult to identify. Little suggests that the base color is $A^y A^y$ combined with dilution alleles at Locus C, either c^{ch} or c^e.[32]

A^y, B, c^{ch}/c^e, D, E, g, m, S, t

Whippet
Color immaterial.
See Greyhound.

Wirehaired Pointing Griffon
Steel-gray with brown markings, frequently chestnut brown or roan, white and brown; white and orange also acceptable. *Disqualification:* Black.

A^s, b, C, D, E, g, m, s^p/s^w, T

Yorkshire Terrier
Born black-and-tan (saddle pattern) and lightens with maturity; black becomes dark steel-blue; tan darker at roots, shading to light-tan at tips of hair.

a^{sa}, B, C, D, E, G, m, S, t

APPENDIX B

A CATALOGUE OF CONGENITAL AND HEREDITARY DISORDERS (BY BREED)

Breed	Mode*	Disorders
Aberdeen terrier		Primary uterine inertia
Afghan hound	R	Cataract (bilateral)
		Elbow joint malformation
	R	Necrotizing myelopathy
Airedale terrier		Cerebellar hypoplasia
		Trembling of hind quarters
		Umbilical hernia
Alaskan malamute		Anemia with chondrodysplasia
	R	Dwarfism
	R	Factor VII deficiency
	R	Hemeralopia
		Renal cortical hypoplasia
American foxhound		Deafness
		Microphthalmia
Antarctic husky	D	Entropion
	SLR	Hemophilia A
Australian shepherd	R	Microphthalmia and multiple colobomas
Basenji	R	Coliform enteritis
		Hemolytic anemia
		Inguinal hernia
	D	Persistent pupillary membrane
		Pyruvate kinase deficiency
		Umbilical hernia
Basset hound	D	Achondroplasia
		Anomaly of third cervical vertebra
		Inguinal hernia
		Platelet disorder
		Primary glaucoma

*Mode of inheritance: R = recessive; D = dominant; ID = incomplete dominance; SLR = sex-linked recessive; and P = polygenic.

Reprinted, by permission, from: "A Catalogue of Congenital and Hereditary Disorders (By Breed)," in *Current Veterinary Therapy IX: Small Animal Practice*, ed. Robert W. Kirk (Philadelphia: Saunders, 1986), 1281–1285.

Breed	Mode*	Disorders
Beagle	SLR	Atopic dermatitis
		Bladder cancer
	ID	Bundle branch block
		Cataract (unilateral)
	D	Cataract with microphthalmia
	P	Cleft lip and palate
		Distemper
	R, P	Epilepsy
	SLR	Factor VII deficiency
		Hemophilia A
		Hypercholesterolemia
		Interverterbral disc disease
		Lymphocytic thyroiditis
	R	Mononephrosis
		Multiple epiphyseal dysplasia
		Necrotizing panotitis
	P	Otocephalic syndrome
	R	Primary glaucoma
	P	Pulmonic stenosis
		Renal hypoplasia
	R	Retinal dysplasia
	R	Short tail
		Thyroiditis
		Unilateral kidney aplasia
Bedlington terrier		Renal cortical hypoplasia
	R	Retinal dysplasia
Bernese sennehound	P	Cleft lip and palate
Black and tan coonhound	SLR	Hemophilia B
Bloodhound		Distemper
Blue tick hound		Globoid cell leukodystrophy
Border collie		Central progressive retinal atrophy
Boston terrier	R	Aortic and carotid body tumors
		Cataract (bilateral)
		Craniomandibular osteopathy
		Hemivertebra
		Mastocytoma
		Oligodendroglioma
		Patellar luxation
		Pituitary tumor
Boxer		Abnormal dentition (extra incisor)
		Aortic and carotid body tumors
		Aortic stenosis
		Atrial septal defects
	SLR	Cystinuria
		Dermoid cysts
		Endocardial fibroelastosis

Breed	Mode*	Disorders
Boxer (continued)	P	Fibrosarcoma Gingival hyperplasia Histiocytoma Melanoma Oligodendroglioma Persistence of right venous valve Pulmonic stenosis Subaortic stenosis Superficial corneal ulcer
Brussels griffon		Short skull
Bull mastiff		Abnormal dentition (extra incisor)
Bull terrier	R	Deafness Inguinal hernia Umbilical hernia
Cairn terrier	SLR R SLR SLR	Craniomandibular osteopathy Cystinuria Globoid cell leukodystrophy Hemophilia A Hemophilia B Inguinal hernia
Ceylon		Hairlessness
Chihuahua	SLR R	Collapsed trachea Dislocation of the shoulder Hemophilia A Hydrocephalus Hypoplasia of dens [sic?] Mitral valve defects Patellar luxation Pulmonic stenosis
Cocker spaniel	P R P R D R P	Behavioral abnormalities Cataract (bilateral) Cataract with microphthalmia Cleft lip and palate Cranioschisis Distichiasis Factor X deficiency Hip dysplasia Hydrocephalus Inguinal hernia Intervertebral disk disease Over- and undershot jaw Patent ductus arteriosis Primary glaucoma Primary peripheral retinal dystrophy Renal cortical hypoplasia Skin neoplasms

Breed	Mode*	Disorders
Cocker spaniel (continued)	R	Tail abnormalities
		Umbilical hernia
	P	Ununited anconeal process
Collie		Bladder cancer
	R	Collie eye anomaly
	R	Cyclic neutropenia
		Deafness
	R,P	Epilepsy
	SLR	Hemophilia A
		Inguinal hernia
	ID	Iris heterochromia
		Microphthalmia
		Nasal solar dermatitis
		Optic nerve hypoplasia
	P	Patent ductus arteriosis
		Umbilical hernia
	D	Achondroplasia
Dachshund	P	Cleft lip and palate
	SLR	Cystinuria
		Deafness
		Diabetes mellitus
		Ectasia syndrome
		Intervertebral disk disease
	ID	Iris heterochromia
		Microphthalmia
		Osteopetrosis
		Over-and undershot jaw (longhaired Dachshund)
		Renal hypoplasia
Dalmatian		Atopic dermatitis
		Deafness
	R	Excess uric acid excretion
		Globoid cell leukodystrophy
Doberman pinscher		His bundle degeneration
		Polycystic fibrous dysplasia
		Renal cortical hypoplasia
		Spondylolisthesis
		Liver copper storage disease
		Persistent primary hyperplastic vitreons
English bulldog		Abnormal dentition (extra incisor)
		Anasarca
		Arteriovenous fistula
	P	Cleft lip and palate
		Hemivertebra
	R	Hydrocephalus
		Hypoplasia of trachea
		Mitral valve defects
		Oligodendroglioma

Breed	Mode*	Disorders
English bulldog (continued)	 R	Predisposition to dystocia Pulmonic stenosis Short skull Short tail Spina bifida
English cocker spaniel	SLR R R	Hemophilia A Juvenile amaurotic idiocy Neuronal ceroid lipofuscinosis
English springer spaniel	D ID R	Cutaneous asthenia Factor XI deficiency Retinal dysplasia
Foxhound		Deafness Osteochondrosis of spine
Fox terrier	R	Ataxia Atopic dermatitis Deafness Dislocation of the shoulder Esophageal achalasia Glaucoma Goiter Lens luxation Oligodontia Pulmonic stenosis
French bulldog		Hemivertebra
German shepherd	 P D P SLR R,P SLR P R P P P D	Atopic dermatitis Behavioral abnormalities Cataract (bilateral) Cleft lip and palate Cystinuria Dermoid cyst Ectasia syndrome Enostosis Epilepsy Esophageal achalasia Eversion of nictitating membrane Hemophilia A Hip dysplasia Pancreatic insufficiency Persistent right aortic arch Pituitary dwarfism Renal cortical hypoplasia Subaortic stenosis Ununited anconeal process Von Willebrand's disease
German shorthaired pointer	R R	Amaurotic idiocy Eversion of nictitating membrane

Breed	Mode*	Disorders
German shorthaired pointer (continued)	D	Fibrosarcoma Lymphedema Melanoma Subaortic stenosis
Golden retriever	D	Cataract (bilateral) Cataract with microphthalmia
Gordon setter		Generalized progressive retinal atrophy
Great Dane	SLR ID P	Cystinuria Deafness Eversion of nictitating membrane Iris heterochromia Mitral valve defects Spondylolisthesis Stockard's paralysis
Great Dane x bloodhound		Paralysis of the hind limbs
Greyhound	SLR R	Esophageal achalasia Hemophilia A Predisposition to dystocia Short spine
Griffon		Dislocation of the shoulder
Griffon bruxellois x dachshund		Susceptibility to rickets
Irish setter	SLR R SLR R	Carpal subluxation Generalized myopathy Generalized progressive renal atrophy Hemophilia A Persistence of right aortic arch Quadriplegia with amblyopia
Irish terrier	SLR	Cystinuria
Jack Russell terrier		Ataxia Lens luxation
Keeshond	P R,P P	Conus septal defects Epilepsy Mitral valve defects Tetralogy of Fallot
Kerry blue	 P	Hair follicle tumor Ununited anconeal process
King Charles spaniel		Diabetes mellitus
Labrador retriever	 ID SLR SLR R	Carpal subluxation Cataract (bilateral) Craniomandibular osteopathy Cystinuria Hemophilia A Retinal dysplasia

Breed	Mode*	Disorders
Labrador x American foxhound		Diaphragmatic hernia
Labrador x poodle	D	Lymphedema
Lhasa apso		Inguinal hernia Renal cortical hypoplasia
Mexican, Turkish, and Chinese breeds	D	Hairlessness
Miniature pinscher		Dislocation of the shoulder
Miniature poodle	R SLR R P	Achondroplasia Cerebrospinal demyelination Cystinuria Dislocation of the shoulder Ectasia syndrome Ectodermal defect Generalized progressive retinal atrophy Globoid cell leukodystrophy Hypoplasia of dens Partial alopecia Patellar luxation Patent ductus arteriosis
Miniature schnauzer	R D	Cataract (bilateral) Pulmonic stenosis Von Willebrand's disease
Mongrel	 SLR	Black hair follicular dysplasia Cystinuria Multiple cartilaginous exostoses
Newfoundland	 P	Eversion of nictitating membrane Subaortic stenosis
Norwegian dunkerhound		Deafness Microphthalmia
Norwegian elkhound	R	Generalized progressive retinal atrophy Keratoacanthoma Renal cortical hypoplasia
Old English sheepdog	R	Cataract, bilateral
Otterhound	ID	Platelet disorder
Pekingese		Distichiasis Hypoplasia of dens Inguinal hernia Intervertebral disk disease Short skull Trichiasis Umbilical hernia

Breed	Mode*	Disorders
Pointer		Bithoracic ectomelia
	R	Cataract (bilateral)
	R	Neuromuscular atrophy
	R	Neurotropic osteopathy
		Umbilical hernia
Pomeranian		Dislocation of the shoulder
		Hypoplasia of dens
		Patellar luxation
	P	Patent ductus arteriosus
		Tracheal collapse
Poodle (see also miniature, standard, and toy poodle)		Atopic dermatitis
	P	Behavioral abnormality
	SLR	Cystinuria
		Distichiasis
	R	Epilepsy
	P	Patent ductus arteriosus
Pug		Male pseudohermaphroditism
		Trichiasis
Rhodesian ridgeback		Dermoid sinus
Rottweiler		Diabetes mellitus
St. Bernard		Aphakia with multiple colobomas
		Dermoid cysts of cornea
		Eversion of nictitating membrane
	SLR	Hemophilia A
	SLR	Hemophilia B
	P	Stockard's paralysis
St. Bernard x Great dane		Paralysis of the hind limbs
Samoyed		Atrial septal defects
		Diabetes mellitus
	SLR	Hemophilia A
		Pulmonic stenosis
Scottish terrier		Bladder cancer
		Atopic dermatitis
		Achondroplasia
		Craniomandibular osteopathy
	SLR	Cystinuria
		Deafness
		Melanoma
		Primary uterine inertia
	R	Scottie cramp
	D	Von Willebrand's disease
Sealyham terrier		Atopic dermatitis
		Lens luxation
	R	Retinal dysplasia
Shetland sheepdog		Bladder cancer

Breed	Mode*	Disorders
Shetland sheepdog (continued)	R	Collie eye anomaly
	SLR	Hemophilia A
		Hip dysplasia
	ID	Iris heterochromia
		Nasal solar dermatitis
	P	Patent ductus arteriosus
Shiba inu	R	Short spine
Shih tzu	P	Cleft lip and palate
		Renal cortical hypoplasia
Siberian husky	ID	Iris heterochromia
Silver grey collie		Cyclic neutropenia
	ID	Iris heterochromia
Skye terrier	R	Hypoplasia of the larynx
Springer spaniel	D	Ehlers-Danlos syndrome
	ID	Factor XI deficiency
	R	Retinal dysplasia
Staffordshire bull terrier	R	Cataract (bilateral)
	P	Cleft lip and palate
Standard poodle	R	Cataract (bilateral)
Swedish lapland	R	Neuronal abiotrophy
Swiss dogs		Generalized progressive retinal atrophy
Swiss sheepdog	P	Cleft lip and palate
Tervueren shepherd	R	Epilepsy
Toy poodle		Ectasia syndrome
		Fibrosis of the plantaris muscle
	R	Generalized progressive retinal atrophy
		Patellar luxation
	P	Patent ductus arteriosus
		Tracheal collapse
Vizsla	SLR	Hemophilia A
Weimaraner		Eversion of nictitating membrane
		Fibrosarcoma
	SLR	Hemophilia A
		Melanoma
		Spinal dysraphism
		Umbilical hernia
Welsh corgi	SLR	Cystinuria
		Generalized progressive retinal atrophy
		Predisposition to dystocia
West Highland white terrier		Atopic dermatitis
		Craniomandibular osteopathy
	R	Globoid cell leukodystrophy
		Inguinal hernia

Breed	Mode*	Disorders
Whippet		Partial alopecia
Yorkshire terrier	R	Hypoplasia of dens Patellar luxation Retinal dysplasia
All breeds	D	Blood group incompatibility
Brachycephalic breeds		Pituitary cysts Stenotic nares and elongated soft palate
Giant breeds		Elbow dysplasia Hip dysplasia Osteogenic sarcoma
Many breeds	P SLR D	Behavioral abnormalities Cryptorchidism Demodectic mange Dewclaws Ectropion Elbow dysplasia (especially large and giant breeds)
Many miniature breeds		Collapsed trachea Glycogen storage disease Legg-Calvé-Perthes syndrome Patellar luxation Predisposition to dystocia Tracheal collapse
Miscellaneous		White breed deafness

NOTES

PREFACE

1. Robert J. Hritzo, "Copper Toxicosis Announcement, AKC Delegates Meeting, March 14, 1995" (American Kennel Club communication sent to Scottsdale Dog Fanciers Association, Scottsdale, Arizona, photocopy).

CHAPTER 1. EVOLUTIONARY GENETICS

1. John C. Avise, *Molecular Markers, Natural History, and Evolution* (New York: Chapman & Hall, 1994), 3–4, 9; M. Verma and S. K. Dutta, "DNA Sequences Encoding Enolase Are Remarkably Conserved from Yeast to Mammals," *Life Sciences* 55 (1994): 893.

2. Rosie Mestel, "Ascent of the Dog," *Discover* 15 (October 1994): 93.

3. R. K. Wayne, W. G. Nash, and S. J. O'Brien, "Chromosomal Evolution of the *Canidae*. 2. Divergence from the Primitive Carnivore Karyotype," *Cytogenetics and Cell Genetics* 44 (1987): 134–141.

4. Ibid. R. K. Wayne, W. G. Nash, and S. J. O'Brien, "Chromosomal Evolution of the *Canidae*. 1. Species with High Diploid Numbers," *Cytogenetics and Cell Genetics* 44 (1987): 123–133.

5. Cornelis Naaktgeboren, "Dogs," in *Grzimek's Encyclopedia of Mammals*, 5 vols., ed. Bernhard Grzimek and Sybil P. Parker (New York: McGraw-Hill, 1990), 4:59.

6. Wayne, Nash, and O'Brien, "Chromosomal Evolution of the *Canidae*. 1. Species with High Diploid Numbers," 123.

7. D. Gottelli et al., "Molecular Genetics of the Most Endangered Canid: The Ethiopian Wolf *Canis Simensis*," *Molecular Ecology* 3 (1994): 301–312.

8. Jennifer Sheldon, *Wild Dogs: The Natural History of the Nondomestic* Canidae (San Diego: Academic Press, 1992), 41.

9. Roberta L. Hall, *Wolf and Man* (New York: Academic Press, 1978), 156, 182; P. S. Gipson, "Coyotes and Related Canis in the Southeastern United States with a Comment on Mexican and Central American Canis," in *Coyotes. Biology, Behaviour, and Management*, ed. M. Bekoff (New York: Academic Press, 1978), 193–194.

10. Gipson, "Coyotes," 195; R. K. Wayne, "Molecular Evolution of the Dog Family," *Trends in Genetics* 9 (1993): 223–224; M. S. Roy et al., "The Use of Museum Specimens to Reconstruct the Genetic Variability and Relationships of Extinct Populations," *Experientia* (Basel) 50 (1994): 551; M. S. Roy et al., "Patterns of Differentiation and Hybridization in North American Wolflike Canids, Revealed by Analysis of Microsatellite Loci," *Molecular Biology and Evolution* 11 (1994): 553; Howard J. Stains, "Distribution and Taxonomy of the *Canidae*," in *The Wild Canids*, ed. M. W. Fox (New York: Van Nostrand Reinhold, 1975), 7.

11. Stains, *"Canidae,"* 6.

12. N. W. G. Macintosh, "The Origin of the Dingo: An Enigma," in *The Wild Canids*, ed. M. W. Fox (New York: Van Nostrand Reinhold, 1975), 93, 94, 95, 99, 106.

13. Stains, *"Canidae,"* 6; Bernhard Grzimek and Eberhard Trumler, "Dingo," in *Grzimek's Encyclopedia of Mammals*, 5 vols., ed. Bernhard Grzimek and Sybil P. Parker (New York: McGraw-Hill, 1990), 4:100; Eberhard Trumler, "Domesticated Dog," in *Grzimek's Encyclopedia of Mammals*, 5 vols., ed. Bernhard Grzimek and Sybil P. Parker (New York: McGraw-Hill, 1990), 4:80.

14. John Paul Scott and John F. Fuller, *Genetics and the Social Behavior of the Dog* (Chicago: University of Chicago Press, 1965), 62; Stains, *"Canidae,"* 5; Naaktgeboren, "Dogs," 4:54.

15. Naaktgeboren, "Dogs," 4:52.

16. Stains, *"Canidae,"* 7; Sheldon, *Wild Dogs*, 25.

17. N. A. Iljin, "Wolf-Dog Genetics," *Journal of Genetics* 42 (1941): 360.

18. A. B. Chiarelli, "The Chromosomes of the *Canidae*," in *The Wild Canids*, ed. M. W. Fox (New York: Van Nostrand Reinhold, 1975), 50.

19. Gottelli et al., "Molecular Genetics of the Most Endangered Canid," 301–312.

20. Wayne, "Molecular Evolution of the Dog Family," 223; N. Lehman et al., "Introgression of Coyote Mitochondrial DNA into Sympatric North American Gray Wolf Populations," *Evolution* 45 (1991): 104; Avise, *Markers*, 391.

21. C. Manwell and C. M. A. Baker, "Origin of the Dog: From Wolf or Wild *Canis Familiaris*," *Speculations in Science and Technology* 6 (1983): 213.

22. Chiarelli, *"Canidae,"* 52.

23. Frederick Eberhard Zeuner, *A History of Domesticated Animals* (New York: Harper & Row, 1963), 101–102.

24. Michael W. Fox, *The Dog: Its Domestication and Behavior* (New York: Garland STPM Press, 1978), 249–250.

25. Naaktgeboren, "Dogs," 4:59.

26. Zeuner, *Domesticated Animals*, 83.

27. Macintosh, "Dingo," 97.

28. Fox, *The Dog*, 241.

29. Zeuner, *Domesticated Animals*, 31, 80, 84; Scott and Fuller, *Genetics and the Social Behavior of the Dog*, 39, 42.

30. Juliet Clutton-Brock, "Origins of the Dog: Domestication and Early History," in *Domestic Dog: Its Evolution, Behaviour and Interactions with People*, ed. James Serpell (Cambridge: Cambridge University Press, 1995), 10–11.

31. Zeuner, *Domesticated Animals*, 87–88.

32. Ibid., 95–98, 99–101; Scott and Fuller, *Genetics and the Social Behavior of the Dog*, 35.

33. Konrad Z. Lorenz, "Foreword," in *The Wild Canids*, ed. M. W. Fox (New York: Van Nostrand Reinhold, 1975), ix.

34. Maxwell Riddle, *Dogs Through History* (Fairfax, Va.: Denlinger's, 1987), 105.

35. R. V. Azua. "How Many Dog Breeds Existed in Prehispanic Mexico?" *Veterinaria—Mexico* 25, no. 1 (1994): 1–11, abstract in *Biological Abstracts* 98, Issue 1 (1995): 4236.

36. William Pferd III, *Dogs of the American Indians* (Fairfax, Va.: Denlinger's, 1987), 74–75, 76.

37. Mestel, "Ascent of the Dog," 96.

38. Raymond Coppinger and Richard Schneider, "Evolution of Working Dogs," in *Domestic Dog: Its Evolution, Behaviour and Interactions with People*, ed. James Serpell (Cambridge: Cambridge University Press, 1995), 33–34.

39. Heini Hediger, *Wild Animals in Captivity* (London: Butterworth, 1950), 141.

40. Ibid., 143–145.

41. Clyde Keeler, "Genetics of Behavior Variations in Color Phases of the Red Fox," in *The Wild Canids*, ed. M. W. Fox (New York: Van Nostrand Reinhold, 1975), 400–401, 413.

42. D. K. Belyaev and L. N. Trut, "Some Genetic and Endocrine Effects of Selection for Domestication in Silver Foxes," in *The Wild Canids*, ed. M. W. Fox (New York: Van Nostrand Reinhold, 1975), 418.

43. Ibid., 420.

44. D. K. Belyaev and P. M. Borodin, "The Influence of Stress on Variation and Its Role in Evolution," *Biologisches Zentralblatt* 100 (1982): 708–710.

45. N. K. Popova et al., "Evidence for the Involvement of Central Serotonin in Mechanism of Domestication of Silver Foxes," *Pharmacology, Biochemistry and Behavior* 40 (1991): 751; L. L. Vasilyeva and K. V. Svechnikov, "Blood Serotonin Level in Domestic Silver Foxes as a Major-Gene Marker of Domestic Behavior," *Genetika* 29, no. 3 (1993): 375; Belyaev and Trut, "Some Genetic and Endocrine Effects of Domestication," 421.

46. Keeler, "Red Fox," 406, 413.

47. Belyaev and Trut, "Some Genetic and Endocrine Effects of Domestication," 416–417.

48. Ibid., 421.

49. D. K. Belyaev, G. K. Isakova, and L. N. Trut, "Influence of Selection for Behavior on Early Embryonic Development of Silver-Black Foxes," *Doklady Biological Sciences* 290 (1986): 565–567.

50. L. N. Trut, "The Variable Rates of Evolutionary Transformations and Their Parallelism in Terms of Destabilizing Selection," *Journal of Animal Breeding and Genetics* 105 (1988): 83–84.

51. Ibid.; D. K. Belyaev and L. N. Trut, "Genetic Interrelationships of Specific Changes in Standard Coloring of Silver-Black Foxes ('Singes' and 'Stars') Arising in the Process of Domestication," *Soviet Genetics* 27 (1986): 97–100.

52. Belyaev and Trut, "Genetic Interrelationships," 99–100.

53. Trut, "Variable Rates of Evolutionary Transformations," 86–87.

54. Mestel, "Ascent of the Dog," 94.

CHAPTER 2. BEHAVIORAL GENETICS

1. Linda Partridge, "Genetics and Behaviour," in *Genes, Development and Learning*, ed. T. R. Halliday and P. J. B. Slater (New York: W. H. Freeman, 1983), 26–28.

2. Cynthia Dawn Arons, "Genetic Variability Within a Species: Differences in Behavior, Development, and Neurochemistry among Three Types of Domestic Dogs and Their F_1 Hybrids" (Ph.D. diss., University of Connecticut, 1989), abstract in *Dissertation Abstracts International*, assession no. AAI9013302, SilverPlatter.

3. George N. M. Gurguis et al., "Biogenic Amine Distribution in the Brain of Nervous and Normal Pointer Dogs: A Genetic Animal Model of Anxiety," *Psychopharmacology* 3 (1990): 297, 300–301.

4. Michael W. Fox, *The Dog: Its Domestication and Behavior* (New York: Garland STPM Press, 1978), 167, 171; Heini Hediger, *Wild Animals in Captivity* (London: Butterworth, 1950), 141.

5. "Music of the Hemispheres," *Discover* 15 (March 1994): 15.

6. A. S. Clarke and M. L. Schneider, "Prenatal Stress Has Long-Term Effects on Behavioral Responses to Stress in Juvenile Rhesus Monkeys," *Developmental Psychobiology* 26 (1993): 293-304.

7. Fox, *The Dog,* 162–163, 166.

8. Ibid., 163, 165.

9. Ibid., 164.

10. Ibid., 164, 175.

11. Hediger, *Wild Animals in Captivity,* 168.

12. Fox, *The Dog,* 158–159.

13. John Paul Scott and John F. Fuller, *Genetics and the Social Behavior of the Dog* (Chicago: University of Chicago Press, 1965), 22.

14. I. I. Poletaeva, N. V. Popova, and L. G. Romanova. "Genetic Aspects of Animal Reasoning." *Behavior Genetics* 23 (1993): 467–475.

15. Cornelis Naaktgeboren, "Jackals," in *Grzimek's Encyclopedia of Mammals,* 5 vols., ed. Bernhard Grzimek and Sybil P. Parker (New York: McGraw-Hill, 1990), 4: 108.

16. Fox, *The Dog,* 145.

17. Ibid., 147–148.

18. Ibid., 146.

19. Cornelis Naaktgeboren, "Dogs," in *Grzimek's Encyclopedia of Mammals,* 5 vols., ed. Bernhard Grzimek and Sybil P. Parker (New York: McGraw-Hill, 1990), 4:54.

20. James Serpell and J. A. Jagoe, "Early Experience and the Development of Behaviour," in *Domestic Dog: Its Evolution, Behaviour and Interactions with People,* ed. James Serpell (Cambridge: Cambridge University Press, 1995), 81.

21. Ibid., 84.

22. Eberhard Trumler, "Domesticated Dog," in *Grzimek's Encyclopedia of Mammals,* 5 vols., ed. Bernhard Grzimek and Sybil P. Parker (New York: McGraw-Hill, 1990), 4:92.

23. Ibid., 96–97.

24. Ibid., 97.

25. Serpell and Jagoe, "Early Experience and the Development of Behaviour," 83.

26. Scott and Fuller, *Genetics and the Social Behavior of the Dog,* 384; Fox, *The Dog,* 159–160.

27. Malcolm B. Willis, *Genetics of the Dog* (London: H. F. & G. Witherby, 1989), 259.

28. Scott and Fuller, *Genetics and the Social Behavior of the Dog,* 222.

29. Ibid., 387.

30. Ibid., 223, 256, 258.

31. Willis, *Genetics,* 273; Fox, *The Dog,* 93.

32. Leon Fradley Whitney, *How to Breed Dogs,* 3d ed. (New York: Howell Books, 1971), 246–248, 251–252, 255–256.

33. T. Marchlewski, "Genetic Studies on the Domestic Dog," *Bulletin International de l'Académie Polonaise des Sciences et des Lettres, Classe des Sciences Mathématiques et Naturelles, Série B* 2 (1930): 129.

34. Whitney, *How to Breed Dogs,* 243; Marchlewski, "Genetic Studies," 130.

35. Whitney, *How to Breed Dogs,* 241–243; Marchlewski, "Genetic Studies," 130.

36. Scott and Fuller, *Genetics and the Social Behavior of the Dog,* 185–186, 378, 384.

37. D. Buchenauer, "Some Aspects of Genetic Fixed Behavior in Farm Animals," *Deutsche Tieraerztliche Wochenschrift* 97 (1990): 247–249, abstract in *Biological Abstracts* 90, Issue 9 (1990): 98938.

CHAPTER 3. CYTOGENETICS

1. E. B. Wilson, "The Cell in Development and Heredity," 1925. Quoted in Karl Drlica, *Understanding DNA and Gene Cloning: A Guide for the Curious,* 2d ed. (New York: John Wiley & Sons, 1992), xi; Drlica, *Understanding DNA,* 2.

2. Carl Zimmer, "First Cell," *Discover* 16 (November 1995): 70–74.

3. H. C. Macgregor, *An Introduction to Animal Cytogenetics* (New York: Chapman & Hall, 1993), 3.

4. F. W. Nicholas, *Veterinary Genetics* (Oxford: Clarendon Press, 1987), 99–100.

5. Ibid., 138.

6. Joseph Levine and David Suzuki, *The Secret of Life: Redesigning the Living World* (Boston: WGBH Educational Foundation, 1993), 32.

7. Robert J. Hritzo, "Copper Toxicosis Announcement, AKC Delegates Meeting, March 14, 1995" (American Kennel Club communication sent to Scottsdale Dog Fanciers Association, Scottsdale, Arizona, photocopy).

8. Louis Levine, *Biology of the Gene,* 3d ed. (St. Louis: C. V. Mosby, 1980), 230; D. K. Belyaev and P. M. Borodin, "The Influence of Stress on Variation and Its Role in Evolution," *Biologisches Zentralblatt* 100 (1982): 708–710.

9. R. H. Schaible, "A Dalmatian Study," *Pure-Bred Dogs/American Kennel Gazette* 98 (April 1981): 49–50.

10. Robert Plomin, J. C. DeFries, and G. E. McClearn, *Behavioral Genetics: A Primer,* 2d ed. (New York: W. H. Freeman, 1990), 127; David T. Suzuki and Anthony J. F. Griffiths, *An Introduction to Genetic Analysis* (San Francisco: W. H. Freeman, 1976), 189; Tingqing Zhang, "Reproduction-Related Chromosomal Aberrations in Domestic Animals in the USA (United States)" (Ph.D. diss., University of Minnesota, 1993), abstract in *Dissertation Abstracts International,* assession no. AAI9411287, SilverPlatter.

11. B. Mayr et al., "Offspring of a Trisomic Cow," *Cytogenetics and Cell Genetics* 44 (1987): 229–230.

CHAPTER 4. MENDELIAN GENETICS

1. T. A. Brown, *Genetics: A Molecular Approach* (London: Van Nostrand Reinhold, 1989), 279.

2. David T. Suzuki et al., *An Introduction to Genetic Analysis,* 4th ed. (New York: W. H. Freeman, 1989), 73.

3. Ibid., 72–73.

4. David T. Suzuki and Anthony, J. F. Griffiths, *An Introduction to Genetic Analysis* (San Francisco: W. H. Freeman, 1976), 37.

5. Cecie Starr, *Biology: Concepts and Applications,* 2d ed. (Belmont, Cal.: Wadsworth Publishing, 1994), 111.

CHAPTER 5. MOLECULAR GENETICS

1. Cecie Starr, *Biology: Concepts and Applications,* 2d ed. (Belmont, Cal.: Wadsworth Publishing, 1994), 143.

2. T. A. Brown, *Genetics: A Molecular Approach* (London: Van Nostrand Reinhold, 1989), 41–42, 232.

3. Joseph Levine and David Suzuki, *The Secret of Life: Redesigning the Living World* (Boston: WGBH Educational Foundation, 1993), 12, 23.

4. Starr, *Biology,* 167.

5. Ibid., 168.

6. Ibid., 169.

7. Levine and Suzuki, *Secret of Life,* 25.

8. Karl Drlica, *Understanding DNA and Gene Cloning: A Guide for the Curious,* 2d ed. (New York: John Wiley & Sons, 1992), 2.

9. D. S. Falconer, *Introduction to Quantitative Genetics* (New York: Ronald Press, 1960), 24–25; Malcolm B. Willis, *Genetics of the Dog* (London: H. F. & G. Witherby, 1989), 295; David J. Merrell, *The Adaptive Seascape: The Mechanism of Evolution* (Minneapolis: University of Minnesota Press, 1994), 186.

10. Levine and Suzuki, *Secret of Life,* 79.

11. Drlica, *Understanding DNA and Gene Cloning,* 42.

12. Gary Francione, "Cloning Breeds Contempt and Adulation. We Claim to Eschew `Unnecessary Suffering,' So Why Are We So Eager to Exploit Animals in Cloning Procedures?" *Chicago Tribune,* 7 March 1997, sec. 1, p. 23; Tim Radford, "Scientists Scorn Sci-Fi Fears over Sheep Clone," *Guardian* (Manchester), 24 February 1997, sec. 1, p. 7.

13. Levine and Suzuki, *Secret of Life,* 24.

CHAPTER 6. QUANTITATIVE GENETICS

1. David J. Merrell, *The Adaptive Seascape: The Mechanism of Evolution* (Minneapolis: University of Minnesota Press, 1994), 160–161.

2. R. Rieger, A. Michaelis, and M. M. Green, *Glossary of Genetics,* 5th ed. (New York: Springer-Verlag, 1991), 388.

3. F. W. Nicholas, *Veterinary Genetics* (Oxford: Clarendon Press, 1987), 203–210.

4. D. F. Patterson et al., "A Single Major-Gene Defect Underlying Cardiac Conotruncal Malformations Interferes with Myocardial Growth During Embryonic Development: Studies in the CTD Line of Keeshond Dogs," *American Journal of Human Genetics* 52 (1993): 388-397.

5. Roy Robinson, *Genetics for Dog Breeders,* 2d ed. (New York: Pergamon Press, 1990), 218; Malcolm B. Willis, *Genetics of the Dog* (London: H. F. & G. Witherby, 1989), 246.

6. S. D. Verryn and J. M. P. Geerthsen, "Heritabilities of a Population of German Shepherd Dogs with a Complex Interrelationship Structure," *Theoretical and Applied Genetics* 75 (1987): 144–146.

7. David T. Suzuki et al., *An Introduction to Genetic Analysis,* 4th ed. (New York: W. H. Freeman, 1989), 654.

8. Claude Pieau, "Temperature Variation and Sex Determination in Reptiles," *BioEssays* 18 (January 1996): 19–26.

9. Merrell, *The Adaptive Seascape,* 6.

10. Ibid.

11. Ibid., 27.

12. Roy Robinson, *Genetics for Cat Breeders,* 3d ed. (London: Pergamon Press, 1991), 66.

CHAPTER 7. POPULATION GENETICS

1. David J. Merrell, *The Adaptive Seascape: The Mechanism of Evolution* (Minneapolis: University of Minnesota Press, 1994), 161.

2. F. W. Nicholas, *Veterinary Genetics* (Oxford: Clarendon Press, 1987), 154, 156.

3. D. S. Falconer, *Introduction to Quantitative Genetics* (New York: Ronald Press, 1960), 24–25; Malcolm B. Willis, *Genetics of the Dog* (London: H. F. & G. Witherby, 1989), 295.

4. Norman V. Rothwell, *Understanding Genetics*, 4th ed. (Oxford: Oxford University Press, 1988), 624.

5. Ibid., 630–631.

6. Ibid., 638.

7. Ibid., 640.

8. Ibid.

9. Ibid., 639, 641.

10. Ibid., 639, 640–641; Merrell, *The Adaptive Seascape,* 43–45, 89.

11. John C. Avise, *Molecular Markers, Natural History, and Evolution* (New York: Chapman & Hall, 1994), 204, 367, 369.

12. Franz Pirchner, "Genetic Structure of Populations. 1. Closed Populations or Matings Among Related Individuals," in *General and Quantitative Genetics,* ed. A. B. Chapman (New York: Elsevier, 1985), 246; Falconer, *Quantitative Genetics,* 270–271.

13. Falconer, *Quantitative Genetics,* 270; Avise, *Markers,* 367, 369.

14. Pirchner, "Genetic Structure," 247.

15. Ibid., 244, 246; Falconer, *Quantitative Genetics,* 244, 248, 252; Nicholas, *Veterinary Genetics,* 274–275, 372–374.

16. John Paul Scott and John F. Fuller, *Genetics and the Social Behavior of the Dog* (Chicago: University of Chicago Press, 1965), 405–406.

17. Pirchner, "Genetic Structure," 247.

18. Falconer, *Quantitative Genetics,* 60, 247, 277.

19. Nicholas, *Veterinary Genetics,* 376; Joseph Levine and David Suzuki, *The Secret of Life: Redesigning the Living World* (Boston: WGBH Educational Foundation, 1993), 57, 58.

20. Cecie Starr, *Biology: Concepts and Applications,* 2d ed. (Belmont, Cal.: Wadsworth Publishing, 1994), 199.

21. Jeffrey P. Cohn, "Surprising Cheetah Genetics," *Bioscience* 36, no. 6 (1986): 358.

22. Ibid.

23. Ibid.

24. Levine and Suzuki, *Secret of Life,* 59.

25. Ibid.; Avise, *Markers,* 369.

26. Stephen J. O'Brien et al., "East African Cheetahs: Evidence for Two Population Bottlenecks?" *Proceedings of the National Academy of Sciences* 84, no. 2 (1987), 508; Marilyn Menotti-Raymond and Stephen J. O'Brien, "Dating the Genetic Bottleneck of the African Cheetah," *Proceedings of the National Academy of Sciences* 90, no. 8 (1993): 3172.

27. Levine and Suzuki, *Secret of Life,* 57.

28. W. J. Dodds et al., "The Frequencies of Inherited Blood and Eye Diseases as Determined by Genetic Screening Programs," *Journal of the American Animal Hospital Association* 17 (1981): 697.

CHAPTER 8. COAT COLORS AND MARKINGS

1. Clarence Little, *The Inheritance of Coat Color in Dogs* (Ithaca, N.Y.: Comstock Publishing, 1957), 75.

2. Roy Robinson, *Genetics for Dog Breeders*, 2d ed. (New York: Pergamon Press, 1990), 124–125; Phillip D. Sponenberg, "Inheritance of the Harlequin Color in Great Dane Dogs," *Journal of Heredity* 76 (1985): 224–225; N. O. O'Sullivan and R. Robinson, "Harlequin Colour in the Great Dane Dog," *Genetica* 78 (1973): 215–218.

3. Robinson, *Genetics*, 125.

4. Ibid., 122–123, 132; Malcolm B. Willis, *Genetics of the Dog* (London: H. F. & G. Witherby, 1989), 70–71, 74; Little, *Coat Color*, 73, 95–96.

5. Robinson, *Genetics*, 121; Little, *Coat Color*, 24.

6. Little, *Coat Color*, 45; Robinson, *Genetics*, 121; Willis, *Genetics*, 67, 101.

7. Little, *Coat Color*, 75.

8. Ibid., 92–95; Robinson, *Genetics*, 133; R. H. Schaible, "A Dalmatian Study," *Pure-Bred Dogs/American Kennel Gazette* 98 (April 1981), 48–52.

9. Johan Gallant, *Schnauzers—Standard, Giant, Miniature* (Golden, Col.: Alpine Publications, 1996), 93; Beverly Piscino and Gloria Lewis, *Miniature Schnauzers* (Neptune City, N. J.: T.F.H. Publications, 1990), 21–22, 24; Donald Draper, personal communication to Virginia Alexander.

10. Willis, *Genetics*, 65–66.

11. Eugene A. Carver, "Coat Color Genetics of the German Shepherd Dog," *Journal of Heredity* 75 (1984): 247–252; Robinson, *Genetics*, 153; American Belgian Tervuren Club, *The Complete Belgian Tervuren* (New York: Howell Books, 1990), 120–121.

12. Little, *Coat Color*, 57–58; Robinson, *Genetics*, 133.

13. Robinson, *Genetics*, 113.

14. Ibid., 115–116.

15. Ibid., 116, 171.

16. Ibid., 135–136.

17. Ibid., 136.

18. Ibid., 134–135.

19. Ibid., 60–61.

20. A. Iljin, "Wolf-Dog Genetics," *Journal of Genetics* 42 (1941): 366–368.

21. Carver, "Coat Color," 251.

22. Ibid., 248, 250; Robinson, *Genetics*, 136–138.

23. Robinson, *Genetics*, 136–137.

24. Ibid., 138–139.

25. Marca Burns and Margaret N. Fraser, *Genetics of the Dog* (Philadelphia: Lippincott, 1966), 60.

CHAPTER 9. COAT TYPES AND QUALITIES

1. Malcolm B. Willis, *Genetics of the Dog* (London: H. F. & G. Witherby, 1989), 117.

2. In a June 1995 discussion on the heredity of Weimaraner coats, Hans Schmidt shared his personal observations and those of other German breeders.

3. Leon Fradley Whitney, *How to Breed Dogs*, 3d ed. (New York: Howell Books, 1971), 275.

4. Ibid., 281–282.

5. Ibid., 276.

6. Ibid., 278.

7. Ibid., 279.

8. Marca Burns and Margaret N. Fraser, *Genetics of the Dog* (Philadelphia: Lippincott, 1966), 40; Anna Katherine Nicholas, *Book of the Poodle* (Neptune City, N.J.: T.F.H. Publications, 1982), 337.

9. Whitney, *How to Breed Dogs*, 279.

10. Willis, *Genetics*, 117–118; T. Pullig, "Inheritance of Whorls in Cocker Spaniels. A Preliminary Report," *Journal of Heredity* 41 (1950): 239–242.

11. Whitney, *How to Breed Dogs*, 285–286.

CHAPTER 10. STRUCTURAL TRAITS

1. Leon Fradley Whitney, *How to Breed Dogs*, 3d ed. (New York: Howell Books, 1971), 311.

2. T. Marchlewski, "Genetic Studies on the Domestic Dog," *Bulletin International de l'Académie Polonaise des Sciences et des Lettres, Classe des Sciences Mathématiques et Naturelles, Série B* 2 (1930): 120–121, 123; Malcolm B. Willis, *Genetics of the Dog* (London: H. F. & G. Witherby, 1989), 103.

3. N. A. Iljin, "Wolf-Dog Genetics," *Journal of Genetics* 42 (1941): 383–385.

4. Michael W. Fox, *The Dog: Its Domestication and Behavior* (New York: Garland STPM Press, 1978), 93.

5. Marchlewski, "Genetic Studies," 120, 127.

6. Whitney, *How to Breed Dogs*, 314.

7. R. B. Kelley, *Sheep Dogs: Their Breeding, Maintenance and Training* (Sydney: Angus & Robertson, 1949), 23, 47.

8. Willis, *Genetics*, 106.

9. Ibid., 109.

10. Ibid.

11. Ibid.

12. Ibid., 112–113.

13. Whitney, *How to Breed Dogs*, 312–313.

14. Marchlewski, "Genetic Studies," 126.

15. Ibid., 125–126.

16. Ibid., 125, 126.

17. Ibid., 126.

18. Willis, *Genetics*, 105–106.

19. Whitney, *How to Breed Dogs*, 292–293.

20. William G. Whittick, *Canine Orthopedics* (Philadelphia: Lea & Febiger, 1974), 147.

21. Ibid.

22. Willis, *Genetics*, 104–105.

23. Pere Alberch, "Developmental Constraints: Why St. Bernards Often Have an Extra Digit and Poodles Never Do," *American Naturalist* 126 (1985): 430–431.

24. Kelley, *Sheep Dogs*, 27; Fox, *The Dog*, 93.

25. Whitney, *How to Breed Dogs*, 306.

26. Fox, *The Dog*, 93.

27. Willis, *Genetics*, 198.

CHAPTER 11. CONTROL OF GENETIC DISORDERS

1. Norman R. Schneider, "Teratogenesis and Mutagenesis," in *Current Veterinary Therapy VIII: Small Animal Practice,* ed. Robert W. Kirk (Philadelphia: W. B. Saunders, 1986), 162–163.

2. David T. Suzuki et al., *An Introduction to Genetic Analysis,* 4th ed. (New York: W. H. Freeman, 1989), 654.

3. Schneider, "Teratogenesis," 171.

4. Association of Veterinarians for Animal Rights, *Canine Consumer Report* (Vacaville, Cal.: Association of Veterinarians for Animal Rights, 1994).

5. J. J. Kaneko, D. R. Cordy, and G. Carlson, "Canine Hemophilia Resembling Classic Hemophilia A," *Journal of the American Veterinary Medical Association* 150 (1967): 15–21.

6. E. A. Corley, "Role of the Orthopedic Foundation for Animals in the Control of Canine Hip Dysplasia," *Veterinary Clinics of North America* 22 (1992): 581.

7. Frances O. Smith, "Screening for Genetic Defects," *Pure-Bred Dogs/American Kennel Gazette* 111 (August 1994): 47.

8. Donald L. Piermattei and Steven P. Arnoczky, *Patellar Luxation Registry: General Procedures and Classification* (Columbia, Mo.: Orthopedic Foundation for Animals, n.d.), pamphlet.

9. Ray Nachreiner, *OFA: Canine Thyroid Registry* (Columbia, Mo.: Orthopedic Foundation for Animals, n.d.), pamphlet.

10. Orthopedic Foundation for Animals, *OFA: Congenital Heart Disease Registry* (Columbia, Mo.: Orthopedic Foundation for Animals, n.d.), pamphlet.

11. K. C. Barnett, "Inherited Eye Disease in the Dog and Cat," *Journal of Small Animal Practice* 29 (1988): 463.

12. Donald D. Draper, J. P. Kluge, and W. J. Miller, "Clinical and Pathological Aspects of Spinal Dysraphism in Dogs," in *Proceedings of the Twentieth World Veterinary Congress, Thessalonika, 1975* (Thessalonika: G. Papageorgeiou, 1975), 134.

13. Marie McCarren, "The Glucokinase Connection," *Diabetes Forecast,* November 1992, 30.

14. Malcolm B. Willis, *Genetics of the Dog* (London: H. F. & G. Witherby, 1989), 356.

CHAPTER 12. CONGENITAL DISORDERS

1. James J. Nora and F. Clarke Fraser, *Medical Genetics: Principles and Practice,* 2d ed. (Philadelphia: Lea & Febiger, 1981), 309; Josef Warkany, *Congenital Malformations* (Chicago: Year Book Medical Publishers, 1971), 629–631, 637–640.

2. Roy Robinson, *Genetics for Dog Breeders,* 2d ed. (New York: Pergamon Press, 1990), 218; Malcolm B. Willis, *Genetics of the Dog* (London: H. F. & G. Witherby, 1989), 278–279.

3. Willis, *Genetics,* 59; V. N. Meyers-Wallen and D. F. Patterson, "Disorders of Sexual Development in Dogs and Cats," in *Current Veterinary Therapy X: Small Animal Practice,* ed. Robert W. Kirk (Philadelphia: W. B. Saunders, 1989), 1268.

4. Meyers-Wallen and Patterson, "Disorders of Sexual Development," 1268.

5. Ibid.

6. Robinson, *Genetics,* 246.

7. A. C. Palmer, J. E. Payne, and M. E. Wallace, "Hereditary Quadriplegia and Amblyopia in the Irish Setter," *Journal of Small Animal Practice* 14 (1973): 343–352.

8. C. W. Foley, J. F. Lasley, and B. D. Osweiler, *Abnormalities of Companion Animals: Analysis of Heritability* (Ames: Iowa State University Press, 1979), 139; Warkany, *Congenital Malformations,* 752–753; Marca Burns and Margaret N. Fraser, *Genetics of the Dog* (Philadelphia: Lippincott, 1966), 89; H. Preston Hoskins, J. V. Lacroix, and Karl Mayer, eds., *Canine Medicine,* 2d ed. (Santa Barbara: American Veterinary Publications, 1959), 185.

9. Hoskins, Lacroix, and Mayer, *Canine Medicine,* 185; Warkany, *Congenital Malformations,* 752–753; Burns and Fraser, *Genetics,* 89; Orthopedic Foundation for Animals, *OFA: Congenital Heart Disease Registry* (Columbia, Mo.: Orthopedic Foundation for Animals, n.d.), pamphlet; Foley, Lasley, and Osweiler, *Abnormalities,* 139.

10. Foley, Lasley, and Osweiler, *Abnormalities,* 55; Frances O. Smith, "Screening for Genetic Defects," *Pure-Bred Dogs/American Kennel Gazette* 111 (August 1994): 48.

11. D. F. Patterson et al., "A Single Major-Gene Defect Underlying Cardiac Conotruncal Malformations Interferes with Myocardial Growth During Embryonic Development: Studies in the CTD Line of Keeshond Dogs," *American Journal of Human Genetics* 52 (1993): 388.

12. Warkany, *Congenital Malformations,* 459–463, 470–472; D. F. Patterson, "Canine Congenital Heart Disease: Epidemiology and Etiological Hypotheses," *Journal of Small Animal Practice* 12 (1971): 280–281.

13. Smith, "Screening for Genetic Defects," 48.

CHAPTER 13. COMMON HEREDITARY PROBLEMS

1. R. D. Jolly et al., "Screening for Genetic Diseases: Principles and Practice," *Advances in Veterinary Science and Comparative Medicine* 25 (1981): 265–266; F. W. Nicholas, *Veterinary Genetics* (Oxford: Clarendon Press, 1987), 327.

2. Roy Robinson, *Genetics for Dog Breeders,* 2d ed. (New York: Pergamon Press, 1990), 242–243.

3. Nicholas, *Veterinary Genetics,* 89–90; W. J. Dodds, "Canine Von Willebrand's Disease," *Journal of Laboratory and Clinical Medicine* 76 (1970): 713–721; Sharon L. Raymond et al., "Clinical and Laboratory Features of a Severe Form of Von Willebrand Disease in Shetland Sheepdogs," *Journal of the American Veterinary Medical Association* 197 (1990): 1342.

4. C. W. Foley, J. F. Lasley, and G. D. Osweiler, *Abnormalities of Companion Animals: Analysis of Heritability* (Ames: Iowa State University Press, 1979), 43; Jolly et al., "Screening," 264.

5. Raymond et al., "Von Willebrand Disease," 1345; Clarence M. Fraser, ed. *Merck Veterinary Manual,* 6th ed. (Rahway, N.J.: Merck, 1986), 57; Foley, Lasley, and Osweiler, *Abnormalities,* 44; Malcolm B. Willis, *Genetics of the Dog* (London: H. F. & G. Witherby, 1989), 246.

6. Nicholas, *Genetics,* 327–328; Jolly et al., "Screening," 266; W. J. Dodds et al., "The Frequencies of Inherited Blood and Eye Diseases as Determined by Genetic Screening Programs," *Journal of the American Animal Hospital Association* 17 (1981): 702.

7. James J. Nora and F. Clarke Fraser, *Medical Genetics: Principles and Practice,* 2d ed. (Philadelphia: Lea & Febiger, 1981), 313–314.

8. American College of Veterinary Ophthalmologists, *Ocular Disorders Proven or Suspected to be Hereditary in Dogs* (N.p.: American College of Veterinary Ophthalmologists, 1992), 17, 104.

9. Ibid., 17; Willis, *Genetics,* 222; Robinson, *Genetics,* 212.

10. Robinson, *Genetics,* 212–213.

11. Willis, *Genetics,* 223–224; Jolly, "Screening," 268.

12. Robinson, *Genetics,* 213; Willis, *Genetics,* 224–225; American College of Veterinary Ophthalmologists, *Ocular Disorders,* 9.

13. American College of Veterinary Ophthalmologists, *Ocular Disorders,* 9, 183.

14. Willis, *Genetics,* 224–225.

15. Ibid., 226.

16. Ibid.

17. Ibid., 227; K. C. Barnett, "Comparative Aspects of Canine Hereditary Eye Disease," *Advances in Veterinary Science and Comparative Medicine* 20 (1976): 43.

18. Robinson, *Genetics,* 211.

19. K. C. Barnett, "Inherited Eye Disease in the Dog and Cat," *Journal of Small Animal Practice* 29 (1988): 469.

20. Foley, Lasley, and Osweiler, *Abnormalities,* 69–71; Barnett, "Comparative Aspects," 43; American College of Veterinary Ophthalmologists, *Ocular Disorders,* 11, 12.

21. D. D. Lawson, "Canine Distichiasis," *Journal of Small Animal Practice* 14 (1972): 475; Barnett, "Comparative Aspects," 44; Josef Warkany, *Congenital Malformations* (Chicago: Year Book Medical Publishers, 1971), 355; Foley, Lasley, and Osweiler, *Abnormalities,* 83.

22. W. Jean Dodds, "Autoimmune Thyroid Disease," *Dog World* 77 (April 1992): 36.

23. Ibid., 36, 38.

24. Ibid., 38.

25. Ibid., 36; Ellen N. Behrend, "Hypothyroidism in Dogs," *Pedigree Breeder Forum* 4, no. 3 (1995): 3, 4; Frances O. Smith, "Screening for Genetic Defects," *Pure-Bred Dogs/American Kennel Gazette* 111 (August 1994): 49.

26. G. B. Schnelle, "Some New Disease in Dogs," *American Kennel Gazette* 52 (1935): 25; Smith, "Screening for Genetic Defects," 47; W. H. Riser, "The Dog as a Model for the Study of Hip Dysplasia: Growth, Form, and Development of the Normal and Dysplastic Hip Joint," *Veterinary Pathology* 12 (1975): 235.

27. Riser, "The Dog as a Model," 235, 279.

28. Ibid., 248.

29. Ibid., 258.

30. Ibid. (italics added).

31. Orthopedic Foundation of America, "30 Years of Progress: OFA Data Confirm Dramatic Improvements in Dog Hips," Letter, July 1, 1997.

32. Ibid.

33. Willis, *Genetics,*151.

34. Riser, "The Dog as a Model," 279, 318.

35. Ibid., 279, 318.

36. Ibid., 260 (italics added).

37. Ibid., 317.

38. Ibid., 239, 259, 318, 320.

39. Ibid., 259.

40. Ibid., 260.

41. Ibid., 321.

42. Ibid., 242, 246–247.

43. Ibid., 244, 253.

44. Ibid., 251.

45. Ibid., 246; Willis, *Genetics*, 157–160.

46. Nicholas, *Veterinary Genetics*, 314; Håkan Kasström, "Nutrition, Weight Gain and Development of Hip Dysplasia," *Acta Radiologica, Supplementum* 344 (1975): 135–179.

47. Riser, "The Dog as a Model," 251.

48. Ibid., 252–253, 256.

49. Ibid., 254.

50. Ibid., 247.

51. Wayne H. Riser, and Harry Miller, *Canine Hip Dysplasia and How to Control It* (Philadelphia: OFA Publications, 1966), 24–25, 77–78.

52. Riser, "The Dog as a Model," 246–248.

53. Nicholas, *Veterinary Genetics*, 331.

54. Ibid.

55. Willis, *Genetics*, 155–156.

56. E. A. Corley, "Role of the Orthopedic Foundation for Animals in the Control of Canine Hip Dysplasia," *Veterinary Clinics of North America* 22 (1992): 585, 588.

57. Willis, *Genetics*, 148.

58. Corley, "Role of the Orthopedic Foundation for Animals," 590–591.

59. Gail K. Smith, "Method of Assessing Canine Hip Dysplasia," *U.S. Patent* 5,482,055.

60. Corley, "Role of the Orthopedic Foundation for Animals," 588.

61. Fraser, *Merck Veterinary Manual*, 548; E. A. Corley, T. M. Sutherland, and W. D. Carlson, "Genetic Aspects of Canine Elbow Dysplasia," *Journal of the American Veterinary Medical Association* 153 (1968): 543.

62. J. W. Alexander, *Leonard's Orthopedic Surgery of the Dog and Cat* (Philadelphia: W. B. Saunders, 1985), 193.

63. Ibid., 193–194; William G. Whittick, *Canine Orthopedics* (Philadelphia: Lea & Febiger, 1974), 157–158.

64. Fraser, *Merck Veterinary Manual*, 546–547; Geoffrey West, *Encyclopedia of Animal Care*, 11th ed. (Baltimore: Williams and Wilkins, 1975), s.v. "osteochondrosis", Alexander, *Orthopedic Surgery*, 185.

65. S. Guthrie and H. G. Pidduck, "Heritability of Elbow Osteochondrosis Within a Closed Population of Dogs," *Journal of Small Animal Practice* 31 (1990): 93, 96; V. P. Studdert, et al., "Clinical Features and Heritability of Osteochondrosis of the Elbow in Labrador Retrievers," *Journal of Small Animal Practice* 32 (1991): 557, 562.

66. Klaus Dämmrich, "Relationship Between Nutrition and Bone Growth in Large and Giant Dogs," *Journal of Nutrition* 12, suppl. (1991): S114–115.

67. Ibid., S114, S118–119.

68. H. A. W. Hazewinkel, "Nutrition in Relation to Skeletal Growth Deformities," *Journal of Small Animal Practice* 30 (1989): 625;
H. A. W. Hazewinkel et al., "Influences of Chronic Calcium Excess on the Skeletal Development of Growing Great Danes," *Journal of the American Animal Hospital Association* 21 (1985): 377; R. C. Nap et al., "Growth and Skeletal Development in Great Dane Pups Fed Different Levels of Protein Intake," *Journal of Nutrition* 12, suppl. (1991): S107.

69. National Research Council, *Nutrient Requirements of Dogs*, rev. ed. (Washington, D.C.: National Academy of Sciences, 1985); H. A. W. Hazewinkel, "Nutrition in Relation to Skeletal Growth Deformities," 629.

CHAPTER 14. SELECTION—THE THEORIES

1. Suzuki et al., *An Introduction to Genetic Analysis*, 4th ed. (New York: W. H. Freeman, 1989), 722; D. S. Falconer, *Introduction to Quantitative Genetics* (New York: Ronald Press, 1960), 186.

2. Falconer, *Quantitative Genetics*, 219, 221.

3. Ibid., 101, 221–224.

4. William D. Hohenboken, "Prediction and Measurement of Response to Selection," in *General and Quantitative Genetics*, ed. A. B. Chapman (New York: Elsevier, 1985), 181; Franz Pirchner, "Genetic Structure of Populations. 1. Closed Populations or Matings Among Related Individuals," in *General and Quantitative Genetics*, ed. A. B. Chapman (New York: Elsevier, 1985), 246.

5. Malcolm B. Willis, *Genetics of the Dog* (London: H. F. & G. Witherby, 1989), 331.

6. Ibid., 338.

7. W. H. Riser, "The Dog as a Model for the Study of Hip Dysplasia: Growth, Form, and Development of the Normal and Dysplastic Hip Joint," *Veterinary Pathology* 12 (1975): 259.

CHAPTER 15. SELECTION—THE ART

1. Dr. James Edwards, address following dinner at Scottsdale Dog Fanciers Association judges' workshop, April 22, 1995.

2. Chris Walkowicz, *The Bearded Collie* (Fairfax, Va.: Denlinger's, 1987), 62; Virginia Alexander and Jackie Isabell, *Weimaraner Ways* (Germantown, Maryland: Sun Star, 1993), 52.

3. Roy Robinson, *Genetics for Dog Breeders*, 2d ed. (New York: Pergamon Press, 1990), 70.

CHAPTER 16. EVALUATION AND RECORDS

1. Virginia Alexander and Jackie Isabell, *Weimaraner Ways* (Germantown, Maryland: Sun Star, 1993), 341.

APPENDIX A. BREED COLORS AND ALLELES

1. American Kennel Club, *The Complete Dog Book*, 18th ed. (New York: Howell Books, 1992). Descriptions are supplemented from Bonnie Wilcox and Chris Walkowicz, *Atlas of Dog Breeds of the World*, 4th ed., 2 vols. (Neptune City, N.J.: T.F.H. Publications, 1993).

2. Clarence C. Little, *The Inheritance of Coat Color in Dogs* (Ithaca, N.Y.: Comstock Publishing, 1957), 170; Roy Robinson, *Genetics for Dog Breeders*, 2d ed. (New York: Pergamon Press, 1990), 147–148.

3. Robinson, *Genetics*, 149.

4. Ibid., 150.

5. Malcolm B. Willis, *Genetics of the Dog* (London: H. F. & G. Witherby, 1989), 76; Robinson, *Genetics*, 150–151; Little, *Coat Color*, 126.

6. Willis, *Genetics*, 77; Chris Walkowicz, *The Bearded Collie* (Fairfax, Va.: Denlinger's, 1987), 53.

7. Willis, *Genetics*, 78; Robinson, *Genetics*, 152–153; American Belgian Tervuren Club, *The Complete Belgian Tervuren* (New York: Howell Books, 1990), 119.

8. Willis, *Genetics,* 78; Robinson, *Genetics,* 152–153; American Belgian Tervuren Club, *Belgian Tervuren,* 119–120.

9. Willis, *Genetics,* 78; Robinson, *Genetics,* 153.

10. Robinson, *Genetics,* 154.

11. Willis, *Genetics,* 78–79; Robinson, *Genetics,* 154; Little, *Coat Color,* 141.

12. Willis, Genetics, 81.

13. Willis, *Genetics,* 82; Robinson, *Genetics,* 155; Little, *Coat Color,* 172.

14. Willis, *Genetics,* 83; Robinson, *Genetics,* 159; Little, *Coat Color,* 114–115.

15. Willis, *Genetics,* 87; Robinson, *Genetics,* 160–161; Little, *Coat Color,* 183.

16. Willis, *Genetics,* 93; Robinson, *Genetics,* 157; M. J. Workman and R. Robinson, "Coat Colors of the Cavalier King Charles Spaniel," *Journal of Animal Breeding and Genetics* 108 (1991): 66–68.

17. Robinson, *Genetics,* 165.

18. Willis, *Genetics,* 89–90; Robinson, *Genetics,* 165–167; Eugene A. Carver, "Coat Color Genetics of the German Shepherd Dog," *Journal of Heredity* 75 (1984): 247–252; Little, *Coat Color,* 148–149.

19. Willis, *Genetics,* 91; Robinson, *Genetics,* 168–169; Phillip D. Sponenberg, "Inheritance of the Harlequin Color in Great Dane Dogs," *Journal of Heredity* 76 (1985): 224–225; Little, *Coat Color,* 150–151.

20. Robinson, *Genetics,* 171.

21. Willis, *Genetics,* 93; Robinson, *Genetics,* 172; Little, *Coat Color,* 184.

22. Roy Robinson, "Inheritance of Coat Color in the German Pinscher Dog," *Genetica* 82 (1990): 57–58; Little, *Coat Color,* 175–176.

23. Willis, *Genetics,* 98; Robinson, *Genetics,* 181; Little, *Coat Color,* 166, 166; Johan Gallant, *Schnauzers—Standard, Giant, Miniature* (Golden, Col.: Alpine Publications, 1996), 93–94; Beverly Piscino and Gloria Lewis, *Miniature Schnauzers* (Neptune City, N.J.: T.F.H. Publications, 1990), 21–22, 24.

24. Willis, *Genetics,* 94–95; Robinson, *Genetics,* 174; Little, *Coat Color,* 152–153.

25. Willis, *Genetics,* 88; Little, *Coat Color,* 137–138; Helen E. Franclose and Nancy C. Swanson, *Norwegian Elkhound* (Fairfax, Va.: Denlinger's, 1974), 69.

26. Leslie Benis, *This is the Puli* (Neptune City, N.J.: T.F.H. Publications, 1976), 159.

27. Robinson, *Genetics,* 178.

28. Willis, *Genetics,* 98; Robinson, *Genetics,* 180–181; Little, *Coat Color,* 155.

29. Willis, *Genetics,* 87; Robinson, *Genetics,* 161; Little, *Coat Color,* 134–135.

30. Robinson, *Genetics,* 170.

31. Ibid., 183; Virginia Alexander and Jackie Isabell, *Weimaraner Ways* (Germantown, MD: Sun Star, 1993), 90–95.

32. Willis, *Genetics,* 101; Robinson, *Genetics,* 185; Little, *Coat Color,* 169.

BIBLIOGRAPHY

Alberch, Pere. "Developmental Constraints: Why St. Bernards Often Have an Extra Digit and Poodles Never Do." *American Naturalist* 126 (1985): 430–433.

Alexander, J. W. *Leonard's Orthopedic Surgery of the Dog and Cat.* Philadelphia: W. B. Saunders, 1985.

Alexander, Virginia, and Jackie Isabell. *Weimaraner Ways.* Germantown, Md.: Sun Star, 1993.

American Belgian Tervuren Club. *The Complete Belgian Tervuren.* New York: Howell Books, 1990.

American College of Veterinary Ophthalmologists. *Ocular Disorders Proven or Suspected to be Hereditary in Dogs.* N.p.: American College of Veterinary Ophthalmologists, 1992.

American Kennel Club. *The Complete Dog Book.* 18th ed. New York: Howell Books, 1992.

Arons, Cynthia Dawn. "Genetic Variability Within a Species: Differences in Behavior, Development, and Neurochemistry Among Three Types of Domestic Dogs and Their F_1 Hybrids." Ph.D. diss., University of Connecticut, 1989. Abstract in *Dissertation Abstracts International.* Assession no. AAI9013302. SilverPlatter.

Association of Veterinarians for Animal Rights. *Canine Consumer Report.* Vacaville, Cal.: Association of Veterinarians for Animal Rights, 1994.

Avise, John C. *Molecular Markers, Natural History, and Evolution.* New York: Chapman & Hall, 1994.

Azua, R. V. "How Many Dog Breeds Existed in Prehispanic Mexico?" *Veterinaria—Mexico* 25, no. 1 (1994): 1–11. Abstract in *Biological Abstracts* 98, Issue 1 (1995): 4236.

Barnett, K. C. "Comparative Aspects of Canine Hereditary Eye Disease." *Advances in Veterinary Science and Comparative Medicine* 20 (1976): 39–67.

———. "Inherited Eye Disease in the Dog and Cat." *Journal of Small Animal Practice* 29 (1988): 462–475.

Behrend, Ellen N. "Hypothyroidism in Dogs." *Pedigree Breeder Forum* 4, no. 3 (1995): 3–8.

Bell, Jerold S. "Identifying and Controlling Defective Genes." *Pure-Bred Dogs/American Kennel Gazette* 110 (July 1993): 82–88.

Belyaev, D. K., and P. M. Borodin. "The Influence of Stress on Variation and Its Role in Evolution." *Biologisches Zentralblatt* 100 (1982): 705–714.

Belyaev, D. K., G. K. Isakova, and L. N. Trut. "Influence of Selection for Behavior on Early Embryonic Development of Silver-Black Foxes." *Doklady Biological Sciences* 290 (1986): 565–567.

Belyaev, D. K., I. N. Oskina, L. N. Trut, and N. M. Bazhan. "Genetics and Phenogenetics of Hormonal Characteristics of Animals. 8. Analysis of Corticosteroid Adrenal Function Variation in Silver Foxes under Selection for Domestication." *Soviet Genetics* 24 (1988): 499–504.

Belyaev, D. K., and L. N. Trut. "Some Genetic and Endocrine Effects of Selection for Domestication in Silver Foxes." In *The Wild Canids,* edited by M. W. Fox, 416–426. New York: Van Nostrand Reinhold, 1975.

———. "Genetic Interrelationships of Specific Changes in Standard Coloring of Silver-Black Foxes ('Singes' and 'Stars') Arising in the Process of Domestication." *Soviet Genetics* 27 (1986): 97–105.

Benis, Leslie. *This is the Puli.* Neptune City, N.J.: T.F.H. Publications, 1976.

Bodner, Elizabeth. "Genetic Status Symbols." *Purebred Dogs/American Kennel Gazette* 109 (September 1992): 52–56.

Brown, T. A. *Genetics: A Molecular Approach.* London: Van Nostrand Reinhold, 1989.

Buchenauer, D. "Some Aspects of Genetic Fixed Behavior in Farm Animals." *Deutsche Tieraerztliche Wochenschrift* 97 (1990): 247–249. Abstract in *Biological Abstracts* 90, Issue 9 (1990): 98938.

Bueler, Lois E. *Wild Dogs of the World.* New York: Stein & Day, 1973.

Burns, Marca, and Margaret N. Fraser. *Genetics of the Dog.* Philadelphia: Lippincott, 1966.

Carver, Eugene A. "Coat Color Genetics of the German Shepherd Dog." *Journal of Heredity* 75 (1984): 247–252.

Chiarelli, A. B. "The Chromosomes of the *Canidae*." In *The Wild Canids*, edited by M. W. Fox, 40–53. New York: Van Nostrand Reinhold, 1975.

Clarke, A. S., and M. L. Schneider. "Prenatal Stress Has Long-Term Effects on Behavioral Responses to Stress in Juvenile Rhesus Monkeys." *Developmental Psychobiology* 26 (1993): 293–304.

Clutton-Brock, Juliet. "Origins of the Dog: Domestication and Early History." In *Domestic Dog: Its Evolution, Behaviour and Interactions with People,* edited by James Serpell, 7–20. Cambridge: Cambridge University Press, 1995.

Cohn, Jeffrey P. "Surprising Cheetah Genetics." *Bioscience* 36 (1986): 358–362.

Coppinger, Raymond, and Richard Schneider. "Evolution of Working Dogs." In *Domestic Dog: Its Evolution, Behaviour and Interactions with People,* edited by James Serpell, 21–47. Cambridge: Cambridge University Press, 1995.

Corley, E. A. "Hip Dysplasia: A Report from the Orthopedic Foundation for Animals." *Seminars in Veterinary Medicine and Surgery (Small Animal)* 2 (1987): 141–151.

———. "Role of the Orthopedic Foundation for Animals in the Control of Canine Hip Dysplasia." *Veterinary Clinics of North America* 22 (1992): 579–593.

Corley, E. A., and P. M. Hogan. "Trends in Hip Dysplasia Control: Analysis of Radiographs Submitted to the Orthopedic Foundation for Animals, 1974 to 1984." *Journal of the American Veterinary Medical Association* 187 (1985): 805–809.

Corley, E. A., T. M. Sutherland, and W. D. Carlson. "Genetic Aspects of Canine Elbow Dysplasia." *Journal of the American Veterinary Medical Association* 153 (1968): 543–547.

Dämmrich, Klaus. "Relationship Between Nutrition and Bone Growth in Large and Giant Dogs." *Journal of Nutrition* 12, suppl. (1991): S114–S121.

DeBlieu, Jan. *Meant to be Wild: The Struggle to Save Endangered Species through Captive Breeding.* Golden, Col.: Fulcrum Publishing, 1991.

Dodds, W. J. "Canine von Willebrand's Disease." *Journal of Laboratory and Clinical Medicine* 76 (1970): 713–721.

———. "Canine Factor X (Stuart-Prower Factor) Deficiency." *Journal of Laboratory and Clinical Medicine* 82 (1973): 560–566.

Dodds, W. J., A. C. Moynihan, T. M. Fisher, and D. B. Trauner. "The Frequencies of Inherited Blood and Eye Diseases as Determined by Genetic Screening Programs." *Journal of the American Animal Hospital Association* 17 (1981): 697–704.

Dodds, W. Jean. "Autoimmune Thyroid Disease." *Dog World* 77 (April 1992): 36–40.

Draper, Donald D., J. P. Kluge, and W. J. Miller. "Clinical and Pathological Aspects of Spinal Dysraphism in Dogs." In *Proceedings of the Twentieth World Veterinary Congress, Thessalonika, 1975*, 134–137. Thessalonika: G. Papageorgeiou, 1975.

Drlica, Karl. *Understanding DNA and Gene Cloning: A Guide for the Curious.* 2d ed. New York: John Wiley & Sons, 1992.

Falconer, D. S. *Introduction to Quantitative Genetics.* New York: Ronald Press, 1960.

Feldmann, D. B., M. M. Bree, and B. J. Cohen. "Congenital Diaphragmatic Hernia in Neonatal Dogs." *Journal of the American Veterinary Medical Association* 153 (1968): 1942–1944.

Fiennes, Richard. *The Order of Wolves.* New York: Bobbs-Merrill, 1976.

Fiennes, Richard, and Alice Fiennes. *The Natural History of the Dog.* London: Weidenfeld & Nicolson, 1968.

Foley, C. W., J. F. Lasley, and G. D. Osweiler. *Abnormalities of Companion Animals: Analysis of Heritability.* Ames: Iowa State University Press, 1979.

Fox, M. W. "Inherited Inguinal Hernia and Midline Defects in the Dog." *Journal of the American Veterinary Medical Association* 143 (1963): 602–604.

Fox, Michael W. *The Dog: Its Domestication and Behavior.* New York: Garland STPM Press, 1978.

Francione, Gary. "Cloning Breeds Contempt and Adulation. We Claim to Eschew `Unnecessary Suffering,' So Why Are We So Eager to Exploit Animals in Cloning Procedures?" *Chicago Tribune*, 7 March 1997, sec. 1, p. 23.

Franclose, Helen E., and Nancy C. Swanson. *Norwegian Elkhound.* Fairfax, Va.: Denlinger's, 1974.

Fraser, Clarence M., ed. *Merck Veterinary Manual.* 6th ed. Rahway, N.J.: Merck, 1986.

Gallant, Johan. *Schnauzers—Standard, Giant, Miniature.* Golden, Col.: Alpine Publications, 1996.

Giger, U., and N. A. Noble. "Determination of Erythrocyte Pyruvate Kinase Deficiency in Basenjis with Chronic Hemolytic Anemia." *Journal of the American Veterinary Medical Association* 198 (1991): 175–176.

Gipson, P. S. "Coyotes and Related Canis in the Southeastern United States with a Comment on Mexican and Central American Canis." In *Coyotes. Biology, Behaviour, and Management*, edited by M. Bekoff, 191–208. New York: Academic Press, New York, 1978.

Gottelli, D., C. Sillero-Zubiri, G. D. Applebaum, M. S. Roy, D. J. Girman, J. Garcia-Moreno, E. A. Ostranders, and R. K. Wayne. "Molecular Genetics of the Most Endangered Canid: The Ethiopian Wolf *Canis Simensis*." *Molecular Ecology* 3 (1994): 301–312.

Grzimek, Bernhard, and Eberhard Trumler. "Dingo." In *Grzimek's Encyclopedia of Mammals*, 5 vols., edited by Bernhard Grzimek and Sybil P. Parker, 4: 100–101. New York: McGraw-Hill, 1990.

Gurguis, George N. M., Ehud Klein, Ivan N. Mefford, and Thomas W. Uhde. "Biogenic Amine Distribution in the Brain of Nervous and Normal Pointer Dogs: A Genetic Animal Model of Anxiety." *Psychopharmacology* 3 (1990): 297–303.

Guthrie, S., and H. G. Pidduck. "Heritability of Elbow Osteochondrosis Within a Closed Population of Dogs." *Journal of Small Animal Practice* 31 (1990): 93–96.

Hall, Roberta L. *Wolf and Man*. New York: Academic Press, 1978.

Hazewinkel, H. A. W. "Nutrition in Relation to Skeletal Growth Deformities." *Journal of Small Animal Practice* 30 (1989): 625–630.

Hazewinkel, H. A. W., S. A. Goedegebuure, P. W. Poulos, and W. T. C. Wolvekamp. "Influences of Chronic Calcium Excess on the Skeletal Development of Growing Great Danes." *Journal of the American Animal Hospital Association* 21 (1985): 377–391.

Hediger, Heini. *Wild Animals in Captivity*. London: Butterworth, 1950.

Hohenboken, William D. "Heritability and Repeatability." In *General and Quantitative Genetics*, edited by A. B. Chapman, 77–119. New York: Elsevier, 1985.

———. "Prediction and Measurement of Response to Selection." In *General and Quantitative Genetics*, edited by A. B. Chapman, 135–149. New York: Elsevier, 1985.

———. "Maternal Effects." In *General and Quantitative Genetics*, edited by A. B. Chapman, 167–186. New York: Elsevier, 1985.

Hoskins, H. Preston, J. V. Lacroix, and Karl Mayer, eds. *Canine Medicine*. 2d ed. Santa Barbara: American Veterinary Publications, 1959.

Hritzo, Robert J. "Copper Toxicosis Announcement, AKC Delegates Meeting, March 14, 1995." American Kennel Club communication sent to Scottsdale Dog Fanciers Association, Scottsdale, Arizona. Photocopy.

Hutt, Frederick B. *Genetics for Dog Breeders*. San Francisco: W. H. Freeman, 1979.

Iljin, N. A. "Wolf-Dog Genetics." *Journal of Genetics* 42 (1941): 359–414.

Jolly, R. D., W. J. Dodds, G. R. Ruth, and D. B. Trauner. "Screening for Genetic Diseases: Principles and Practice." *Advances in Veterinary Science and Comparative Medicine* 25 (1981): 245–276.

Kaneko, J. J., D. R. Cordy, and G. Carlson. "Canine Hemophilia Resembling Classic Hemophilia A." *Journal of the American Veterinary Medical Association* 150 (1967): 15–21.

Kasprisin, Christina Algiere, and Duke O. Kasprisin. *Clinical Human Genetics*. New York: Medical Examination Publishing, 1982.

Kasström, Håkan. "Nutrition, Weight Gain and Development of Hip Dysplasia." *Acta Radiologica, Supplementum* 344 (1975): 135–179.

Keeler, C. E., and H. C. Timble. "The Inheritance of Dew Claws in the Dog." *Journal of Heredity* 29 (1938): 145–148.

Keeler, Clyde. "Genetics of Behavior Variations in Color Phases of the Red Fox." In *The Wild Canids*, edited by M. W. Fox, 399–413. New York: Van Nostrand Reinhold, 1975.

Kelley, R. B. *Sheep Dogs: Their Breeding, Maintenance and Training*. Sydney: Angus & Robertson, 1949.

Kirk, Robert W., ed. "A Catalogue of Congenital and Hereditary Disorders of Dogs (by Breed)." In *Current Veterinary Therapy IX: Small Animal Practice*, edited by Robert W. Kirk, 1281–1285. Philadelphia: W. B. Saunders, 1986.

Lawson, D. D. "Canine Distichiasis." *Journal of Small Animal Practice* 14 (1972): 469–478.

Lehman, N., A. Eisenhawer, K. Hansen, L. D. Mech, R. O. Peterson, P. J. P. Gogan, and R. K. Wayne. "Introgression of Coyote Mitochondrial DNA into Sympatric North American Gray Wolf Populations." *Evolution* 45 (1991): 104–119.

Levine, Joseph, and David Suzuki. *The Secret of Life: Redesigning the Living World*. Boston: WGBH Educational Foundation, 1993.

Levine, Louis. *Biology of the Gene.* 3d ed. St. Louis: C. V. Mosby, 1980.
Little, Clarence C. *The Inheritance of Coat Color in Dogs.* Ithaca, N.Y.: Comstock Publishing, 1957.
Lorenz, Konrad Z. "Foreword." In *The Wild Canids,* edited by M. W. Fox, vii–xii. New York: Van Nostrand Reinhold, 1975.
Macgregor, H. C. *An Introduction to Animal Cytogenetics.* New York: Chapman & Hall, 1993.
Macintosh, N. W. G. "The Origin of the Dingo: An Enigma." In *The Wild Canids,* edited by M. W. Fox, 87–106. New York: Van Nostrand Reinhold, 1975.
Manwell, C., and C. M. A. Baker. "Origin of the Dog: From Wolf or Wild *Canis Familiaris.*" *Speculations in Science and Technology,* 6 (1983): 213–224.
Marchlewski, T. "Genetic Studies on the Domestic Dog." *Bulletin International de l'Académie Polonaise des Sciences et des Lettres, Classe des Sciences Mathématiques et Naturelles, Série B* 2 (1930): 117–145.
Mayr, B., K. Schellander, H. Auer, E. Tesarik, W. Schleger, K. Sasshofer, and E. Glawischnig. "Offspring of a Trisomic Cow." *Cytogenetics and Cell Genetics* 44 (1987): 229–230.
McCarren, Marie. "The Glucokinase Connection." *Diabetes Forecast,* November 1992, 27–28, 30.
Menotti-Raymond, Marilyn, and Stephen J. O'Brien. "Dating the Genetic Bottleneck of the African Cheetah." *Proceedings of the National Academy of Sciences* 90, no. 8 (1993): 3172–3176.
Merrell, David J. *The Adaptive Seascape: The Mechanism of Evolution.* Minneapolis: University of Minnesota Press, 1994.
Mestel, Rosie. "Ascent of the Dog." *Discover* 15 (October 1994): 90–98.
Meyers-Wallen, V. N., and D. F. Patterson. "Disorders of Sexual Development in Dogs and Cats." In *Current Veterinary Therapy X: Small Animal Practice,* edited by Robert W. Kirk, 1262–1269. Philadelphia: W. B. Saunders, 1989.
Murphree, Oddist D. "Inheritance of Human Aversion and Inactivity in Two Strains of the Pointer Dog." *Biological Psychiatry* 7 (1973): 23–29.
Murphree, Oddist D., Charles Angel, Donald C. DeLuca, and J. E. O. Newton. "Longitudinal Studies of Genetically Nervous Dogs." *Biological Psychiatry* 12 (1977): 573–576.
"Music of the Hemispheres." *Discover* 15 (March 1994): 15.
Naaktgeboren, Cornelis. "Dogs." In *Grzimek's Encyclopedia of Mammals,* 5 vols., edited by Bernhard Grzimek and Sybil P. Parker, 4: 52–61. New York: McGraw-Hill, 1990.
———. "Jackals." In *Grzimek's Encyclopedia of Mammals,* 5 vols., edited by Bernhard Grzimek and Sybil P. Parker, 4: 107–109. New York: McGraw-Hill, 1990.
Nachreiner, Ray. *OFA: Canine Thyroid Registry.* Columbia, Mo.: Orthopedic Foundation for Animals, n.d. Pamphlet.
Nap, R. C., H. A. W. Hazewinkel, G. Voorhout, W. E. Van Den Brom, S. A. Goedegebuure, and A. T. Van't Klooster. "Growth and Skeletal Development in Great Dane Pups Fed Different Levels of Protein Intake." *Journal of Nutrition* 12, suppl. (1991): S107–S113.
National Research Council. *Nutrient Requirements of Dogs.* Rev. ed. Washington, D.C.: National Academy of Sciences, 1985.
Nicholas, Anna Katherine. *Book of the Poodle.* Neptune City, N.J.: T.F.H. Publications, 1982.

Nicholas, F. W. *Veterinary Genetics.* Oxford: Clarendon Press, 1987.

Nora, James J., and F. Clarke Fraser. *Medical Genetics: Principles and Practice.* 2d ed. Philadelphia: Lea & Febiger, 1981.

O'Brien, Stephen J., David E. Wildt, Mitchell Bush, Timothy M. Caro, Clare FitzGibbon, Issa Agoundey, and Richard E. Leakey. "East African Cheetahs: Evidence for Two Population Bottlenecks?" *Proceedings of the National Academy of Sciences* 84, no. 2 (1987), 508–511.

Orthopedic Foundation for Animals. *OFA: Congenital Heart Disease Registry.* Columbia, Mo.: Orthopedic Foundation for Animals, n.d. Pamphlet.

———. "30 Years of Progress: OFA Data Confirm Dramatic Improvements in Dog Hips." Letter, July 1, 1997.

O'Sullivan, N. O., and R. Robinson. "Harlequin Colour in the Great Dane Dog." *Genetica* 78 (1989): 215–218.

Palmer, A. C., J. E. Payne, and M. E. Wallace. "Hereditary Quadriplegia and Amblyopia in the Irish Setter." *Journal of Small Animal Practice* 14 (1973): 343–352.

Partridge, Linda. "Genetics and Behaviour." In *Genes, Development and Learning,* edited by T. R. Halliday and P. J. B. Slater, 11–51. New York: W. H. Freeman, 1983.

Patterson, D. F. "Canine Congenital Heart Disease: Epidemiology and Etiological Hypotheses." *Journal of Small Animal Practice* 12 (1971): 263–287.

———. "Congenital Defects of the Cardiovascular System of Dogs: Studies in Comparative Cardiology." *Advances in Veterinary Science and Comparative Medicine* 20 (1976): 1–37.

Patterson, D. F., T. Pexieder, W. R. Schnarr, T. Navratil, and R. Alaili. "A Single Major-Gene Defect Underlying Cardiac Conotruncal Malformations Interferes with Myocardial Growth During Embryonic Development: Studies in the CTD Line of Keeshond Dogs." *American Journal of Human Genetics* 52 (1993): 388–397.

Pearson, K., and C. H. Usher. "Albinism in Dogs." *Biometrika* 21 (1929): 144–163.

Pfaffenberger, Clarence. *The New Knowledge of Dog Behavior.* New York: Howell Books, 1963.

Pferd, William III. *Dogs of the American Indians.* Fairfax, Va: Denlinger's, 1987.

Pieau, Claude. "Temperature Variation and Sex Determination in Reptiles." *BioEssays* 18 (January 1996): 19–26.

Piermattei, Donald L., and Steven P. Arnoczky. *Patellar Luxation Registry: General Procedures and Classification.* Columbia, Mo.: Orthopedic Foundation for Animals, n.d. Pamphlet.

Pirchner, Franz. "Genetic Structure of Populations. 1. Closed Populations or Matings Among Related Individuals." In *General and Quantitative Genetics,* edited by A. B. Chapman, 227–250. New York: Elsevier, 1985.

Piscino, Beverly, and Gloria Lewis. *Miniature Schnauzers.* Neptune City, N. J.: T.F.H. Publications, 1990.

Plomin, Robert, J. C. DeFries, and G. E. McClearn. *Behavioral Genetics: A Primer.* 2d ed. New York: W. H. Freeman, 1990.

Poletaeva, I. I., N. V. Popova, and L. G. Romanova. "Genetic Aspects of Animal Reasoning." *Behavior Genetics* 23 (1993): 467–475.

Popova, N. K., N. N. Voitenko, A. B. Kulikov, and D. F. Avgustinovich, "Evidence for the Involvement of Central Serotonin in Mechanism of Domestication of Silver Foxes." *Pharmacology, Biochemistry and Behavior* 40, no. 4 (1991): 751–756.

Pullig, T. "Inheritance of Whorls in Cocker Spaniels. A Preliminary Report." *Journal of Heredity* 41 (1950): 239–242.

Radford, Tim. "Scientists Scorn Sci-Fi Fears over Sheep Clone." *Guardian* (Manchester), 24 February 1997, sec. 1, p. 7.

Raymond, Sharon L., Douglas W. Jones, Marjory B. Brooks, and W. Jean Dodds. "Clinical and Laboratory Features of a Severe Form of Von Willebrand Disease in Shetland Sheepdogs." *Journal of the American Veterinary Medical Association* 197 (1990): 1342–1345.

Riddle, Maxwell. *Dogs Through History.* Fairfax, Va.: Denlinger's, 1987.

Rieger, R., A. Michaelis, and M. M. Green. *Glossary of Genetics.* 5th ed. New York: Springer-Verlag, 1991.

Riser, W. H. "The Dog as a Model for the Study of Hip Dysplasia: Growth, Form, and Development of the Normal and Dysplastic Hip Joint." *Veterinary Pathology* 12 (1975): 229–334.

Riser, Wayne H., and Harry Miller. *Canine Hip Dysplasia and How to Control It.* Philadelphia: OFA Publications, 1966.

Robinson, Roy. "Genetic Aspects of Umbilical Hernia Incidence in Cats and Dogs." *Veterinary Record* 100 (1977): 9–10.

———. "Chinese Crested Dog." *Journal of Heredity* 76 (1985): 217–218.

———. "Inheritance of Colour and Coat in the Belgian Shepherd Dog." *Genetica* 76 (1988): 139–142.

———. "Inheritance of Coat Color in the German Pinscher Dog." *Genetica* 82 (1990): 57–58.

———. *Genetics for Dog Breeders.* 2d ed. New York: Pergamon Press, 1990.

———. *Genetics for Cat Breeders.* 3d ed. London: Pergamon Press, 1991.

Roland, Mark. "Genetic Markers." *AKC Gazette* 113 (August 1996): 54–57.

Rothwell, Norman V. *Understanding Genetics.* 4th ed. Oxford: Oxford University Press, 1988.

Roy, M. S., D. J. Girman, A. C. Taylor, A. C, and R. K. Wayne. "The Use of Museum Specimens to Reconstruct the Genetic Variability and Relationships of Extinct Populations." *Experientia* (Basel) 50, no. 6 (1994): 551–557.

Roy, M. S., E. Geffen, D. Smith, E. A. Ostrander, and R. K. Wayne. "Patterns of Differentiation and Hybridization in North American Wolflike Canids, Revealed by Analysis of Microsatellite Loci." *Molecular Biology and Evolution* 11 (1994): 553–570.

Schaible, R. H. "A Dalmatian Study." *Purebred-Dogs/American Kennel Gazette* 98 (1981): 48–52.

Schneider, Norman R. "Teratogenesis and Mutagenesis." In *Current Veterinary Therapy VIII: Small Animal Practice,* edited by Robert W. Kirk, 161–171. Philadelphia: W. B. Saunders, 1986.

Schnelle, G. B. "Some New Disease in Dogs." *Purebred Dogs/American Kennel Gazette* 52 (1935): 25.

Scott, John Paul, and John F. Fuller. *Genetics and the Social Behavior of the Dog.* Chicago: University of Chicago Press, 1965.

Searle, Anthony Gilbert. *Comparative Genetics of Coat Colour in Mammals.* New York: Academic Press, 1968.

Serpell, James, and J. A. Jagoe. "Early Experience and the Development of Behaviour." In *Domestic Dog: Its Evolution, Behaviour and Interactions with People,* edited by James Serpell, 80–102. Cambridge: Cambridge University Press, 1995.

Sheldon, Jennifer. *Wild Dogs: The Natural History of the Nondomestic* Canidae. San Diego: Academic Press, 1992.

Smith, Frances O. "Screening for Genetic Defects." *Pure-Bred Dogs/American Kennel Gazette* 111 (August 1994): 46–49.

Smith, Gail K. "Method of Assessing Canine Hip Dysplasia." *U.S. Patent* 5,482,055.

Sponenberg, D. P., E. Scott, and W. Scott. "American Hairless Terriers: A Recessive Gene Causing Hairlessness in Dogs." *Journal of Heredity* 79 (1988): 69.

Sponenberg, D. Phillip. "Inheritance of the Harlequin Color in Great Dane Dogs." *Journal of Heredity* 76 (1985): 224–225.

Stains, Howard J. "Distribution and Taxonomy of the *Canidae*." In *The Wild Canids,* edited by M. W. Fox, 3–26. New York: Van Nostrand Reinhold, 1975.

Starr, Cecie. *Biology: Concepts and Applications*. 2d ed. Belmont, Cal.: Wadsworth Publishing, 1994.

Studdert, V. P., R. B. Lavelle, R. B. Beilharz, and T. A. Mason. "Clinical Features and Heritability of Osteochondrosis of the Elbow in Labrador Retrievers." *Journal of Small Animal Practice* 32 (1991): 557–563.

Suzuki, David T., and Anthony J. F. Griffiths. *An Introduction to Genetic Analysis*. San Francisco: W. H. Freeman, 1976.

Suzuki, David T., Anthony J. F. Griffiths, Jeffrey H. Miller, and Richard C. Lewontin. *An Introduction to Genetic Analysis*. 4th ed. New York: W. H. Freeman, 1989.

Trumler, Eberhard. "Domesticated Dog." In *Grzimek's Encyclopedia of Mammals,* 5 vols., edited by Bernhard Grzimek and Sybil P. Parker, 4: 79–94. New York: McGraw-Hill, 1990.

Trut, L. N. "The Variable Rates of Evolutionary Transformations and Their Parallelism in Terms of Destabilizing Selection." *Journal of Animal Breeding and Genetics* 105, no. 2 (1988): 81–90.

Vasilyeva, L. L., and K. V. Svechnikov. "Blood Serotonin Level in Domestic Silver Foxes as a Major-Gene Marker of Domestic Behavior." *Soviet Genetics* 29, no. 3 (1993): 375–383.

Verma, M., and S. K. Dutta. "DNA Sequences Encoding Enolase Are Remarkably Conserved from Yeast to Mammals." *Life Sciences* 55 (1994): 893–899.

Verryn, S. D., and J. M. P. Geerthsen. "Heritabilities of a Population of German Shepherd Dogs with a Complex Interrelationship Structure." *Theoretical and Applied Genetics* 75 (1987): 144–146.

Walkowicz, Chris. *The Bearded Collie*. Fairfax, Va.: Denlinger's, 1987.

Warkany, Josef. *Congenital Malformations*. Chicago: Year Book Medical Publishers, 1971.

Wayne, R. K. "Molecular Evolution of the Dog Family." *Trends in Genetics* 9 (1993): 218–224.

Wayne, R. K., W. G. Nash, and S. J. O'Brien. "Chromosomal Evolution of the *Canidae*. 1. Species with High Diploid Numbers." *Cytogenetics and Cell Genetics* 44 (1987): 123–133.

———. "Chromosomal Evolution of the *Canidae*. 2. Divergence from the Primitive Carnivore Karyotype." *Cytogenetics and Cell Genetics,* 44 (1987): 134–141.

West, Geoffrey. *Encyclopedia of Animal Care*. 11th ed. Baltimore: Williams and Wilkins, 1975.

Whitney, Leon Fradley. *How to Breed Dogs*. 3d ed. New York: Howell Books, 1971.

Whittick, William G. *Canine Orthopedics*. Philadelphia: Lea & Febiger, 1974.

Wilcox, Bonnie, and Chris Walkowicz. *Atlas of Dog Breeds of the World.* 4th ed., 2 vols. Neptune City, N.J.: T.F.H. Publications, 1993.

Willis, M. B. "Genetic Aspects of Dog Behaviour with Particular Reference to Working Ability." In *Domestic Dog: Its Evolution, Behaviour and Interactions with People,* edited by James Serpell, 51–64. Cambridge: Cambridge University Press, 1995.

Willis, Malcolm B. *Genetics of the Dog.* London: H. F. & G. Witherby, 1989.

Workman, M. J., and R. Robinson. "Coat Colors of the Cavalier King Charles Spaniel." *Journal of Animal Breeding and Genetics* 108 (1991): 66–68.

Zeuner, Frederick Eberhard. *A History of Domesticated Animals.* New York: Harper & Row, 1963.

Zhang, Tingqing. "Reproduction-Related Chromosomal Aberrations in Domestic Animals in the USA (United States)." Ph.D. diss., University of Minnesota, 1993. Abstract in *Dissertation Abstracts International.* Assession no. AAI9411287. SilverPlatter.

Zimmer, Carl. "First Cell." *Discover* 16 (November 1995): 70–74.

GLOSSARY

adaptability. The alteration of phenotype without modification of the genotype. An example is the dandelion. At low elevations and temperate climate, a dandelion is erect, with large leaves and flowers; if its seeds are planted at alpine elevations, the dandelions will be compact dwarfs.

additive gene action. [1]A form of allelic interaction in which dominance is absent; the heterozygote is intermediate in phenotype between homozygotes for the alternative alleles. [2]The cumulative contribution of polygenes at all loci toward the expression of a polygenic trait.

additive genetic variance. The averaging effects of substituting one polygene for another. Although additive variance does not always indicate that the genes are, in fact, exhibiting additive gene action, it is a useful working concept for dog breeders.

adenine (A). A nitrogenous base, one member of the base pair A–T (adenine-thymine).

agouti allele. The agouti *(A)* allele at Locus *A* produces a band of light pigment on a shaft of dark hair. The location of the band varies; it may be terminal (end) or subterminal. In dogs, the color of the back and sides is darker than the abdomen, extremities, and head, though the head often has darker markings, and the entire coat lightens very slightly from the puppy to the adult shade.

alike in state. There are different degrees of homozygosity, some derived through being members of the same population and others derived through direct ancestry. Homozygous alleles have the same phenotypic action. For example, the genes that produce the chocolate color in Labrador Retrievers produce brown pigmentation. They are described as alike in state. If two chocolate Labradors are mated, the alleles from the parents are duplicates, and these are described as identical by descent (or simply as identical), and an individual with two identical-by-descent alleles at a specific locus is called an identical homozygote.

allele. Any one of two-or-more alternative forms of a gene occupying the same position (locus) on a particular chromosome. The term is roughly synonymous with gene but useful when discussing several genes at a specific locus.

allelo-. A combining form from Greek, meaning *one another, reciprocal*, or *parallel*, as in allele or allelomorphic.

allelomorphic series. The sequence of relative dominance of alleles that can occupy the same locus. Also called allelic series.

altricial. Helpless at birth and requiring considerable parental care. *Compare with* precocial.

amino acid. Any organic compound composed of an amino group (NH_2) and an acid group. The genetic code directs the synthesis of only twenty amino acids, which are the building blocks of all proteins. *See* genetic code.

amorph. An inactive allele that blocks normal biosynthesis; also called a genetic block.

anagenesis. *See* evolutionary patterns.

anchor gene. A developmental control gene that acts as an on-off switch.

aneuploidy. A chromosomal anomaly in which the number of chromosomes departs from the normal diploid number by less than a whole haploid set.

anticodon. The codon's counterpart on transfer RNA (tRNA) that bonds with a codon unit on the messenger RNA (mRNA) during translation. *Compare with* codon.

antimorph. An allelic action that is opposite to that of the wild or natural type; also called an endomorph.

artificial selection. *See* selection.

associative learning. *See* conditioning.

assortive mating. *See* selection methods or systems, assortive mating.

autosomal trait. A trait determined by a gene located on an autosome. *Compare with* sex-linked trait.

autosome. Any chromosome except the *XY* sex chromosomes. The diploid human genome consists of 23 chromosome pairs (46 chromosomes), of which 22 pairs are autosomes and one pair is sex the chromosomes (the *X* and *Y* chromosomes).

backcross. [1]Breeding to a parent or grandparent. [2]Breeding a crossbred back to a purebred of the same breed as one parent.

badger. A coat color that is a mixture of white, gray, brown, and black hairs.

base pair. The bond formed between two nitrogenous bases (either adenine and thymine or guanine and cytosine). The base pairs, like rungs on a ladder, join two DNA strands into the long, twisted spiral called a double helix.

base sequence. The order of nucleotide bases in a DNA molecule.

behavioral genetics. The study of organisms by means of both genetic and behavioral analysis; it is an interface between the two sciences.

belton. In English Setters, refers to ticked coat color.

bicolored pattern. Produced by the a^t allele, the pattern is characterized by a background of dark pigment with tan points that are located as follows: above each eye; on each cheek; on the lips and lower jaw, extending under the throat; on two spots on the forechest; below the tail; and from the feet to the pasterns and hocks, extending up the inner sides of the legs. Also known as the black-and-tan pattern because it is typical of breeds such as the Rottweiler and Gordon Setter, the pattern also occurs with blue, brown, and isabella as the background color.

black-and-tan pattern. *See* bicolored pattern.

Blenheim. In Cavalier King Charles and English Toy Spaniels, red and white particolor.

blue. The silvery, blue-gray color produced by dilute black pigment with the genotype $B\text{--}dd$.

blue merle. A coat with black patches on a blue-gray background. *See* merle pattern.

borophagine. *See Canidae*.

bottleneck effect. The fluctuation of gene frequency that occurs when a large population passes through a contracted stage and then expands again with an altered gene pool, usually one with reduced variability, as a consequence of genetic drift. *See* genetic drift.

breeding. [1]A combination of selection procedures (choice of breeding animals) and systems of mating (choice of mates). [2]The practical application of genetic analysis for development of lines of domestic animals suited to human purposes.

brindle pattern. Produced by the E^{br} allele, the pattern is characterized by stripes or bars of dark pigment on a background of light pigment.

Canidae. The taxonomic family of doglike species. *Hesperocyon gregarius* or stem (ancestral) dog was the earliest member of the *Canidae* (doglike species) family that originated in the North American tropics about 67 million years ago. About 30 million years ago, it branched into *Leptocyon* and *Borophagus*. The *Leptocyon*, small-game hunters that could also metabolize vegetable matter, evolved over a few million years into wolves, foxes, and other modern members of the *Canidae* family. The borophagine branch, mastiff-sized big-game hunters, became extinct about 2 1/2 million years ago when big game be came scarce.

cataract. The dull, whitish cloudiness of the lens or capsule in one or both eyes that may eventually lead to blindness.

catecholamines. A group of biochemicals that function as neurohormones or neurotransmitters.

cell. The smallest unit of living matter capable of self-perpetuation.

cellular genetics. *See* cytogenetics.

central progressive retinal atrophy (CPRA). A progressive degenerative disease in which death of the photoreceptor cells of the retina is secondary to disease of the underlying pigment epithelium. It progresses slowly, and some animals never become blind. *See also* progressive retinal atrophy.

centromere. The constricted region on the chromosome to which the spindle fibers attach during cell division. Its position on the chromosome is an aid to identification of different species.

chiasma (plural, chiasmata). [1]The visible manifestations of crossovers. [2]Cross-shaped structres that appear between two *nonsister* chromatids as the paired chromosomes begin to separate during the diplotene phase of meiosis I. (From Greek, meaning two lines placed crosswise or diagonally arranged.)

china eye. An eye with a whitish iris. Also called wall eye.

chromatid. While still joined at the centromere during cell division, the new chromosome strand is known as a *chromatid*, and the pair are *sister chromatids*.

chromo-. A combining form from Greek, meaning *color*, as in chromosome.

chromosomal anomaly (aberration). Any irregularity in the structure of a chromosome or in the number of chromosomes that may alter embryonic development. An anomaly is not hereditary unless the germ cells of the ovaries or the testes are affected. Also called a chromosomal mutation.

chromosome. [1]A linear sequence of genetic information. Each chromosome is a single DNA molecule consisting of hundreds to millions of genes. [2]The self-replicating genetic structures of cells containing the cellular DNA that bears in its nucleotide sequence the linear array of genes. In prokaryotes, chromosomal DNA is circular, and the entire genome is carried on one chromosome. Eukaryotic genomes consist of a number of chromosomes whose DNA is associated with different kinds of proteins.

cladogenesis. *See* evolutionary patterns.

classical conditioning. A learned behavioral response to stimulus recognition.

classification. *See* taxonomy.

cleft palate. The failure of the bony plates forming the roof of the mouth to close normally during embryonic development, usually leaving a fissure between the palate and the nasal passages. It is often accompanied by a cleft lip (harelip).

clone. A group of genetically identical cells, all derived from a single ancestor.

cloning. The process of asexually producing a group of cells (clones), all genetically identical, from a single ancestor. In recombinant DNA technology, the use of DNA manipulation procedures to produce multiple copies of a single gene or segment of DNA is referred to as cloning DNA.

closed behavioral program. *See* instinct.

coding strand. The DNA strand that carries the gene's biological information and acts as a template (pattern) for the synthesis of an RNA molecule called a *transcript*.

codominance. The expression of a heterozygous pair that produces a phenotype in which the activity of both genes can be identified in the phenotype by the presence of two *different* gene products. In sickle cell anemia, for example, the gene that causes the disease produces a variant type of hemoglobin, and when heterozygous, both normal and abnormal forms of hemoglobin are found in red blood cells.

codon. The coding unit on messenger RNA (mRNA) that identifies either a specific amino acid or the end of a code sequence.

compensatory mating. *See* selection methods or systems, assortive mating.

conditioning. The modification of behavior so that an act or response previously associated with one stimulus becomes associated with another; also called associative learning.

congenital. Any character or trait that can be identified at birth *or* that is related to the constitution at birth. It is simply a descriptive term that neither includes all hereditary traits nor excludes those caused solely by environmental influences or by developmental accidents.

conserved sequence. A base sequence in a DNA molecule (or an amino acid sequence in a protein) that has remained essentially unchanged throughout evolution.

continuous variance. A phenotype that exhibits no abrupt changes but rather a smooth blending from one extreme to the other.

CPRA. *See* central progressive retinal atrophy.

critical period. A genetically set, age-related stage in which a specific behavioral learning task must be accomplished. Specific events must occur during a narrow time window for an animal's hereditary behavioral development to progress normally. *Compare with* sensitive period.

crossing-over. The reciprocal exchange of segments of genetic material between homologous chromosomes during the prophase of cell division. The genes are still in the same sequence and location on the chromosome, but they have new genetic combinations.

cryptorchidism. The failure of one or both testicles to descend into the scrotal sac—monolateral (unilateral) or bilateral cryptorchidism, respectively.

cytogenetics. The study of genetics by visual analysis of chromosomes and chromosomal aberrations and of other cellular structures that are related to heredity, combining the sciences of cytology and genetics.

cytology. The study of the structure, function, development, and reproduction of cells.

cytoplasm. All of the living parts of the cell outside of the nucleus.

cytosine (C). A nitrogenous base, one member of the base pair G–C (guanine and cytosine).

dapple. In Dachshunds, the dappled pattern produced by the heterozygous *Mm* alleles. *See also* merle.

dark pigment. Eumelanin, the coat pigment that produces black and brown.

deoxyribonucleic acid (DNA). *See* DNA.

dewlap. Loose, pendulous skin on the chin, throat, and neck.

diaphragmatic hernia. An opening in the diaphragm, usually with the protrusion of the stomach and other abdominal organs into the thoracic cavity.

dilution modifiers. The group of polygenes that influences the expression of the recessive dilution alleles (*dd*).

dipl-, diplo-. A combining form from Greek, meaning *twice, double, twin,* or *twofold* as in diploid.

diploid. A full set of genetic material, consisting of paired chromosomes, one chromosome from each parental set. Most animal cells except the gametes have a diploid set of chromosomes. The diploid human genome has 46 chromosomes. *Compare with* haploid.

discontinuous gene. A gene in which the biological information is divided between two or more exons (coding regions) separated by introns (noncoding regions).

discontinuous variance. A phenotype that exhibits the either-or difference typical of dominant and recessive genes, such as black or brown color.

distichiasis. Extra eyelashes that emerge from the meibomian glands along the margin of the eyelid—from one to ten hairs may emerge from a single gland. The number of affected glands varies, ranging from a few extra eyelashes to what appears to be a complete second row.

DNA (deoxyribonucleic acid). [1]The molecule that encodes genetic information. [2]A double chain of linked nucleotides that have three basic components: (*a*) the five-carbon sugar deoxyribose; (*b*) a phosphate; and (*c*) a base. The base portion of the nucleotide may be any one of following four: two—adenine (A) and guanine (G)—have the type of molecular structure called a pyramidine; the others—cytosine (C) and thymine (T)—have a structure called a purine.

DNA sequence. The relative order of base pairs, whether in a fragment of DNA, a gene, a chromosome, or an entire genome.

domesticated animal. An animal belonging to a species that has developed through human selection or interference. *Compare with* tamed animal.

dominant. [1]A gene that, when heterozygous, masks the expression of an unlike gene, and the phenotypic effect is the same in both the homozygote and the heterozygote; however, dominance may be complete, incomplete, or absent. [2]A biochemically active allele.

ectropion. The drooping or sagging of the lower eyelid (sometimes called *haw*) that is characterized by excessive drying of the cornea with overflow of tears.

elbow dysplasia. A developmental anomaly of the elbow joint that is manifested as early osteoarthritis, which may occur bilaterally or unilaterally and with varying degrees of severity. Three conditions that affect the canine elbow joint are regarded as elbow dysplasia: the ununited anconeal process (UAP), the fragmented coronoid process (FCP), and osteochondritis dissecans (OCD) of the medial humeral condyle.

electrophoresis. A method of separating large molecules (such as DNA fragments or proteins) from a mixture of similar molecules. An electric current is passed through a medium containing the mixture, and each kind of molecule travels through the medium at a different rate, depending on its electrical charge and size. Separation is based on these differences. Agarose and acrylamide gels are the media commonly used for electrophoresis of proteins and nucleic acids.

endomorph. A gene in which the action is opposite to that of the wild or natural type; also called an antimorph.

enhancer. *See* polygenes.

entropion. An inward rotation of the eyelid that is characterized by watery eyes, blinking, conjunctivitis, sensitivity to sunlight, pain, and inflammation.

environmental factor. Any factor that cannot be attributed to gene action, such as nutrition, climate, gender, age, size of litter, or embryonic environment.

enzyme. A protein that acts as a catalyst, speeding the rate at which a biochemical reaction proceeds but not altering the direction or nature of the reaction.

epi-. A prefix meaning *upon, over,* or *beside,* as in epistatic.

epilepsy. Any of various disorders marked by disturbed electrical rhythms of the central nervous system and typically manifested by convulsions.

epistasis. [1]The genetic interaction whereby one gene alters or totally masks the phenotypic expression of another gene at a *different locus.* [2]Any type of interaction between genes.

epistatic. An allele that is more dominant (above) than another.

essential amino acids. Amino acids that must be obtained from nutrient sources because they either cannot be synthesized by the body or are synthesized in insufficient quantities.

eukaryote. An organism or cell containing a nucleus and a nuclear membrane. Eukaryotes include all organisms except viruses, bacteria, and blue-green algae. *Compare with* prokaryote.

eumelanin. *See* dark pigment.

evolution. The change in a population's genetic composition over time.

evolutionary genetics. The study of factors that alter a population's genetic composition over time.

evolutionary patterns. The three patterns of evolution have been identified: *anagenesis,* a single line that changes over a period of time, maintaining genetic continuity throughout; *cladogenesis,* a single line gives rise to two or more contemporary species; and *reticulate evolution,* produced by species hybridization.

exon. *See* discontinuous gene.

expressivity. The degree to which the genotype is expressed in the phenotype. An interesting example of the *variable expressivity* of a homozygous trait can be observed in dogs with the black-and-tan pattern. *Compare with* penetrance.

extreme piebald pattern. The characteristic pattern produced by homozygous s^w alleles, ranging from solid white to small, pigmented spots on the ears, around the eyes, and in the tail area.

familial trait. A trait for which the incidence among relatives of affected individuals is higher than the general population because of (*a*) shared genes, (*b*) shared environment, or (*c*) a combination of genes and environment.

fawn. The silvery, brownish gray color produced by dilute brown pigment with the genotype *bbdd.* Also known as *isabella* or *lilac.*

FCP. Fragmented coronoid process. *See* elbow dysplasia.

feral animal. An animal belonging to a domesticated species that has reverted to the wild. The term applies to individuals that have learned to survive through need such as stray dogs and cats, as well as identifiable types such as pariah dogs and mustangs and identifiable subspecies such as the Australian and New Guinea dingoes.

filial. *See* parental generation.

founder effect. The change of gene frequency that occurs when a new population is based on a few individuals who carry only a small fraction of the genetic variation of the parental population.

fragmented coronoid process (FCP). *See* elbow dysplasia.

gamete. A mature germ cell (sperm or ovum) containing one unpaired (*haploid*) set of chromosomes capable of initiating the formation of a new individual by fusion with another gamete.

gametogenesis. The creation of gametes that occurs during meiosis II. In males, the process is known as *spermatogenesis*: each division is equal, and the result is four viable sperm. In females, the process, known as *oogenesis*, produces three polar bodies and only one viable ovum or egg. The polar bodies have little or no cytoplasm and soon disintegrate, whereas the ovum has almost all of the cytoplasm, which also contains some genetic material in the mitochondria.

gene. The basic unit of heredity, a gene is an ordered sequence of nucleotides located in a particular position on a particular chromosome that encodes a protein or RNA molecule. *See* gene expression.

gene bank. A repository for the genes of living organisms, though the term is most commonly applied to repositories for plants. Preservation of the wild and less productive strains of crop plants insures that alternative genetic combinations are available for developing new strains that are resistant to that disease. Seeds are preserved at low temperature and humidity, and living plants are cultivated. Animal gene banks store frozen semen and embryos. *Compare with* gene library.

gene deletion. A mutation in which DNA segments are lost.

gene expression. The process through which the gene's biological information is converted into the structures present and operating in the cell. Expressed genes include those that are transcribed into mRNA and then translated into protein and those that are transcribed into RNA but not translated into protein. *See also* gene product.

gene family. A groups of closely related genes that make similar products.

gene flow. The spread of genes from one breeding population to others as the result of the migration of individuals.

gene frequency. [1]The population's total number of different genes at any given locus. [2]The sum total of the different genes in a given breeding population at a particular time.

gene inversion. A mutation in which DNA segments are reversed.

gene library. A collection of clones carrying a large number (sometimes all) of the genes from a particular organism in order to provide pure samples of genes for the study of recombinant DNA technology. *Compare with* gene bank.

gene mapping. Determination of the relative positions of genes on a DNA molecule and of the distance, in linkage units or physical units, between them.

gene pool. The population's collective genes.

gene product. The biochemical material, either RNA or protein, resulting from expression of a gene. The amount of gene product is used to measure how active a gene is; abnormal amounts can be correlated with disease-causing alleles.

gene splicing. *See* recombinant DNA.

gene therapy. The treatment of genetic enzyme defects by introducing fragments of the DNA directly into the cells, effectively curing the genetic defect.

genetic block. *See* amorph.

genetic code. The sequence of nucleotide bases on mRNA, coded in triplets (codons), that identify an amino acid sequence and directs gene expression. The four nucleotide bases of mRNA—adenine, cytosine, guanine, uracil—are the basis of the genetic code, and they are identified by the initials A, C, G, and U. The 64 codons either specify an amino acid or the end of a protein chain. The 20 amino acids are: alanine (Ala); arginine (Arg); aspargine (Asn); aspartic acid (Asp); cystine (Cys); glutamine (Gin); glutamic acid (Glu); glycine (Gly); histidine (His); isoleucine (Ile); leucine (Leu); lysine (Lys); methionine (Met); phenylalanine (Phe); proline (Pro); serine (Ser); threonine (Thr); tryptophan (Trp); tyrosine (Tyr); valine (Val).

genetic drift. The random changes of gene frequency produced by chance events. Also called random drift.

genetic engineering. [1]The process of creating new genetic combinations. [2]The process of producing recombinant DNA.

genetic modifier. *See* modifier.

genetics. The science dealing with heredity and variation seeking to discover laws governing similarities and differences in individuals related by descent.

geno-. A combining form from Greek, meaning *race, offspring, kind,* or *sex,* as in genotype.

genome. The genetic content of a single *(haploid)* set of chromosomes.

genotype. The entire genetic constitution of an individual or a group, which cannot be directly measured but may be transmitted to the next generation.

germ cells. The cells that produce gametes—found in the testes and ovaries of animals and in the anthers and ovaries of plants.

glaucoma. The elevation of pressure within the eye that leads to damage of the optic disk and gradual loss of vision. The age of onset varies, but it typically develops in middle-aged and older dogs. The two types of primary glaucoma—open-angle and angle-closure—are considered hereditary.

grading up. A system of breeding in which the females on hand are bred to a male of better quality; the best females in each generation are retained and again bred to a male of better quality.

grizzle. Bluish-gray or iron-gray coat color produced by a mixture of black and white hairs. Red grizzle is a mixture of black and red hairs.

guanine (G). A nitrogenous base, one member of the base pair G–C (guanine and cytosine).

haploid. A cell with a complete set of unpaired chromosomes (half the diploid number). *Compare with* diploid.

Hardy-Weinberg law. In a large, random-mating population, the gene frequencies and genotype frequencies are constant—that is, in equilibrium. The ideal Hardy-Weinberg population is based on certain assumptions: *(a)* mating is random and all genotypes produce the same number of offspring; *(b)* there is no mutation; *(c)* there is no selective process that favors one geno type over another; *(d)* there is no addition from other populations or loss through departure; and *(e)* the population is infinitely large. In reality, no population meets all of these conditions, but these assumptions enable geneticists to measure, analyze, and describe populations and the ways they change.

harlequin pattern. In Great Danes, a pattern characterized by ragged black patches on a white background. The harlequin *(H)* allele acts as a modifier and is expressed only in the presence of the *M* (merle) allele.

haw. *See* ectropion.

HD. *See* hip dysplasia.

hemophilia. A hereditary disorder characterized by excessive bleeding. Hemophilia A (classic hemophilia) is caused by a deficiency of clotting factor VIII; hemophilia B (Christmas disease) is caused by a deficiency of clotting factor IX.

heritability. [1]Capable of being inherited or of passing by inheritance. [2]The percentage of the variation seen in the expression of a character or trait that can be attributed to genetic factors; the value may also be given as a decimal number ranging from 0 to 1.

hetero-. A combining form from Greek, meaning *other* or *different*, as in heterozygous.

heterosis. The marked vigor—characterized by greater survival, fertility, or capacity for growth—that is often shown by the offspring of genetically dissimilar parents. It is a fundamental genetic phenomenon; its opposite is inbreeding depression. Also called hybrid vigor.

heterozygote. The noun form of heterozygous.

heterozygous. Having different alleles at one or more loci on homologous chromosomes.

hip dysplasia (HD). The malformation of the hip joint of variable severity: *subluxation* is the slight displacement of the joint; *luxation* is the total dislocation of the joint.

homeo-. A combining form from Greek, meaning *like* or *similar*, as in homeostasis.

homeostasis. The ability to maintain physiological processes within normal limits despite varying external conditions.

homo-. A combining form from Greek, meaning *one, same, common,* or *alike*, as in homozygous and homologous.

homologous chromosomes. A pair of chromosomes containing the same linear gene sequences, each derived from one parent.

homozygote. The noun form of homozygous.

homozygous. Having identical alleles at one or more loci on homologous chromosomes.

hybrid. In the broadest definition, the product of the mating of genetically differentiated forms, usually different species. In the narrowest definition, an individual that is heterozygous at one or more loci.

hybrid vigor. *See* heterosis.

hybrid zone. A region in which genetically distinct populations meet and produce progeny of mixed ancestry—natural hybridization.

hypermorph. An allele that produces an excess of genetic product.

hypomorph. An allele that functions imperfectly; also called a leaky gene.

hypostatic. An allele that is less dominant than another.

hypothyroidism. A deficiency of the thyroid hormone. Screening tests can identify two types of hypothyroidism—idiopathic and autoimmune (Hashimoto's) thyroiditis—both with a variable age of onset.

identical by descent. *See* alike in state.

imprinting. A rapid learning process that takes place early in the life of a social animal and activates a hereditary behavioral pattern. It is similar to instinct in that the behavior is innate, but unless activated within a limited period of time, the behavioral potential is lost.

in vitro. Outside a living organism.

in vivo. Inside a living organism.

inbreeding. [1]The mating of individuals more closely related to one another than the average relationship within the population. [2]The mating of closely related individuals, usually sibling or parent-progeny matings.

inbreeding coefficient. The probability of homozygosity by descent expressed as a percentage.

inbreeding depression. The reduction of fertility and vigor associated with increased homozygosity; it is the opposite of heterosis.

incomplete dominance. The expression of heterozygous alleles that produces an intermediate phenotype.

incomplete penetrance. *See* penetrance.

independent culling levels. *See* selection methods or systems, independent culling levels.

individual selection. *See* selection methods or systems, individual selection.

inhibitor. *See* polygenes.

insight learning. A type of learning characterized by problem solving.

instinct. Also called a closed behavioral program, an instinct is a natural pattern that is complete and functional the first time it is invoked.

interphase. The period in the cell cycle preceding division, when DNA is replicated in the nucleus.

introgression. The dispersion of the genes from a different species among a population through hybridization.

intron. *See* discontinuous gene.

Irish spotting pattern. The characteristic pattern produced by homozygous s^i alleles, with white on the muzzle, forehead, chest, abdomen, feet, and tail tip.

isabella. The silvery, brownish-gray color produced by dilute brown pigment with the genotype *bbdd*. Also known as *fawn* or *lilac*.

isoallele. An allele that has no obvious effect.

karyo-. A combining form from Greek, meaning *kernel* or *nucleus*, as in karyotype.

karyotype. [1]A special photograph showing the chromosomes of an individual or species arranged in a standard format showing the number, size, and shape of each chromosome type. [2]The sum of the specific characteristics of the chromosomes in a cell of an individual or a related group.

King Charles. In Cavalier King Charles and English Toy Spaniels, black and tan.

law of independent assortment. The inheritance of each paired unit is independent of the others.

law of segregation. The units of heredity exist in pairs, the pairs separate for reproduction, and each parent contributes one unit to the next generation.

leaky gene. *See* hypomorph.

Leptocyon. *See Canidae*.

lethal gene. A gene that causes the death of the embryo or fetus when homozygous.

light pigment. Phaeomelanin, the coat pigment that produces yellow and red colors.

like-to-like mating. *See* selection methods or systems, assortive mating.

lilac. The silvery, brownish gray color produced by dilute brown pigment with the genotype *bbdd*. Also known as *fawn* or *isabella*.

linebreeding. The mating of related individuals in which the closeness of the relationship is highly variable.

linkage. The proximity between two or more genes on the same chromosome; the closer together they are, the lower the probability that they will be separated during meiosis and the higher the probability that they will be inherited together.

linkage map. A map of the relative positions of genetic loci on a chromosome, determined on the basis of how often the loci are inherited together.

locus (plural, loci). The site or location that an allele occupies on a chromosome.

luxation. *See* hip dysplasia.

major genes. A somewhat archaic term for genes that produce a readily identifiable effect on the phenotype and can be studied by Mendelian methods. The phenotype is characterized by *discontinuous variance*—that is, the either-or phenotypic difference produced by dominant-recessive pairs such as the alleles for black or brown coat color. *Compare with* minor genes.

marker. A gene or DNA segment that appears in more than one form in a population. Markers occupy an identifiable physical location on a chromosome and can be easily identified either by a gene product or by other means. Markers are used as a point of reference when mapping new loci.

mass selection. *See* selection methods or systems, individual selection.

maternal effect. Everything that affects the progeny's phenotype that is directly attributable to the dam, such as the uterine environment, maternal antibodies, quantity and quality of milk, number of littermates, and transmission of worms and disease.

mating barrier. The preference for mating within the same species.

meio-. A combining form from Greek, meaning *less than* or *to make smaller than,* as in meiosis.

meiosis. The process of cell division by which cells prepare for sexual reproduction by reducing the parental chromosome number by half—that is, from the diploid (paired) number to the haploid (unpaired) number.

meiosis I. The first maturation division or reduction division.

meiosis II. The second maturation division, also known as *gametogenesis*—the creation of gametes.

Mendelian genetics. [1]The study of single-gene heredity in which each gene is inherited as a distinct unit and produces an identifiable effect. [2]The study of *particulate* (that is, minute separate particles) *heredity*, characterized by easily classified units of heredity.

Mendelian ratios. The varying probabilities of occurrence of different dominant recessive combinations.

merle pattern. Produced by the heterozygous alleles (*Mm*), the pattern is characterized by irregular, dark patches against a lighter background that is a mixture of normal and pigment-deficient hairs. The classic expression is the *blue merle,* with irregular black patches against a blue background. When homozygous (*MM*), there is additional loss of pigment producing an almost all-white coat called the *white merle;* the dogs usually have impaired hearing and vision and are sometimes sterile.

messenger RNA (mRNA). The RNA that serves as a template for protein synthesis. *See* genetic code.

metaphase. A stage in mitosis or meiosis during which the chromosomes are aligned along the equatorial plane of the cell.

microsatellite. A segment of DNA that contains a repeating nucleotide pattern that is highly genetically variable and is used as a marker.

migration. The transfer of genes through the movement of individuals from one population to another.

mimic effects. Two or more independently inherited alleles that produce similar or identical phenotypes. *Compare with* phenocopy.

minor genes. A somewhat archaic term for genes that produce such small effects that their individual actions cannot be easily identified. They are, however, paired, and they are transmitted in a Mendelian fashion. *Compare with* major genes.

mito-. A combining form from Greek, meaning *thread*, as in mitochondria or mitosis.

mitochondria (singular, mitochondrion). Oval or elongated structures in cell cytoplasm that produce energy; known as the powerhouses of the cell.

mitochondrial DNA (mtDNA). The circular or ring-shaped DNA molecules in mitochondria that are transmitted to offspring through the cytoplasm of the ova.

mitosis. The process of cell division that duplicates the chromosome pairs and apportions a set of each pair to the two daughter cells.

modifiers. Polygenes that affect the expression of alleles at an identifiable locus. The modifiers are usually designated as *plus* and *minus*.

molecular genetics. The study of the structure and function of genes at the molecular level.

mono-. A combining form from Greek, meaning *one, single,* or *alone,* as in monomorphism.

monomorphism. In a population, the occurrence of only one phenotypic form. *Compare with* polymorphism.

monorchidism. A contraction of monolateral cryptorchidism. *See* cryptorchidism.

-morph. A combining form from Greek, meaning *one characterized by a specified form,* such as monomorphism and polymorphism.

mRNA. *See* messenger RNA.

mtDNA. *See* mitochondrial DNA.

multifactorial trait. *See* polygenic trait.

multigene families. Gene clusters of related units of biological information.

mutable gene. A gene that has a significant rate of spontaneous mutation.

mutagen. Any physical or chemical agent that causes mutations.

mutant type. Any phenotype that is not typical of a wild species.

mutation. Any alteration of the genome, chromosome, or gene.

natural selection. *See* selection.

neurohormone. Any biochemical produced by or acting on nerve tissue.

neurotransmitter. A substance that transmits nerve impulses across neural synapses and influences behavior by initiating or modifying the transmission of nerve impulses.

nick. A mating that produces superior offspring.

nitrogenous base. A nitrogen-containing molecule having the chemical properties of a base.

noncoding strand. The DNA strand that does not carry the gene's biological information.

nucleotide. A subunit of DNA or RNA consisting of a nitrogenous base (adenine, guanine, thymine, or cytosine in DNA; adenine, guanine, uracil, or cytosine in RNA), a phosphate molecule, and a sugar molecule (deoxyribose in DNA and ribose in RNA). Thousands of nucleotides are linked to form a DNA or RNA molecule.

nucleus. The cellular organelle in eukaryotes that contains the genetic material.

observational learning. The ability to learn by observing the behavior of another.

OCD. *See* osteochondritis dissecans and elbow dysplasia.

omphalocele. A herniation of the abdominal organs into the umbilical cord.

oncogene. A gene, one or more forms of which is associated with cancer. Many oncogenes are involved, directly or indirectly, in controlling the rate of cell growth.

oogenesis. *See* gametogenesis.

operant conditioning. A response learned through trial and error.

osteochondritis dissecans (OCD). A disease of immature joints that is characterized by separation of the cartilage from the underlying bone, lameness, and degeneration of the joint. It occurs most often in the shoulder, it also occurs in the elbow, stifle, and hock. *See* elbow dysplasia.

osteochondrosis. A disease that affects the calcification of developing bones and is characterized by degeneration and necrosis, followed by regeneration and recalcification.

outcrossing. The mating of relatively unrelated individuals. It increases heterozygosity and creates new genetic combinations by bringing together genes from diverse source.

parental generation. Identified as *P*, the term for the parental generation offspring is *filial*. The first generation of descendants is called the first filial or F_1 generation, and the second generation is known as the second filial or F_2 generation.

particulate heredity. *See* Mendelian genetics.

patellar luxation. The dislocation of the patella, the bone in the stifle joint that corresponds with the human knee. Either one or both rear legs may be affected.

penetrance. The percentage (or proportion) of individuals with a given genotype that exhibit the associated phenotype. For example, if 100 percent show the expected phenotype, the gene has 100 percent penetrance. If less than 100 percent show the phenotype, the genotype has incomplete penetrance. *Compare with* expressivity.

performance selection. *See* selection methods or systems, individual selection.

phaeomelanin. *See* light pigment.

phenocopy. Having a phenotype that resembles a genetic trait but is produced by environmental damage to the developing embryo or growing youngster. *See* teratogen. *Compare with* mimic effects.

phenotype. [1]The observable and measurable expression of genetic traits. [2]The total of all traits, including the molecular, cellular, anatomical, physiological, and behavioral traits that are expressed from conception to reproduction and death and which are determined by the interaction of genetic and environmental factors.

piebald spotting pattern. The characteristic pattern produced by homozygous s^p alleles, with pigmented spots and widely variable areas of white.

pleiotropy. The phenomenon of a single allele causing a number of distinct and seemingly unrelated phenotypic effects.

-ploid. A combining form from Greek, meaning *fold*, as in diploid (twofold) or triploid (threefold).

poly-. A combining form from Greek, meaning *many, much, abounding in,* or *often,* as in polynucleotide, polyploid, or polymorph.

polygenes. Genes that function as a group to collectively control the expression of a trait. Although the effect of each is small, they function in groups that have similar effects on the phenotype. The expression of polygenes is characterized by *continuous variance*—that is, having no abrupt change from one extreme to another, blending in a smooth phenotypic transition, with slight discontinuities that may be blurred by the environmental factors. It is conventional to regard polygenes as having plus or minus effects. The plus polygenes act as *enhancers* (*intensifiers, extension genes*) that intensify the phenotypic effect; the minus polygenes act as *reducers* (decrease the phenotypic effect) or as *inhibitors* (completely block phenotypic expression).

polygenic trait. A trait with a variable phenotype that is produced by the interaction of numerous genes. Polygenic (many genes) traits are also known as *multifactorial* (many factors) traits, which implies the influence of other factors. Although the terms are usually used synonymously, there is a slight difference of semantic emphasis.

polymerase (DNA or RNA). Enzymes that catalyze the synthesis of nucleic acids on preexisting nucleic acid templates, assembling RNA from ribonucleotides or DNA from deoxyribonucleotides.

polymorphism. In a population, the occurrence of several phenotypic forms associated with the alleles of one gene or homologs of one chromosome. *Compare with* monomorphism.

polynucleotide. A chain of nucleotides.

polyploid. A cell with one-or-more extra chromosomes.

population. A breeding group with genes that have continuity from one generation to the next.

population genetics. The study of the genetic composition of populations, Mendelian gene frequencies, and factors that alter gene and genotype frequencies through the use of mathematical models to analyze the effects of mutation, selection, migration, and drift.

positive assortive mating. *See* selection methods or systems, assortive mating.

PRA. *See* progressive retinal atrophy.

precocial. Having a high degree of independence at birth. *Compare with* altricial.

prepotency. The ability to consistently and predictably transmit specific traits to progeny.

Prince Charles. In Cavalier King Charles and English Toy Spaniels, black, tan, and white (tricolor).

progeny testing. Rating genetic value of individuals according to the quality of their offspring from several different mates—the more offspring, the better.

progressive retinal atrophy (PRA). A progressive, degenerative disease of the visual cells of the retina that leads to blindness. *See also* centralized progressive retinal atrophy.

prokaryote. An organism or cell that lacks a nucleus and a nuclear membrane such as bacteria and blue-green algae. *Compare with* eukaryote.

protein. A large molecule composed of one or more chains of amino acids in a specific order; the order is determined by the base sequence of nucleotides in the gene coding for the protein. Proteins are required for the structure, function, and regulation of the body's cells, tissues, and organs, and each protein has unique functions. Examples are hormones, enzymes, and antibodies.

pseudo-Irish pattern. With homozygous S alleles, the most extreme expression of the minus modifiers—that is, the greatest amount of white—that resembles the Irish spotting pattern.

pseudogenes. DNA nucleotides that have lost the ability to function.

pure line. A population that breeds true for a particular trait or traits.

purine. A nitrogen-containing, single-ring, basic compound that occurs in nucleic acids. The purines in DNA and RNA are adenine and guanine.

pyrimidine. A nitrogen-containing, double-ring, basic compound that occurs in nucleic acids. The pyrimidines in DNA are cytosine and thymine; in RNA, cytosine and uracil.

quantitative genetics. The study of traits that are characterized by continuous variation.

random drift. *See* genetic drift.

random mating. Each member of the population has an equal opportunity of mating with any individual of the opposite sex.

recessive. A gene that is expressed only when paired (homozygous) with a matching recessive.

recombinant DNA molecules. A combination of DNA molecules of different origin that are joined using recombinant DNA technologies.

recombinant DNA technology. Procedures used to join together DNA segments in a cell-free system (an environment outside a cell or organism). Under appropriate conditions, a recombinant DNA molecule can enter a cell and replicate there, either autonomously or after it has become integrated into a cellular chromosome.

recombination. The process by which progeny derive a combination of genes different from that of either parent. In higher organisms, this can occur by crossing-over.

reducer. *See* polygenes.

regulatory regions or sequence. A DNA base sequence that controls gene expression.

replication. The synthesis of DNA molecules.

replication origin. The break in the base pairing of the two DNA chains that initiates replication; the break progresses, possibly in both directions, along the length of the DNA molecule.

reticulate evolution. *See* evolutionary patterns.

retinal dysplasia. An abnormality leading to retinal detachment at birth or shortly afterward, causing blindness.

ribonucleic acid (RNA). *See* RNA.

ribosomal RNA (rRNA). The class of RNA molecules present in both the small and large subunits of ribosomes.

ribosome. A cell structure that synthesizes proteins.

RNA (ribonucleic acid). A single chain of linked nucleotides that have three basic components: the five-carbon sugar ribose; a phosphate; and a base. The base portion of the nucleotide may be any one of four kinds: adenine (A), guanine (G), cytosine (C), and uracil (U). Found in the nucleus and cytoplasm of cells, RNA plays an important role in protein synthesis and other chemical activities of the cell. There are several classes of RNA molecules, including messenger RNA, transfer RNA, ribosomal RNA, and other small RNAs, each serving a different purpose.

rRNA. *See* ribosomal RNA.

ruby. In Cavalier King Charles and English Toy Spaniels, a rich red.

rufus polygenes. The group of polygenes that influences the expression of light pigment, producing shades ranging from pale yellow to rich mahogany. The genes are expressed in the presence of both genotypes that produce yellow (A^s–ee and A^y–E–) as well as in the presence of the bicolored and the saddle patterns.

saddle pattern. Produced by the a^{sa} allele, the pattern is characterized by a V-shaped saddle of dark pigment over the back and sides, with areas of tan on the extremities and face. The saddle is typically darker at birth and lightens with maturity, and the size of the area covered by dark pigment ranges considerably.

selection. The differential reproduction that changes a population's gene frequencies. With *artificial selection*, the differential is imposed by human intervention. *Natural selection* is the natural process in which the probability of reproduction is often enhanced by traits that promote survival, which is why it is also known as *survival of the fittest*.

selection index. *See* selection methods or systems, total score index.

selection methods or systems.
>   **assortive mating.** A method of breeding based on selection for specific phenotypes. The mating of animals with similar phenotypes tends to produce offspring that resemble the parents and is also known as like-to-like, type-to-type, or positive assortive mating; the goal is to reinforce desired traits. The mating of animals with dissimilar phenotypes tends to produce offspring that resemble either or both parents and is also known as unlike-to-unlike or compensatory mating; the goal is to avoid reinforcing undesired traits.
>
>   **independent culling levels.** A system of breeding selection that sets a minimum standard for a spectrum of traits, discarding all animals that are below the minimum for all characters.
>
>   **individual selection.** A system of breeding selection that concentrates on improving only one trait. Also called mass selection and performance selection.
>
>   **tandem selection.** A system of breeding selection that concentrates on improving only one trait, and after improvement, selects for another trait.
>
>   **total score index.** A system of breeding selection in which each trait is assigned a numerical value. Also called selection index.

selection response. The difference between the average of the parental population and the average of their offspring.

self-colored. A term used by dog fanciers meaning a solid-colored coat.

sensitive period. Genetically set, age-related periods of special vulnerability during which long-lasting behavioral effects can be caused by environmental factors such as maternal deprivation. The developmental time boundaries are less rigid than critical periods, and behavioral responses acquired during this period can be modified or even reversed, though never without some difficulty. *Compare with* critical period.

sequence. *See* base sequence.

sex chromosomes. The *X* and *Y* chromosomes that determine gender in mammals. *Compare with* autosomes.

sex-limited trait. A trait for which the visible expression is limited to one gender even though the genes may be transmitted by both parents.

sex-linked trait. A trait that is produced by the genes on the *X* or *Y* chromosomes. The more recent, and more precise, terms are *X*-linked and *Y*-linked traits. *Compare with* autosomal trait.

single-gene trait. A trait with a clearly identifiable phenotype that is produced by a mutant allele at a single locus.

social organization, types of canine. Three types have been identified: type I, solitary except for breeding and raising young (foxes); type II, permanent pair bonds with occasional pack bonds (coyote, jackal, dingo); and type III, permanent pair and pack bonds (wolf).

-soma. A combining form from Greek, meaning *size* or *form of body,* as in chromosome.

somatic cells. Any cell in the body except gametes and their precursors.

species. A group of individuals that share a common gene pool and are bound together by bonds of mating and heritage. Among other things, the concept of species is based on the ability to produce fertile offspring when partners are freely chosen.

spermatogenesis. *See* gametogenesis.

stasi-. A combining form from Greek, meaning *posture* or *position*, as in epistatic or hypostatic.

stem (ancestral) dog. *See* Canidae.

subluxation. *See* hip dysplasia.

survival of the fittest. *See* selection.

swimmer's syndrome. A disorder of nursing puppies that is characterized by a flattened sternum and sliding, swimming movement.

tamed animal. An animal in which the flight tendency has been eliminated and which has become emotionally stable and comfortable in the presence of humans. *Compare with* domesticated animal.

tandem selection. *See* selection methods or systems, tandem selection.

taxonomy. The orderly classification of plants and animals according to their presumed natural relationships. The taxonomic classification of the domestic dog is as follows: kingdom *Animal*, subkingdom *Metazoa*, phylum *Chordata*, subphylum *Vertebrata*, class *Mammalia*, order *Carnivora*, family *Canidae* (doglike species), and genus *Canis*, and species *familiaris f.* (forma, meaning not a natural form).

temperament. The constellation of inherited tendencies, which interact with early life experiences, that determine behavior and the potential ability to form and maintain social relationships in later life.

teratogen. Any substance, agent, or process—*anything*—that interferes with normal prenatal development. This broad term includes genetic disorders and chromosomal anomalies. It also includes purely mechanical factors that interfere with normal development; for example, restriction of fetal movement by uterine crowding or insufficient amniotic fluid can cause pressure leading to the deformity of a limb.

teratology. Stems from the Greek word *teras*, meaning monster or marvel, so it literally means the study of monstrosities. In modern usage, however, teratology is the study of congenital malformations and marked deviations from normal.

test breeding. The mating to a known producer of a specific trait to discover whether or not the individual also carries the trait.

tetraploid (tetraploidy). Having four sets of chromosomes. Tetraploidy tends to be both stable and fertile.

threshold effect. A trait that develops only if the additive effects of the contributory alleles exceed a critical number. Dominant genes, additive genes, or even recessive genes can have thresholds for expression. The phenotypes are characterized by discontinuous variance, which is why they are also known as all-or-none traits.

thymine (T). A nitrogenous base, one member of the base pair A–T (adenine-thymine).

ticking. The pattern of tiny flecks of pigmented hair in otherwise nonpigmented (white) areas. The areas are white at birth, with ticking appearing within a few weeks. Ticking ranges from a few flecks to so many that the dog appears to be roan (a fairly even mixture of white and colored hairs); the roan effect is particularly evident in longhaired dogs.

total score index. *See* selection methods or systems, (total score index).

transcript. The single-stranded chain of messenger RNA (mRNA) that is assembled on a DNA template.

transcription. The first phase of gene expression in which DNA acts as a template (pattern) for the synthesis of an mRNA molecule. *Compare with* translation.

transfer RNA (tRNA). A class of RNA having structures with triplet nucleotide sequences that are complementary to the triplet nucleotide coding sequences of mRNA. The role of tRNAs in protein synthesis is to bond with amino acids and transfer them to the ribosomes, where proteins are assembled according to the genetic code carried by mRNA.

translation. The second phase of gene expression in which mRNA directs the synthesis of proteins from amino acids. *Compare with* transcription.

translocation. The insertion of a chromosomal segment into another part of the same chromosome or into a different one.

trichiasis. Normal eyelashes that curve inward, irritating the cornea and causing chronic eye inflammation.

tricolor. A coat of three colors, usually white, black, and brown.

triploid (triploidy). Having three complete sets of chromosomes.

trisomy. The addition of an extra chromosome to one of the homologous pairs.

tRNA. *See* transfer RNA.

tubary dog. A diminutive, prehistoric type first identified in the remains of the Swiss lake dwellers and believed to be the ancestor of the maltese-type toys and the small terriers.

tweed pattern. In Australian Sheepdogs, a pattern characterized by the typical merle patchwork of dark spots on lighter areas. Although each light-colored area has a uniform color, there may be three or more patches, each of a different shade. The tweed (*Tw*) allele acts as a modifier and is expressed only in the presence of the *M* (merle) allele.

type-to-type mating. *See* selection methods or systems, assortive mating.

UAP. Ununited anconeal process. *See* elbow dysplasia.

umbilical hernia. A soft, skin-covered protrusion of the intestine through a weakness in the abdominal wall at the umbilicus. Umbilical hernias range in severity from very minor ones that close without surgery to very severe ones.

umbrous polygenes. The group of polygenes that influences the expression of black-tipped hairs in the A^y–E– yellows, producing a range of shades from nearly gold to a dark, shaded sable. The genes appear to have no effect on the A^s–ee yellows.

unlike-to-unlike mating. *See* selection methods or systems, assortive mating.

ununited anconeal process (UAP). *See* elbow dysplasia.

uracil. A nitrogenous base normally found in RNA but not DNA; uracil is capable of forming a base pair with adenine.

variable expressivity. *See* expressivity.

virus. A noncellular biological entity that can reproduce only within a host cell. Viruses consist of nucleic acid covered by protein; some animal viruses are also surrounded by a membrane. Inside the infected cell, the virus uses the synthetic capability of the host to produce progeny virus.

von Willebrand's disease (vWD). A hereditary disorder characterized by abnormally slow blood clotting owing to a deficiency of factor VIII. It differs from hemophilia A in that there is a decreased level of the von Willebrand factor (vWF) and low platelet retention (adhesiveness).

vWD. *See* von Willebrand's disease.

wall eye. An eye with a whitish iris. Also called china eye.

wheaten. Fawn, pale yellow, or straw color.

white merle. *See* merle.

wild type. The phenotype typical of a species.

wild-type allele. The allele that is most frequent in a population.

X-linked trait. *See* sex-linked trait.

Y-linked trait. *See* sex-linked trait.

zygo-. A combining form from Greek, meaning *yoke* or *pair*, as in zygote, heterozygous, or homozygous.

zygote. A fertilized egg, which has the full complement of paired chromosomes and genetic material.

INDEX

Page numbers in **boldface** font indicate figures; page numbers in *italic* font indicate tables.

adaptability, 89
additive gene action, 82, 85-86, 204
additive genetic variance, 85, 178, 182
adenine (A), 67, 68, 69, 75
adrenaline (epinephrine), 16, 17
AKC (American Kennel Club), 41, 152-153, 158, 199-200, 207-208, *208*
allele, 60, 103, *104*, 105, **105**, *224*
altricial species, 24
American College of Veterinary Ophthalmologists, 170
American Kennel Club. *See* AKC
amino acids, 69, 71
anagenesis, 2
anchor genes, 78
anticodon, 71
Arabian wolf (*Canis lupus arabs*), 10, 11
arctic fox (*Alopex lagopus*), 3
Aristotle, 6
Asian wolf (*Canis lupus pallipes*), 7
assortive mating, 89–90, 198–199
atn deficit dtentioisorder, 21
autosomal trait, 59
autosome, 59
Avery, Oswald T., 65

backcrossing, 197
bacteria, 39, 69, 78, 79
bat-eared fox (*Otocyon megalotis*), 3
Bateson, William, 1
behavior, 8, 10, 24, 28, 34, 199. *See also* learning
    environment and, **32**
    hereditary disorders, 21
    social, bonds, 27–28
    social, organization, 27
    social, patterns, 15, 23
    traits, 26–35
        anxiety, 34
        heritability, 35
        smiling, **21**
        temperament, 203
        timidity, 34
        trainability, 33–34

behavioral development, critical periods, 28
    early socialization, 213
    human bonding, 30–31, **31**
    juvenile, 32–33
    neonatal, **29**, 29–30
    sensitive periods, 28–29, *30*
    socialization, 23–24, 30–32
    stages of, 28–29
    transition, 30
behavioral genetics, 19
biochemical tests, 155
bison, 39
bites, 140, **141**
bleeding disorders, 59, 60, 149, 154, 155, 165–167
blue (coat color), 107
blue hen, 196, 197
blue merle, 109
blue-green algae, 39
body language, 28
body type, hip dysplasia and, 180, 182
Borophagus, 2
bottleneck effect, 95–96, 208
brain, 19–20, 22
breed aptitude, 203
breed knowledge, 204
breed type, 203, 207
breeder, 101–102, 191, 205
breeding program, evaluation of, 211
    adult record, **221-222**, 222, *224*
    age for, 214
    breed aptitude, 213–214
    comparisons, **219**
    conformation, 215–217
    health, 212, 213
    movement, 217
    overall, 217, 219–220
    photography, **214**, 215
    puppies, 211–222
    puppy record, 213, *215*, **216**
    shoulders, **218**
    temperament, 213–214
    veterinary examination, 212, **212**, 213
    produce records, 220, 222
    puppy testing, 213–214
British Kennel Club, 158

311

brood bitch, 205, 206
brown (coat color), 105
bush dog (*Speothos venaticus*), 3

cancer, cell division and, 41, 78, 79
Canidae, 2–3
canine wobbler syndrome, 189
Canine Eye Registration Foundation (CERF), 152, 199
Canine Molecular Genetics Project (CMGP), 41
captive breeding, 99
cardiac abnormalities, 86, 87, 153, 163–164, 212, 213
cataract, 169–170
catecholamines, 20
cats, 23–24, 39, 61, 165
cattle, 39, 51, 165, 193, 194, 196
cell division, 38, 41, 49
    meiosis, 43, **44**, 45, **46**, 48
    mitosis, 41, **42**
cell membrane, 37, 38
cell nucleus, 37
cells, 37–38, 41
cells, mitochondria. *See* mitochondria
central progressive retinal atrophy (CPRA), 169
centromere, 41
centrosome, 37
CERF (Canine Eye Registration Foundation), 152, 199
checkerboards (Punnett squares), 56, **56**, 57, 85
cheetahs, 100–101
chickens, 24, 98, 194
chimpanzees, 19, 21, 25
chocolate (coat color), 105
chromatids, 43, **43**, 45
chromosomes, 38, 40, 48–51. *See also* crossing over and linkage
    abnormalities of, 50–51, 147
    DNA and, 65, 67
    DNA replication and, 75–76
    homologous, **43**, 43, 48
    numbers, 39, 41, 43, 50, 51
    structural changes of, 50, **51**
cladogenesis, 2
cleft palate, 148, 157–158
clones, 79–80
CMGP (Canine Molecular Genetics Program), 41
coat, 126
    corded, 128–130, **129**
    cowlicks, 134, **134**
    curly, 132, **133**
    density, 131
    feathering, 132, **133**
    hairless, 11, 13, 60, **130**, 130–131
    kinky, 132, **132**
    longhaired, 125, 126–130, **127**, **128**
    powderpuff, **130**, 130–131
    ripple coat, 134–135, **135**
    shorthaired, 125–126, **126**
    stockhaarig, 126
    stripping, 125
    texture, 131
    topcoat, 125, 127, 129
    undercoat, 125, 126, 127–128, 129, 131
    wavy, 131, **132**
    whorls, 134, **134**
    wirehaired, **125**, 125–126
    wooly, 128–129, **129**
codominance, 58, **58**, **62**, 74, 75
codon, 69, 71
color genetics, 103
compensatory mating, 199
complete dominance, 55, 57, 73, 74
condor, California, 99
congenital, 157
congenital disorders. *See specific disorders*
continuous variance, 113–114
copper toxicosis, 41, 155
cornaz, 111
Correns, Carl, 53
coyote (*Canis latrans*), 4, **5**, 13, 26, 27–28, 31
    hybrids, 6, 7, 39, 139, 145
CPRA (central progressive retinal atrophy), 169
crab-eating fox (*Cerdocyon thous*), 3
Crick, Francis, 65
crossing-over, 15–16, 48, 48–49
cryptorchidism, 86, 148, **158**, **159**, 158–160, 164, 211, 213
cytogenetics, 37
cytology, 37
cytoplasm, 37, 76
cytosine (C), 67, 68, 69, 75

dapple pattern, 109
dark-eyed white, 122
Darwin, Charles, 1, 7, 88
DDT resistance, 2, 96–97
dentition, 140, **141**
developmental adaptability, 89
dewclaws, 144, 144–145
dewlaps, 142
diabetes, 154
diaphragmatic hernia, 161, 163, 212, 213
differentiation of cells, 48, 148
dilution, modifiers, 82, 122
dilution of pigment, *See* Locus *C*, Locus *D*, Locus *G*, and modifiers

dingo, 5, 7, 26, 27, 31
dire wolf *(Canis dirus)*, 4
distichiasis, 149, 170–171, **171**, 172, 213
DNA, 2, 65, 68, 75
    base pairs, 67, 71, 75, 77
    compared with RNA, 69
    extranuclear, 14, 75–77
    hereditary disorders, testing for, 55, 201–202
    mitochondrial (mtDNA), 14, 75–77
    recombinant technology, 80
    replication, 75–77, **76**, 78–79
    structure, **66**
    studies in dogs, 14
dogs *(Canis familiaris, Canis lupus f. familiaris)*, 3, 5, 7, 61
    breed evolution, 9–14
    breed preferences, 24–25
    chromosome numbers, 39
    evolution, 7–9
    list of prehistoric, 9
    purebred population, 91
domesticated animal, 7
domestication, dogs, 7–9
    foxes, 15–17
    selective evolution and, 14–17
dominance, allelic series, 103
    codominance, **58**, 58, **62**, 74, 75
    complete, 55, 57, **73**, 74
    dominant-recessive genetic combinations, 57
    gene expression and, 73–74
    incomplete, 57, **58**, 61, **62**, 74, **74**
donkey, 39
dopamine, 17, 20
Down's syndrome (trisomy 21), 51
dwarfism, 144

ears, 139, **140**
ectropion, 170
Edward's syndrome, (trisomy 18), 51
egg-rolling instinct, 24
Egyptians, 8–9, 98
elbow dysplasia, 152–153, 183–185
elbow joint, parts of, **187**
embryo, 22, 48, 60, 147, 101
embryonic period, 148
endangered species, 99–101
endocrine system, genes, effect on 20
entropion, 170
environment, behavior, 15, 22
    brain structure, effect on, 14–15, 22
    developmental effect, 88
environmental adaptability, 89
environmental factors, 49, 88–90, 137, 148, 204
epilepsy, 167

epinephrine (adrenaline), 16, 17
epistasis, 81, 105
equilibrium, 94
Eskimos, 6
Ethiopian wolf *(Canis simensis)*, 3, 4
evolution, 1, 2
evolution, *Canidae* and, 2–3, 50
    chromosomal rearrangements and, 2, 50
    population and, 91
evolutionary genetics, 1
expressivity, 55
expressivity, variable, 55, 85
eye color, 123
eye, parts of, **168**
eyelash abnormalities, **169**

factor IX deficiency, 165
factor VIII deficiency, 166
factor VIII deficiency, 166
factor X deficiency, 155, 165
familial patterns, 21, 148, 162, 168, 172
familiality, distinguishing from heritability, 88
family, 196
fawn (coat color), 107
FCP (fragmented coronoid process), 183, 184
Federation Cynologique International (FCI), 126
feet, **145**
fennec fox *(Vulpes zerda)*, 3
feral, 5, 7
fertility, 194
fetal period, 148
fetus, 48, 60
filial (F_1, F_2) generations, 54
flecking (Dalmatian spotting), **114**, 115
flews, 142, **143**
fossils, 5, 6, 8
founder effect, 95–96, 101, 208
foxes, 2, 3, 22, 27
fragmented coronoid process (FCP), 183, 184
frogs, 89, 97–98
frozen canine semen, 197
fruit fly *(Drosophila melanogaster)*, 19–20, 39, 96–97
fur farms, foxes, 15, 16

Gauls, 6
geese, 24, 99
gender (sex) inheritance, 59, **59**
gene bank, 101
gene expression, 68–75, 81
gene flow, 94
gene frequency, 91–96, 97, 191, 199. *See also* genetic drift, random drift, migration, selection

gene library, 79
gene mapping, 68
gene pool, 91, 94, 96, 197
gene products, 71, 73–74
gene therapy, 73
genes, 2, 38, 67–68, 78. *See also* dominance, recessive genes
genes, behavior, effect on, 19–21
genes, brain structure, effect on, 19
genes, patterns of single-gene inheritance, **59**
genetic clock, 17, 20, 90
genetic code, 68–69, *70*, 76
genetic disorders. *See specific disorders*
genetic diversity, 91, 92, 94, 95, 96–102, 197, 198, 208
genetic drift, 1, 91, 92, 94–96, 207, 208
genetic engineering, 73, 79–80
genetics, 1
genome, 41, 91–92
genotype, 55
glaucoma, 170
Golgi bodies, 37
grading up, 196–197
gray wolf (*Canis lupus lupus*), 3, **4**, 11
ground squirrels, 98
growth rate, hip dysplasia and, 180, 182
guanine (G), 67, 69, 75

haploid chromosomes, 50
Hardy-Weinberg law, 92
head, 137, 139–140, 142–14
hemophilia, 59, 60, 149, 154, 155, 165–166
hereditary disorders, 21, 101, 145–149. *See also specific disorders*
    control programs, 153–156, 166–167
    lists, 149, 154, *249–258*
    mode of inheritance, 154–155
    screening methods, 155–156
heritability, 87–88, 193, 194
hernias, 161–163, 211, 213
herring gull, 24
Hesperocyon gregarius, 2
heterosis, 97, 98, 101
heterozygote, 54, 97
heterozygous advantage, 93–94
hip dysplasia, 85, 152, 172–186, 203
    pelvic muscle mass, *181, 183*
    trends, *175–178*
    X-rays, **185**
homeostasis, 20, 97–98, 100
homozygote, 54
hormones, 54
horses, 61, 165, 194, 197
Human Genome Project, 41

humans, heterozygosity of, 96
hunting, 8, 25, 26, 34–35, 199
Huntington's chorea, 22
hybrids, 2, 6, 7, 14, 28, 34, 39
    canines, interfertility of, 4–6, 7, 14
    hybrid zones, 6
hypothyroidism, 153, 172

ice ages, 3, 5, 8, 100
inbreeding, 97, 98–99, 101, 102, 192, 197–198
inbreeding coefficient, 197
inbreeding depression, 98, 101, 197, 198
incest, 97–98
incomplete dominance, 57, **58**, 61, **62**, 74, 74
incomplete penetrance, 55
independent culling levels, 193, *194*
Indian wolf (*Canis lupus pallipes*), 3, 10
individual selection, 192–193
introgression, 6
isabella (coat color), 107
Ischermak-Seysenegg, Erich von, 53

jackal, black-backed (*Canis mesomelas*), 3, 4
jackal, golden (*Canis aureus*), 3, 4, 26–27, 39
jackal, side-striped (*Canis adjustus*), 3, 4
jackals, 6, 7, 10, 14, 27
Jackson Laboratory, 28, 29, 33–34, 98–99
joint laxity, hip dysplasia and, 181, 182, 184, 185

karyotypes, 6, 40, **40**, 58, 60

law of independent assortment, 54, 63
law of segregation, 54, 63
learning, 20, 23
    associative learning, 25, 31
    closed behavioral programs, 24
    conditioning, 25
    imprinting, 23–25, **35**
    insight learning, 26
    instincts, 19, 24
    observational learning, 26
    problem solving, 26
Leber's optic atrophy, 77
leg length, 143–144
Leptocyon, 2
Lesch-Nyhan syndrome, 21
lethal genes, 60, 110, 130–131
like-to-like mating, 198–199
lilac (coat color), 107
linebreeding, 198
linkage, **49**, 49–50
liver (coat color), 105
livestock, 98, 101
locus (plural, *loci*), 60, 61, 103

Locus *A*, 60, 62, 106, 116–118
    agouti allele *(A)*, 116, **117**, 122
    bicolored pattern *(aᵗ)*, 54, 55, 107, **119**, 117–118
    black (dominant) *(Aˢ)*, 117
    black (recessive) *(a)*, 62, 118
    interactions with Locus *E*, 119, 120, **120**, 121
    saddle pattern *(aˢᵃ)*, 107, 117, **118**
    series, heterozygous interactions, 118
    yellow (dominant) *(Aʸ)*, 116
Locus *B*, 60, 106, **106**
Locus *C*, 111–112
    albino *(c)*, 111, 112
    blue-eyed albino *(cᵇ)*, 111
    chinchilla dilution *(cᶜʰ)*, 111, 112, **112**
    extreme dilution *(cᵉ)*, 111, 112
Locus *D*, 61, **106**, 106–107
Locus *E*, 62, 118–121
    black mask *(Eᵐ)*, 118, 119
    brindle pattern *(Eᵇʳ)*, 118, 119, **120**
    extension *(E)*, 118, 120
    interactions with Locus *A*, 119, 120, **120**, 121
    restriction *(e)*, 120–121
Locus *G*, 107, **107**
Locus *M*, 109–111
    harlequin pattern, 60, 62, 110, **110**, 111
    merle pattern *(M)*, 109, **109**
    tweed pattern, 110–111
Locus *P*, 111
Locus *R*, 111
Locus *S*, 112–115
    extreme piebald spotting *(sʷ)*, 105, 112, 115, **115**
    Irish spotting pattern *(sⁱ)*, 105, 112, **113**, 114
    piebald spotting *(sᵖ)*, 55, 85, 105, 112, 114, **115**
    pseudo-Irish pattern, 114
    solid or self color *(S)*, 105, 112, **113**, 114
Locus *T*, ticking, **108**, 109
luxation, 172
lysosomes, 37

major genes, 82, 90
malaria, 94
maned wolf *(Chrysocyon brachyurus)*, 3
markers, 68
mass selection, 192–193
maternal effects, 49, 88, 102
maternal qualities, 194
McCarty, Maclyn, 65
McLeod, Colin M., 65

meiosis, 43, **44**, 45, **46**, 48
melanin, 17
Mendel, Gregor Johann (1822–1884), 1, 38, 53–54, 58, 60, 61, 63
Mendelian genetics, 54, 55
    inheritance, 76
    laws, 54, 56, 57, 58, 63
    patterns, 81
    ratios, 56, 57, 86
mental disorders, 21
merle pattern *(M–)*, 109
mice, 21, 26, 61, 98, 99
microsatellite, 68
migration, 1, 91, 92, 94, 208
mimic effects, 62
minor genes, 82, 90
mitochondria, 37, 38, 45, 75–77
mitosis, 41, **42**
modifiers, 82, 113, 122
molecular genetics, 2, 65
monkeys, 2, 23, 24
monorchidism, 158
moose, imprinting, 24
Morgan, Thomas Hunt, 38–39
Morris Animal Foundation, 41
mosquitos, 2
mule, 39
multifactorial traits, 81
multifocal retinal dysplasia, 169
multigene families, 67–68
museum specimens, 99, 100
mutant type, 78
mutations, 1, 50, 77–78, 91, 92, 93–94, 96–97
    DDT resistance, 2, 96–97
    mutable gene, 78, 154
    natural rates of, 77–78, 92
    recurrent, 92
    spontaneous, 154
    stress and, 16
    types of, 77
myoclonus epilepsy with ragged red fibers (MERRF), 77

necks, 142, **143**
Nene (Hawaiian goose), 99
nervous system, 19–20
neurohormone, 17, 20, 23
neurotransmitter, 20
nick, 196, 197, 200
norepinephrine, 16, 17, 20, 23
nose color, 106
nuclear sclerosis, 169
nucleotide, 67
nutrition, 88–90, 189–190

OCD (osteochondritis dissecans), 183, 184–185, 189
OFA (Orthopedic Foundation for Animals), 41, 199. *See also* hip dysplasia.
    registries, congenital heart disease, 153, 163
    DNA, 153
        elbow dysplasia, 152–153
        hip dysplasia, 151
        patellar luxation, 153
        thyroid disease, 153
oocyte, 76
oogenesis, 45
oomphalocele, 161
operant conditioning, 25
origin of life, 2
Orthopedic Foundation for Animals (OFA). *See* OFA
osteochondritis dissecans (OCD), 183, 184–185, 189
outcrossing, 198–199

parakeets, 61–62, 97, 99
parental generation (P), 54
patellar luxation, 153, 185
Patou's syndrome (trisomy 13), 51
patterning effect, selection and, 208
patterns of evolution, 2
Pavlov, Ivan, 25
pedigree analysis, 199–200, 206
pellagra, 88, 148
pelvic muscle mass, hip dysplasia and, 180, *181*, 182, *183*
penetrance, 55
PennHIP, 184
performance selection, 192–193
peroxisomes, 37
phenocopies, 147
phenotype, 5–6, 14–15, 22, 55, 88–90
phenylketonuria (PKU), 22
phosphofructokinase deficiency, 155
physical structure, selection and, 203
pigment, dark pigment (eumelanin), 105
pigment, light pigment (phaeomelanin), 105
PKU (phenylketonuria), 22
pleiotropy, 109
Pliny, 6
plus-and-minus polygenes, 85, 113–114
polygenes, 82
    plus-and-minus effects, 85, 113–114
        polygenic traits, 81, 82, **83**, **84**, 85, 87–88, 137, 143
        rufus, 112, 121
        saddle variation, 121
        umbrous, 121
polymorphic, 96
polynucleotide, 67, 68
population, selection and, 192–194, 197, 198, 207–208
population size, 94–95, 193–194
populations, 91, 92, 94–95, 97–98, 151
positive assortive mating, 198–199
PRA (progressive retinal atrophy), 155, 168
precocial species, 24
pregnancy, care during, 148
prenatal, environment, 22
prepotency, 200
problem solving, 23, 26, 33–34
progeny testing, 201–202
progressive retinal atrophy (PRA), 155, 168
Punnett squares (checkerboards), 56, **56**, 57, 85
pure line, 91
purebred population, 192

quantitative genetics, 81, 91, 193, 194, 199

rabbits, 61, 62
raccoon dog (*Nyctereutes procyonoides*), 3
random assortment, 45, *45*, 48
random drift, 1, 91, 92, 94–96, 207, 208
random-mating, 92, 191
rats, 22, 23, 25, 26, 99
recessive genes, 21, 56, 98
records
    adult record, **221-222**, 222, 224
        puppy record, 213, *215*, **216**
        veterinary examination, 212, **212**, 213
        produce records, 220, 222
red fox (*Vulpes vulpes*), 3, 14, 15, 16
red wolf (*Canis rufus*), 2, 4–5
registries, congenital heart disease, 153
    DNA registry, 153
    elbow dysplasia, 152–153
    eye disorders, 152
    hip dysplasia, 151
    patellar luxation, 153
    thyroid disorders, 153
renal dysplasia, 155, 169
reproduction, 14–15, 43, 48, 96, 98, 101
    asexual reproduction, cloning, 43
    fertilization, **47**, 48
    mate preference and, 25
    semen, frozen, 101
resistance, evolution and, 2
reticulate evolution, 2
retroviruses, 73
ribosomes, 37–38, 69, 71

risk assessment, *201*, 201–202
RNA, 68, **69**, *69*
    messenger RNA (mRNA), 71–73
    ribosomal RNA (rRNA), 71–73
    transfer RNA (tRNA), 71
robin, 25

schizophrenia, 21
seals, 100
seizures, causes, 167
selection, 191
    art of, 203–204
    artificial selection, 191
    bloodlines, 206–207
    breed population, 207–208
    breed quality, 207
    breeding, foundation, 204–206
    environmental factors and, 89–90
    gene frequency and, 92–94, 192, 194, 207. *See also* genetic diversity
    gene pool and, 197
    genetic drift and, 94–95
    goals, 208–209
    natural, 1, 97, 191
    pedigree analysis, 199–200, 206
    planning matings, 209–210
selection for tameness, effect of, 15–17
selection index, 193–194
selection limit, 192
selection procedures, 192–196. *See also* systems of mating
selection response, 191–192
serotonin, 15, 20
sex-limited trait, 59, 60, 159
sex-linked disorders, hemophilia, 165
sex-linked recessives, 59, 60, **61**
sheep, 20, 39, 79–80, 193
sickle cell anemia, 58, 74, 77, 93–94
silver foxes, 15–17, 20
size, 143–144
skull types, 8, 14, 137, 139, **139**, 140
species, 6
species, identification, 24–25, 30
sperm, abnormal, inbreeding, 98
spermatogenesis, 45
spinal dysraphism, 116
stem, ancestral dog, 2
stool eating, 26
stress, 15–16, 20–21, 23–24, 48, 49
structural traits, 137, 139
    anatomical terms, **138**
    bites, 140, **141**
structural traits, body, 142–145

dentition, 140, **141**
dewclaw, **144**, 144–145
dewlaps, 142
dwarfism, 144
ears, 139, **140**
environmental factors, 137
feet, **145**
flews, 142, **143**
head, 137, 139–140, 142–143
leg length, 143–144
necks, 142, **143**
polygenic, 137, 143
size, 143–144
skull types, 137, 139, **139**, 140
tails, 145, **146**
stud dog, 205, 206
subluxation, 172
Sutton, Walter S., 38
swimmer' syndrome, 160–161, **161**
swimming, imprinting for, 25
swine, selection, 193
systems of mating, 196–199. *See also* selection procedures
systems of mating, 202

tails, 145, **146**
tamed animal, 7
tandem selection, 193
tapetum, 169
taxonomy, 3
Tay-Sachs disease, 21–22
temperament, hip dysplasia and, 180, 182
teratogen, 147
teratogenic agents, 22, 147–148, 149, 157–158, 159, 161, 162, 163, 164
    table of, *150–151*
teratology, 147
tetraploid chromosomes, 50, 51
thalassemia, 94
threshold effect, 85–86, **86**, 87, 158–159
thymine (T), 67, 75
Tibetan wolf (*Canis lupus chanco*), 11
ticking, 108
total score index, 193–194, *195, 196*
Tourette's syndrome, 22
transcriptase, reverse, 73
transcription, 70–73, **71**
translation, 70–73, **72**
translocation, 50
trichiasis, 170–171
triploid chromosomes, 50
trisomy, 51
tweed pattern, 110–111

twins, identical, 48, 79
type-to-type mating, 198–199
tyrosine, 17

UAP (ununited anconeal process), 183, 184
umbilical hernia, 161–163, **162**, 164
unlike-to-unlike mating, 199
ununited anconeal process (UAP), 183, 184
uracil (U), 69
uric acid metabolism, 49–50

variable expressivity, 55
variance, additive genetic variance, 82, 85
    continuous, 81–82, 85–86, 87–90
    discontinuous, 81–82, 85–86
    environmental, 89–90
viruses, 69, 73
von Willebrand's disease, 155, 166–167
Vries, Hugo de, 53

wall eyes, 109
Watson, James, 65
weight, hip dysplasia and, 180, 182
white merle, 109–110
wild type, 78, 116
Wilmut, Ian, 79
wolf, Arabian (*Canis lupus arabs*), 10, 11
    Asian (*Canis lupus pallipes*), 7
    coyote (*Canis latrans*). *See under* coyote
    dire (*Canis dirus*), 4
    Ethiopian (*Canis simensis*), 3, 4
    gray (*Canis lupus lupus*), 3, 4, 11
    Indian (*Canis lupus pallipes*), 3, 10
    red (*Canis rufus*), 2, 4–5
    Tibetan (*Canis lupus chanco*), 11
wolves, 2, 5–6, 19, 28, 31–32, 33, 98, 182
    hybrids, 6, 7, 14, 39
    range of, 4, 11
    social bonds, 27–28
    social organization, 27
    subspecies, number of, 4, 5
    tamed, 8, 26, 33
worms, 69

X chromosome, 21, **40**, 59

Y chromosome, **40**, 59
yeasts, 69

zoo animals, 14–15
zygote, 48

DOG TYPES AND BREEDS

Page numbers in **boldface font** indicate figures; page numbers in *italic* font indicate tables.

Aberdeen Terrier, *249*
Affenpinscher, 223
Afghan Hound, 11, 119, 127, **128**, 223
    hereditary disorders, *175*, 187, *249*
Airedale Terrier, 117, 223, 225
    hereditary disorders, 172, 174, *175*, *249*
Akita, 11, 13, 174, *175*, 225
Alaskan Malamute, 7, 11, 13, 14, 137, 225
    hereditary disorders, 144, 174, *175*, *249*
alaunt, 11
alsatian (type), 11, 139
American Cocker Spaniel, 12, 85, 127, 144, 155. *See also* Cocker Spaniel and English Cocker Spaniel
American Eskimo Dog, 13, 14
American Foxhound, 225, *249*. *See also* English Foxhound and Foxhound
American Hairless Terrier, coat, 130
American Rat Terrier, 130
American Staffordshire Terrier, 225
American Water Spaniel, 12, 116, 225
Anatolian Shepherd Dog, 225
Antarctic husky, *249*
Australian Cattle Dog, 226
Australian Kelpie, 226
Australian Shepherd, 109, 110–111, *175*, 226, *249*
Australian Terrier, 226

Basenji, 10, 11, 34, 99, 155, 226, *249*
Basset Hound, 12, 137, 160, 226
    hereditary disorders, 144, 170, 187, *249*
Beagle, 12, 34, 99, 121, 139, 145, 226–227
    hereditary disorders, 144, 169, 170, *250*
Bearded Collie, 95, **95**, 107, 127, 208, 227
    hereditary disorders, 174, *175*
Bedlington Terrier, 107, 227
    hereditary disorders, v, 41, 155, 169, *250*
Belgian Malinois, 227
Belgian Sheepdog, *175*, 227
Belgian Tervuren, 118, 119, 174, *175*, 227, 257
Berganese Shepherd, 12
Bernese Mountain Dog, 155, 174, *175*, 228
Bernese Sennehound, *250*
Bichon Frise, 12, 228
Black and Tan Coonhound, 54, 228, *250*
Bloodhound, 12, 13, 34, 131, 134, 143, 228
    hereditary disorders, 174, *175*, 187, *250*
Blue-ticked Hound, **109**, 142, *250*

Border Collie, 20, 140, 145, 169, 228, *250*
Border Terrier, 228
Borzoi, 11, 12, 13, 131, **132**, 137, 228
Boston Terrier, 12, 13, 137,144, 229, *250*
Bouvier des Flanders, 174, *175*, 229
Boxer, 119, 134, 140, 144, 172, 229, *250-251*
Briard, 169, 229
Brittany, 55, 114, 145, *175*, 229
Brussels Griffon, 229–230, *251*
Bull Terrier, 13, 122, 230, *251*
Bulldog, 8, 12, 13, 14, 137, 140, 230
    hereditary disorders, 144, 160, *252-253*
Bullmastiff, 140, 144, 174, *175*, 230, *251*

Cairn Terrier, color alleles, 230, *251*
Canaan Dog, 10, 230
Cardigan Welsh Corgi. *See* Welsh Corgi (Cardigan)
Cavalier King Charles Spaniel, 12, 230. *See also* English Toy Spaniels.
Chesapeake Bay Retriever, 12, 174, *175*, 230
Chihuahua, 11, 13, 14, 24, 230–231, *251*
Chinese Crested, 13, 60, **130**, 130, 131, 231
Chinese Shar-Pei, 231
Chow Chow, 11, 121, 174, *176*, 231
Chuvatch, 12
Clumber Spaniel, 115, 122, 231
Cocker Spaniel, 13, 25, 55, 99, 118, 121, 123, 132, 134, 142, 145, 231–232. *See also* English Cocker Spaniel and American Cocker Spaniel.
    hereditary disorders, 165, 169, 170, 172, *176*, *251-252*
collie (type), 10, 11, 139, 169
Collie, 35, 109, 114, 121, **127**, 137, 232
    hereditary disorders, 174, *176*, *252*, *257*
Curly-Coated Retriever, 12, 116, 132, **133**, 232

Dachshund, 14, 109, 137, 232–233
    hereditary disorders, 144, 168, 172, *252*
Dalmatian, 62, 108, **114**, 115, 121, 233
    hereditary disorders, 49–50, *176*, *252*
Dandie Dinmont Terrier, 107, 233
dingo (type), 9, 10
Doberman Pinscher,106, 107, 117, **119**, 134, 140, 233
    hereditary disorders, 155, 166, 172, *176*, *252*

English bulldog. *See* Bulldog
English Cocker Spaniel, 127, 233–234. *See also* American Cocker Spaniel and Cocker Spaniel
    hereditary disorders, 170, *176*, *253*

English Foxhound, 234. *See also* American Foxhound and Foxhound
English Setter, 108, 121, 174, *176*, 234
English Springer Spaniel, 114, 234
    hereditary disorders, 155, 170, *176*, *253*, *257*
English Toy Spaniel, 234
Eskimo dog. *See* American Eskimo Dog

Field Spaniel,121, 235
Finnish Spitz, 11, 13, 235
Flat-Coated Retriever, color alleles, 235
Fox Terrier, 235, 144, *253*
foxhound (type), 13
Foxhound, 12, 13, 131, *253*. *See also* American Foxhound and English Foxhound
French Bulldog, 137, 235, *253*

gazehound (type), 10, 11
German pointer (type), 142
German Shepherd Dog, 31, 62, 88, 117, 119, 122, 126, 131, 139, 140, 142, 145, 199, 235–236
    hereditary disorders, 166, *176*, 178, 187, *253*
German Shorthaired Pointer, 34, 108, 137, 139, 236
    hereditary disorders, *176*, *253-254*
German Wirehaired Pointer, *176*, 236
Giant Schnauzer, 112, 116, 127, 174, *176*, 236. *See also* Miniature Schnauzer and Standard Schnauzer
Golden Retriever, 13, 101, 121, 152, 236
    hereditary disorders, 172, 174, *176*, 187, 188, *254*
Gordon Setter, 55, 117, 121, 236
    hereditary disorders, 168, 174, *176*, *254*
Great Dane, 12, 13, 14, 189, 191
    color, 60, 62, 109, 110, **110**, 119, 236–237
    hereditary disorders, 172, 174, *177*, 187, *254*
Great Pyrenees, 12, 13, 115, 122, 144–145, 174, *177*, 237
Greater Swiss Mountain Dog, 237
greyhound (type), 8–9, 10, 13
Greyhound, 11, 13, 92, 113, 119, **120**, 123, 137, 191, 237
    hereditary disorders, 174, *254*
Griffon, *254*

Harrier, 237. *See also* English Foxhound
Havanese, 237
hound (type), 9, 131, 139
husky (type), 7, 14

hyrcanian, 11

Ibizan Hound, 10, 13, 237
Inca Hairless Dog, 130
Irish Setter, color, 114, 121, 132, 238
    hereditary disorders, 155, 160, 168, 172, 174, *177, 254*
Irish Terrier, 238, *254*
Irish Water Spaniel, 12, 132, **132**, 238
Irish Wolfhound, 11, 187, *187*, 238
Italian Greyhound, 11, 13, 238

Jack Russell terrier, *254*
Japanese Chin, 114, 238

Karelian Bear Dog, 11
Keeshond, 11, 13, 86, 116, 163, *177*, 238, *254*
Kerry Blue Terrier, 107, 239, *254*
King Charles Spaniel, 144, *254*
Komondor, 12, 13, **129**, 129–130, 239
Kuvasz, 12, 25, 239

Labrador Retriever, 12, 106, 121, 132, 207, 239
    hereditary disorders, 169, 174, *177*, 187, 188, *254*
Lakeland Terrier, 239
Lhasa Apso, 155, 239, *255*
Lowchen, 239–240

malamute. *See* Alaskan Malamute
maltese (type), 8
Maltese, 11, 13, 115, 128, **128**, 240
Manchester Terrier, 155, 240
Maremma, 12, 14
mastiff (type), 8–9, 11–12
Mastiff, 12, 139, 140, 240
Mexican Hairless, 13, 14
Miniature Bull Terrier, 240. *See also* Bull Terrier
Miniature Pinscher, color alleles, 240
Miniature Poodle, 12, 14, 128–129, 132, 144
    color, 121, 240–241
    hereditary disorders, 144, 155, 170, 172, *177, 255, 256*
Miniature Schnauzer, 85, 112, 116, **125**, 127, 241. *See also* Giant Schnauzer and Standard Schnauzer
    hereditary disorders, 172, *255*
molossian, 11

New Guinea Highland dog (*Canis f. hallstromi, Canis lupus f. hallstromi*), 5
Newfoundland, 12, 13, 145, 241–242
    hereditary disorders, 174, *177*, 187, *255*
Norfolk Terrier, color alleles, 242

Norwegian dunkerhound, hereditary disorders, 255
Norwegian Elkhound, 11, 13, 112, 116, **117**, 131, 242
    hereditary disorders, 168, 170, 174, *177, 255*
Norwich Terrier, 242

Old English Sheepdog, 11, 107, 127, **127**, 145, 242
    hereditary disorders, 172, 174, *177, 255*
Otterhound, 242, *255*

Papillon, 12, 242
pariah dog (*Canis indicus*), 5, 7, 9, 10–11, 12
Pekingese, 12, 112, 137, 140, 144, 160, 242, *255*
Pembroke Welsh Corgi. *See* Welsh Corgi (Pembroke)
Peruvian Inca Orchid, 130
Petit Basset Griffon Vendeen, 242
Pharaoh Hound, 10, 243
pointer (type), 13
Pointer, 20, 34, 50, 121, 132, 137, 139, 142 243
    hereditary disorders, 144, *256*
Pomeranian, 11, 13, 112, 243, *256*
Poodle. *See* Miniature Poodle, Standard Poodle, and Toy Poodle
Portuguese Water Dog, 12, 243
Pug, 12, 13, 119, 137, 140, 144, 243, *256*
Puli, 12, 129–130, 174, *177*, 243
Pyrenean Shepherd, 12

retriever (type), 13, 169, 216
Rhodesian Ridgeback, 174, *177*, 243, *256*
Rottweiler, 12, 13, 117, 191, 207, 244
    hereditary disorders, 174, *177, 256*
Russian Laika, 11
Russian Ovtcharka, 11

Saint Bernard, 12, 126, 145, 244
    hereditary disorders, *177*, 187, *256*
Saluki, 11, 13, 132, **133**, 244
Samoyed, 11, 13, 115, 122, 244
    hereditary disorders, 144, 170, *177, 256*
Schipperke, 244
schnauzer. *See* Giant Schnauzer, Miniature Schnauzer, and Standard Schnauzer
Scottish Deerhound, 11, 244
Scottish Terrier, 155, 166, 244, *256*
Sealyham Terrier, 169, 245, *256*
segusierhund, 12
setter (type), 12, 131, 216
Shar Planinetz, 20
sheep-guarding (type), 10, 12

sheep-herding (type), 11
sheepdog (type), 8–9
Shetland Sheepdog, 34, 99, **109**, 121, 127, 245
    hereditary disorders, 155, 166, 172, *178*, 256-257
Shiba Inu, 5, 11, 245, *257*
Shih Tzu, 155, 245, *257*
Siberian Husky, 11, 14, 20, 116, 170, *178*, 245, *257*
Silky Terrier, 245
Skye Terrier, 245, *257*
Soft Coated Wheaten Terrier, 155, 245
spaniel (type), 12
Spinoni Italiani, 246
spitz (type), 11, 12
Springer Spaniel. *See* English Springer Spaniel
Staffordshire Bull Terrier, 13, 246, *257*
Standard Poodle, 12, 14, 128–129, **129**, 132, 144
    color, 121, 246
    hereditary disorders, 144, 155, 172, *177*, 256, *257*
Standard Schnauzer, 112, 116, 127, *178*, 246. *See also* Giant Schnauzer and Miniature Schnauzer
Sussex Spaniel, 54, 246
Swedish lapland, *257*
Swiss sheepdog, *257*

Talchichi, 13
terrier (type), 8, 11, 13
Tibetan Mastiff, 11
Tibetan Spaniel, 246
Tibetan Terrier, 13, 246
toy (type), 10, 11, 12, 13
Toy Manchester Terrier, 246
Toy Poodle, 12, 14, 121, 128–129, 132, 144, 247
    hereditary disorders, 144, 155, 168, 172, *177*, 256, *257*
tubary dog, 8, 11

Valee, 12
Vizsla, 13, *178*, 247, *257*

water dogs, 12
Weimaraner, 13, 25, 31, 32, 35, 95, 97, 149, 126, 131, 134, 135, **135**, 142, 144, 145, 197, 199, 208, 215, 216
    color, 82, 107, 108, **108**, 114, 116, 122, 247
    hereditary disorders, 144, 171, 174, *178*, *257*
Welsh Corgi (Cardigan), 109
Welsh Corgi (Pembroke), 155
Welsh Corgi, *257*

Welsh Springer Spaniel, 170, 174, 247
Welsh Terrier, 247
West Highland White Terrier, 112, 174, *178*, 247, *257*
Whippet, 11, 119, 126, **126**, 197, 248, *258*
Wire Fox Terrier, 99
Wirehaired Pointing Griffon, 248

Xoloitzcuintli (Mexican Hairless), 13, 130

Yorkshire Terrier, 128, 169, 248, 258x